Bankruptcy Law and Practice

Grace A. Luppino, J.D.

Robert A. Smith, J.D.

PEARSON

Boston Columbus Indianapolis New York San Francisco Amsterdam
Cape Town Dubai London Madrid Milan Munich Paris Montréal Toronto
Delhi Mexico City São Paulo Sydney Hong Kong Seoul Singapore Taipei Tokyo

Editorial Director: Andrew Gilfillan
Senior Acquisitions Editor: Gary Bauer
Editorial Assistant: Lynda Cramer
Program Manager: Tara Horton
Director of Marketing: Dave Gesell
Marketing Manager: Thomas Hayward
Marketing Assistant: Les Roberts
Project Management Team Lead: Bryan Pirrmann
Production Project Manager: Susan Hannahs
Operations Supervisor: Mary Fischer
Operations Specialist: Deidra Skahill
Senior Art Director: Diane Ernsberger
Cover Designer: Studio Montage
Cover Art: Kentoh/Shutterstock
Full-Service Project Management: Integra Software Services Pvt. Ltd
Composition: Integra Software Services Pvt. Ltd
Printer/Binder: Edwards Brothers Malloy, Jackson Road
Cover Printer: Lehigh-Phoenix Color
Text Font: 11/13 Minion Pro Regular

Credits and acknowledgments borrowed from other sources and reproduced, with permission, in this textbook appear on the appropriate page within the text.

Acknowledgements of third party content appear on page with the borrowed material, which constitutes an extension of this copyright page.

Unless otherwise indicated herein, any third-party trademarks that may appear in this work are the property of their respective owners and any references to third-party trademarks, logos or other trade dress are for demonstrative or descriptive purposes only. Such references are not intended to imply any sponsorship, endorsement, authorization, or promotion of Pearson's products by the owners of such marks, or any relationship between the owner and Pearson Education, Inc. or its affiliates, authors, licensees or distributors.

Library of Congress Cataloging-in-Publication Data

Luppino, Grace A., author.
  Bankruptcy law and practice for paralegals/Grace A. Luppino, Robert A. Smith.—1e.
    pages cm
  ISBN 978-0-13-381727-0
  ISBN 0-13-381727-X
  1. Bankruptcy—United States.   2. Legal assistants—United States—Handbooks, manuals, etc.
I. Smith, Robert A. (Lawyer) author.   II. Title.
  KF1524.85.L87 2016
  346.7307′8—dc23
                                                        2015016131

10 9 8 7 6 5 4 3 2 1

ISBN-10:   0-13-381727-X
ISBN-13: 978-0-13-381727-0

Dedication

*To my grandfather Joseph Luppino, who taught me the value of a dollar,
and to my father, Rocco Luppino, who taught me how to use a credit card responsibly.*

Grace A. Luppino

*To my parents, Mary Ann Piwczynski-Smith
and Robert A. Smith, Sr., who provided me with a solid moral foundation
and sound money management skills.*

Robert A. Smith

BRIEF TABLE OF CONTENTS

TABLE OF CONTENTS

CHAPTER 4   The Automatic Stay   43

CHAPTER 5   The Means Test   54

CHAPTER 6   Chapter 7 Bankruptcy: Liquidation   66

CHAPTER 15   The Bankruptcy Client: Initial Intake and Related Matters   198

Appendixes

PREFACE

Bankruptcy Law and Practice for Paralegals

A paralegal textbook on the subject of bankruptcy is not exactly a spellbinding page-turner. Although the subject lacks the sex appeal of criminal or family law, bankruptcy law is a growing area of practice and the field provides great employment opportunities for a well-trained paralegal student. This text presents the rules and code references you will need to know to be effective in a bankruptcy law firm and will provide you with working experience doing the tasks and procedures you will be called upon to perform in a practice. In preparation for writing this book, we began by researching job descriptions for bankruptcy paralegals. This research helped us determine the scope of this textbook and helped ensure that, upon successful completion of this course, you will have developed the job skills required by the bankruptcy profession across the nation.

Bankruptcy paralegals engage in a lot of client interaction. They gather information, interview clients, and prepare the forms needed to file and process the bankruptcy. Attorneys hiring bankruptcy paralegals expect them to have a strong knowledge of the rules and procedures of the U.S. Bankruptcy Court and U.S. district courts and experience with e-filing through the PACER system. They also should be able to prepare the bankruptcy petition and accompanying schedules and draft motions and responses. Bankruptcy paralegals should be familiar with popular bankruptcy software programs such as Best Case, EZ-Filing, New Hope's Bankruptcy 2014, and other useful Internet resources. Equally important, because bankruptcy deals with financial issues and representations made to the court under oath and penalty of law, a bankruptcy paralegal must possess a strong grasp of ethics and how to avoid malpractice claims and sanctions against the attorney.

The goal of this textbook, *Bankruptcy Law and Practice for Paralegals*, is to prepare paralegals to enter the workforce, possessing a solid knowledge of the various aspects of substantive bankruptcy law and a firm grasp of its procedural components. To meet this challenge, this textbook is divided into two parts, one on law and the other on practice. The first part provides a concise overview of the bankruptcy code along with the various changes and updates. The second part contains detailed chapters that explain client relations, ethics, and preparation of the bankruptcy petition and accompanying documents and includes an introduction to electronic filing and bankruptcy software. Practical exercises and vignettes familiarize the student with the procedures involved in processing a client's bankruptcy matter and focus on the paralegal's role throughout the life cycle of a bankruptcy from the initial client interview through the filing of the petition, schedules, and other forms and motions.

Chapter 17 of *Bankruptcy Law and Practice for Paralegals* includes a detailed case study of a married couple, Christina and Otto Schuler, who own a small business and experience a series of calamities that affect both their personal and business finances. Examination of the Schulers' case allows students to apply what they have learned in the substantive chapters, solve ethical issues, and practice preparation of bankruptcy-related schedules and forms.

To make a somewhat dry subject interesting, we include examples of celebrity and popular store bankruptcy filings and direct students to review these documents and answer relevant questions in the end-of-chapter exercises. The text includes statutory references, interesting and relevant case law, and current events as they relate to bankruptcy law.

The chapter entitled "Bankruptcy Intersections" examines the adverse effects a bankruptcy case can have on a variety of other legal issues the client might be facing. Complex bankruptcy proceedings that intersect with other areas of the law can require referrals to attorneys who specialize in those fields or involve other specialists. Although this chapter will not make the student an expert, it will acquaint him or her with at least enough information to issue-spot matters to bring to the attorney's attention immediately.

Finally, in keeping with the pervasive role of social networking in our culture, the text addresses some of the unique and ethical implications that Facebook, Twitter, and other forms of technology bring to the field of bankruptcy practice.

Organization and Coverage

Bankruptcy Law and Practice for Paralegals is divided into two parts. Part 1 is titled "Bankruptcy Law," and provides the paralegal student with a solid foundation in substantive bankruptcy law. Part 2, titled "Bankruptcy Practice," addresses topics such as legal ethics, the role of the paralegal, client intake, drafting petitions and other forms, motion practice, and electronic resources to acquaint the student with the practical aspects of a busy bankruptcy practice.

Part 1 Bankruptcy Law

Chapter 1, Introduction to Bankruptcy, begins with a definition of bankruptcy directly followed by a discussion of its very human causes. The next section takes the reader through a brief history of bankruptcy, describing debtors' prisons and illustrating the forward thinking of our country's forefathers to empower Congress to legislate relief in what we know today as our modern bankruptcy law. The chapter concludes with the goals of bankruptcy, the most important of which is to provide the debtor with a fresh start.

Chapter 2, Sources of Bankruptcy Law, begins with a section on the jurisdiction and structure of the bankruptcy court and the role of the various participants who either work within or enter the system. The chapter gives a brief overview of the bankruptcy process, starting with the client's decision to file for bankruptcy and progressing to the discharge or dismissal of the bankruptcy case. The chapter ends with an introduction to bankruptcy mediation.

Chapter 3, Introduction to the Bankruptcy System, explains the operative chapters of the Bankruptcy Code, specifically distinguishing the differences between liquidation and reorganization bankruptcy filings. The chapter introduces paralegal students to the primary and secondary sources of bankruptcy law and explains how the Bankruptcy Abuse Prevention and Consumer Protection Act of 2005 affected the Bankruptcy Code.

Chapter 4, The Automatic Stay, addresses the basic legal principles of the Automatic Stay with detailed discussion about how it protects both debtors and creditors alike.

Chapter 5, The Means Test, explains why Chapter 7 relief is not automatic and provides the student with a comprehensive overview of the origin and purpose of this preliminary calculation. The student also gains a basic understanding of the definition of *abuse* as it applies to bankruptcy law.

Chapter 6, Chapter 7 Bankruptcy: Liquidation, illustrates the most common bankruptcy petitions filed in busy consumer-oriented practices—voluntary Chapter 7 cases. This chapter provides the reader with the foundation of a voluntary Chapter 7 liquidation proceeding and a detailed discussion of the Means Test.

Chapter 7, Chapter 13 Bankruptcy: Debt Restructuring for Individuals, provides the reader with the foundation of a Chapter 13 reorganization proceeding for an individual with regular income. Many individuals file for Chapter 13 because they are not eligible to file for Chapter 7 liquidation. However, a growing number of individual filers are choosing Chapter 13 because they not only can repay some of their debts, but they would like to use a repayment plan to assist them with making mortgage, car, and student loan payments more manageable. In this chapter, we also discuss other, less known, benefits available to a debtor under this chapter of the Bankruptcy Code and detail the inception and life cycle of a repayment plan.

Chapter 8, Chapter 11 Bankruptcy: Reorganization, introduces the reader to Chapter 11 of the Bankruptcy Code, which deals with the reorganization of debt to allow debtors to restructure their debt and pay back their creditors. The chapter concludes with an overview of the Hostess bankruptcy case along with an application of the legal principles of Chapter 11 reorganizations.

Chapter 9, Bankruptcy Creditors: Rights, Restrictions, and Responsibilities, identifies the most common types of creditors paralegals encounter in a bankruptcy practice. It addresses the classifications of creditors, creditors' rights, and the amounts they may receive in a bankruptcy case. The creditors' responsibility to provide proof of its claim is also reviewed. Finally, this chapter explores creditors' response to the Automatic Stay and their rights in overcoming this protection afforded to the debtor.

Chapter 10, Voidable Preferences and Fraudulent Transfers, helps students understand the power the Bankruptcy Code has with respect to pre-petition and postpetition transfers the debtor makes. Chapter 10 summarizes the right the trustee has to reverse any unlawful transfer of property the debtor makes, and it describes the differences between preferences and fraudulent transfers. Chapter 10 explains the process by which the trustee may pursue the transferee for the property or money that was transferred unlawfully and helps identify the defenses a transferee may assert against the trustee in a voidable transfer action.

Chapter 11, Dismissal, Conversion, and Closing a Bankruptcy, addresses the various ways in which bankruptcy cases end and are closed in the eyes of the bankruptcy court. It also addresses circumstances that might necessitate reopening the bankruptcy case so the court can take a second look.

Chapter 12, The Bankruptcy Discharge, guides students in understanding the power the Bankruptcy Code has with respect to discharging certain debts. Chapter 12 summarizes the types of debt that are nondischargeable and describes the difference between denial of discharge and nondischargeable debt. The chapter explains the right and the process by which a creditor can bring an action against a debtor to declare certain debts nondischargeable and identifies the actions a debtor might take that would cause a denial of discharge.

Chapter 13, Bankruptcy Intersections, looks at several other areas of law that can affect the typical bankruptcy case. Even the most specialized boutique practice will encounter many intersections that must be addressed either by the bankruptcy attorney or a specialist in the respective field. Although this chapter is not exhaustive of all bankruptcy intersections, it will help the paralegal recognize some of these issues, particularly the exposure to criminal charges.

Part 2 Bankruptcy Practice

Chapter 14, Bankruptcy Law Ethics and the Role of the Paralegal, begins with a discussion of the four C's, the most common ethical issues that arise in bankruptcy practice: conflict of interest, competency, confidentiality, and compensation. The role of the bankruptcy paralegal is defined, as is that of the bankruptcy petition preparer. More important, this chapter equips paralegal students with the knowledge required to avoid engaging in the unauthorized practice of law when working in the field of bankruptcy.

Chapter 15, The Bankruptcy Client: Initial Intake and Related Matters, begins with a short discussion of the psychology of bankruptcy and how paralegals can assure clients that the fresh start afforded by a bankruptcy discharge is protected in our Constitution. The chapter then discusses the initial interview process. It emphasizes the importance of disclosure and describes how clients who conceal or fail to disclose assets and income to the bankruptcy court risk having their cases dismissed and the possibility of facing criminal fraud charges. The chapter highlights the traps inherent in the use of social networking and includes sections about important matters related to the establishment of the attorney–client relationship in the bankruptcy practice.

Chapter 16, Electronic Resources for Bankruptcy Practice, discusses how technology has dramatically changed the way legal services are rendered. This chapter looks at how bankruptcy documents are prepared and filed online and addresses the use of bankruptcy software. This chapter also discusses the importance of becoming familiar with bankruptcy software tutorials because different forms of bankruptcy software are used in different offices, depending on the preferences of the law firm. The student is exposed to some of the online resources that keep paralegals informed of the changes in bankruptcy law and practice and that bankruptcy law professionals use in answering day-to-day questions.

Chapter 17, Petitions, Schedules, and Other Forms, explains, in detail, the important documents necessary to file a bankruptcy case through the example of a fictitious couple in the throes of bankruptcy, Christina and Otto Schuler. The chapter provides the student with the Schulers' detailed financial information to be captured in the appropriate forms, requiring him or her to prepare the Schulers' bankruptcy petition and related documents, using a student version of Best Case software, available at http://bestcase.com/edu/students. Students are then equipped with a drafted bankruptcy petition and other relevant documents to include in their professional portfolio.

Chapter 18, Motion Practice and Adversary Proceedings in Bankruptcy, introduces students to motion practice in bankruptcy court and acquaints them with some of the most common motions. The chapter explains the reasons for filing such documents and how the bankruptcy court addresses them. Chapter 17 also includes an introduction to adversary proceedings and a discussion of the most common types creditors, U.S. trustees, and debtors file.

Pedagogical Features

End-of-chapter material has been organized into four sections: "Chapter Summary," "Concept Review and Reinforcement," "Building Paralegal Skills," and "Building a Professional Portfolio."

- **Chapter Summary** This section provides the student with a quick summary of the chapter.
- **Concept Review and Reinforcement** This section lists the key terms defined and discussed in the chapter. Knowledge of the language of bankruptcy is essential for working in a busy bankruptcy practice. "Reviewing Key Concepts" provides students with a list of review questions that reemphasize the major aspects of bankruptcy law and procedure discussed in the chapter.
- **Building Your Paralegal Skills** Bridging the gap between legal theory and practice requires an understanding of the practical application of bankruptcy law. In the "Cases for Review" section, carefully selected cases address an important concept covered in the chapter. The fact patterns in these cases cover scenarios that students might encounter in the workplace.
- **Building a Professional Portfolio** This section presents students with a scenario through various portfolio exercises that simulate some of the tasks they might be asked to perform in a law office. The student is then asked to generate documents that he or she can show prospective employers during a job search. The portfolio exercise in Chapter 15 culminates with the student drafting a bankruptcy petition and other relevant documents, demonstrating to a prospective employer that the student has grasped not only the theory of bankruptcy law but also its practical application.

Student Resources

- **Best Case® Bankruptcy Software Access** Students may download the free educational version of Best Case® Bankruptcy software and learn the basics of using the software at http://bestcase.com/edu/students. A free online demonstration is available that shows how to prepare a voluntary petition and other bankruptcy schedules and forms, open a new client file, and use the Best Case Means Test Calculator. Training exercises contained on the website can also be used to practice preparing a sample voluntary petition and corresponding schedules, Statement of Financial Affairs, and complete an exercise in electronic filing.

Instructor Supplements

- **Instructor's Manual with Test Bank** This supplement includes content outlines for classroom discussion, teaching suggestions, and answers to selected end-of-chapter questions from the text. It also contains a Word document version of the test bank.
- **TestGen** This computerized test-generation system gives you maximum flexibility in creating and administering tests in hard copy, electronically, or

online. It provides state-of-the-art features for viewing and editing test bank questions; dragging a selected question into a test you are creating; and printing sleek, formatted tests in a variety of layouts. Select test items from test banks included with TestGen for quick test creation or write your own questions from scratch. TestGen's random generator provides the option to display different text or calculated number values each time questions are used.

- **PowerPoint presentations** Our presentations offer clear, straightforward outlines and notes to use for class lectures or study materials. Photos, illustrations, charts, and tables from the book are included in the presentations when applicable.

To access supplementary materials online, request an instructor access code. Go to www.pearsonhighered.com/irc to register for one. Within 48 hours after registering, you will receive a confirming email that includes your code. After you have received your code, visit the site and log on for full instructions about downloading the materials you wish to use.

Alternate Versions

eBooks. This text is also available in multiple eBook formats, including Adobe Reader and *CourseSmart*. *CourseSmart* is an exciting new choice for students looking to save money. As an alternative to purchasing the printed textbook, students can purchase an electronic version of the same content. With a *CourseSmart* eTextbook, students can search the text, make notes online, print out reading assignments that incorporate lecture notes, and bookmark important passages for later review. For more information, or to purchase access to the *CourseSmart* eTextbook, visit www.coursesmart.com.

ACKNOWLEDGMENTS

We wish to thank reviewers of this book, who provided many helpful comments and insights that have been incorporated into this edition.

We wish to thank the following people for their support and encouragements in making this book a reality:

Gary Bauer at Pearson; Elisa Rogers at 4development, and Stephanie Raga at Integra-Chicago.

Our colleagues Frank Farina, M.A., D.P.E.; and Renée L. Duff, Esq. for their technical assistance and support.

Special thanks from Grace A. Luppino to her family for their patience and support and to Christina Maturi for her sense of humor and constant encouragement to "keep typing!"

Special thanks from Robert A. Smith to Ruth Ann Schuler, M.S.; Michael F. Smith, M.B.A.; Marcus Smith; Nitin Acharya, M.S.; and Linda Dunkerley, M.S.; for their endless support and positive influence.

Our very special thanks to Amanda Sager for her research assistance and review of the manuscript. Also, thank you to paralegal students Joseph Esposito, Nina Pizzola, Carmen Baldwin, and Jasmine Salters for their review and input from the student's perspective.

Grace A. Luppino
Robert A. Smith

ABOUT THE AUTHORS

GRACE A. LUPPINO graduated from Quinnipiac University School of Law in 1990 and received an AS in Paralegal Studies and BS in Business Administration from Sacred Heart University. Prior to becoming an attorney, she worked as a paralegal and court advocate for victims of domestic violence. She practiced child protection and family law and is coauthor of *Family Law and Practice*, 4th edition, published by Pearson Education. Ms. Luppino has been a paralegal instructor for more than 20 years and currently practices intellectual property law.

ROBERT A. SMITH earned his BA from Central Connecticut State University and his JD from Quinnipiac University School of Law. He currently maintains a law practice in Branford, Connecticut. In addition to representing a diverse group of clients, Attorney Smith is also a paralegal instructor. He teaches courses in Bankruptcy Law, Tort Law, Real Property Law, Civil Litigation, and Legal Research and Writing.

chapter 1
INTRODUCTION TO BANKRUPTCY

In 2009, decorated British army Major Willard Foxton watched his entire life savings vanish. Foxton had invested his hard-earned money with Bernard Madoff, a criminal who perpetrated the largest investor fraud in history. While Madoff enjoyed the high life, his Ponzi scheme resulted in a loss of approximately $50 billion in investor money. Although Foxton survived the French Foreign Legion and the loss of an arm as a result of his military service, he could not survive the embarrassment and humiliation of a penniless existence. Foxton ended his life with a single gunshot wound to the head, leaving a suicide note which specifically made reference to his despair over his financial problems. Foxton is not alone. A report issued by the U.S. Centers for Disease Control and Prevention and published in the American Journal of Public Health in 2011 revealed that suicide rates increase during periods of economic crisis. Suicides nearly quadrupled during the Great Recession of 2008, with their root causes attributable to the increase in unemployment and foreclosure.

The lawyers and paralegals who work in the area of bankruptcy law assist clients through a system that was created by our forefathers as legal and societal relief for the destitute. Without it, we would still have debtors' prisons and an even larger number of the financially desperate ending their own lives. Although the public may at times malign the bankruptcy system as an easy way out for the irresponsible, the reality is that it provides a very important safety valve for those whose circumstances could befall any one of us.

LEARNING OBJECTIVES

After studying this chapter, you should be able to:

1. Understand the definition of bankruptcy.

2. Recognize the causes of modern-day bankruptcy filings.

3. Explain the historical roots of bankruptcy law.

4. Give examples of the goals of the American bankruptcy system.

Introduction

Chapter 1 begins with a definition of bankruptcy directly followed by a discussion of its very human causes. The next section takes the reader through a brief history of bankruptcy, describing the debtors' prisons and illustrating the keen insight of our forefathers to empower Congress to legislate relief in what we know today as our modern bankruptcy law. The chapter concludes with the goals of bankruptcy, the most important of which is to provide the debtor with a fresh start.

Bankruptcy Defined

A **bankruptcy** is a legal procedure established under federal law that allows a financially distressed individual, business, or municipality to obtain debt relief by either liquidating its assets or restructuring its debt so its creditors may be paid. It is an official, legal declaration of an individual's or business's inability to meet its financial obligations. The word *bankruptcy* is a combination of two Latin terms, *bankus* and *ruptus,* literally meaning "broken bench." *Banca rotta,* as the Italians called it, or *banquerotte,* in French, described a common practice in the Middle Ages in which indebted merchants would have the benches from which they sold their goods literally smashed and destroyed by angry creditors as a symbol of their insolvency.

The Causes of Bankruptcy

Statistics compiled by the United States courts revealed that in 2013 alone, 1,071,932 bankruptcies were filed in this country. There is a common misconception that individuals and businesses that file for bankruptcy are over-extended, irresponsible money managers who want to get out of paying their debts. Although this may be true in many cases, a look at the causes of bankruptcy helps change that perception with the realization that the average person is only one tragedy away from financial devastation.

Despite the best of intentions, a business or individual may decide that filing for bankruptcy is the only viable solution in situations when an insolvency event, such as excessive income taxes and fines, large lawsuit judgment, or catastrophic illness, takes place. Other reasons for seeking bankruptcy protection include loss of employment, death of a spouse or main wage earner, divorce or separation, natural disasters, living beyond one's means, economic conditions, or business failures.

Regardless of the reason, no one is immune. Clients oftentimes take comfort in learning that they are not the only ones filing for bankruptcy. The bankruptcy laws of the United States provide a legal and legitimate vehicle for a fresh start. Here is a list of a few famous people and corporations that filed for bankruptcy protection:

- Cyndi Lauper
- DMX
- Mary J. Blige
- Meatloaf
- Michael Vick
- TLC
- Vince McMahon
- Walt Disney
- Warren Sapp
- Willie Nelson
- Blockbuster LLC
- Fruit of the Loom, Inc.
- Hostess Brands, Inc.
- Kmart Corporation
- Los Angeles Dodgers

- Marvel Entertainment Group
- Pepsi Cola Company
- Regal Cinemas, Inc.
- Sbarro, Inc.
- Six Flags, Inc.

MEDICAL REASONS

According to a 2009 study published in *The American Journal of Medicine*, entitled "Medical Bankruptcies in the United States," 62.1% of all bankruptcies in 2007 were filed because of medical reasons. In a journal of *Health Affairs* study published in 2013, for example, individuals diagnosed with cancer were more than two and a half times more likely to file for federal bankruptcy protection than those without cancer. Many families, dependent on two incomes, may face financial problems when one of the breadwinners must leave work due to illness. Some families have to mortgage their home to pay for medical expenses and soon find themselves facing the specter of both foreclosure and bankruptcy.

Interestingly, most medical debtors are middle class, have college educations, and own their own homes. What was most revealing about this study, however, was that three-quarters of these debtors actually had health insurance coverage. Some medical debtors are underinsured or carry high deductibles, which result in financial devastation when faced with high out-of-pocket expenses. Economic disaster can also occur when an insured employee gets sick and is unable to work for medical reasons. Although the Consolidated Omnibus Budget Reconciliation Act (COBRA) allows an employee to maintain his or her health insurance for a period of 18 months after leaving the job, the reality is that COBRA payments are expensive and, even if the former employee can pay them, coverage typically expires after those 18 months.

LOSS OF EMPLOYMENT

Loss of employment by either the debtor or the debtor's spouse is another leading cause of bankruptcy filings. Job loss translates into millions of Americans faced with tough decisions when deciding how to allocate unemployment benefits and other resources. For many families, buying food and maintaining some form of shelter takes precedence over purchasing health insurance, the cost of which may be out of reach. Many turn to using credit cards to purchase the basic necessities when cash is scarce or depleted. The financial picture worsens when the period of unemployment is prolonged or the individual is underemployed in a low-paying job and is unable to make ends meet.

The old saying that "two can live cheaper than one" is a downright lie. In the book *The Two-Income Trap: Why Middle-Class Parents Are Going Broke*, by Elizabeth Warren (now U.S. Senator from Massachusetts) and Amelia Tyagi, the authors show how rising costs such as child care, health care, student loans, taxes, a second vehicle, and home ownership are leaving families with much less discretionary income left over after these expenses are paid. The two-income family is most vulnerable to bankruptcy if one of the spouses loses his or her job. According to the authors, families are five times more likely to file for bankruptcy and three times more likely to watch their homes go into foreclosure. The authors go on to say that more children will watch their parents go through bankruptcy than through a divorce.

DIVORCE OR SEPARATION

Now compound the two-income trap with a 50% divorce rate in the United States. According to the American Bar Association, the primary reason for divorce is money problems. The financial dilemmas that families face on a day-to-day basis can lead to conflict that results in stress on the marriage. Divorce or separation forces couples, who were already under financial stress, to support two households with the same amount of money, or even less if one or both have suffered a job loss. Divorced individuals under court orders to pay alimony or child support may legitimately be unable to make these payments, which results in lack of income for the custodial parent who has to shoulder the responsibility of supporting the children. Noncustodial parents may sometimes be subjected to court-ordered wage garnishments, leaving little money left over for other expenses. Without adequate employment or support, many turn to credit cards to pay their basic expenses and dig themselves deeper into debt. Others may be saddled with debts incurred by current or former spouses because both may be held legally responsible for many debts incurred during the marriage.

Filing for bankruptcy, however, does not provide an absolute fresh start for many divorced individuals. Court orders for alimony and child support, known in bankruptcy law as domestic support obligations, as well as student loans cannot be discharged in bankruptcy.

DEATH OF A SPOUSE OR MAIN WAGE EARNER

Surviving spouses or cohabitating partners may be forced to seek bankruptcy protection when a spouse or main wage earner in the family dies. Often, families rely on two incomes to survive, and even if both spouses or partners are employed, the death of one may result in the inability of the other to maintain the family's current lifestyle. Although it is advisable from an estate planning perspective to maintain life insurance for the benefit of the family in the event of a major wage earner's death, this is not always possible. There may be no room in the family budget to pay for the cost of premiums, or the spouse or partner may be uninsurable due to preexisting illness or other circumstances.

NATURAL DISASTERS

Natural disasters such as earthquakes, floods, and tornadoes destroy homes, automobiles, and personal property and displace businesses, families, and individuals for extended periods. Many homeowners are unaware that special coverage is required for damage caused by some natural disasters. Victims of natural disasters, who may have lost everything, not only have to worry about rebuilding their lives, but also are responsible for debts they had before disaster struck. In his article entitled "Bankruptcy Filing Rates after a Major Hurricane," *Nevada Law Journal*, vol. 6, p. 7, (2005), Professor Robert M. Lawless studied the bankruptcy rates from the 18 hurricanes that caused over $1 billion in damage between 1980 and 2004. His study found that the bankruptcy filing rates increased in the affected areas in the 12 to 36 months after the incidents.

LIVING BEYOND ONE'S MEANS

Some individuals and families have to file for bankruptcy because they live far beyond their means, spending much more than they earn. According to

"Overspending in America: Statistics and Facts," by *The Credit Examiner*, December 30, 2012, 52% of Americans are spending more than they earn. The reasons people overextend themselves vary. Some try to "keep up with the Joneses" whether they live next door or are within social or professional circles. Some debtors engage in "retail therapy" to help alleviate melancholy or depression; others may be compulsive shopaholics in need of professional psychological counseling. Some debtors gamble excessively, only to find that the lure of the casino and broken promises of lotteries and scratch-off tickets can lead to devastating financial consequences. This may be particularly true of those who are recently widowed or just lonely and may resort to wagering as a means of therapy. Others have too much access to credit cards, do not live within a budget or set financial goals, or just have difficulty saying no.

A 2008 study, "Household Consumption and Personal Bankruptcy," by University of California Davis Graduate School of Management professor Ning Zhu, suggests that the overspending habits of American households is what makes them more vulnerable to unexpected events. Very often, lifestyle expenses are financed with loans and credit cards, which will eventually catch up with the debtor, especially if coupled with a job loss, illness, or other personal tragedy. Businesses can also be prone to overspending when a business plan, or lack thereof, may have underestimated the inherent costs of entrepreneurship.

ECONOMIC CONDITIONS

The cyclical nature of the economy translates into either a boom or bust for businesses and individuals. Whether the economy affects the overall market or a specific sector, debtors can sometimes find themselves victims of circumstances beyond their control. For example, during the 9/11 attacks on the United States, the federal government grounded all airlines and closed all airports for fear that there were more suicide bombers who would wreak havoc on the nation. The airports eventually reopened, but travelers were leery about air travel. The aftermath was so bad that on September 22, 2001, the Air Transportation Safety and System Stabilization Act was enacted to save the airline industry with billions in the form of immediate assistance and loan guarantees. Add to the mix the SARS epidemic, rising fuel costs, increased expenses for airport security, and an economic recession, and the result has been economic disaster for the airlines. Many sought refuge in U.S. bankruptcy courts, with some airlines, such as Northwest Airlines, United Airlines, Delta Air Lines, and US Airways, restructuring their debt to survive.

POOR MONEY MANAGEMENT

Some individuals as well as businesses must file for bankruptcy simply because they are poor money managers, have made very bad financial decisions in their lives, or have delegated their finances to unqualified or unethical individuals. Poor money management often includes abusing credit cards, spending far beyond one's means, and failing to accumulate savings, even though the ability to do so exists. The consequences of poor money management affect even those in our society who are, by the public's estimation, perceived as wealthy. The perfect examples are well-compensated athletes, celebrities, or lottery winners who have lost their fortunes and been forced into bankruptcy.

Those who make a lot of money in our society have their own issues to contend with when it comes to money management. Celebrities and athletes, for instance, may have difficulties with budgeting. These individuals are typically paid in lump sums for activities such as going on tour to promote a new album, appearing in a new blockbuster movie, fighting for the heavy weight championship of the world, or receiving an advance on a new bestseller. From these lump sums, they have to pay all those who provide them with goods and services. Some may also support friends, relatives, or hangers-on and opportunists who want to take advantage of their status. Others have to contend with frivolous lawsuits filed by plaintiffs eager to reach into a famous person's deep pocket. Those who invest their money may entrust someone with questionable ethics who will mismanage funds or even steal from them. Some celebrities invest in business industries they know nothing about only to watch them fail. Finally, some just have horrible spending habits. For some, the amount of money earned is irrelevant. The more they make, the more they spend, not realizing that fame and fortune is here today and gone tomorrow.

Many can restructure, reemerge, or rebound from bankruptcy. Football player Michael Vick, for example, filed for bankruptcy even though he was ranked by *Forbes* magazine in 2012 as the fourth highest-paid athlete, earning the sum of $37.5 million. Vick filed for Chapter 11 in July 2008 and since has been able to restructure his debt and make a financial comeback. Others, however, have not been that lucky, especially if their celebrity status has faded and they have lost their earning power.

BUSINESS FAILURES

Another cause of bankruptcy is the failure of a business. From corporate giants to small mom-and-pop enterprises, businesses fail for a variety of reasons. The most common reasons are poor management, lack of adequate capital, or economic circumstances. The statistics on new-business failure rates are not encouraging. According to the Small Business Administration, 7 out of 10 new businesses survive at least 2 years, half at least 5 years, a third at least 10 years, and a quarter stay in business 15 years or more. Debtors who own small or personal businesses may find that despite efforts to protect themselves from personal liability by organizing as limited liability companies or corporations, the failure of a business venture can result in having to file for personal bankruptcy. What happens in these cases is that these budding entrepreneurs often sign a **personal guarantee**. A personal guarantee is an agreement signed by a business owner that allows the creditor to pursue the personal assets of the owner for the debts the business entity owes. Therefore, if the business is unable to pay its debts, the business owner can be sued in his or her personal capacity.

For example, a client wants to open a quilting supply shop and forms a limited liability company called Quilting Bees, LLC. The client now wants to rent commercial space for her new business. The lease for the commercial space includes a personal guarantee, which means that the client promises to be personally liable under the terms of the agreement. If she is unable to pay the rent and other expenses associated with her commercial lease, her landlord may sue her in her personal capacity. This puts the client's home, car, bank accounts, investments, and other assets in jeopardy. The consequences can be devastating and may require the client to file for personal bankruptcy to liquidate or repay the debt.

Unfortunately, clients who are eager and excited about starting their own business may sign personal guarantees for the purpose of obtaining financing, commercial space, or business credit cards. Many seek the advice of an attorney *after* they have signed on the dotted line instead of at the beginning stages of

personal guarantee
An agreement signed by a business owner that allows the creditor to pursue the personal assets of the owner for the debts the business entity owes, so if the business is unable to pay its debts, the business owner is sued in his or her personal capacity.

organizing their small businesses. From the lender's perspective, requiring borrowers to sign a personal guarantee makes good business sense, especially with new businesses. Attorneys can assist in not only explaining to the client the consequences of the personal guarantee, but also in negotiating the modification of these provisions in contracts as well as providing other valuable business advice. The attorney might also advise the client to explore what is known as **personal guarantee insurance**. This is insurance coverage purchased to minimize the risk of loss to a business owner's personal assets in the event that the liquidated business assets cannot satisfy debts owed to a creditor. The insurance may cover a percentage of the business debts so that the personal consequences to the owner are not so severe and require filing a personal bankruptcy.

personal guarantee insurance
Insurance coverage purchased to minimize the risk of loss to a business owner's personal assets in the event that the liquidated business assets cannot satisfy debts owed to a creditor. The insurance may cover a percentage of the business debts so that the personal consequences to the owner are not so severe they require filing a personal bankruptcy.

Contemporary Bankruptcy Law: A Brief History

There is an old saying by an anonymous author that goes something like this: "You have to know where you've been before you know where you're going." That is why most books on bankruptcy law begin with some type of brief or comprehensive history on the subject. It was the events of the past that really helped shape our modern bankruptcy laws and their various incarnations. Contemporary bankruptcy law as we know it is a form of relief. It is the legal process that stops the never-ending onslaught of harassing creditors' phone calls, alleviates the crushing weight of financial debt, and offers the debtor a fresh start. Debtors who had fallen on hard times, however, were not always treated with compassion by various legal systems. Instead, punishment was the answer rather than reasonable solutions that balanced the interests of both debtors and creditors.

The Bible, however, expecting people to pay their debts, did strike a balance, encouraging compassion for those in financial distress as well as the Old Testament mandate of relieving debtors from their obligations every seven years.

> If a countryman of yours becomes so poor with regard to you that he sells himself to you, you shall not subject him to a slave's service.
>
> Leviticus 25:35 *(New American Standard Bible)*

> At the end of every seven years you shall grant a remission of debts. This is the manner of remission: every creditor shall release what he has loaned to his neighbor; he shall not exact it of his neighbor and his brother, because the LORD's remission has been proclaimed.
>
> Deuteronomy 15:1–2 *(New American Standard Bible)*

The ancient Romans were not so forgiving. One gruesome punishment was dismembering the debtor's body and dividing it among the creditors in proportion to the debt owed. Other practices included banishing or imprisoning the family or selling them into slavery, where they were forced to work until they paid off their debt.

ENGLISH ROOTS AND THE EMERGENCE OF THE AMERICAN LEGAL SYSTEM

Attorneys and paralegals in the United States are well acquainted with the English roots of American jurisprudence, which included antiquated and inhumane laws regarding the treatment of debtors. In 1542, King Henry VIII instituted the practice

debtors' prison
A special facility where individuals who were in debt were incarcerated.

of incarcerating individuals who were in debt in special facilities called **debtors' prisons**. The reasoning behind the debtors' prisons was that families would come forth and pay the prisoner's debt. The debtor in turn owed the prison for room and board, which increased the amount of debt owed. Some debtors turned to their families, who paid off the debt to spare their loved ones. What if the prisoner had no family or had one that was equally destitute? The debtors' prisons were the quintessential catch-22: how can debtors pay their bills if they are locked up? There were several solutions to this conundrum. If the debtor had any assets, some could be seized by creditors in satisfaction of the debt. Some became indentured servants who had to work off their debt to earn their release. Those who had a trade or had goods to sell were given what we would call a day pass to leave prison, work, and make money to be applied toward the debt. Some prisoners languished in prison, and unless they had family that could provide them with food and clothing, they were left to die.

English writer Charles Dickens, known for his holiday classic, *A Christmas Carol*, wrote about one of England's most notorious debtors' prisons, Marshalsea, in his novel, *Little Dorrit*. Dickens' father fell into debt and was incarcerated in Marshalsea, an experience that had a long-lasting effect on the author, who vowed never to follow in his footsteps. In *Little Dorrit*, Dickens describes the prison at the beginning of Chapter 6 of *Book One the First*, aptly named "Poverty."

> Thirty years ago there stood, a few doors short of the church of Saint George, in the borough of Southwark, on the left-hand side of the way going southward, the Marshalsea Prison. It had stood there many years before, and it remained there some years afterwards; but it is gone now, and the world is none the worse without it. It was an oblong pile of barrack building, partitioned into squalid houses standing back to back, so that there were no back rooms; environed by a narrow paved yard, hemmed in by high walls duly spiked at top. Itself a close and confined prison for debtors, it contained within it a much closer and more confined jail for smugglers. Offenders against the revenue laws, and defaulters to excise or customs who had incurred fines which they were unable to pay, were supposed to be incarcerated behind an iron-plated door closing up a second prison, consisting of a strong cell or two, and a blind alley some yard and a half wide, which formed the mysterious termination of the very limited skittle-ground in which the Marshalsea debtors bowled down their troubles.

Chapter 6 of *Book One the First*: "Poverty"

The first English bankruptcy law was passed in 1570 in response to the overcrowding of the debtors' prisons and their increasing unpopularity among the general public. In 1705, the Statute of Anne provided some relief for debtors who were agreeable to making payment arrangements with their creditors. Those who were not, however, were executed. Under English law, only creditors could commence a bankruptcy case against a debtor, and debtors had to be merchants to qualify for bankruptcy relief, which left individual debtors still subject to the indignity of the debtors' prison.

Many fled England and other parts of Europe to escape incarceration, paying their way by coming to America as **indentured servants**. An indentured servant is an individual who pays for his or her passage, including expenses and maintenance,

indentured servant
An individual who paid for his or her passage, including expenses and maintenance, by contracting to work for a period of years for his or her sponsors.

by contracting to work for a period of years for his or her sponsors. The definition is framed in the present tense because there are many accounts of undocumented immigrants who still to this day make similar arrangements in exchange for the opportunity to come to the United States.

The colonies also adopted the English practice of incarcerating debtors until they were able to pay off their debts. James Oglethorpe, founder of the Georgia colony, established this territory as a refuge from the debtors' prison. In 1729, a friend of Oglethorpe's was imprisoned because he could not pay his debts. If an inmate wanted fairly decent accommodations while serving his sentence, he had to pay for it. Because Oglethorpe's friend had no money, he was forced to share a cell with a prisoner who had smallpox and eventually died from the disease himself. Having witnessed the deplorable conditions and their consequences, Oglethorpe embarked on a campaign to reform the debtors' prisons in London. Unhappy with the treatment of the poor in England, Oglethorpe and his influential friends established the Georgia colony in 1732, where debtors would be given a fresh start and the opportunity to start a new life without the fear of being imprisoned or having to endure years of indentured servitude to earn their freedom. Over time, the institution of debtors' prison was looked upon with disgust and outrage, and many voices demanded reform. New York was the first to abolish the debtors' prisons formally in 1831 with others eventually following its lead.

Prior to passage of the U.S. Constitution, the governing document of the country was the Articles of Confederation. There was no mention of bankruptcy in the Articles, so the states were left to establish their own laws regulating the relationships between debtors and creditors. The differences in state law, however, made business relationships unpredictable, especially in a commercially expanding republic. The Founding Fathers saw the need for coherent, uniform laws on bankruptcy that would be compatible with the regulation of interstate commerce and prevent fraud when the parties or their property could be removed to different states. Finally, in 1789, the U.S. Constitution went into effect, authorizing Congress to enact bankruptcy laws if it elected to do so. The bankruptcy clause was adopted in the Constitution with literally no debate or opposition. Congress was granted the power

> [T]o establish a uniform Rule of Naturalization, and uniform Laws on the subject of Bankruptcies throughout the United States;
>
> To make all Laws which shall be necessary and proper for carrying into Execution the foregoing Powers, and all other Powers vested by this Constitution in the Government of the United States, or in any Department or Officer thereof.
>
> *Article I, Section 8*

Although the Constitution went into effect in 1789, it was not until a decade later that Congress passed the first bankruptcy law in 1800.

MODERN-DAY DEBTORS' PRISONS

Although debtors' prisons were abolished by the federal government in 1833, there are many who argue that debtors' prisons have reemerged in modern times. It is important to note at the outset of this section that states are allowed to create their own laws regarding imprisonment of individuals for failure to pay child support as well as fines and penalties incurred through the criminal justice system. Critics of this practice however, argue that imprisoning the poor is a waste of government resources and creates a new host of problems when the debtors reenter society.

A 2010 investigative report by the American Civil Liberties Union, *In for a Penny: The Rise of America's New Debtors' Prisons,* reported that the financial crisis has led states and counties to be more aggressive in the assessment and collection of legal financial obligations, which are "fines, fees, and costs associated with a criminal sentence." The report cites abuses of civil liberties in an effort to fill government coffers in Louisiana, Michigan, Georgia, Ohio, and Washington. Debtors are incarcerated on charges of contempt, which are levied by the judge when one fails to obey a court order by not paying sums owed to the court. Some debtors face these charges without proper legal representation even though they are exposed to possible incarceration.

In April 2013, the American Civil Liberties Union of Ohio issued a report entitled *The Outskirts of Hope: How Ohio's Debtors' Prisons Are Ruining Lives and Costing Communities.* The allegations here are that several courts in Ohio, without due process, incarcerate individuals who are unable to pay fines and costs. When the fines go unpaid, the individual is incarcerated on charges of contempt of court and are denied a hearing to determine their financial ability to meet their obligations. The ACLU report claims that debtors' prisons are alive today, incarcerating the poor at a cost to the taxpayers far beyond the original debt owed.

Ohio is not the only state where claims of incarcerating the poor have arisen. In Missouri, payday lenders have found a way to use the courts to enforce debt collection. **Payday loans** are short-term, high-interest loans made usually to financially strapped individuals who need an infusion of cash for one reason or another between paychecks. The assumption is that when payday rolls around, the borrowers will make good on their debt. Unfortunately, some individuals who literally live from paycheck to paycheck are unable to pay and are sued in civil court by the lender. Although the bill of rights in Missouri's constitution declares that "no person shall be imprisoned for debt, except for nonpayment of fines and penalties imposed by law," creditors who obtain civil judgments against debtors call them into court for examination to determine whether they have any assets that can be seized to satisfy the debt. When some debtors do not appear for the hearing, the creditor's attorney asks the judge to order them to be arrested and held until the next court date or until they can post bond. These orders are called body attachments in Missouri and have been criticized by many. Creditors, on the other hand, argue that this is the only way they can force payment by debtors who dodge the system.

payday loans
Short-term, high-interest loans made usually to financially strapped individuals who need an infusion of cash for one reason or another between paychecks.

The Goals of Bankruptcy Law

Bankruptcy law and procedure in the United States seeks to accomplish several goals, taking into consideration the interests of both debtors and creditors.

1. A Fresh Start for the Debtor

Bankruptcy is the remedy that is sought when the debtor is so financially distressed that the only reasonable solution is to seek relief from the debts. The United States Supreme Court has recognized that the main purpose of bankruptcy law is to give debtors a fresh start.

This Court has certainly acknowledged that a central purpose of the Code is to provide a procedure by which certain insolvent debtors can reorder their affairs, make peace with their creditors, and enjoy "a new opportunity in life with a clear field for future effort, unhampered by the pressure and discouragement of preexisting debt." *Grogan v. Garner*, 498 US 279 (1991)

As long as the debtor complies with the Bankruptcy Code, a **fresh start** consists of the debtor either having the debt once owed wiped away or being given the opportunity to reorganize the debt owed in a manageable and realistic manner.

fresh start
The ultimate goal in bankruptcy, by which the debtor obligations are either wiped away or the debtor is given the opportunity to reorganize the debt owed in a manner more manageable and realistic, given his or her financial circumstances.

2. Efficient Administration of Bankruptcy Proceedings

Bankruptcy law provides for an efficient, official, and judicially supervised procedure of administering the bankruptcy case. Some creditors would be cheated out of their rightful share if debtors and creditors were left to their own devices in settling matters when debtors are unable to pay their bills. Bankruptcy law has established procedures for filing the bankruptcy action and provides a venue for interested parties to settle their grievances regarding the debtor's insolvency in an organized, civilized manner.

3. Preserving the Bankruptcy Estate

It is the role and function of the bankruptcy trustee to maintain control over the bankruptcy estate and preserve any of the debtor's available assets for the benefit of the creditors or other interested parties. Bankruptcy trustees have the authority to take control of the assets, investigate fraud, uncover hidden assets, and recover fraudulently transferred property.

4. Protection and Fair Treatment of Creditors

There is no doubt that many debtors would prefer to abandon their obligations and leave their creditors with unpaid bills. Although one of the main goals of bankruptcy is to provide the debtor with a fresh start, the trade-off for participation in the system is the protection and fair treatment of creditors. This is accomplished by the bankruptcy court's supervision and administration of the bankruptcy case as well as the fact that it provides creditors with the opportunity to participate in the process. Creditors are also afforded fair treatment in the settlement and distribution of the debtor's assets and are protected when debtors with sufficient income are required to pay their debts instead of having them totally discharged. Although in some cases creditors walk away from these proceedings with nothing, in others, they may be paid a portion of the debt or the entire debt in a restructured manner. Creditors are also protected by laws that allow them literally to force an uncooperative debtor into what is known as an involuntary bankruptcy.

You may recall our account of Major Willard Foxton's despair over his financial loss in the introduction to this chapter. His case, like so many, exemplifies how we as a human race have withstood wars, physical impairments, deaths, and illnesses. However, financial ruin can result in the ultimate in humiliation and feelings of despair. It is hoped that, after reading this chapter, you realize that financial ruin can occur at any point in our lives for a number of reasons that, in many instances, are beyond our control. The Bankruptcy Code provides a very important safety valve for those whose circumstances could befall any one of us.

CHAPTER **SUMMARY**

A bankruptcy is a legal procedure established under federal law that allows a financially distressed individual, business, or municipality to obtain debt relief by either liquidating its assets or restructuring its debt so its creditors may be paid. The causes of bankruptcy include medical reasons, loss of employment, divorce or separation, natural disasters, living beyond one's means, economic conditions, poor money management, and business failures.

Historically, debtors who fell on hard times were not always treated with compassion by various legal systems. Instead, punishment was the answer rather than reasonable solutions that balanced the interests of both debtors and creditors. Some debtors were incarcerated in debtors' prisons. Although the federal government abolished debtors' prisons in 1833, many argue that debtors' prisons have reemerged in modern times.

Bankruptcy law and procedure in the United States seek to accomplish several goals, taking into consideration the interests of both debtors and creditors. They include a fresh start for the debtor, efficient administration of bankruptcy proceedings, preservation of the bankruptcy estate, and protection and fair treatment of creditors.

CONCEPT REVIEW AND REINFORCEMENT

KEY **TERMS**

bankruptcy
debtors' prison
fresh start

indentured servant
payday loans
personal guarantee

personal guarantee insurance

REVIEWING **KEY CONCEPTS**

1. Define the term *bankruptcy* and explain the roots of its definition.
2. Describe common misconceptions regarding individuals and businesses that file for bankruptcy.
3. List the main causes of bankruptcy and briefly describe each one.
4. Describe the circumstances in American history that led to the abolition of debtors' prisons.
5. Read the bankruptcy clause of the U.S. Constitution provided in this chapter. What is its purpose?
6. Explain why some critics believe that debtors' prisons have emerged in modern-day society.
7. What are payday loans and what are some of the problems that can arise for debtors as a result of these arrangements?
8. What is the main remedy debtors seek by filing for bankruptcy?
9. One of the goals of bankruptcy is to preserve the bankruptcy estate. What does this mean?
10. How does the bankruptcy process protect the interests of creditors?

chapter 2
SOURCES OF BANKRUPTCY LAW

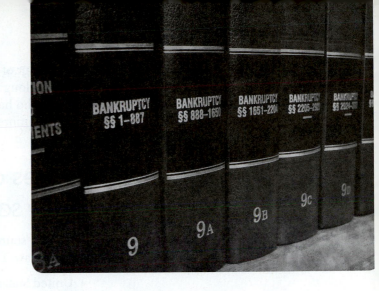

Glinda McNeal is a first-year student at Riverside Community College. She is studying to become a paralegal. She has always had an interest in the law and has a healthy curiosity for the workings of our legal system. For instance, her sister recently purchased a home, and Glinda was there for her sister every step of the way, providing moral support. She also absorbed a great deal about the law behind the financial transaction and title conveyance to her sister. Last year, one of Glinda's closest friends filed for Chapter 7 bankruptcy. She paid close attention to the process of filing the petition as well as to the court proceedings. She was also intrigued by the automatic stay and the immediate relief it offered debtors. Her friend's experience prompted Glinda to learn more about the sources of bankruptcy law. She decided to enroll in a bankruptcy course in the paralegal program at her college. Her professor started the course with a brief history on the origins of the U.S. Bankruptcy Code. Read on to learn more about the sources of bankruptcy law in the United States.

LEARNING OBJECTIVES

After studying this chapter, you should be able to:

1. Recognize the primary and secondary sources of bankruptcy law.

2. Distinguish among the various types of bankruptcy filings available under the operative chapters of the Bankruptcy Code.

3. Explain how the Bankruptcy Abuse Prevention and Consumer Protection Act of 2005 affected the bankruptcy system.

4. Compare and contrast liquidations and reorganizations.

Introduction

Chapter 2 introduces the reader to the sources of bankruptcy law, the foundation on which legal professionals base their services to clients. In these pages, the primary and secondary sources of bankruptcy law are identified and explained in the context of their relevance to legal practice. The Bankruptcy Code and its universal and the operative chapters are also introduced. The reader will learn that filing for bankruptcy does not necessarily mean that the debtor has lost everything. The Bankruptcy Code provides a vehicle for debtors either to liquidate or reorganize, thus making the repayment of their obligations more manageable. The Bankruptcy Code comprises nine chapters, six of which deal with the different types of bankruptcy filings.

It is the job of the bankruptcy attorney to determine which bankruptcy chapter is most appropriate for the client to file. This chapter also includes a section on the Bankruptcy Abuse Prevention and Consumer

Protection Act of 2005, the most sweeping amendments to the Bankruptcy Code since 1978, along with a discussion of its effects on the practice of bankruptcy law. Paralegals who have a clear understanding of the law and its application will find that they are more productive and more efficient on the job.

Sources of Bankruptcy Law

PRIMARY SOURCES

The primary sources of bankruptcy law are legal resources that contain the actual bankruptcy law. They consist of:

- United States Constitution
- Bankruptcy Code
- Federal Rules of Bankruptcy Procedure
- Federal Rules of Bankruptcy Appellate Procedure
- Local rules of bankruptcy procedure
- State laws regarding bankruptcy exemptions
- Case law

The United States Constitution

As discussed in Chapter 1, *U.S. Const. art. I, § 8* gives Congress the exclusive authority to pass laws regulating bankruptcy. This means that federal law controls the area of bankruptcy, and attorneys and paralegals who practice in this field must become familiar with the appropriate legal research sources to represent clients effectively. Many of the laws bankruptcy practitioners use on a day-to-day basis include the **Bankruptcy Code** and the **Federal Rules of Bankruptcy Procedure**.

Bankruptcy Code

The bankruptcy laws, or statutes, created by Congress are found in Title 11 of the official *United States Code* or in the similarly titled unofficial *U.S.C.A.* published by Thomson-West or *U.S.C.S.* published by LexisNexis. Bankruptcy practitioners commonly refer to it as the Bankruptcy Code or just the Code. Congress passed major bankruptcy legislation in 1800, 1841, 1867, 1898, and 1978, but for purposes of modern-day bankruptcy practice, the 1978 Code and its various amendments is the foundation for American bankruptcy law. The most important amendments to the Code were made in 2005 with the passage of the **Bankruptcy Abuse Prevention and Consumer Protection Act** or, more informally, **BAPCPA**.

The Bankruptcy Code is divided into two classes of chapters, the **universal chapters** and the **operative chapters**. The universal chapters consist of Chapters 1, 3, and 5 and function as an instruction manual or rule book; the remaining chapters of the Code are known as the operative chapters. Chapter 1 includes definitions and general provisions such as who may or may not qualify as a debtor and the powers of the bankruptcy court. It is of particular importance to note that the definition of any bankruptcy term found in Chapter 1 will prevail over a conflicting definition of the same term found outside the Bankruptcy Code.

Bankruptcy Code
The bankruptcy laws, or statutes, created by Congress are found in Title 11 of the official United States Code or in the similarly titled unofficial U.S.C.A. published by Thomson-West or U.S.C.S. published by LexisNexis.

Federal Rules of Bankruptcy Procedure (FRBP)
A supplement to the Bankruptcy Code that includes the mechanics of processing a bankruptcy case. It is abbreviated in the formal *Bluebook* citation form as **Fed. R. Bankr. P.** or the more informal **FRBP** and is often referred to by legal practitioners as the Bankruptcy Rules.

Bankruptcy Abuse Prevention and Consumer Protection Act of 2005 (BAPCPA)
Legislation that was enacted in April of 2005 that made several sweeping changes to the Bankruptcy Code.

universal chapters
Chapters 1, 3, and 5 of the Bankruptcy Code, which operate as an instruction manual or rule book of sorts with regard to the remaining chapters of the code, known as the operative chapters.

operative chapters
Sections of the Bankruptcy Code that define the specific types of bankruptcy filings a debtor may file, depending on his or her eligibility and income level.

Chapter 3 addresses issues surrounding the administration of the bankruptcy estate, the powers of the bankruptcy court, the eligibility and compensation requirements of the trustee, the meeting of the creditors (otherwise known as a *341 meeting*) and the creditors' examination of the debtor under oath.

Chapter 5 is concerned primarily with creditors' claims and the obligations and benefits available to the debtor. This chapter governs issues concerning the creditors' priority status in the case of unsecured debt and determining to what extent a creditor's claim is secured. Chapter 5 includes provisions and language that intend to protect the individual debtor from discrimination in employment by both government and private employers. More specifically, 11 U.S.C. 525 states, in part, that:

> [A] governmental unit may not deny, revoke, suspend, or refuse to renew a license, permit, charter, franchise, or other similar grant to, condition such a grant to, discriminate with respect to such a grant against, deny employment to, terminate the employment of, or discriminate with respect to employment against, a person that is or has been a debtor under this title or a bankrupt or a debtor under the Bankruptcy Act.

Subsection (b), of 11 U.S.C. §525, further states that:

> No private employer may terminate the employment of, or discriminate with respect to employment against, an individual who is or has been a debtor under this title, a debtor or bankrupt under the Bankruptcy Act, or an individual associated with such debtor or bankrupt, solely because such debtor or bankrupt:
>
> 1. is or has been a debtor under this title or a debtor or bankrupt under the Bankruptcy Act;
> 2. has been insolvent before the commencement of a case under this title or during the case but before the grant or denial of a discharge; or
> 3. has not paid a debt that is dischargeable in a case under this title or that was discharged under the Bankruptcy Act.

Bankruptcy Code 11 U.S.C. § 525(a) specifically excludes the Perishable Agricultural Commodities Act, 7 U.S.C. 499 (a) *et. seq.*(2011) from the Code's provisions. Under state law, dealers who purchase or receive products from agricultural producers, such as farmers, must be licensed. These laws provide protection for producers by ensuring that producers are paid and preventing unfair trade practices. If a dealer fails to pay the producer, the producer has the right to file a claim against the dealer. The Perishable Agricultural Commodities Act allows for the revocation of a license for the failure to pay in full for produce purchases. Congress created this exception after lobbying efforts from the agricultural industry and its concerns requested that only financially responsible firms be granted licenses in the perishable agricultural commodity business. It permits termination of a license upon a bankruptcy discharge unless the Secretary of Agriculture "finds upon examination of the circumstances of [the] bankruptcy that such circumstances do not warrant such termination."

The operative chapters discussed in this text include Chapters 7, 11, and 13 and relate to specific types of bankruptcy filings a debtor may file, depending on his or her eligibility and income level. Chapter 15 of the Bankruptcy Code applies to

cross-border insolvency cases
A term that refers to cases filed under Chapter 15 of the Bankruptcy Code. Chapter 15 applies to debtors and creditors and other parties in interest where more than one country is involved.

debtors and creditors and other parties of interest where more than one country is involved. Cases filed under Chapter 15 are sometimes referred to as the **cross-border insolvency cases**. Chapter 15 went into effect on October 17, 2005, after passage of the Bankruptcy Abuse Prevention and Consumer Protection Act of 2005.

Bankruptcy Abuse Prevention and Consumer Protection Act of 2005

The Bankruptcy Abuse Prevention and Consumer Protection Act of 2005, or BAPCPA (pronounced *bap-see-pa*), represents the most significant and sweeping change in the Bankruptcy Code to date and largely affects the process by which debtors file for bankruptcy protection. BAPCPA went into effect on October 17, 2005. The opinions regarding this legislation held by legal scholars and practitioners in the field have varied from negative to positive. Prior to 2005, there was a strong perception that Chapter 7 of the Bankruptcy Code was being abused by individual debtors who had amassed credit card debt and were looking for an easy way out. Although this might have been the case in some instances, Congress was of the opinion that it would be more advantageous for bankruptcy filers to be held accountable for at least some portion of their bills if they qualified according to their income level. It is also important to note that prior to and during the time of BAPCPA's passage, members of the credit card industry were involved in supporting and writing the law.

In an attempt to avoid serial filers from taking advantage of the bankruptcy laws, BAPCPA requires Chapter 7 filers to wait for a period of 8 years after receiving a discharge before they may file again. Furthermore, Chapter 13 filers must wait for a period of 6 years after receiving a discharge.

BAPCPA also places greater responsibility on bankruptcy attorneys to vouch for representations made by their clients with regard to their debts. Bankruptcy attorneys are now required to conduct a reasonable investigation or inquiry into the statements their debtor clients make and may face sanctions by the court or risk dismissal of their client's case if misrepresentations have been made to the court. No longer can an attorney merely take his or her client at his or her word regarding the truthfulness of what is contained in the bankruptcy schedules. Critics of this new requirement seem to be dissatisfied with the lack of guidance from BAPCPA with regard to how to verify the truthfulness of a client's statement or assertion. However, it would appear that practitioners, exercising good judgment and reason, should be reasonably able to verify their client's assertions, as they would in any case, before the court when financial dollar amounts are relied on in rendering judgments.

BAPCPA also requires individual filers to attend pre-petition credit counseling from an approved credit counseling agency. The debtor must also attend a two-hour debtor education course (sometimes referred to as financial management course) again just prior to receiving his or her discharge of debt. The U.S. Department of Justice website provides a directory of approved credit counseling agencies that are listed by state. Many of the agencies are run online and consist of a mixture of online counseling and over-the-phone counseling. The cost for these mandatory courses has been reduced significantly. Courses are now available for as little as $5.00 per certificate for credit counseling and $8.00 per household for debtor education. A certificate of credit counseling completion must be included with the bankruptcy petition, along with an "Exhibit D – Individual Debtor's Statement of Compliance with Credit Counseling Requirement." If the individual debtor is filing jointly, each spouse must file his or her own Exhibit D.

Next, and arguably, the most significant change was the income requirement for Chapter 7 filers and the introduction of the Means Test. This new requirement is intended to reduce the number of Chapter 7 filers because it places restrictions on the income level of the individual debtor based on his or her household income. The basic purpose of the Means Test is to determine whether the debtor is truly broke and deserving of Chapter 7 relief. Each state has a set median income requirement that Chapter 7 filers must meet to file for Chapter 7 liquidation. If an individual's income is above the median set by his or her state, he or she is required to take the Means Test, which will allow him or her to deduct certain government-approved living expenses from their income. After taking the Means Test, the debtor will know how much monthly disposable income he or she has left after deducting the allowed expenses. If the debtor's monthly disposable income is below a certain level, the debtor may file Chapter 7. If the monthly disposable income is above a certain level, the debtor must file under Chapter 13.

With regard to the various state exemptions, and in an effort to prevent what is known as forum shopping, BAPCPA now requires debtors to have lived in their home state for a period of 730 days to be eligible to use that state's exemptions.

LIQUIDATION versus REORGANIZATION

LIQUIDATION

A **liquidation** bankruptcy is filed by a debtor who has very little or no ability to pay back his or her debts and whose income level is low enough to qualify under the BAPCPA. Before filing, the debtor must attend court-approved credit counseling. This type of filing requires the debtor to turn over his or her nonexempt property to the **bankruptcy trustee**. The trustee in turn arranges for the sale of the property according to the Code and distributes the proceeds to the creditors.

Nonexempt property is property that becomes part of the bankruptcy estate and may be sold by the bankruptcy trustee to raise funds to pay back creditors in an orderly fashion. Some examples of nonexempt property include cash, stocks, bonds, family heirlooms and collectibles, and a vacation home. **Exempt property** is property the debtor is allowed to keep despite having filed for bankruptcy. Some examples of exempt property may include automobiles (under a certain value), a portion of the equity in the debtor's home, household appliances, and reasonably necessary clothing and household furnishings.

After all the debtor's creditors are paid, the debtor must attend a second mandatory debtor education course before receiving a discharge. Liquidation bankruptcy cases can last from four to six months or longer, depending on such factors as the quantity of the debtor's nonexempt property items and the number of creditors. A **no-asset case** is one in which the debtor has no nonexempt property. The majority of liquidation cases filed fall into the no-asset category.

REORGANIZATIONS

A **reorganization** is a procedure by which a business or individual restructures, or reorganizes, debt over a long period of time. The purpose behind this restructuring

liquidation
A bankruptcy filing by a debtor who has very little or no ability to pay back his or her debts and whose income level qualifies under the Bankruptcy Abuse Prevention and Consumer Protection Act of 2005. The goal of the liquidation bankruptcy is to discharge the debtor's debt, resulting in a fresh start.

bankruptcy trustee
An individual appointed by the bankruptcy court, who is responsible for arranging the sale of the debtor's property and distributing the proceeds to the creditors.

nonexempt property
Property that becomes part of the bankruptcy estate and may be sold by the bankruptcy trustee to raise funds to pay back creditors.

exempt property
Property that is exempt from seizure by creditors.

no-asset case
A bankruptcy case in which most of the debtor's assets are exempt from the proceedings, leaving no nonexempt property for the trustee to sell.

reorganization
A bankruptcy in which the business or individual filing works closely with the bankruptcy court, directly or with the assistance of a bankruptcy attorney, to restructure or reorganize debt.

plan of reorganization
A process by which the debtor creates a plan designed to restructure the financial claims owed to the creditor so that the debtor's business may remain viable and stand on its own without the legal protections of a Chapter 11 filing.

is to make repayment of the debt more manageable under the terms of a repayment plan, or **plan of reorganization**.

Most often, a debtor and his or her attorney must file several plans of reorganization with the bankruptcy court before the court approves the plan. Once approved, the debtor is required to make monthly payments to the bankruptcy trustee pursuant to the plan. The trustee then makes payments to the creditors.

One of the biggest advantages of a reorganization is that the debtor is allowed to remain in control over his or her assets. This proves especially helpful when the debtor is a business and would like to continue to run its business while being at least temporarily relieved from most creditors' claims or aggressive collection attempts. In addition, the business debtor may be able to suspend making installment payments temporarily on such things as rent and business equipment during reorganization. The debtor in a reorganization case is referred to as a **debtor in possession (DIP)** because of the control retained over most aspects of its business and assets. For the individual debtor, a reorganization plan helps the individual who has regular income by allowing him or her to retain nonexempt assets while making more manageable repayments.

debtor in possession (DIP)
An individual or business that files for Chapter 11 relief while it still has control over its assets and continues operating without having to seek court approval.

The Operative Chapters

Chapters 7, 9, 11, 12, 13, and 15 are known as the operative chapters of the Bankruptcy Code. The following section includes a brief introduction to each chapter, its eligibility requirements and benefits, and its drawbacks.

CHAPTER 7

Chapter 7 is the operative chapter that deals exclusively with liquidation. Individuals, partnerships, and certain types of businesses that plan to close their operations and rid themselves of debt may file under Chapter 7. Chapter 7 gives the debtor an opportunity to eliminate most of his or her unsecured debt relatively quickly and attain what is known as a fresh start after receiving a **discharge of debt**. Some debt, such as priority unsecured debt, will not be discharged.

discharge of debt
A ruling issued by a bankruptcy judge that releases the debtor from liability and prohibits the creditor from pursuing any legal action to collect those debts.

Chapter 7 liquidation is also known as a straight bankruptcy, total bankruptcy, or complete bankruptcy. It is the chapter of the Bankruptcy Code that most people think about when they hear the word *bankruptcy* because it involves a liquidation of certain items owned by the debtor. The United States Trustee appoints and supervises a Chapter 7 trustee, who has the specific function of collecting the debtor's nonexempt assets and selling off those assets to raise money to pay off creditors in their order of priority. Finally, this leaves the court to discharge the remaining debts.

Most Chapter 7 filings are classified as no-asset cases because many Chapter 7 filers either have very little in the way of assets, or all the assets the debtor has are classified as exempt. Typically, a no-asset case, as mentioned previously, can be resolved in as little as 4 months.

A debtor may convert his or her Chapter 7 case to a Chapter 11, 12, or 13 at any time, provided he or she qualifies and has not previously converted the case from a Chapter 11, 12, or 13 bankruptcy. The court may also, on request by an interested party (e.g., creditor), and after proper notification and a hearing, convert a debtor's case to a Chapter 11 proceeding. The bankruptcy court may not convert a debtor's case to a Chapter 12 or 13 unless the debtor has consented to such a conversion. The Bankruptcy Code also contains language that operates to protect soldiers and sailors overseas from having their Chapter 7 case dismissed or converted to another bankruptcy chapter in their absence. The Bankruptcy Code states as follows: "A Chapter 7 case cannot be dismissed or converted based on any form of means testing if the debtor is a disabled veteran and the indebtedness occurred primarily during a period of active duty or while the debtor was performing a homeland defense activity." 11 U.S.C. §707(b)(2)(D)(i)&(ii).

CHAPTER 9

Chapter 9 is designed to assist a municipality, school district, town, city, and county with restructuring its debts and to shield itself from the collections efforts of its creditors. Prior to a Chapter 9 filing, the municipality debtor must negotiate with its creditors. If the debtor cannot reach an agreement with its creditors, it may then file for bankruptcy under Chapter 9. Chapter 9 filings are similar to other reorganization filings such as Chapters 11 and 13 in that the municipality debtor must compose and file a plan of adjustment with the court and, after that plan is approved, the municipality becomes bound to all of its creditors.

In a Chapter 9 case, the bankruptcy court has considerably less power over the actions of the debtor than it does in other chapters. The court has no authority to direct the way in which the municipality raises funds, nor does it have the power to impede any of the political powers the debtor may hold. If a Chapter 9 plan of reorganization is not successfully negotiated or if the debtor has difficulty keeping up with its payments to the creditors, it does not have the option to liquidate. As with the other chapters of the Bankruptcy Code, the bankruptcy court has the power to dismiss a Chapter 9 filing that was not filed in good faith. The Bankruptcy Court also has the power to disapprove of a Chapter 9 repayment plan that was not proposed in good faith. Further, the bankruptcy court has taken the position that it cannot interfere with the operations of the debtor nor with the debtor's use of its property and revenues. This is at least partly because in a Chapter 9 case, there is no property of the estate and thus no estate to administer.

Chapter 9 filings have been historically rare. In fact, roughly 140 Chapter 9 cases have been filed across the United States since 1980. Furthermore, a municipality's eligibility to file Chapter 9 is limited from state to state and depends on whether the municipality is authorized by the state to be a Chapter 9 debtor. In an already strained economy and with the continuing hardships faced by many communities across the nation, what was once a relatively rare occurrence, may, unfortunately, become slightly more commonplace.

Since January 2010, the following municipalities have filed for bankruptcy: San Bernardino, California; Mammoth Lakes, California; Stockton, California; Jefferson County, Alabama; Harrisburg, Pennsylvania; Central Falls, Rhode Island; and Boise County, Idaho. Add to this list the Motor City, Detroit, Michigan, as the one municipality to make international headlines as the largest Chapter 9 bankruptcy filing in the history of the United States. On Thursday, July 18, 2013, after enduring many years of an economic downturn and on the verge of defaulting on nearly $14 billion dollars in public debt, the city of Detroit, Michigan, filed for Chapter 9 bankruptcy protection. Since the 1960s, when the auto industry slowly began moving away from the city, Detroit has seen a decrease in property values and an increase in crime. What was once a thriving industrial hub with a population of 2 million in the early 1950s is now a city of roughly 700,000 inhabitants.

Detroit has the highest tax rate of any other city in the state of Michigan, with the smallest number of services for its citizens in exchange for that high tax rate. On November 7, 2014, the bankruptcy court confirmed the city's plan of reorganization, going into effect some time in December 2014. The plan is not without its challengers, however, with retired city employees requesting a stay of the implementation while they appeal on the grounds that the decision would result in deep cuts to their pension benefits.

CHAPTER 11

Chapter 11 cases, sometimes referred to as reorganization cases, are most often filed by businesses (sole proprietorships, partnerships, and corporations) to reorganize their debt while retaining all their assets and continuing to do business. The fact that the business debtor is allowed to retain the assets of the business as well as operate and oversee the day-to-day operations of the business is the reason a Chapter 11 debtor is sometimes referred to as a debtor in possession, or DIP (articulated D-I-P). In a small percentage of cases, individuals may file under Chapter 11 but must meet the credit counseling and other requirements of the Bankruptcy Code prior to filing. The DIP is treated by the bankruptcy court as a **fiduciary** with similar powers to that of a Chapter 11 trustee. The fiduciary role that the debtor in possession takes on includes the duty to report to the court on such issues as business accountings, examining creditors' claims, and filing business tax returns. The U.S. trustee oversees the debtor in possession throughout this process.

Chapter 11 allows more flexibility than Chapter 13 for individuals who own more than one parcel of real property or do not meet the requirements of either Chapter 7 or Chapter 13. As in all reorganization cases, the debtor in a Chapter 11 case is required to develop and file a plan of reorganization with the bankruptcy court. This plan includes the debtor's proposal regarding how the debt will be paid. Unlike a Chapter 13 plan, a Chapter 11 plan is not limited to a 3- to 5-year period.

Creditors' representatives form a creditors' committee to represent their interests in discussions, negotiations, and evaluation of the plan, which ultimately must be approved by the bankruptcy court. The debtor's reorganization plan is often developed or proposed in a way that reduces the amount owed to the creditors and spreads the payments made to the creditors over a period of time. It is usually a good idea for the debtor to involve its creditors in this process because many debtors find that their plans for reorganization are more readily accepted by their creditors when they had input in its implementation. Along with the plan for reorganization, the Chapter 11 debtor must file a **disclosure statement**, which must include information such as the financial details of the debtor's business, enough to allow the creditors to determine how their interests will be affected under the proposed plan.

In the case of most business filings, the goal of a Chapter 11 case is to allow the business debtor an opportunity to restructure its debt and ultimately save its business. However, most recently, there has been an increase in the number of cases that begin as Chapter 11 reorganizations and end up in liquidation. Factors such as the economy and the increased administrative costs imposed by the Bankruptcy Abuse Prevention and Consumer Protection Act of 2005 may have contributed to this trend.

fiduciary
One who holds a position of trust and generally manages the money of another person or persons and has similar powers to those of a Chapter 11 trustee.

disclosure statement
A document that lists all the mandatory disclosures required in 11 U.S.C. § 527, Section 527. It includes information such as the financial details of the debtor's business, enough to allow the creditors to determine how their interests will be affected.

CHAPTER 12

Congress added Chapter 12 to the Bankruptcy Code in 1986 as a temporary solution for family farmers and those involved in the fishing industry who were experiencing credit problems and facing the loss of their property and equipment as a result. Bankruptcy filings under this chapter comprise a very small percentage of bankruptcy filings each year. To qualify under this chapter, individuals or businesses must be engaged in the fishing or farming industry, have regular income, and have a total debt not exceeding $1,757,475 for those involved in the fishing industry and a total debt not exceeding $3,792,650 for farmers. Chapter 12 is now a permanent chapter of the Bankruptcy Code.

Chapter 12 requires the debtor to formulate and propose a reorganization plan or debt repayment plan for court and creditor approval. After the repayment plan is approved by the court, the onus is on the debtor to maintain his or her plan payments in a timely manner. Failure to do so can result in a dismissal of the case or a conversion of the case to a Chapter 7 liquidation. Much like Chapter 11, the goal of a Chapter 12 case is to allow the family farmer or fisher an opportunity to restructure debt and ultimately save his or her business. A trustee oversees the implementation of the plan.

CHAPTER 13

Chapter 13, sometimes referred to as the wage-earner plan, is a reorganization plan that is available for individuals who have regular income and who have sufficient disposable income each month to maintain a repayment plan. To file under Chapter 13, an individual debtor or married couple must have secured debts not exceeding $1,149,525 and unsecured debts not exceeding $383,175 (as of April 1, 2013). The individual must complete individual or group credit counseling from an approved credit counseling agency within 180 days of filing for Chapter 13. Only individuals are eligible to file for bankruptcy protection under Chapter 13. The definition of *individual* includes sole proprietors but excludes limited liability companies, partnerships, or corporations. A sole proprietor is generally a debtor operating a business either in his or her own name or under a fictitious name. It does not have the corporate or partnership designation prohibiting a Chapter 13 filing and may take advantage of Chapter 13 when the sole proprietor has both personal and business debts.

To be considered **regular income**, the debtor's income does not have to be from traditional employment to qualify as such. Pension payments, public benefits, domestic support (child support and alimony), unemployment benefits, social security, and payments received from royalties and rents can all qualify as regular income that can be used to fund a Chapter 13 repayment plan. A debtor's **disposable income** is the income left over after deducting allowable expenses and is determined by the Means Test. The Means Test will be discussed in detail in Chapter 5 of this text. The debtor is expected to devote his or her entire disposable income to the payment of unsecured claims and may not incur any new debt without first informing the trustee. It is the responsibility of the trustee to distribute the proceeds collected from the debtor to the creditors in accordance with the repayment plan.

Chapter 13 is an advantageous chapter for debtors who owe nondischargeable debts such as child support and taxes or debts that are difficult to discharge such as student loans. Once again, the debtor proposes a plan that includes how debts owed

regular income
Debtor's income from traditional employment as well as pension payments, public benefits, domestic support (child support and alimony), unemployment benefits, social security, and payments received from royalties and rents.

disposable income
Income remaining after the debtor pays for certain expenses the Bankruptcy Code allows such as mortgage payments, health insurance payments, medical bills, and food bills.

to the creditors are to be paid off over a period of 3 to 5 years. The bankruptcy court must approve the plan before any payments can be made. The debtor makes payments directly to the trustee, who distributes the payments to the creditors. After the plan payments are complete, the debtor's unsecured debt is discharged. Although student loan debt is generally considered unsecured debt, it is typically not subject to discharge. Moreover, student loans are often paid just pennies on the dollar in Chapter 13 cases. Therefore, the balance of the debt survives discharge.

DOLLAR AMOUNT ADJUSTMENTS

The threshold dollar amounts for certain figures in the Bankruptcy Code are adjusted every 3 years to reflect the changes in the Consumer Price Index published by the Department of Labor. Examples of bankruptcy matters affected by the dollar amount adjustments include:

- Certain maximum values of property that a debtor may claim as exempt
- Calculation of the Means Test for Chapter 7 debtors
- Definition of a small-business debtor
- Duration of a Chapter 13 plan
- Eligibility of a debtor to file under Chapters 12 and 13
- Maximum amount of certain claims entitled to priority
- Minimum aggregate value of claims needed to commence an involuntary bankruptcy
- Value of luxury goods and services deemed nondischargeable
- Where the trustee may commence certain proceedings to recover a money judgment or property

The dollar amount adjustments became effective on April 1 of the three-year interval period. New figures went into effect on April 1, 2013, and are due for another adjustment on April 1, 2016. (11 U.S.C. §104) It is important for legal professionals to keep these adjustment dates in mind because the changes reflect the rendering of bankruptcy services to clients.

Federal Rules of Bankruptcy Procedure

Fed. R. Bankr. P. (FRBP)
The **Federal Rules of Bankruptcy Procedure** is a supplement to the Bankruptcy Code that includes the mechanics of processing a bankruptcy case. It is abbreviated in the formal *Bluebook* citation form as **Fed. R. Bankr. P.** or the more informal **FRBP** and are often referred to by legal practitioners as the "Bankruptcy Rules."

The Federal Rules of Bankruptcy Procedure includes the mechanics of processing a bankruptcy case and was adopted by order of the United States Supreme Court as a supplement to the Bankruptcy Code. It is abbreviated in the formal *Bluebook* citation form as **Fed. R. Bankr. P.** or the more informal **FRBP** and is often referred to by legal practitioners as the Bankruptcy Rules. Fed. R. Bankr. 1001 defines the scope of the rules.

Fed. R. Bankr. P. 1001 Scope of Rules and Forms, Short Title

The Bankruptcy Rules and Forms govern procedure in cases under title 11 of the United States Code. The rules shall be cited as the Federal Rules of Bankruptcy Procedure and the forms as the Official Bankruptcy Forms. These rules shall be construed to secure the just, speedy, and inexpensive determination of every case and proceeding.

OFFICIAL BANKRUPTCY FORMS

The United States courts require debtors, as well as creditors and other claimants, to use the **Official Bankruptcy Forms**. These forms are available free of charge and in PDF through the United States Courts website. Fed. R. Bankr. P. 9009 states that forms may be combined and contents rearranged; however, they must be consistent with Rules of Bankruptcy Procedure as well as the Bankruptcy Code. Care should be taken when scripting the forms to ensure that all the necessary portions of the Official Forms, including declarations made under penalty of law, are included in the scripted form.

> **Fed. R. Bankr. P. 9009 Forms**
>
> Except as otherwise provided in Rule 3016(d), the Official Forms prescribed by the Judicial Conference of the United States shall be observed and used with alterations as may be appropriate. Forms may be combined and their contents rearranged to permit economies in their use. The Director of the Administrative Office of the United States Courts may issue additional forms for use under the Code. The forms shall be construed to be consistent with these rules and the Code.

Official Bankruptcy Forms
The forms that are approved by the Judicial Conference of the United States that include the Petition, Schedules of the debtors assets and debts, and Statement of Financial Affairs.

LOCAL RULES

The federal judicial district courts have the authority under the Federal Rules of Bankruptcy Procedure to create their own procedural rules for facilitating the bankruptcy process in that particular judicial district as long as they are consistent with the federal rules. Paralegals working in bankruptcy law offices should quickly become familiar with the local rules that govern the federal courts in their respective states. Local bankruptcy rules may be found on the official website of the bankruptcy court located in that U.S. district. The following section of the Federal Rules of Bankruptcy Procedure lays the groundwork for the local bankruptcy rules.

STATE LAW

Although bankruptcy is primarily governed by federal law, state law does affect bankruptcy practice. Statutes regulating the debtor–creditor relationship, for example, are state-specific. State law also governs state exemptions. An exemption is the value of property that a debtor is allowed to keep when filing for bankruptcy. If the debtor's district court rules have adopted state exemptions, the debtor may claim either federal or state exemptions, whichever is more advantageous to the debtor. Common exemptions include exemption for real property called homestead, wages, automobiles, and personal property.

BANKRUPTCY CASE LAW

Bankruptcy court decisions may be retrieved online using a legal research service such as LEXIS and WESTLAW as well as in *West's Bankruptcy Reporter, CCH Bankruptcy Law Reporter*, and *Collier Bankruptcy Cases*. Some bankruptcy court cases may also be found on various Internet websites. Reviewing bankruptcy court decisions is a valuable tool in determining how the federal courts interpret the Bankruptcy Code as well as are other primary sources of bankruptcy law.

SECONDARY SOURCES

Secondary sources are helpful when research is necessary to obtain some understanding or background regarding a bankruptcy issue. Although secondary sources are not cited as law, they are of great assistance, especially when starting at square one on a bankruptcy topic. Secondary sources include treatises such as *Norton Bankruptcy Law and Practice* (Westlaw) and *Collier on Bankruptcy* (LexisNexis) and legal encyclopedias such as *American Jurisprudence Second* and *Corpus Juris Secundum*, both of which have topic sections dedicated to bankruptcy law.

INTERNET

Several Internet websites are very helpful for attorneys and paralegals working in the field of bankruptcy law. Some useful websites include *The American Bankruptcy Institute, Findlaw, Legal Information Institute (LII) Cornell Law School, U.S. Bankruptcy Courts,* and *U.S. Trustee Program.* Another valuable resource is using an Internet search engine such as Google or Bing to locate bankruptcy law blogs or bar association articles written by bankruptcy law practitioners. These sites often provide useful information, including invaluable case summaries, articles on statutory or procedural changes, and practice pointers.

You may recall Glinda McNeal, the eager new bankruptcy law student from the beginning of this chapter. Her interest in this subject area began with her connection to someone experiencing financial difficulty. Most of us, from time to time, have known someone who struggled to pay his or her bills, lost a job, or went through a foreclosure, a person who piqued our interest in how one can deal with such tough financial situations. We hope that after reading this chapter, your interest in this subject has grown as well. Knowing the very foundations of this area of law and how those foundations evolved into the complex, yet manageable, current Bankruptcy Code helps us become better advocates for those in financial need.

CHAPTER **SUMMARY**

The primary sources of bankruptcy law include the United States Constitution, Bankruptcy Code, Federal Rules of Bankruptcy Procedure, Federal Rules of Bankruptcy Appellate Procedure, local rules of bankruptcy procedure, state laws regarding bankruptcy exemptions, and case law. The universal chapters of the Bankruptcy Code consist of Chapters 1, 3, and 5 and function as an instruction manual or rule book. Chapters 7, 9, 11, 12, 13, and 15 are known as the operative chapters of the Bankruptcy Code.

The Bankruptcy Abuse Prevention and Consumer Protection Act of 2005, or BAPCPA, (pronounced *bap-see-pa*), represents the most significant and sweeping change to the Bankruptcy Code to date and largely affects the process by which debtors file for bankruptcy protection. BAPCPA went into effect on October 17, 2005. The changes BAPCPA ushered in include waiting periods to prevent serial bankruptcy filings, greater responsibility on bankruptcy attorneys for representations made on behalf of clients regarding their debts, mandatory pre-petition counseling and debtor education course, the Means Test calculation, and longer residency requirements to qualify for state exemptions.

A liquidation bankruptcy is filed by a debtor who has very little or no ability to pay back his or her debts and whose income level is low enough to qualify under the Bankruptcy Abuse Prevention and Consumer Protection Act of 2005. A reorganization is the procedure by which a business or individual restructures, or reorganizes, his or her debt with the goal of developing a plan of reorganization. Secondary sources include treatises, legal encyclopedias, and resources found on the Internet such as case summaries, articles on statutory or procedural changes, and practice pointers.

CONCEPT REVIEW AND REINFORCEMENT

KEY **TERMS**

Bankruptcy Abuse Prevention
  and Consumer Protection Act
  of 2005 (BAPCPA)
Bankruptcy Code
bankruptcy trustee
cross-border insolvency cases
debtor in possession (DIP)
discharge of debt

disclosure statement
disposable income
exempt property
Fed. R. Bankr. P. (FRBP)
Federal Rules of Bankruptcy
  Procedure (FRBP)
fiduciary
liquidation

no-asset case
nonexempt property
Official Bankruptcy Forms
operative chapters
plan of reorganization
regular income
reorganization
universal chapters

REVIEWING **KEY CONCEPTS**

1. Name the most relevant Bankruptcy Code revision and amendments for modern-day bankruptcy law.
2. Using the Internet, locate and review Fed. R. Bankr. P. 1001 and define the scope of the bankruptcy rules.
3. Fed. R. Bankr. P. 9009 indicates an exception regarding the use of Official Bankruptcy Forms in Fed. R. Bankr. P. 3016(d). Locate this section of the rules on the Internet and explain this exception.
4. Explain how local rules affect a bankruptcy case.
5. Explain how state laws affect federal bankruptcy practice.

BUILDING YOUR PARALEGAL SKILLS

CASE **FOR REVIEW**

In Re Francisco, 390 B.R. 700 (B.A.P.10th Cir. 2008)

BUILDING A PROFESSIONAL PORTFOLIO

PORTFOLIO **EXERCISES**

You work for the law offices of Brian Burgh, LLC, and your firm represents the debtor Sam Greene. Sam Greene is an individual debtor with primarily consumer debts. Draft a letter to the client on behalf of your supervising attorney explaining the differences between Chapter 7 and Chapter 13 bankruptcy filings. Be sure to inform the client of the pre-petition responsibilities he must fulfill.

LEARNING OBJECTIVES

After studying this chapter, you should be able to:

1. Understand the jurisdiction and basic structure of the bankruptcy court.

2. Explain the roles of the bankruptcy participants.

3. Describe the bankruptcy process.

4. Summarize the three important Bankruptcy Code sections that apply to debt relief agencies.

5. Describe the role of bankruptcy mediation.

Tyquan Wilson worked for many years as a supervisor in a high-end clothing store in Manhattan. With the continuing decline of the economy, his store began to see a steady drop in sales approximately 2 years ago. Although the store managed to survive for a while, it eventually filed for Chapter 11 bankruptcy and had to lay off Tyquan as part of its downsizing and restructuring process. Having heard so much about his former employer's bankruptcy and eventually being forced to file for bankruptcy himself, Tyquan developed an interest in the process and wanted to help other people going through similar financial struggles. Tyquan enrolled at his local community college in its paralegal program and chose bankruptcy law as one of his electives. One of the first things Tyquan's instructor did in his bankruptcy class was lay out the structure of the bankruptcy court system and the various participants in the bankruptcy process, including the debtor, the bankruptcy court, the trustees, and the creditors. Read on to gain a basic knowledge of the American bankruptcy system.

Introduction

Bankruptcy law and practice is like a pocket watch packed with so many gears, all moving at the same time, that it is difficult to describe one part without having an understanding of the whole. Therefore, a basic knowledge of the bankruptcy system is crucial at the beginning of this textbook to provide the paralegal student with enough introductory information to comprehend the chapters that follow. This chapter begins with a section on the jurisdiction and structure of the bankruptcy court and the roles of the various participants who either work within or eventually enter the system. A brief overview of the bankruptcy process is presented, starting with the actual decision to file for bankruptcy and progressing all the way to the discharge or dismissal of the bankruptcy case. This chapter also includes an introduction to bankruptcy mediation and bankruptcy appeals.

Throughout this chapter, references are made to the **Bankruptcy Abuse Prevention and Consumer Protection Act of 2005,** or **BAPCPA**. BAPCPA amendments represent the most sweeping changes to Bankruptcy Code since the enactment of the Bankruptcy Reform Act of 1978. In light of these significant changes, this chapter looks at the relevant sections under BAPCPA that classify bankruptcy attorneys and their firms as debt relief agencies, placing new requirements and restrictions on those who practice bankruptcy law.

Bankruptcy Abuse Prevention and Consumer Protection Act of 2005 (BAPCPA)
Legislation that was enacted in April of 2005 that made several sweeping changes to the Bankruptcy Code.

Bankruptcy Court Jurisdiction and Structure

For purposes of this section, the term **jurisdiction** is defined as the power or authority of a court to hear and resolve a case. The federal courts, or U.S. district courts, have exclusive jurisdiction over bankruptcy cases, with 94 federal judicial districts throughout the United States. When a court has exclusive jurisdiction, it is the only court that may hear this particular type of case. Therefore, state courts do not have jurisdiction over bankruptcy cases. The federal district courts are the first-tier courts in the federal system and function as the trial courts. A trial court is where the case is first heard in the court system, where the facts are presented before a judge or jury. The U.S. district courts are the federal trial courts and therefore have the authority to hear both civil and criminal cases. Bankruptcy courts are structured as special units *within* the U.S. District Court system. There is at least one bankruptcy court per federal judicial district. Larger judicial districts, such as California for example, have four bankruptcy courts, which serve the Central, Eastern, Northern, and Southern districts of California.

jurisdiction
The power or authority of a court to hear and resolve a case.

The Bankruptcy Participants

THE BANKRUPTCY ESTATE

All of the debtor's legal and equitable interest in property at the moment the bankruptcy petition is filed creates the **bankruptcy estate**. A bankruptcy estate is a new legal entity separate from the debtor; much like a probate estate in the field of trusts and estates. The bankruptcy estate also includes property and income that is acquired after the commencement of the case, so it is important for clients filing for bankruptcy to be aware of their obligations to inform the attorney of any after-acquired property. According to Bankruptcy Code 11 U.S.C. §541, the bankruptcy estate consists of:

bankruptcy estate
All the legal and equitable interests a debtor may own in property at the time he or she files a Chapter 7 petition. It also includes any property the debtor receives within 180 days of the filing date of the petition.

- Property owned by the debtor, either in his or her possession or possession of another (e.g., real estate, bank accounts, stocks and bonds, patents, copyrights, and trademarks).
- Property the debtor is entitled to receive (e.g., wages, commissions, and tax refunds).
- Profits or appreciation in value generated by the property of the estate (e.g., rents and interest).
- Property that was fraudulently transferred prior to the bankruptcy filing (e.g., debtor sells his motorcycle to his cousin for $1.00 or quitclaims his interest in real property to a family member).

- Preferential payments made to creditors prior to the bankruptcy filing (e.g., debtor pays debt owed to his favorite supplier).
- Property acquired within 180 days after the bankruptcy filing (e.g., life insurance proceeds, inheritance).
- Community property.

The Debtor

debtor
An individual, corporation, partnership, or municipality seeking relief in the bankruptcy court from debts owed to creditors.

The central participant in the bankruptcy process is the debtor. For the purpose of bankruptcy law, a **debtor** may be an individual, corporation, partnership, or municipality seeking relief in bankruptcy court from debts owed to creditors. Bankruptcy Code 11 U.S.C. § 101 (13) defines a debtor as a "person or municipality concerning which a case under this title has been commenced." Bankruptcy Code 11 U.S.C. § 101 (41) defines a person as an individual, partnership, and corporation but does not include governmental unit. Only a person who is domiciled or has a principal place of business or property in the United States, or is a municipality, may file for bankruptcy protection under 11 U.S.C. §109 of the Bankruptcy Code.

Many debtors voluntarily petition the bankruptcy court when they are unable to pay their debts. Some debtors are subjected to an involuntary bankruptcy when their creditors force them into the process because they are unable to pay the debts owed, and creditors are afraid that the debtors might squander the remaining assets.

The Creditors and Creditors' Committee

claims
A creditor's right to receive payment for debts owed by debtors.

Creditors are individuals or business entities who are owed debts by debtors who have been unable to meet their obligations. Creditors have **claims** against the bankruptcy estate after a voluntary or involuntary bankruptcy petition is filed with the court. This means that they have a right to receive payment. These claims, however, are subject to other provisions of the Bankruptcy Code, which may limit or eliminate the claims owed or paid to the creditor. The Bankruptcy Code defines claims in 11 U.S.C. §101(5)(A) and (B):

(5) The term "claim" means—
(A) right to payment, whether or not such right is reduced to judgment, liquidated, unliquidated, fixed, contingent, matured, unmatured, disputed, undisputed, legal, equitable, secured, or unsecured; or
(B) right to an equitable remedy for breach of performance if such breach gives rise to a right to payment, whether or not such right to an equitable remedy is reduced to judgment, fixed, contingent, matured, unmatured, disputed, undisputed, secured, or unsecured.

Creditors or the classification of claims in a bankruptcy case fall into three major categories:

secured creditors
Creditors that have a claim against the debtor, and the property is secured as collateral in exchange for extension of credit.

- **Secured creditor** A secured creditor holds a claim against the debtor's property as collateral in exchange for extension of credit. For example, the bank loans the debtor money to purchase a car. The debtor falls behind on the car payments and, as a result, the bank, as a secured creditor, has the right to repossess the car. A bank loan for a home mortgage also puts the bank in the position of a secured creditor.

- **Unsecured creditor** An unsecured creditor holds a claim against the debtor, but there is no collateral in exchange for the extension of credit. For example, some credit cards are, by their terms, considered unsecured debt. Under these credit card agreements, the bank is an unsecured creditor and does not have the right to repossess the goods. This is one of the reasons interest rates for unsecured credit cards are so high; the bank is taking a risk by not securing the goods the consumer purchases. Not all credit cards, however, are classified as unsecured debts. Some are secured under the terms of an often overlooked clause in the credit card agreement called a **purchase money security interest (PMSI)**. A PMSI clause gives the creditor the right to repossess the goods if the debtor does not make payments in a timely fashion. Popular stores such as Best Buy, Sears, and Circuit City, to name a few, include these clauses in their credit card agreements. Even if the debt is discharged in bankruptcy, the creditor still has the right to repossess the goods. In reality, repossession of the goods is rare. Most creditors do not want to amass large amounts of used, repossessed goods but, instead, use the clause as a threat to encourage debtors to make payments. These debts may be reaffirmed or resumed by the debtor after a bankruptcy so that the debtor may retain possession of the goods.
- **Priority creditor** A priority creditor is an unsecured creditor whose claims take precedence over the claims of other creditors. Examples of some of the debts that receive priority in a bankruptcy case include domestic support obligations such as alimony and child support, bankruptcy court administrative expenses, employee wages, and taxes.

A **creditors' committee** is a group that represents creditors that have claims against a business in a bankruptcy proceeding. The creditors' committee is divided between secured and unsecured creditors.

The Bankruptcy Court

The **bankruptcy court** is a unit of the U.S. District Court; it is where the bankruptcy petition is filed and the system in which the bankruptcy case is processed.

The Bankruptcy Judge

The **bankruptcy judge** presides over bankruptcy proceedings, serving a 14-year term. The role of the bankruptcy judge is to hear arguments and resolve issues among the parties, rule on motions, conduct hearings, determine whether debtors qualify for relief under the Bankruptcy Code, administer rules under Bankruptcy Procedures and Bankruptcy Code, and determine whether a debtor should receive a discharge. The chief judge of the bankruptcy court is responsible for ensuring that both federal and local bankruptcy court rules are followed and that the administrative aspects of the court run smoothly and efficiently.

The United States Trustee

Bankruptcy cases are administered under the auspices of the United States trustee. The **United States trustee** is a federal official employed by the government and appointed by the U.S. Attorney General. There are 21 regional U.S. trustees offices

unsecured creditor
A creditor whose debt is not secured by collateral.

purchase money security interest (PMSI)
A clause in a credit card agreement that gives the creditor the right to repossess the goods if the debtor does not make payments in a timely fashion.

priority creditor
A creditor to whom no type of collateral is pledged by the debtor to satisfy the loan if the debtor defaults on payment; an unsecured creditor whose claims take precedence over the claims of other creditors.

creditors' committee
A group appointed by the United States trustee that represents creditors that have claims against a business in a bankruptcy proceeding. The creditors' committee is divided between secured and unsecured creditors.

bankruptcy court
A unit of the U.S. District Court where the bankruptcy petition is filed and the system in which the bankruptcy case is processed.

bankruptcy judge
An individual who presides over the bankruptcy proceedings, serving for a 14-year term, whose role is to hear arguments and resolve issues among the parties, rule on motions, conduct hearings, determine whether debtors qualify for relief under the Bankruptcy Code, administer rules under Bankruptcy Procedures and Bankruptcy Code, and determine whether a debtor should receive a discharge.

United States trustee
A federal official employed by the government and appointed by the U.S. Attorney General, who is responsible for enforcing the civil provisions of the bankruptcy laws of the United States by supervising the administration of bankruptcy cases and the functions of private trustees.

located throughout the federal district courts except for the states of Alabama and North Carolina. (In these two states, a bankruptcy administrator oversees the administration of bankruptcy cases.) The U.S. trustee is responsible for enforcing the civil provisions of the bankruptcy laws of the United States by supervising the administration of bankruptcy cases and the functions of private trustees. The main goal of the U.S. trustee is to preserve the integrity of the bankruptcy process. The U.S. trustee monitors each bankruptcy case to ensure that the Bankruptcy Code is properly enforced and prevent fraud and abuse by reviewing petitions and schedules filed with the bankruptcy court. He or she conducts audits to determine whether further investigation is required in suspicious filings. U.S. trustees have more involvement in Chapter 11 cases, in which they monitor proceedings related to business reorganizations and individual Chapter 11 cases.

U.S. trustees and Assistant U.S. trustees are appointed by the Attorney General, serve for a five-year term, and may be removed from office if necessary. Criminal violations of bankruptcy law are not prosecuted by the U.S. trustees; rather, the case is referred to federal law enforcement for investigation and sent to the United States Attorney for prosecution. The U.S. Trustee Program's responsibilities under the Bankruptcy Abuse Prevention and Consumer Protection Act of 2005 (BAPCPA) include the implementation of a means test to determine whether a debtor's filing for Chapter 7 is eligible for liquidation of his or her debt or is required to file for Chapter 13 repayment plan.

The Private Trustee

private trustees
Appointed by the U.S. trustee to administer bankruptcy estates filed under Chapters 7, 12, and 13. Private trustees are not considered government employees but are private attorneys who are supervised by and work in conjunction with the U.S. trustee.

The role of the private trustee is different from that of the U.S. trustee. **Private trustees** are appointed by the U.S. trustee to administer bankruptcy estates filed under Chapters 7, 11, and 13. Private trustees are not considered government employees but are private attorneys supervised by and who work in conjunction with the U.S. trustee. There are two types of private trustees. One is a **panel trustee**, who serves on a panel in a particular judicial district and is assigned Chapter 7 bankruptcies and functions similarly to an executor in a probate estate. The duties of the panel trustee consist of collecting the debtor's nonexempt assets, liquidating them to raise funds, and distributing whatever is left over to the creditors in order of priority. **Standing trustees** are responsible for administering Chapters 11 and 13 bankruptcies in designated geographic areas within the judicial district. Standing trustees who administer Chapter 13 cases review the financial status of the debtor, make recommendations to the bankruptcy court regarding confirmation of the debtor's repayment plan, collect money from debtors, and make payments to creditors pursuant to a bankruptcy court repayment plan. No trustees are appointed in Chapter 11 cases in which the debtor serves as its own trustee unless cause exists, in which case, the U.S. trustee or creditor can motion the court for the appointment of a case trustee.

panel trustee
An individual who serves on a panel in a particular judicial district and is assigned Chapter 7 bankruptcies and functions similarly to an executor in a probate estate.

standing trustees
An individual responsible for administering Chapter 12 and Chapter 13 bankruptcies in designated geographic areas within the judicial district.

bankruptcy examiner
An individual appointed by the court in Chapter 11 cases to scrutinize the financial affairs of a debtor.

The Bankruptcy Examiner

The **bankruptcy examiner** is appointed by the court in Chapter 11 cases to look into the financial affairs of a debtor. The examiner is responsible for investigating claims of fraud, dishonesty, incompetence, mismanagement, or misconduct. Although the examiner is appointed at the request of any affected party in a bankruptcy case, an examiner must be appointed by the court when the debtor's unsecured debts exceed $5,000,000.

The Bankruptcy Attorney

A **bankruptcy attorney** may represent a debtor, creditor, or another interested party in a bankruptcy proceeding. The bankruptcy attorney has many responsibilities, which begin with the initial consultation and the rendering of legal advice to the client. He or she assesses the client's financial situation and advises the client on the best course of action to take regarding debt relief. Filing for bankruptcy, however, is not always the answer. The attorney will interview the client to determine whether there are any viable alternatives to filing for bankruptcy, such as negotiating a debt settlement with creditors, debt consolidation, or advising the client on how to adjust his or her spending for the purposes of paying down debt. When a bankruptcy attorney is retained, the Fair Debt Collection Practices Act requires the debt collector to cease contacting the debtor when it knows the debtor has retained legal counsel. The debtor or the attorney can so advise the creditor. A large part of the bankruptcy attorney's job is to prepare the bankruptcy petition for filing. The attorney prepares the client for any issues that may arise at the creditors' meeting. Other functions of the debtor's attorney can include preparing, filing, and arguing motions, negotiating settlement agreements, reviewing documents, and attending confirmation hearings.

bankruptcy attorney
An attorney who represents a debtor, creditor, or other interested party in a bankruptcy proceeding.

The Bankruptcy Paralegal

Bankruptcy paralegals are nonattorneys who work under the direct supervision of an attorney, who will hold them accountable to Bankruptcy Code regulations. They must be highly organized individuals who are knowledgeable in bankruptcy law and able to handle the demands of a fast-paced, paper-intensive practice. Paralegals who work for bankruptcy law practices spend a lot of time dealing with clients and must remember that they cannot advise clients on questions of law. Although bankruptcy paralegals cannot give clients legal advice, they may perform a wide range of support functions for the attorney that include obtaining information for the filing of petitions and schedules, drafting documents, handling correspondence and docket management, and attending hearings with the attorney and client.

bankruptcy paralegal
A nonattorney who works under the supervision of a bankruptcy lawyer.

The Bankruptcy Petition Preparer

Bankruptcy Code 11 U.S.C. §110(a)(1) defines a **bankruptcy petition preparer** as "a person, other than an attorney for the debtor or an employee of such attorney under the direct supervision of such attorney, who prepares for compensation a document for filing." Debtors who are cash strapped and short of funds may seek the assistance of a bankruptcy petition preparer to type the petition and schedules. Debtors then file the initiating documents and represent themselves before the bankruptcy court. Bankruptcy petition preparers, however, cannot give legal advice. They can only enter information as it is provided to them on the bankruptcy forms and can only charge a reasonable fee. Some run afoul of state unauthorized practice of law statutes when they tell clients what chapter to file, what exemptions to claim, or whether they should file at all. Local bankruptcy court rules limit what the bankruptcy petition preparer can charge, with nominal fees ranging from $100 to $150. The Bankruptcy Abuse Prevention and Consumer Protection Act of 2005 places strict requirements on preparers as well as penalties for those who fail to comply with the statute.

bankruptcy petition preparer
A person, other than an attorney for the debtor or an employee of such attorney under the direct supervision of such attorney, who prepares for compensation a document for filing.

Paralegals work under the direct supervision of an attorney and therefore are not considered bankruptcy petition preparers under the definition of the Bankruptcy Code. This does not, however, stop a paralegal from engaging in this enterprise outside of the confines of the law office as bankruptcy petition preparers, which will subject them to Bankruptcy Code regulations. The concerns of the U.S. bankruptcy courts regarding bankruptcy petition preparers are expressed in excerpts of the following article.

Increased Use of Bankruptcy Petition Preparers Raises Concerns

Text Size

U.S. bankruptcy courts increasingly are concerned with abuses committed by some non-lawyers in the business of helping prepare bankruptcy filing documents for a fee …

… The U.S. Trustee Program, part of the Department of Justice, features a warning on its website (Justice.gov) for those who might seek help filing for bankruptcy protection.

"Non-attorney bankruptcy petition preparers may type bankruptcy documents with information supplied by the debtor. They may not provide legal services, such as helping you choose whether to file under Chapter 7 or Chapter 13 or identifying your property that is exempt from the reach of creditors," it states. "Bankruptcy petition preparers may advertise their services under 'document preparation services' and similar categories of services, but not under 'legal services.' If a bankruptcy petition preparer offers to provide legal services to you or fails to disclose that he or she is not an attorney and may not provide legal services, please report this to a U.S. Trustee Program field office."

Efforts to thwart fraud by Bankruptcy Petition Preparers are hampered in some districts by cultural differences. "Our challenge is exacerbated by the large Latino population who confuses notaries with 'notarios' because 'notarios' actually can carry out simple legal functions in Central America," … "Some of our BPPs just advertise as 'notarios' and reel them in." …

Source: United States Courts Website, dated June 18, 2012

The Debt Relief Agency

debt relief agency
Any person who provides any bankruptcy assistance to an assisted person in return for the payment of money or other valuable consideration, or who is a bankruptcy petition preparer.

This term is fairly new to bankruptcy law and first appeared in the Bankruptcy Abuse Prevention and Consumer Protection Act of 2005. Bankruptcy Code 11 U.S.C. 101(12A) defines **debt relief agency**, which, for purposes of the legal profession, includes attorneys. A debt relief agency is "any person who provides any bankruptcy assistance to an assisted person in return for the payment of money or other valuable consideration, or who is a bankruptcy petition preparer… ." A debt relief agency provides bankruptcy assistance to an "assisted person," which, according to 11 U.S.C. § 101(3), means "any person whose debts consist primarily of consumer debts and the value of whose nonexempt property is less than $150,000." Bankruptcy Code 11 U.S.C. § 101(3) (4A) defines "bankruptcy assistance" as:

… any goods or services sold or otherwise provided to an assisted person with the express or implied purpose of providing information, advice, counsel, document preparation, or filing, or attendance at a creditors' meeting or appearing in a case or proceeding on behalf of another or providing legal representation with respect to a case or proceeding under this title.

Many bankruptcy attorneys have opposed the inclusion of attorneys under the definition of a debt relief agency. They contend that it would confuse the public and impose additional burdens on attorneys. Another complaint was that BAPCPA violates an attorney's constitutional First Amendment right to free speech in regulating the communications between attorney and client. One of the practices that the passage of the BAPCPA sought to prevent is clients being advised to run up their credit cards in anticipation of filing for bankruptcy. Under the BAPCPA, debt relief agencies cannot encourage a client who is anticipating filing bankruptcy to incur any further debt. Although this provision prevented bankruptcy attorneys from engaging in this practice, it also barred them from providing clients with practical advice. For example, if the client's car breaks down and this is his or her only means of transportation to get to work to pay the bills, an attorney, as a debt relief agency, could not advise the client to do the practical thing and buy a car.

In 2010, the United States Supreme Court, in the case of *Milavetz, Gallop & Milavetz, P.A. v. United States*, 559 U.S. 229 (2010), held that attorneys who provide bankruptcy assistance to persons are considered debt relief agencies under the BAPCPA and therefore subject to its regulations and prohibitions. The Court determined that "bankruptcy assistance" includes services that are commonly performed by attorneys such as giving legal advice or document preparation. The Court, however, also addressed the issue of advising clients contemplating bankruptcy to incur more debt and held that clients may be advised to incur more debt when doing so is for a valid purpose.

Bankruptcy paralegals should take special note of the requirements and prohibitions under this statute, as well as relevant sections of the state's code of professional responsibility, if the paralegal's duties include drafting bankruptcy retainer agreements and/or are taking charge of arranging for law office advertisements.

Three important Bankruptcy Code sections apply to debt relief agencies: 11 U.S.C. §§ 526, 527, and 528. Bankruptcy attorneys who charge any fees or receive any other valuable consideration in the course of providing bankruptcy assistance are considered debt relief agents and must comply with these three Code sections. Retainer agreements that do not comply with the Bankruptcy Code are considered void and may not be enforced by any federal or state court or by any other person other than the client. The debt relief agency may be held liable to the assisted person in the amount of any fees or charges received in connection with providing bankruptcy assistance, actual damages, and reasonable attorneys' fees and costs if the agency intentionally or negligently failed to comply with these provisions of the Bankruptcy Code.

Debt Relief Agency Restrictions

Bankruptcy Code 11 U.S.C. § 526 places certain restrictions on debt relief agencies. The debt relief agency must:

- Provide all of the services promised to the assisted person
- Properly advise the assisted person regarding the benefits and risks that may result if the client files for bankruptcy

- Refrain from advising the assisted person to make untrue or misleading statements in a document filed in a case or proceeding
- Refrain from advising the assisted person to incur more debt in contemplation of filing bankruptcy (except for a valid purpose)

Debt Relief Agency Disclosures

Debt relief agencies are also required to provide assisted persons with mandatory disclosures and notices under 11 U.S.C. § 527. Under this section, debt relief agencies must provide written notices to the client "not later than 3 business days after the first date on which a debt relief agency first offers to provide any bankruptcy assistance services to an assisted person." Pursuant to 11 U.S.C. §§ 527(a)(2) and (b), these disclosures shall include disclosure statements that:

(A) all information that the assisted person is required to provide with a petition and thereafter during a case under this title is required to be complete, accurate, and truthful;

(B) all assets and all liabilities are required to be completely and accurately disclosed in the documents filed to commence the case, and the replacement value of each asset as defined in section 506 must be stated in those documents where requested after reasonable inquiry to establish such value;

(C) current monthly income, the amounts specified in section 707 (b)(2), and, in a case under chapter 13 of this title, disposable income (determined in accordance with section 707 (b)(2)), are required to be stated after reasonable inquiry; and

(D) information that an assisted person provides during their case may be audited pursuant to this title, and that failure to provide such information may result in dismissal of the case under this title or other sanction, including a criminal sanction.

(b) A debt relief agency providing bankruptcy assistance to an assisted person shall provide each assisted person at the same time as the notices required under subsection (a)(1) the following statement, to the extent applicable, or one substantially similar. The statement shall be clear and conspicuous and shall be in a single document separate from other documents or notices provided to the assisted person:

"IMPORTANT INFORMATION ABOUT BANKRUPTCY ASSISTANCE SERVICES FROM AN ATTORNEY OR BANKRUPTCY PETITION PREPARER.

"If you decide to seek bankruptcy relief, you can represent yourself, you can hire an attorney to represent you, or you can get help in some localities from a bankruptcy petition preparer who is not an attorney. THE LAW REQUIRES AN ATTORNEY OR BANKRUPTCY PETITION PREPARER TO GIVE YOU A WRITTEN CONTRACT SPECIFYING WHAT THE ATTORNEY OR BANKRUPTCY PETITION PREPARER WILL DO FOR YOU AND HOW MUCH IT WILL COST. Ask to see the contract before you hire anyone.

"The following information helps you understand what must be done in a routine bankruptcy case to help you evaluate how much service you need. Although bankruptcy can be complex, many cases are routine.

"Before filing a bankruptcy case, either you or your attorney should analyze your eligibility for different forms of debt relief available under the Bankruptcy Code and which form of relief is most likely to be beneficial for you. Be sure you understand the relief you can obtain and its limitations. To file a bankruptcy case, documents called a Petition, Schedules, and Statement of Financial Affairs, and in some cases a Statement of Intention, need to be prepared correctly and filed with the bankruptcy court. You will have to pay a filing fee to the bankruptcy court. Once your case starts, you will have to attend the required first meeting of creditors where you may be questioned by a court official called a 'trustee' and by creditors.

"If you choose to file a chapter 7 case, you may be asked by a creditor to reaffirm a debt. You may want help deciding whether to do so. A creditor is not permitted to coerce you into reaffirming your debts.

"If you choose to file a chapter 13 case in which you repay your creditors what you can afford over 3 to 5 years, you may also want help with preparing your chapter 13 plan and with the confirmation hearing on your plan which will be before a bankruptcy judge.

"If you select another type of relief under the Bankruptcy Code other than chapter 7 or chapter 13, you will want to find out what should be done from someone familiar with that type of relief.

"Your bankruptcy case may also involve litigation. You are generally permitted to represent yourself in litigation in bankruptcy court, but only attorneys, not bankruptcy petition preparers, can give you legal advice."

(c) Except to the extent the debt relief agency provides the required information itself after reasonably diligent inquiry of the assisted person or others so as to obtain such information reasonably accurately for inclusion on the petition, schedules or statement of financial affairs, a debt relief agency providing bankruptcy assistance to an assisted person, to the extent permitted by nonbankruptcy law, shall provide each assisted person at the time required for the notice required under subsection (a)(1) reasonably sufficient information (which shall be provided in a clear and conspicuous writing) to the assisted person on how to provide all the information the assisted person is required to provide under this title pursuant to section 521, including—

(1) how to value assets at replacement value, determine current monthly income, the amounts specified in section 707 (b)(2) and, in a chapter 13 case, how to determine disposable income in accordance with section 707 (b)(2) and related calculations;

(2) how to complete the list of creditors, including how to determine what amount is owed and what address for the creditor should be shown; and

(3) how to determine what property is exempt and how to value exempt property at replacement value as defined in section 506.

(d) A debt relief agency shall maintain a copy of the notices required under subsection (a) of this section for 2 years after the date on which the notice is given the assisted person.

Debt Relief Agencies Requirements

Bankruptcy Code 11 U.S.C § 528 imposes statutory requirements on debt relief agencies to address the issue of misleading advertising and prevent consumer confusion. One of the requirements of this section of the Code is to provide clients with a fully executed written contract within five business days after the bankruptcy assistance is first provided to the client and before the bankruptcy filing. The contract must clearly and conspicuously:

- Disclose in any advertisement of bankruptcy assistance services or of the benefits of bankruptcy directed to the general public (whether in general media, seminars or specific mailings, telephonic or electronic messages, or otherwise) that the services or benefits are with respect to bankruptcy relief under this title.
- Use the following statement, or a substantially similar statement, in such advertisement: "We are a debt relief agency. We help people file for bankruptcy relief under the Bankruptcy Code."

An Overview of the Bankruptcy Process and Proceedings

A basic knowledge of the bankruptcy process and proceedings is important to understand the legal principles, statutes, case law, and practical aspects as presented in this textbook. Some topics outlined in this section will receive greater coverage in the chapters ahead; however, a basic overview is essential for a better understanding of the topic.

THE DECISION TO FILE FOR BANKRUPTCY

The bankruptcy process begins with a decision made by either the debtor, who is in financial distress and is seeking relief from obligations owed to the creditor, or a creditor who is owed a debt and seeks to force the debtor into meeting the obligation. Although the goal of bankruptcy law is to provide the debtor with a fresh start, the goal may be achieved in different ways. In some cases, the debtor's obligations may be discharged, relieving the debtor of having to pay creditors. In other situations, a debtor's obligations may be paid or restructured in some manner.

PRE-PETITION CREDIT COUNSELING

pre-petition credit counseling
The legal requirement mandating that debtors must participate in consumer credit counseling prior to filing the bankruptcy petition.

When a debtor is filing for bankruptcy, the he or she is required by law to participate in consumer credit counseling known as **pre-petition credit counseling** or pre-filing counseling within 180 days before the petition is filed or risk having the petition dismissed by the bankruptcy court. There are exceptions to this rule in cases when the debtor:

- Provides a certification of exigent circumstances explaining that an immediate filing was required and the debtor was unable to obtain counseling within the prior five days
- Is disabled or incapacitated and as a result cannot participate in the process
- Establishes that there is no qualified counseling agency within the court district
- Is disabled or on active military service in a combat zone

The credit counseling agency must be approved by the federal government and involves evaluation of the debtor's financial status, adoption of a budget, and investigation of alternatives to filing for bankruptcy. A certificate of completion must be filed with the court.

BANKRUPTCY PETITION

A debtor may voluntarily choose to start bankruptcy proceedings, or the debtor's creditors may determine that the time has come to force the debtor into an involuntary bankruptcy to recover some of the debt owed. Most petitions, however, are initiated by debtors who cannot meet their obligations. Whether the bankruptcy is voluntary or involuntary, the proceeding in bankruptcy court begins with filing the **bankruptcy petition**. This is the initiating document that is filed along with a filing fee in the bankruptcy court of the federal district where the debtor is domiciled or resides with the intent to remain permanently. The petition includes Schedules and the Statement of Financial Affairs, among other documents, which includes information regarding the debtor's assets, liabilities, expenses, and a list of creditors to whom debts are due.

The petition must indicate what type of bankruptcy relief the debtor is seeking. Choosing the type of relief to apply for in a bankruptcy petition requires a determination of eligibility as well as the burdens and benefits involved. A debtor may apply for bankruptcy relief under various chapters of the Bankruptcy Code. As discussed in the previous chapter, a debtor may be eligible for a Chapter 7 liquidation or a Chapter 11 reorganization or liquidation, Chapter 12 for family farmers and fishers with regular income, a Chapter 13 repayment plan, and a Chapter 9 for municipalities seeking to restructure their debt and propose a repayment plan.

One of the best advantages of filing the bankruptcy petition is that the creditors are immediately notified that an Automatic Stay has now gone into effect. The **Automatic Stay** stops the debt collection process in its tracks. The creditor cannot proceed against the debtor in any way unless the creditor comes into the bankruptcy court and has the stay lifted or removed.

MEETING OF THE CREDITORS

The first court appearance the debtor makes in a Chapter 7 or Chapter 13 filing is at a **meeting of the creditors** or **341 hearing**, named after Section 341 of the Bankruptcy Code. Here, the debtor is sworn under oath to tell the truth and answer questions the U.S. trustee, trustee, and creditors pose regarding information contained in the bankruptcy petition and schedules. The trustee may also require the debtor to produce further documentation. All debtors filing for Chapter 7 or Chapter 13 bankruptcy relief are required to attend a creditors meeting. Failure to attend a creditors meeting will result in dismissal of the bankruptcy case. The 341 hearing is not held before a judge in a courtroom but, rather, before the trustee.

CONFIRMATION HEARINGS

In a **confirmation hearing,** the bankruptcy court judge approves a plan for repayment filed in Chapter 13 and Chapter 11 cases. Creditors may file an objection to the repayment plan and appear before the court to argue against its implementation.

bankruptcy petition
The initiating document that is filed along with a filing fee in the bankruptcy court of the federal district where the debtor is domiciled or resides with the intent to remain permanently. The petition includes Schedules and the Statement of Financial Affairs, among other documents, which includes information regarding the debtor's assets, liabilities, expenses, and a list of creditors to whom debts are due.

Automatic Stay
An injunction against the debtor's creditors and claimants that stops all court lawsuits and collection efforts against the debtor until the stay is lifted or removed by the bankruptcy court or the case ends.

meeting of the creditors (341 hearing)
The first court appearance the debtor makes in a bankruptcy case. This meeting may also be referred to as the **341 meeting,** named after the Bankruptcy Code section where it is found. The debtor must attend this meeting or face the possibility that the court will dismiss his or her case.

MOTIONS OR ADVERSARY PROCEEDINGS

Most bankruptcy cases progress smoothly toward discharge; however, situations may arise that require the court's intervention. Debtors, creditors, and trustees may file motions or other actions in the course of the bankruptcy proceedings. A **motion** is a request filed by a party in a legal case when a court ruling is required on important issues or in contested matters requiring a resolution by the judge. An **adversary proceeding** may also be filed in a bankruptcy matter by the debtor, creditor, or trustee. In an adversary proceeding, a party files a separate lawsuit within the bankruptcy case, which the judge must resolve before the case may proceed to discharge.

PRE-DISCHARGE DEBTOR EDUCATION COURSE

The debtor is required to take a **debtor education course**, also referred to as a **financial management course** that provides information about using credit responsibly, managing money, and staying on a budget. This course must be completed before the bankruptcy court addresses the final disposition of the bankruptcy case. Courses are available online for a nominal fee and generate a certificate of completion that must be filed with the bankruptcy court.

DISCHARGE OR DISMISSAL

The **discharge**, the ultimate goal in a Chapter 7 bankruptcy case, occurs when the judge issues a discharge order, an important document releasing the debtor from liabilities, which clears the way for a fresh start. The court issues a discharge of debtor, which officially declares that the debtor's obligations have been discharged in bankruptcy proceedings. In cases in which the court has determined that the debtor is not entitled to a discharge, the judge enters a **dismissal**. This means that the court has closed the case and the debtor does not get the benefit of a fresh start. The debtor's obligations are still due, and the court will take no further action on the case. Note that a discharge is not entered in Chapter 7 business cases.

BANKRUPTCY MEDIATION

Mediation is a form of alternate dispute resolution. The parties seek to resolve their legal dispute through means other than expensive and time-consuming litigation. It is a nonadversarial proceeding that provides the parties with the opportunity to resolve their differences with the assistance of a **mediator**. The mediator is a neutral party and does not act like a judge. Instead, the mediator facilitates a discussion between the parties and proposes possible solutions. The goal of the mediation is a compromise by which both parties engage in a give-and-take process to find a solution that works for both. This is not always easy to accomplish because one or both parties may not be so enthusiastic about mediating; however, nothing binds the parties until they have actually produced a signed settlement agreement.

Many bankruptcy courts throughout the country use mediation to facilitate the resolution of disputes. The Bankruptcy Code authorizes the bankruptcy court to implement the mediation process; however, the rules governing the procedural aspect are dictated by local rules.

---

motion
A request filed by a party in a legal case when a court ruling is required on important issues or in contested matters requiring a resolution by the judge.

adversary proceeding
A separate lawsuit filed within a bankruptcy case, which must be resolved by the judge before the case may proceed to discharge. An adversary proceeding in a bankruptcy case is treated much like a civil lawsuit would be treated.

debtor education course (financial management course)
A mandatory course for debtors filing for Chapter 7 relief that must be completed within 60 days of the initial date set for the meeting of creditors.

discharge
A document issued by a bankruptcy judge that releases the debtor from liability and prohibits the creditor from pursuing any legal action to collect those debts.

dismissal
Where the bankruptcy court has closed the case and the debtor does not get the benefit of a fresh start. The debtor's obligations are still due and the court will take no further action on the case.

mediation
A form of alternate dispute resolution by which the parties seek to resolve their legal dispute through means other than expensive and time-consuming litigation.

mediator
A neutral party who facilitates a discussion between the parties in mediation and proposes possible solutions.

The parties may agree to mediation at any point in the bankruptcy process, and there is a trend in the bankruptcy courts for judges to refer contested bankruptcy cases for mandatory, court-ordered mediation. Although the bankruptcy court judge may order the parties to participate in the mediation process, it is up to the parties to determine whether they wish to accept any proposals. What is important is that the parties participate in the mediation in good faith. Although the bankruptcy courts have not developed clear standards on how to assess good-faith participation, good faith does require attendance and participation, and the parties must send someone to the mediation conference who has the authority to settle the case.

In 2012, U.S. Bankruptcy Court Judge Robert Drain, assigned to the *Hostess Brands, Inc.*, bankruptcy, refused to approve its liquidation and ordered management and the bakers' union to go to mediation to attempt to settle their differences. The judge was concerned with the prospective loss of 18,000 jobs if the parties could not agree on some compromise. Ultimately, the management and the bakers' union came to an impasse, and the company was forced to file for liquidation. Although the bankruptcy court may order the parties to participate in the process, mediation is not binding. As illustrated in the *Hostess* case, if the mediation process is not successful, the parties can seek other remedies.

Maintaining the confidentiality of the mediation proceedings and the documents involved is also crucial because it encourages the parties to negotiate in good faith with a candid and open exchange of the issues without the fear of having it used against them in later court proceedings.

This is accomplished by an agreement by the parties that what goes on during the mediation session is kept confidential. The prevailing rule is that confidential information or materials created for the mediation process, with some exceptions, are generally not released to third parties.

For example, it has been determined that documents prepared for use in confidential bankruptcy mediation proceedings cannot be obtained for use in a divorce settlement, as illustrated in a case involving the sale of the Los Angeles Dodgers. The famous baseball team avoided bankruptcy after striking a deal with their owner Frank McCourt to sell the team for $2 billion to Guggenheim Partners and former basketball star Magic Johnson.

The mediation proceedings in the LA Dodgers case were successful, and the bankruptcy court approved the team's Chapter 11 plan in April 2012. The team, however, was sold 6 months after McCourt and his wife, Jamie, settled their divorce case. Jamie McCourt petitioned the family court to reopen her divorce case and set aside the judgment because the $131 million divorce settlement was based on a fraudulent fair market value of the couple's assets, which included interest in the baseball team. She filed a discovery request in the family case to obtain copies of the mediation documents so she could prove that her husband deliberately undervalued his interest in the LA Dodgers in the divorce proceedings.

Attorneys representing the LA Dodgers moved quickly and requested an emergency hearing seeking an order from the bankruptcy court to prevent the documents from being released. In 2013, U.S. Bankruptcy Judge Kevin Gross in Wilmington, Delaware, agreed, stating that the reason for enforcing the order was because "it was an essential ingredient in the success" of resolving the LA Dodgers potential bankruptcy.

CASE **3.1** In re Los Angeles Dodgers LLC, No. 11-12010
(Bankr. D. Del. Dec. 15, 2011)

KEVIN GROSS, U.S.B.J.

... Mediation and Settlement

As the parties became ever more entrenched in what the Court could see would become a protracted, expensive and non-productive struggle over the control of the Dodgers, the Court determined that mediation was essential for the benefit of Debtors' estate. The Court was also mindful that a negotiated business settlement could benefit MLB. The Court turned to recently retired United States District Court Judge Joseph J. Farnan, Jr. (the "Mediator") to bring his considerable skills, knowledge, experience and business savvy to a mediation. Debtors and MLB agreed to privately mediate, given the public attention to the matter. Later the Court entered an Order confirming and making public the mediation. After the Mediator guided MLB and Debtors through months of negotiations, on November 2, 2011, MLB, Debtors and the Committee reached a settlement (the "Settlement'). The Settlement, which the Court was only recently asked to approve and which is scheduled for hearing in the near future, provides, *inter alia*, for the sale of the Dodgers pursuant to a plan of reorganization on or before April 30, 2012 ..."

BANKRUPTCY APPEALS

final order
A court order that resolves the dispute between the parties.

interlocutory order
An interim or temporary court order on issues that arise during the case.

Bankruptcy Appellate Panel (BAP)
Units of the federal courts of appeal, consisting of three-judge panels.

Litigants in a bankruptcy case who believe that an error was committed generally may appeal final and interlocutory orders issued by the bankruptcy courts on the federal district court level. A **final order** resolves the dispute between the parties, whereas an **interlocutory order** resolves interim or temporary orders on issues that arise during the case. Bankruptcy appeals, however, are not treated in the same manner as ordinary federal appeals. A bankruptcy case may be subject to review by either the U.S. District Court *or* the Bankruptcy Appellate Panel. U.S. district courts serve in an appellate capacity and have authority to hear bankruptcy appeals. Bankruptcy appellate panels, on the other hand, were created under the Bankruptcy Reform Act of 1978 and currently exist in the 1st, 6th, 8th, 9th, and 10th Circuits. In these circuits, both parties must agree to have the appeal heard by the **Bankruptcy Appellate Panel (BAP)**. BAPs are units of the federal courts of appeal and consist of three-judge panels. Parties in bankruptcy matters have the right to appeal decisions rendered by the U.S. District Court and bankruptcy appellate panels to the appropriate U.S. Circuit Courts of Appeals. Another important aspect regarding bankruptcy appeals is that under the BAPCPA, Circuit Courts of Appeal were granted the authority to hear appeals directly from the bankruptcy court at the federal district court level if certain conditions are met.

petition for writ of certiorari
A document filed with the U.S. Supreme Court by the petitioner, asking the Court to review the lower court's decision.

Finally, appeals from the U.S. Circuit Courts of Appeal are heard before the United States Supreme Court, the highest court in the land. The Court however, must agree to hear the appeal, by either granting or denying a party's **petition for writ of certiorari**. A petition for writ of certiorari is a document filed with the U.S. Supreme Court by the petitioner, asking the Court to review the lower court's decision. If the Supreme Court grants certiorari, the Court will hear the case and will affirm, reverse, or remand all or portions of the lower court's decision. A denial of certiorari means that the lower court decision stands.

From the beginning of this chapter, recall Tyquan Wilson's experience in one of his first bankruptcy law classes. After a brief history and timeline for the evolution of modern-day bankruptcy law, it is helpful to learn about the various parties involved in a bankruptcy in addition to the bankruptcy process itself. Although many students have a glib understanding of how the bankruptcy process works from what they hear on television or what friends and family may be experiencing, most are unaware of the existence and roles of such individuals as the Chapter 13 and the Chapter 7 trustee. New students are often surprised to hear that individual debtors are required to take pre-petition credit counseling and that it is tougher to file for Chapter 7 today than it was over ten years ago. As Mr. Wilson will attest, too often, students tend to skip the introductory sections in their textbooks, and they miss the foundation and tools that these chapters give them to master the material in later chapters.

CHAPTER **SUMMARY**

Bankruptcy courts are structured as special units *within* the U.S. District Court system. There is at least one bankruptcy court per federal judicial district. The parties involved in a bankruptcy case include the bankruptcy estate, which is a separate legal entity created after the bankruptcy petition is filed. The central participant in the bankruptcy process is the debtor. A debtor may be an individual, corporation, partnership, or municipality seeking relief in the bankruptcy court from debts owed to creditors. Creditors have claims against the bankruptcy estate, and a creditors' committee is a group that represents creditors that have claims against a business in a bankruptcy proceeding.

The bankruptcy petition is filed in the bankruptcy court, where the bankruptcy judge presides over the proceedings. The United States Trustee is a federal official employed by the government and appointed by the U.S. Attorney General. The U.S. trustee is responsible for enforcing the civil provisions of the bankruptcy laws of the United States by supervising the administration of bankruptcy cases and the functions of private trustees. Private trustees are appointed by the U.S. trustee to administer bankruptcy estates filed under Chapters 7, 11, and 13. They are not considered government employees but are private attorneys who are supervised by and work in conjunction with the U.S. trustee. The bankruptcy examiner is appointed by the court in Chapter 11 cases to examine the financial affairs of a debtor. The examiner is responsible for investigating claims of fraud, dishonesty, incompetence, mismanagement, or misconduct.

A bankruptcy attorney may represent a debtor, creditor, or other interested party in a bankruptcy proceeding. The bankruptcy paralegal is not an attorney but works under the supervision of a bankruptcy lawyer. Title 11 U.S.C. §101(12A) of the Bankruptcy Code defines debt relief agency, which includes attorneys. Three important Bankruptcy Code sections apply to debt relief agencies, 11 U.S.C. §§ 526, 527, and 528. Bankruptcy attorneys that charge any fees or receive any other valuable consideration in the course of providing bankruptcy assistance must comply with these three Code sections.

The bankruptcy process begins with the decision to file for bankruptcy after all other viable alternatives have been explored. The debtor must participate in pre-petition credit counseling before the bankruptcy petition is filed. After the bankruptcy petition is filed, the Automatic Stay goes into effect, stopping all collections actions by creditors unless the bankruptcy court has lifted these restrictions.

The first court appearance the debtor makes in a Chapter 7 or Chapter 13 filing is at a meeting of the creditors, or 341 hearing. At a confirmation hearing, the bankruptcy court judge approves a plan for repayment filed in Chapter 13 and Chapter 11 cases. Most bankruptcy cases progress smoothly toward discharge; however, situations may arise that require the court's intervention. These interventions include motions and adversary proceedings.

The debtor is required to take a financial management course that provides information about using credit responsibly, managing money, and staying on a budget. This course must be completed before the bankruptcy court addresses the final disposition of the bankruptcy case.

In the discharge, the ultimate goal in a Chapter 7 bankruptcy case, the judge issues a discharge order, an important document releasing the debtor from liabilities, which clears the way for a fresh start. The court issues a discharge of debtor, which officially declares that the debtor's obligations have been discharged in bankruptcy proceedings. In cases when the court has determined that the debtor is not entitled to a discharge, the judge enters a dismissal. This means that the court has closed the case, and the debtor does not get the benefit of a fresh start.

Many bankruptcy courts throughout the country use mediation to facilitate the resolution of disputes. Litigants in a bankruptcy case who believe that an error was committed generally may appeal final and interlocutory orders issued by the bankruptcy courts on the federal district court level.

CONCEPT REVIEW AND REINFORCEMENT

KEY TERMS

adversary proceeding
Automatic Stay
Bankruptcy Abuse Prevention
   and Consumer Protection Act
   of 2005 (BAPCPA)
Bankruptcy Appellate Panel (BAP)
bankruptcy attorney
bankruptcy court
bankruptcy estate
bankruptcy examiner
bankruptcy judge
bankruptcy paralegal
bankruptcy petition
bankruptcy petition preparer

claims
creditors' committee
debt relief agency
debtor
debtor education course
   (financial management
   course)
discharge
dismissal
final order
interlocutory order
jurisdiction
mediation
mediator

meeting of the creditors
   (341 hearing)
motion
panel trustee
petition for writ of certiorari
pre-petition credit counseling
priority creditor
private trustees
purchase money security interest
   (PMSI)
secured creditors
standing trustees
United States trustee
unsecured creditor

REVIEWING KEY CONCEPTS

1. What is the difference between a U.S. trustee and a private trustee?
2. Review 11 U.S.C. §541 as provided in this chapter and list five assets that are considered part of the bankruptcy estate.
3. What is a claim and how is it defined? Define secured creditor, unsecured creditor, and priority creditor.
4. Using an Internet search engine such as Google or Bing, locate 11 U.S.C. §704 and list five duties of the Chapter 7 trustee.
5. Explain the roles of the bankruptcy attorney and paralegal.

6. What are some of the ethical issues that apply to the role of bankruptcy petition preparers?
7. Are law firms that practice bankruptcy law considered debt relief agencies?
8. Summarize the three important Bankruptcy Code sections that apply to debt relief agencies.
9. Describe the bankruptcy mediation process.
10. Describe the difference between a final order and an interlocutory order.

BUILDING YOUR PARALEGAL SKILLS

CASE FOR REVIEW

Milavetz, Gallop & Milavetz, P.A. v. United States, 559 U.S. 229 (2010)

BUILDING A PROFESSIONAL PORTFOLIO

PORTFOLIO EXERCISES

You work for Attorney Gregory J. Kaplan, who has just opened a new office in your state, dedicated to bankruptcy law practice. You are helping Attorney Kaplan create the necessary forms to serve his clientele and find that he needs an attorney/client retainer agreement. Using a sample form found through an Internet search engine such as Google or Bing, draft a bankruptcy retainer agreement for a Chapter 7 case, for your supervising attorney's review, that complies with the requirements in 11 U.S.C §§ 526, 527, and 528.

chapter 4
THE AUTOMATIC STAY

Recently, Alexandro and Flora Hernandez have fallen on hard times. Alexandro was laid off from his job as lead architect at Kitchens and More, LLC. His attempts at working independently in his field have proven difficult. Many folks are tightening their belts due to the poor economy. Consumers are simply putting off updating their kitchens and bathrooms with the latest interior design trends until the economy improves. A year ago, Flora was diagnosed with breast cancer and has been undergoing treatment. She had to stop working last month due to the effects of the chemotherapy.

Unfortunately, the Hernandezes have been unable to meet their financial obligations and do not see any improvement in the near future. They have become overwhelmed by the numerous phone calls and threatening letters from collection agencies. Their mortgage company has been threatening to file foreclosure soon because they have fallen several months behind in their mortgage payments. Another concern plaguing the Hernandez couple is the threat that the repo man will repossess their car, the only means of transportation they have and necessary to transport Flora to her doctor's appointments.

They decide to hire a bankruptcy attorney, who explains what the Automatic Stay is and the immediate affect it will have on their creditors. The attorney files a petition on their behalf with the bankruptcy court. After the petition is filed, the bankruptcy court clerk notifies the creditors that the couple has filed for bankruptcy. The creditors must cease all collections activities now that the Automatic Stay has gone into effect. This includes collections-related phone calls and letters as well as all efforts to repossess their car. Mr. and Mrs. Hernandez think this is fabulous news and are so relieved to hear this. But wait a moment. Although the Automatic Stay stops the immediate collection efforts of all their creditors, will it keep all their creditors quiet? Is it permanent for all creditors? Read on and find out.

LEARNING OBJECTIVES

After studying this chapter, you should be able to:

1. Recognize the purpose of the Automatic Stay.

2. Identify the most common exceptions to the Automatic Stay encountered in law practice.

3. Explain the duration of the Automatic Stay.

4. Summarize the consequences for violating the Automatic Stay.

Introduction

Debtors experiencing financial difficulties and unable to pay their bills are often subjected to collection attempts that may include aggressive and relentless phone calls and letters from creditors. The stress, embarrassment, and humiliation associated with collection efforts may be overwhelming, especially when there are multiple creditors seeking payment. When debtors and creditors cannot reach an out-of-court settlement, creditors may have to resort to civil lawsuits, foreclosures, repossessions, and garnishments. Creditors, on the other hand, are put in a position of vying for a piece of the debtor's dwindling resources when balances are owed to multiple creditors.

This chaotic collections environment results in a race to the courthouse during which creditors are not guaranteed an orderly distribution of the debtors' assets. Debtors who cannot pay their debts often turn to the bankruptcy court for relief. After the bankruptcy petition is filed, the status known as the Automatic Stay goes into effect. This chapter discusses the basic legal principles of the Automatic Stay and how it serves to protect both debtors and creditors. It is the most fundamental and immediate benefit of filing for bankruptcy protection in that it stays, or stops, any further legal proceedings against the debtor, maintaining a financial status quo until issues between the debtors and creditors are resolved on a level playing field.

The Automatic Stay: An Introduction

Automatic Stay

An injunction against the debtor's creditors and claimants that stops all court lawsuits and collection efforts against the debtor until the stay is lifted or removed by the bankruptcy court or the case ends.

Filing the bankruptcy petition with the court clerk's office automatically stays, or stops, any further action against the debtor. This is known as the **Automatic Stay**; it is an injunction against the debtor's creditors and claimants and requires no court action on the part of the debtor other than actually filing the petition. After the debtor has filed for bankruptcy, 11 U.S.C. §362(a) prohibits creditors from engaging in the following actions until the stay is lifted, or removed, by the bankruptcy court or the case ends:

- Commencement or continuation of any judicial, administrative, or other action or proceedings against the debtor
- Collections proceedings (includes phone calls and sending default or demand letters)
- Enforcements of judgments against the debtor or against any property of the estate of judgment obtained before the bankruptcy case was commenced
- Any actions to obtain possession of property of the estate or of property from the estate or to exercise control over property of the estate
- Any act to create, perfect, or enforce any lien against property of the estate arising from pre-bankruptcy claims
- Any act to collect, assess, or recover a claim against the debtor that arose before the commencement of the case is stayed
- Set-off of indebtedness owed to the debtor before commencement of the bankruptcy proceeding
- Commencement or continuation of a proceeding before the United States tax court concerning the debtor

The debtor does not need to file a motion or initiate any type of court action for the Automatic Stay to take effect. The Automatic Stay is found in 11 U.S.C. §362 and is one of the most recognized and most important sections of the Bankruptcy Code. The Automatic Stay immediately goes into effect when the bankruptcy petition is filed, and its function is to prohibit the collection and enforcement of collections against the debtor temporarily.

Filing the bankruptcy petition creates the **property of the estate**, which encompasses all the legal and equitable interests of the debtor in property the debtor owns anywhere or in anyone's possession. The property of the estate is now under the control and supervision of the trustee or what is known as a debtor in possession in Chapter 11 cases. When the Automatic Stay goes into effect, creditors and third parties may not exercise any form of control over property that is subject to the bankruptcy administration process. The Automatic Stay, however, is not permanent; it is temporary in that it suspends any creditor collections or court actions *while the Stay is in effect.*

The bankruptcy court clerk notifies the creditors listed on the schedules filed along with the bankruptcy petition. (See Exhibit 4-1 Notice of Automatic Stay.) Therefore, an important function of the bankruptcy legal team is to conduct a thorough inquiry regarding the debtor's existing creditors along with their correct addresses and sums due for notification purposes.

The Automatic Stay benefits the debtor because it immediately halts any collection activity or enforcement. The debtor now has breathing room to proceed with bankruptcy liquidation or, in the case of a business debtor, the opportunity to reorganize its debt and stay in business. Creditors also benefit from the Automatic Stay because it freezes the assets of the bankruptcy estate and prevents the debtor's property from being unfairly divided among its creditors. It eliminates the creditors' race to the courthouse by providing an orderly process of validating creditors' claims. The opening chapter scenario illustrates how the Automatic Stay affects the debtor after the bankruptcy petition is filed.

> **property of the estate**
> Encompasses all the legal and equitable interests of the debtor in property the debtor owns anywhere or in anyone's possession.

EXCEPTIONS TO THE AUTOMATIC STAY

It is important to understand that the Automatic Stay does not prohibit all legal and collections actions against a debtor. In fact, there are 28 exceptions to the Automatic Stay under 11 U.S.C. §362(b) that allow certain actions to commence or continue after the debtor has filed for bankruptcy protection. The most common exceptions encountered in law practice include the following.

- **Criminal Law Exception** The commencement or continuation of any criminal action or proceeding against an individual who has committed a crime under the laws of the federal or state government is not stayed under the Bankruptcy Code.
- **Family Law Exception** One of the most common exceptions to the Automatic Stay concerns family law matters. The Automatic Stay does not prohibit the commencement or continuation of a civil action or proceeding:
  - (i) for the establishment of paternity.
  - (ii) for the establishment or modification of an order for domestic support obligations.
  - (iii) concerning child custody or visitation.
  - (iv) for the dissolution of a marriage, except to the extent that such proceeding seeks to determine the division of property that is property of the estate.
  - (v) regarding domestic violence.

> **criminal law exception**
> An exception to the Automatic Stay. The commencement or continuation of any criminal action or proceeding against an individual who has committed a crime under the laws of the federal or state government is not stayed under the Bankruptcy Code.

> **family law exception**
> One of the most common exceptions to the Automatic Stay, concerning family law matters.

EXHIBIT 4.1

UNITED STATES BANKRUPTCY COURT
For the District of Colorado

In re:) Bankruptcy No._____
)
) Petition Filing Date _____
)
)   Chapter 7   **G**
)   Chapter 11   **G**
)   Chapter 12   **G**
                          Debtor(s).)   )   Chapter 13   **G**

Notice of Automatic Stay

_____
       (Name of Creditor or Business on Whom this Notice is being Served)

_____
                          (City, State, and Zip Code)

YOU ARE HEREBY NOTIFIED that the above-named debtor(s) have filed a voluntary
petition in this Court. In accordance with Title 11, U.S.C. § 301, the petition
constitutes an Order for Relief as of the date shown above. Additionally, pursuant
to U.S.C. § 362(a), all creditors of the debtor(s) are stayed from any act, the
commencement or continuation of any act, enforcement of any lien or judgment obtained
against the debtor(s) or the property of their estate, or any court proceeding with
respect to the enforcement of a lien or judgment against the debtor(s) or the
property of their estate from and after the filing date of the bankruptcy petition,
except as otherwise provided for by U.S.C. § 362(b).

   Relief from the automatic stay may be sought by filing a motion in this Court
pursuant to U.S.C. § 362(d).

_____
        (Signature of Pro Se Debtor or Counsel for the Debtor(s))

_____
     (Pro Se Debtor's/Counsel's Address, including City, State, and Zip Code)

_____
               (Pro Se Debtor's/Counsel's Telephone Number)

Certificate of Service
   There undersigned hereby certifies that a true and correct copy of the above-
captioned <u>Notice of Automatic Stay</u> was mailed **G** (or hand-delivered **G** or sent via
facsimile transmission **G**) [check which box applies] by depositing the same in the
United States Postal Service mail, postage prepaid, addressed to the above-named party.

Dated:_____   _____
                                                            Signature

44444444444444444444444444444444444444444444444444444444444444444444444444444444
Instructions
   Prepare the caption of this Notice exactly as it is shown on the original
petition, inserting the case number, chapter number, and date the petition was filed.
Insert the full name and address of the party on whom this Notice is being served.
Sign and complete the Pro Se debtor's/counsel's address and telephone number block.
Make a copy of the Notice and deliver it to the intended party. Sign and date the
Certificate of Service. File the original Notice with the Clerk of the Bankruptcy
Court. Use a separate form for each party noticed. The original Notice will be
"Filed-stamped" by the Clerk only after service has been completed.

Child and spousal support are often collected through wage garnishment and seizure of tax refunds. When the debtor has filed for bankruptcy under Chapter 7 liquidation, collection of child and spousal support is not affected by the Automatic Stay; however, these sums may be subjected to a reorganization under Chapter 13. Note, however, that property division is not stayed under the family law exceptions.

- **Taxing Authority Exception**   The Automatic Stay prohibits acts to collect a tax or to create, or perfect, or enforce a tax lien, so the Internal Revenue Service or other taxing authority may not garnish a debtor's wages, issue tax liens, or seize a debtor's property under the Automatic Stay. The taxing authority may proceed with the continuation of audits to determine tax liability, demand the filing of tax returns, issue tax deficiency notices, and assess taxes due and demand payment for said amounts.

- **Eviction Exception**   Debtors who file for bankruptcy protection and are behind on their rent are concerned with the question of what effect the Automatic Stay will have on eviction proceedings. The answer to this question depends on the status of the eviction proceedings against the tenant debtor. Although the Automatic Stay prohibits most evictions, two residential eviction exceptions allow the property owner to proceed with the eviction without violating the Automatic Stay. The first becomes effective if the property owner obtained a judgment for possession prior to the bankruptcy filing and the judgment is based on a lease or rental agreement. The other exception comes into play when the eviction is based on the tenant's use of illegal controlled substances on the property or his or her actions that damage the property. Under these circumstances, the property owner may proceed with the eviction against the debtor. If neither of these two residential eviction exceptions applies, the property owner cannot commence an eviction proceeding unless the bankruptcy court lifts the Automatic Stay.

taxing authority exception
Exception to Automatic Stay regarding taxes owed.

eviction exception
An exception to the Automatic Stay, allowing the property owner to proceed with an eviction.

CHAPTER 13: CO-DEBTOR AUTOMATIC STAY EXCEPTION

Protection under the Automatic Stay is also extended to the co-debtors of a debtor in Chapter 13 cases and remains in effect until the debtor's case is closed. This is often referred to as the **co-debtor stay**. The co-debtor stay applies only when the debt incurred is a consumer debt. A perfect example would be someone who co-signs a car loan for the debtor, for the debtor's personal use. The co-debtor is entitled to protection from the creditor's reach even though the co-debtor is not a party to the bankruptcy case. Creditors who wish to pursue a legal action against the co-debtor must first file for relief from the Automatic Stay and obtain an order from the bankruptcy court.

Co-debtors, however, may be held responsible for debts incurred in the ordinary course of business. For example, John, in his individual capacity, co-signs a loan to his corporation. If the corporation files for bankruptcy protection, John is not afforded the same protection, and the creditor may proceed against him in his individual capacity. In Chapter 7 cases, however, creditors are free to proceed against a co-debtor after the debtor's bankruptcy case has been discharged.

co-debtor stay
Legal protection under the Automatic Stay that is also extended to the co-debtors of a debtor in Chapter 13 cases and remains in effect until the debtor's case is closed.

Duration of the Stay

The general rule is that the Automatic Stay remains in effect until:

1. The bankruptcy court judge lifts or removes it upon formal request of the creditor.
2. The debtor's case is dismissed or closed.
3. The debtor's property is no longer included in the property of the estate.
4. The debtor is granted or denied a discharge.

The Automatic Stay typically terminates 90 to 100 days after the bankruptcy petition is filed in no asset cases filed under Chapter 7 of the Bankruptcy Code. In Chapter 13 cases, however, the Automatic Stay remains in effect for the duration of the matter.

Serial Filers and the Automatic Stay

Prior to the enactment of the Bankruptcy Abuse Prevention and Consumer Protection Act of 2005 (BAPCPA), Chapter 13 debtors would engage in the practice of filing several bankruptcy petitions to buy time as they either reorganized their business affairs or eventually lost their property. BAPCPA amended the Bankruptcy Code to address this issue by placing limitations on the duration of the Automatic Stay when the debtor is a repeat or serial filer.

A situation may arise when a debtor files for bankruptcy and, within one year of that first case's dismissal, files a second bankruptcy case. The presumption under 11 U.S.C. § 362(c) (3) is that the second case is filed in bad faith, and the Automatic Stay expires 30 days after filing the second bankruptcy petition. Typically, these debtors have no real intention of filing for bankruptcy but, rather, seek refuge under the Automatic Stay at the expense of their creditors. To extend the Automatic Stay beyond the 30-day limit, the debtor must file a motion with the bankruptcy court and prove, by clear and convincing evidence, that the second petition was filed in good faith.

A debtor who has filed two or more bankruptcies within a period of one year is presumed to be filing that case in bad faith. Under the provisions of 11 U.S.C. § 362(c) (4), the Automatic Stay does not go into effect at all unless the debtor can convince the bankruptcy court, by clear and convincing evidence, that this third bankruptcy is being filed in good faith. In the following example, assume that all the filings take place within a period of one year.

EXAMPLE

Max Praxton ("Praxton") defaults on his mortgage loan with Homeowner's Choice Finance Company ("Homeowners'"). Homeowners tries to foreclose on the property, so Praxton files for bankruptcy. When Praxton files, the Automatic Stay goes into effect and stops all foreclosure proceedings. Praxton's bankruptcy case is dismissed, and Homeowners' files a second foreclosure action. Praxton files for bankruptcy a second time. This time, the Automatic Stay remains in effect for only 30 days, and to extend it, Praxton must motion the court. Let us assume that the bankruptcy court dismissed the second case. Homeowners' attempts once again to foreclose, but Praxton now files a third bankruptcy petition. Remember that the Automatic Stay does not take effect because of the presumption that the third petition is filed in bad faith unless Praxton can prove otherwise. Homeowners' attorneys now file a motion to dismiss the third bankruptcy because Praxton is acting in bad faith by abusing the bankruptcy process solely to avoid foreclosure on his home. The bankruptcy court dismisses Praxton's third petition.

Relief from the Automatic Stay

Creditors are prohibited from unilaterally defying the Automatic Stay. As stated in the previous section, the Automatic Stay remains in effect until it is lifted by order of the bankruptcy court pursuant to Section 362(c) of the Bankruptcy Code.

Creditors typically seek **relief from the Automatic Stay** or, in essence, have it lifted or removed by the court, for the following reasons.

relief from the Automatic Stay
Creditors request the Automatic Stay to be lifted or removed by the court.

1. The creditors' interest in the property is not adequately protected.
2. The property in question is depreciating in value.
3. The debtor has no equity in the property, and the property is not needed for reorganization under Chapter 13.

Secured creditors are among those who frequently seek relief from the Automatic Stay. Remember that a secured creditor is one who extends credit with the assurance that if the debt is not paid, the creditor may seize the debtor's property, or collateral, and sell it to satisfy the debt. These assurances come in the form of a mortgage, lien, pledge, or other form of security interest. By obtaining relief from the Automatic Stay, a secured creditor may be free to retrieve the debtor's collateral, for example, by repossessing a car or foreclosing on a home.

The creditor accomplishes relief from the Automatic Stay by filing a motion with the bankruptcy court to lift it. The motion must show cause; that is, the creditor must provide the court with the reasons he or she is seeking relief from the Automatic Stay. Along with the motion, the creditor must also provide notice to the debtor and other interested parties of the filing so the court can hear their objections. Preliminary hearings on the motion are heard within 30 days after the motion is filed, with a final hearing scheduled within another 30 days thereafter.

Hearings on such motions can be quite heated as the parties vigorously defend their competing interests. It is up to the bankruptcy court judge to balance the interests of the parties when determining whether the Automatic Stay should be lifted. If the bankruptcy court lifts the Automatic Stay, this does not mean that the property in question is removed from the bankruptcy estate or that the creditor may now seize the asset. Simply stated, the creditor may now seek resolution of the conflict in question by the remedies available under the laws of the state that has jurisdiction in the matter. Furthermore, the bankruptcy court is not limited to terminating the Automatic Stay; it may also modify or place conditions on it. Therefore, creditors must proceed with caution in exercising their state rights so that the bankruptcy court's order is followed.

Termination of the Automatic Stay by Operation of Law

In addition to termination of the Automatic Stay by order of the bankruptcy court, the Automatic Stay may also terminate by operation of law under the provisions of 11 U.S.C. § 362(h)(1). The BAPCPA amendments to the Bankruptcy Code subject a debtor who has filed for bankruptcy protection under Chapter 7 to termination of the Automatic Stay if he or she fails to file a **Statement of Intentions** regarding secured property. A Statement of Intentions is a form filed in a Chapter 7 case that informs the creditors, trustee, and the bankruptcy court of how the debtor intends to deal with the secured debts within the context of the bankruptcy. Recall that a secured debt allows a creditor to repossess the debtor's property as collateral. Homes and automobiles are examples of property most typically repossessed by creditors. Bankruptcy Code 11 U.S.C. §521(a)(2) requires that the debtor:

Statement of Intentions
A form filed in a Chapter 7 case that informs the creditors, trustee, and bankruptcy court of how the debtor intends to deal with secured debts within the context of the bankruptcy.

> [W]ithin thirty days after the date of the filing of a petition under chapter 7 of this title or on or before the date of the meeting of creditors, whichever is earlier, or within such additional time as the court, for cause, within such period fixes, file with the clerk a statement of his intention with respect to the retention or surrender of such property and, if applicable, specifying that such property is claimed as exempt, that the debtor intends to redeem such property, or that the debtor intends to reaffirm debts secured by such property;

The consequence of not filing a Statement of Intentions in a timely manner results in an immediate termination of the Automatic Stay. The legal effect removes the property as part of the bankruptcy estate and places it within reach of the creditors.

Violating the Automatic Stay

Creditors' attempts to collect, sue, foreclose, repossess, garnish, evict, or engage in any other actions in the name of debt collection of property under the Automatic Stay are considered void and have no legal effect. Specifically, Section 362(a) of the Bankruptcy Code prohibits any acts "to obtain possession of property of the estate or of property from the estate or to exercise control over property of the estate" or "to collect, assess, or recover a claim against the debtor that arose before the commencement of the case." The bankruptcy court has the discretion to determine which acts constitute a violation of the Automatic Stay. A violation of the Automatic Stay must be proven by the debtor, who must show that:

1. The creditor violated the automatic stay.
2. The violation was willful. (The creditor acted deliberately with the knowledge that the debtor has filed a bankruptcy petition.)
3. The debtor was injured by the violation.

In the following case, a verbal exchange in a bar was more than the creditor bargained for when comments regarding the debtor's filing for bankruptcy were made in a social setting.

CASE 4.1 In Re Chad Ehlinger, Debtor, No. 12-01680, (Bankr. N. D. Iowa Mar. 19, 2013)

Debtor filed a Chapter 7 bankruptcy petition on September 7, 2012. One of his creditors is Bullock Ag Service, Inc. – LaMotte. William Bullock is currently the manager of the Bullock Ag Service, Inc. – Preston store. His brother Travis Bullock manages the LaMotte store, but William Bullock managed it during the time that Debtor accrued the debt there. Both Bullocks were involved in attempting to collect the judgment the LaMotte store obtained against Debtor prepetition. There is no dispute that Debtor filed bankruptcy because of the Bullock prepetition collection efforts. William Bullock acknowledged he received notice of Debtor's bankruptcy filing and was reminded by counsel to stop any collection efforts. As a businessman, Mr. Bullock understands the effects of a bankruptcy filing and the automatic stay of further collections.

On October 27, 2012, the Saturday before Halloween, William Bullock entered Debtor's bar, the County Line, at approximately midnight. A band was playing at the bar that night. Mr. Bullock was on a bus tour to various area bars to attend costume contests with his wife, neighbors and friends. The bus made an unscheduled stop at the County Line. Mr. Bullock entered the bar for the purported purpose of using the restroom.

The parties dispute what happened next. Debtor testified that Mr. Bullock approached the area of the bar where he could get behind the bar, but didn't actually go behind the bar. He stated that Mr. Bullock appeared intoxicated and was talking loudly, yelling and swearing. Debtor stated he had previously witnessed Mr. Bullock drinking and becoming louder as he became intoxicated. Debtor testified Mr. Bullock yelled something about Debtor filing bankruptcy against him, loud enough for the entire bar to hear. Debtor had Mr. Bullock escorted out of the bar.

William Bullock testified that he entered the bar and went straight to the restroom. While he was there, he saw what he thought was a drug transaction between two people who had a baggie of white powder. Mr. Bullock testified that he went up to the bar to report this to someone behind the bar and to buy a soda with cash he had in his hand. He had been drinking prior in the evening but had stopped by this time. He stated that when he tried to report the illegal activity in the restroom to someone behind the bar, he was roughly escorted out, causing him to drop the cash in his hand. Mr. Bullock denied yelling or talking loudly or swearing or mentioning Debtor's bankruptcy....

The filing of a bankruptcy petition automatically stays a variety of acts to collect or otherwise enforce a prepetition debt. 11 U.S.C. § 362(a). The automatic stay stops all collection efforts and all harassment to give the debtor a breathing spell from the financial pressures that led to the bankruptcy filing.... If a creditor violates the automatic stay, the debtor is entitled to recover damages, costs and attorney fees. 11 U.S.C. § 362(k). To prevail under § 362(k), the debtor must show: (1) the creditor violated the automatic stay; (2) the violation was willful; and (3) the debtor was injured by the violation.... A violation is willful "when the creditor acts deliberately with knowledge of the bankruptcy petition."

... [T]he Court finds William Bullock willfully violated the automatic stay by his actions on October 27, 2012....

Sanctions for Violating the Automatic Stay

The sanctions for violating the Automatic Stay are found in 11 U.S.C. §362(k), under which, an individual debtor who is injured by a willful violation of the Automatic Stay provisions of §362 is entitled to recover actual damages, costs, and attorney's fees as well as punitive damages in some cases. This section of the Bankruptcy Code, however, only applies to individuals, so a corporation may not recover damages.

Creditors who have engaged in activities that could be deemed a violation of the Automatic Stay may argue that they did not receive notice regarding the filing of the bankruptcy petition. It is vital for the debtor's attorney and the paralegal staff working on a client's bankruptcy matter to obtain the correct address for notice purposes. Although the billing address is often noted on the client's invoice, this may not be the best address to which to send notification of the bankruptcy. A letter should also be sent to the collection agency if the creditor has turned the debt over for collection. In addition, some bankruptcy attorneys also make it a practice to notify the creditors immediately that their client has filed for bankruptcy so that the creditor will receive notice prior to the bankruptcy court clerk's notification of the filing. Letters immediately faxed or emailed to creditors provide clients with immediate relief from harassing phone calls and letters.

Recall the Hernandez couple from the beginning of the chapter. Unfortunately, their situation is not much different from what many Americans are experiencing. Like many Americans, the Hernandezes felt on top of the world with a larger than average income and little financial worries until illness and a bad economy struck. They must have felt some type of relief after learning about the Automatic Stay from their bankruptcy attorney. The Automatic Stay will undoubtedly provide protection for the Hernandez couple from most of their debts. However, as you are now aware, certain debts and collections efforts, particularly their looming mortgage foreclosure, may not be barred by the Automatic Stay for the life of their bankruptcy filing. They need to be prepared for the reality that their mortgage company, depending on such factors as the amount of equity in the home and balance owed on the note, among other factors, may successfully seek relief from the Automatic Stay.

CHAPTER **SUMMARY**

Filing the bankruptcy petition with the court clerk's office automatically stays, or stops, any further action against the debtor. This is known as the Automatic Stay, an injunction against the debtor's creditors and claimants that stops all court lawsuits and collection efforts against the debtor until the bankruptcy court lifts, or removes, the stay or the case ends.

The Automatic Stay does not prohibit all legal and collections actions against a debtor. In fact, 28 exceptions to the Automatic Stay allow certain actions to be commenced or continued even after the debtor has filed for bankruptcy protection.

The Automatic Stay remains in effect until it is lifted or removed by the bankruptcy court judge upon formal request of the creditor, the debtor's case is dismissed or closed, the debtor's property is no longer included in the property of the estate, or the debtor is granted or denied a discharge.

Creditors are prohibited from unilaterally defying the Automatic Stay; however, the creditor obtains relief from the Automatic Stay by filing a motion with the bankruptcy court to remove it. The motion must show cause; the creditor must provide the court with the reasons he or she is seeking relief from the Automatic Stay. In addition to termination of the Automatic Stay by order of the bankruptcy court, the Automatic Stay may also terminate by operation of law. Creditors' attempts to collect, sue, foreclose, repossess, garnish, evict, or engage in any other actions in the pursuit of debt collection are considered void and without legal effect. The sanctions for violating the Automatic Stay include the ability for the debtor to recover actual damages, costs, and attorney's fees as well as punitive damages in some cases.

The Bankruptcy Code has placed limitations on the duration of the Automatic Stay in cases involving repeat, or serial, filers. When a debtor has filed for bankruptcy twice in one year and the first bankruptcy was dismissed, the Automatic Stay remains in effect for only thirty days, requiring the debtor to motion the court for an extension. When the debtor has filed for bankruptcy two or more times in one year and the previous cases were dismissed, the Automatic Stay does not go into effect unless the debtor can convince the court that he or she is not acting in bad faith.

CONCEPT REVIEW AND REINFORCEMENT

KEY TERMS

Automatic Stay	eviction exception	relief from the Automatic Stay
co-debtor stay	family law exception	Statement of Intentions
criminal law exception	property of the estate	taxing authority exception

REVIEWING KEY CONCEPTS

1. What is the Automatic Stay and what effect does it have on a bankruptcy case?
2. How does the Automatic Stay protect both debtors and creditors?
3. What types of actions are stayed under 11 U.S.C. §362(a)?
4. What are the four most common exceptions to the Automatic Stay encountered in law practice?
5. What is the co-debtor stay?
6. State the general rule regarding the duration of the Automatic Stay.
7. What effect has the enactment of BAPCPA had on repeat bankruptcy filers?
8. Why do creditors typically seek relief from the Automatic Stay?
9. How may the Automatic Stay be terminated by operation of law?
10. What are the consequences for violating the Automatic Stay?

BUILDING YOUR PARALEGAL SKILLS

CASE FOR REVIEW

Citizens Bank of Maryland v. Strumpf, 516 U.S. 16, 18 (1995)

BUILDING A PROFESSIONAL PORTFOLIO

PORTFOLIO EXERCISES

You work as a paralegal for the law office of Maria Castillo. Your bankruptcy client, Benjamin Ayala, has failed to pay court-ordered child support of $450.00 per month to his wife, Claudia, for a period of 9 months. Ayala just filed for bankruptcy under Chapter 7 and has called the office to find out whether his former wife can garnish his wages. She keeps threatening him every time they exchange the children during visitation, but this time he thinks she will follow through. He can barely make ends meet as it is now. Does any exception to the Automatic Stay apply in Mr. Ayala's case? Draft a letter to Mr. Ayala on behalf of Attorney Castillo, responding to his inquiry.

chapter 5
THE MEANS TEST

LEARNING OBJECTIVES

After studying this chapter, you should be able to:

1. Understand why relief in Chapter 7 is not automatic.

2. Describe the Means Test, its origin, and its purpose.

3. Comprehend the Means Test calculation in a Chapter 7 case.

4. Understand how "abuse" is defined in bankruptcy law.

5. Explain the Means Test in Chapter 13 cases.

Sandra and Karl Wickes live far beyond their means. Despite great careers and considerable income, they are always struggling to pay their bills. Sandra is a commercial transaction attorney and Karl is a successful plastic surgeon. They live in Hillendale Village, an exclusive gated community, and are members of the local country club. Their finances started getting out of control when Karl decided to upgrade his practice to attract a more high-end clientele. The costs for the renovation were triple the initial estimate but Karl was determined to see this project to its completion. Sandra became resentful of Karl's spending and decided to upgrade her wardrobe and go on an expensive cruise with her girlfriends from law school.

The spending spree continued until both exhausted any savings they had and maxed out their credit cards to the point that not only were they unable to obtain credit, but Karl's renovation plans had to be put on hold due to lack of funds. Things got so bad that they decided to file for bankruptcy. Sandra recalled taking a bankruptcy course in law school back in 2003, and she is certain that they can wipe out all their debt in a Chapter 7 liquidation. Karl and Sandra made an appointment with Sandra's old law school buddy, Sarah Martin, who told them that the law has changed since Sandra last took a bankruptcy course. Attorney Martin explained that the means test would determine whether they would be eligible for Chapter 7. Perplexed, Sandra asked, "What's a means test?" Read on to find out.

Introduction

Bankruptcy Abuse Prevention and Consumer Protection Act of 2005 (BAPCPA)
Legislation that was enacted in April of 2005 that made several sweeping changes to the Bankruptcy Code.

Prior to the passage of the **Bankruptcy Abuse Prevention and Consumer Protection Act of 2005 (BAPCPA)**, practically any debtor who wanted to file for Chapter 7 protection could do so. Today, relief under a Chapter 7 liquidation bankruptcy is not automatic. When Congress enacted BAPCPA, it included an amendment to the Bankruptcy Code that required prospective debtors to prove that they are financially worthy of a total discharge of their debt or that they possess the ability to pay back their obligations. Prior to the passage of BAPCPA, debtors were allowed to choose which type of bankruptcy petition to file with the court. Most debtors chose to file under Chapter 7 because a discharge would, in effect, wipe out all their debt. Under these circumstances, debtors could easily abuse the bankruptcy system, and many did. The banking and credit card industry aggressively lobbied for reform of the Bankruptcy Code to address these types of abuses specifically. Congress's intent in implementing the Bankruptcy Code and the BAPCPA is to prevent individuals who are perfectly capable of paying their debts from liquidating, thus avoiding many of their obligations, while their creditors are left unpaid.

The law now requires debtors to pass a **Means Test**, which is a formula designed to determine whether debtors have the ability to restructure their debt and make payments to creditors. One of the purposes of the Means Test is to determine whether the debtor can afford to pay 25% of his or her income on nonpriority, unsecured debt. The Means Test consists of a series of financially related questions and formulas designed to determine whether debtors qualify for Chapter 7.

Means Test
A formula designed to determine whether debtors have income and the ability to restructure their debt and pay off their creditors.

The Means Test applies only to individuals whose debt is primarily consumer debt and is designed to calculate current monthly disposable income. The current monthly disposable income figure determines whether the debtor is in a position to enter into a repayment plan. Debtors are required to complete a Means Test when they file for either Chapter 7 or Chapter 13. For Chapter 13 filers, the Means Test determines the debtor's repayment plan. For Chapter 7 filers, the Means Test compares the debtor's annual income to the median income of households of similar size in their state. This information is easily obtained from tables located on the Department of Justice U.S. Trustee Program website in the Census Bureau Median Family Income by Family Size section. If the debtor's annual income is less than the median income for his or her state, no further calculations of the Means Test need to be completed. If the debtor's annual income is greater than the state median income, additional calculations in the Means Test form must be completed to determine whether the debtor is eligible to file for Chapter 7.

Prevention of Abuse in Bankruptcy

One of the main reasons behind the passage of the BAPCPA was to prevent abusive and fraudulent bankruptcy filings. In drafting this legislation, Congress provided the bankruptcy court with the discretion to dismiss a bankruptcy case for abuse or, with the debtor's consent, convert the case to a Chapter 11 or Chapter 13 bankruptcy under 11 U.S.C. §707 (b). The United States trustees, panel trustees, bankruptcy administrators, creditors, or other parties in interest may motion to have the case dismissed or converted under Chapter 11 or Chapter 13 if the court finds that granting relief under Chapter 7 would be considered abuse.

There are two official forms for calculating the Means Test in a bankruptcy case. The first form is used for debtors filing for Chapter 7 and is calculated on *Official Form B22A Chapter 7 Statement of Current Monthly Income and Means-Test Calculation*. Completing *Official Form B22A* determines whether there is a presumption of abuse, no presumption of abuse, or the presumption is temporarily unavailable. The second form is *Official Form B22C Chapter 13 Statement of Current Monthly Income and Calculation of Commitment Period and Disposable Income*. This form must be completed by debtors filing under Chapter 13, whether by default because they do not qualify for Chapter 7 or voluntarily because it has been determined that filing for Chapter 13 will allow them to keep some of their assets. Examples of both official forms can be found in Appendix Q.

IS THERE A PRESUMPTION OF ABUSE?

Calculation of the Means Test provides an answer to this question. There are three possible outcomes upon completion of the Means Test:

- There is no presumption of abuse.
- There is a presumption of abuse.
- The presumption is temporarily inapplicable.

1. No Presumption of Abuse

A no presumption of abuse finding means that the debtor may file for Chapter 7. There is, however, an exception to this rule. When considering whether to grant relief to the debtor, the bankruptcy court judge may refuse to do so if it is determined that the debtor filed the petition in bad faith or, based on a totality of the circumstances, the debtor's financial situation demonstrates abuse. Not only may the trustees or judge take issue with the debtor's filing status, but creditors also scrutinize the Means Test in terms of bad faith and totality of the circumstances. Case law constantly evolves regarding this section of the Bankruptcy Code, so it is important to check the relevant case law on this issue.

The Bankruptcy Code does not define the terms *bad faith* or *totality of the circumstances*, which means that Congress has left it up to the courts to supply the definitions based on their assessment of the case. This makes sense because the determination of either is driven by the specific circumstances in each case. For example, in the case of *In re Booker*, 399 B.R. 662 (Bankr. W.D. Mo. 2009), the United States Bankruptcy Court for Western District of Missouri provided some guidance:

> [I]n assessing whether the filing was made in bad faith, this Court should focus more on conduct. Conversely, when assessing whether the case should be dismissed as an abuse based upon the totality of the Debtors' financial circumstances, the Court should consider primarily, if not exclusively, the Debtors' ability to pay....

2. Presumption of Abuse

A presumption of abuse arises when a calculation of the Means Test reveals that the debtor has enough disposable income available to arrange a payment plan with creditors under Chapter 13. This presumption is rebuttable if the debtor can prove that special circumstances exist that qualify him or her for relief under Chapter 7. Bankruptcy Code 11 U.S.C. 707(b)(2)(B) lists two examples of special circumstances: a serious medical condition or a call or order to active duty in the armed forces.

One of the goals of BAPCPA is to require debtors who have regular income and can afford to pay their debts to restructure their obligations and repay their creditors under a Chapter 13 bankruptcy. The function of the Means Test is to determine whether the debtor qualifies for Chapter 7. If a debtor makes more than his or her state's median income, the debtor's case is presumed to be an abuse of the Bankruptcy Code. However, if the debtor can prove through documentation that special circumstances exist, such as showing a decrease in income because overtime is no longer available, he or she can rebut this ruling. He or she could provide evidence through pay stubs, employee notices, or other forms of evidence that the presumption of abuse was unwarranted and thus qualify him or her for Chapter 7 relief.

To rebut the presumption of abuse, the debtor must file an **Affidavit of Special Circumstances**. Special circumstances include the two examples provided by the Bankruptcy Code as well as loss of employment, disability, injury, or unanticipated expenses. In the affidavit, the debtor argues that if such conditions exist, the presumption should not be applied.

Affidavit of Special Circumstances
A sworn document in which the debtor argues that conditions exist, such as loss of employment, disability, injury, or unanticipated expenses, that indicate that the presumption of abuse should not be applied.

3. Presumption is temporarily inapplicable

Under the provisions of the National Guard & Reservist Debt Relief Act of 2008, which amended 11 U.S.C. § 707 (b)(2)(D), Chapter 7 debtors who are reservists or members of the National Guard are temporarily excluded from the Means Test. The debtor will qualify for this exclusion if the active duty or homeland defense activity is for a period of at least 90 days and has occurred after September 11, 2001. This exclusion from the Means Test applies for the duration of the debtor's active duty and for another 540 days after the period of active duty has terminated.

Calculating the Means Test

The following section discusses the Means Test as calculated on *Official Form B22A Chapter 7 Statement of Current Monthly Income and Means-Test Calculation.*

MONTHLY INCOME CALCULATION

The debtor must calculate monthly income from all sources except Social Security benefits; Veteran's Administration disability payments; and payments received for victims of war crimes, crimes against humanity, and domestic or international terrorism. This figure is based on the average of all income sources for a period of six complete months before filing for bankruptcy. For example, if your client, Brian Klein, plans to file for bankruptcy on September 20, the monthly income listed in Official Form B22A is for the period of March 1 to August 31. Two columns are provided in Part II of Form B22A so that the income of both spouses may be included in calculating the Means Test. If the spouses reside together, both spouses' income must be included in the Means Test. Spouses are not required to file a joint bankruptcy petition and, in many situations, only one spouse will file. Regardless, the income of both must be included if they are in the same household. The various types of income that must be included in this calculation include:

- Gross wages, salary, tips, bonuses, overtime, and commissions
- Income from the operation of a business, profession, or farm
- Rent and other real property income
- Interest, dividends, and royalties
- Pension and retirement income
- Unemployment compensation
- Income from all other sources

The debtor's monthly income from Part II is multiplied by 12 to determine the debtor's annual income. Part III requires the debtor to compare his or her annual income to the median income of households of similar size in his or her state. This information is easily obtained from tables located on the Department of Justice U.S. Trustee Program website in the Census Bureau Median Family Income by Family Size section. If the debtor's annual income is less than the median income for his or her state, no further calculations of the Means Test need to be completed. The debtor may now check the box marked "The presumption does not arise" in the section located in the top right portion of Official Form B22A. The debtor may ignore the rest of the Means Test form and go straight to Part VIII. If the debtor's annual income is greater than the state median income, additional calculations in the Means Test form must be completed to determine whether the debtor is eligible for Chapter 7.

The next part of the Means Test addresses the issue of marital adjustment. Married couples may take certain deductions in this section of the Means Test if they have been married for more than six months. Spouses are not required to file for bankruptcy together as joint petitioners. One spouse will often file for bankruptcy because the debt has been mainly incurred by the filing spouse. Even though the spouse is filing a sole bankruptcy petition, he or she must include his or her spouse's income. One of the reasons for avoiding a joint bankruptcy petition is to take advantage of the deductions allowable in this section, which are not available for spouses filing jointly. The nonfiling spouse's income is included in the calculation of current monthly income; however, this section allows the debtor to deduct portions of the nonfiling spouse's income that was not regularly contributed to the household expenses of the debtor or the debtor's dependents. The Bankruptcy Code, however, does not define the term *household expenses* and, as a result, line 17 of Part IV is subject to heavy scrutiny by the U.S. trustee. Keep in mind that the U.S. Trustee can challenge these deductions, as well as any figures included on the Means Test form, in assessing abuse. The following is a list of expenses of the nonfiling spouse that may be deducted in calculating the marital adjustment. This list is not exhaustive, and it's important to check local case law.

- Alimony payments and child support (for nonfiling spouse's dependent children not residing with debtor)
- Attorney's fees
- Business travel, food expenses, and working clothing/uniforms
- Car payments, insurance, and car expenses (for nonfiling spouse's car)
- Cell phone expenses (for nonfiling spouse)
- Entertainment expenses, fitness memberships
- Loan repayments on 401(k)
- Mortgage payments and other real estate–related expenses (for property owned solely by nonfiling spouse)
- Student loan payments (for nonfiling spouse)
- Withholding taxes

CALCULATION OF DEDUCTIONS FROM INCOME

This section of the Means Test allows the debtor to deduct living and debt payment expenses. Part V is divided into four subparts:

- Subpart A: Deductions under Standards of the Internal Revenue Service (IRS)
- Subpart B: Additional Living Expense Deductions
- Subpart C: Deductions for Debt Payment
- Subpart D: Total Deductions from Income

SUBPART A: DEDUCTIONS UNDER STANDARDS OF THE INTERNAL REVENUE SERVICE (IRS)

Allowable living expenses are predetermined and have been established by the Bankruptcy Code. U.S. census and IRS data are available on the U.S. Trustee Program website. (To avoid confusion when reading these standards, please be aware that instead of using the term *debtor*, the IRS Collection Financial Standards uses the word *taxpayer*.) The debtor is allowed to deduct expense amounts according to National and Local Standards. **National Standards** are monthly expense amounts based on nationwide figures and are considered the allowable living expenses depending on the size of the family.

Although determining household income and the number of individuals in a household are important when calculating the Means Test, "household size" is not defined in the Bankruptcy Code. Case law among the various circuits provides three approaches to calculating the size of the debtor's household. A majority of circuit courts use what is known as the **economic unit approach**. This method looks at the household as a single economic unit and takes into account who is making financial contributions and who depends on the debtor for support. A minority of circuits use the U.S. Bureau of the Census's definition, which is basically a head count of everyone who resides in the home. This is called the **heads-on-beds approach**. The **income tax–dependent approach** determines household size by counting the dependents claimed on the debtor's tax return. There are also many wrinkles in determining household size that include, for example, factoring in the contribution or dependency of part-time household members, roommates, and domestic partners. It is important to note that these definitions vary from circuit to circuit, so relevant case law should be researched to determine which approach applies.

National Standards are provided for the following expenses and may not be deducted separately in other sections of the Means Test.

- Apparel and services (such as shoes and clothing, laundry and dry cleaning, and shoe repair)
- Housekeeping supplies (such as laundry and cleaning supplies)
- Lawn and garden supplies
- Meals at home or away (unless unreimbursed business expenses)
- Miscellaneous personal expenses
- Other household products such as cleaning and toilet tissue, paper towels, and napkins
- Out-of-pocket health care expenses
- Personal care products and services (includes hair care products, haircuts and beautician services, oral hygiene products and articles, shaving needs, cosmetics, perfume, bath preparations, deodorants, feminine hygiene products, electric personal care appliances, personal care services, and repair of personal care appliances)
- Postage and stationery and other miscellaneous household supplies

Local Standards are based on the state and county where the debtor lives and will vary from case to case. These amounts may also be found on the U.S. Trustee Program website. When determining amounts for Local Standards, locate the section mentioned previously on the U.S. Trustee Program website and obtain the most current table from the drop-down, state-by-state menu. On the appropriate table for

National Standards
Monthly expense amounts based on nationwide figures and considered allowable living expenses, depending on the size of the family.

economic unit approach
A method adopted by a majority of the circuit courts to calculate the size of the debtor's household. This method looks at the household as a single economic unit and takes into account who is making financial contributions and who depends on the debtor for support.

heads-on-beds approach
A method adopted by a minority of circuit courts to calculate the size of the debtor's household. This method uses the U.S. Bureau of the Census's definition, which is a head count of everyone who resides in the home.

income tax–dependent approach
A method adopted by a minority of circuit courts to calculate the size of the debtor's household by counting the dependents claimed on the debtor's tax return.

Local Standards
Expense costs used in calculating the Means Test that are based on the average housing, utilities, and transportation expenses in the state and county where the debtor lives.

the client's state, locate the county where the client resides to determine the allowable living expenses. Local Standards are provided for the following expenses.

- Housing and utilities standards
- Transportation expense standards

OTHER NECESSARY EXPENSES

Although National and Local Standards are predetermined, requiring the debtor to use those figures regardless of the actual cost of allowable living expenses, the debtor may also deduct monthly actual living expenses in sections of the Means Test calculation form for other necessary expenses. It is important to obtain documentary verification of these expenses from the debtor to justify why the debtor should be entitled to deduct these expenses. The amount deducted is the average monthly expense that the debtor has spent over the six-month period preceding the bankruptcy petition filing. These deductions include:

- Taxes
- Involuntary deductions for employment (such as retirement contributions, union dues, and uniform costs)
- Life insurance
- Court-ordered payments
- Education for employment or for a physically or mentally challenged child
- Child care
- Health care (unreimbursed expenses)
- Telecommunications services (such as basic home telephone service and cell phones)

SUBPART B: ADDITIONAL LIVING EXPENSE DEDUCTIONS

necessary expense test
An inquiry into the expenses needed to provide for the health, welfare, and/or production of income for the debtor and the debtor's family.

Deductible expenses are determined by the **necessary expense test**. This requires an inquiry into whether the expenses are needed to provide for the health, welfare, and/or production of income for the debtor and the debtor's family. The debtor must justify these expenses for the health and welfare of the debtor and/or the debtor's family under the necessary expense test in 11 U.S.C. § 707(b)(2)(A)(ii)(I). As mentioned earlier in this chapter, these figures are scrutinized very carefully, so it is important to obtain documentation from the client verifying these deductions. The additional living expense deductions include:

- Health insurance, disability insurance, and health savings account expenses
- Protection against family violence
- Home energy costs
- Education expenses for dependent children younger than 18
- Additional food and clothing expenses
- Continued charitable contributions

SUBPART C: DEDUCTIONS FOR DEBT PAYMENT

The Bankruptcy Code allows the debtor to deduct average monthly payments for certain secured debts over a five-year period. Secured debts are guaranteed by the actual property, and the debtor agrees to give up the property if the payments cannot be made. There is a lot of litigation surrounding this section of the Means Test because 11 U.S.C. § 707(b)(2)(A)(iii)(I) requires the debtor to calculate the average monthly income that is scheduled as contractually due during this time period. The problem arises when the amount of the secured debt is deducted, but the debtor intends to surrender the collateral to the creditor before the five-year period has elapsed. Debtors tend to argue that the statute allows them to deduct the amounts that are due under the debt agreement rather than those that are actually paid. Creditors and trustees often object to these deductions because they reflect amounts that the debtor will not be making because the collateral or property has been surrendered.

EXAMPLE

Frederick and Elizabeth LaDonne file for Chapter 7 bankruptcy. In Subpart C, line 42 of the Means Test, they list the amount of $2,105.36 as future payments on the mortgage on their principal residence. The LaDonnes, however, intend to surrender their home. The U.S. trustee moves to dismiss their case on fraud grounds. She argues that they should not be allowed to deduct the secured debt payments when the debtors intend to surrender their principal residence. The Bankruptcy Court takes the plain-meaning approach to the Code and rules that the Code requires the debtors to list their expenses as of the date of the petition. The LaDonnes are allowed to deduct from their current monthly income long-term secured debt payments that are allowed on the bankruptcy petition date, regardless of whether they intend to surrender the property securing the debt.

SUBPART D: TOTAL DEDUCTIONS FROM INCOME

Subpart D requires the debtor to total all the deductions allowed by Subparts A, B, and C.

PART VI: DETERMINATION OF PRESUMPTION OF ABUSE

Here the debtor determines whether there is extra income after all the allowable deductions are claimed to arrange for a repayment plan under Chapter 13. If money is left over, the presumption of abuse arises, and the debtor will not be able to file for Chapter 7. If there is no extra income, the debtor qualifies for Chapter 7.

PART VII: ADDITIONAL EXPENSE CLAIMS

A debtor who does not qualify for Chapter 7 because of the calculations in Part VI is allowed to claim additional expenses that are not included in other sections of the Means Test. These expenses are those required for the health and welfare of the debtor and the debtor's family.

PART VIII: VERIFICATION

In this section, the debtor or debtors in a joint petition sign the document under penalty of perjury, declaring that all the information filed in the petition is true and correct.

EXAMPLE: APPLICATION OF THE MEANS TEST USING OFFICIAL FORM B22A

Brian Klein is a new bankruptcy client who lives in New Jersey and wants to file for bankruptcy. His petition will be filed in September 2013. It is important to verify Klein's income for the six months prior to filing the petition in September by obtaining paystubs or other records that justify the figures used for determining his gross income. Let us presume in this example that Klein is laid off from work in June and has been unable to find work. It is recommended that students following this example find the relevant website sections mentioned in this problem for a better understanding of the Means Test and to build the important skill of using the resources that a paralegal encounters on the job.

STEP 1: DETERMINE CLIENT'S CURRENT MONTHLY INCOME (CMI)

Calculating a client's current monthly income (CMI) is determined by taking an average of the client's gross income for the six-month period prior to filing the bankruptcy petition.

Remember that gross income is defined as the income the client earned before taxes and other deductions are subtracted. The next step is to add the client's gross income for this six-month period and divide it by six. This figure yields the client's CMI.

1. Add Klein's gross income for the six months preceding filing the bankruptcy petition.

Month	Brian Klein's Gross Income
March	$2,500
April	$2,500
May	$2,500
June	0
July	0
August	0
Total	$7,500

2. Divide Klein's gross income by six: $7,500 divided by 6 = $1,250. Klein's CMI is $1,250.
3. Multiply Klein's income by 12 to determine his average income: $1,250 \times 12 = $15,000.
4. Klein's average income is $15,000.

STEP 2: DETERMINE WHETHER THE CLIENT MUST TAKE THE MEANS TEST

Locate the Department of Justice website and retrieve the table entitled, "Census Bureau Median Family Income by Family Size." Make sure the table corresponds with the client's filing date. Median income means the median family income both calculated and reported by the Bureau of the Census.

The table includes the median family income for use in completing Official Bankruptcy Form B22A. Locate the client's State and the size of the client's family household.

1. This is the proper table to use in Klein's case because it applies to cases filed "on and after May 1, 2013," and he will be filing his bankruptcy petition in September 2013.
2. Locate the State of New Jersey.
3. Klein represents a family size consisting of "1 Earner." From the table, the New Jersey media income for a one-earner family is $61,146 per year.

State	1 Earner	2 People	3 People	4 People
New Jersey	$61,146	$69,697	$85,016	$103,786

Because Klein's income falls below the median income for a one-earner family, and assuming he has met the other qualifications outlined in this chapter, he does not have to proceed any further with the Means Test and is eligible to file for Chapter 7 bankruptcy. If Klein's income, however, had been too high to be eligible for Chapter 7, deducting expenses from his income could still qualify him under this chapter.

STEP 3: CALCULATING DISPOSABLE INCOME

Suppose Klein's income exceeded $61,146. He would be required to proceed with the Means Test calculation to determine whether he could file for Chapter 7. After the debtor's CMI has been calculated, the next step is to determine the client's monthly disposable income. Disposable income is determined by adding the client's expenses and deducting this figure from the client's CMI. The purpose of calculating disposable income is to determine whether the client is financially able to pay off the existing debt over a three- to five-year period under a court-monitored Chapter 13 repayment plan or, instead, qualify for a Chapter 7 liquidation bankruptcy.

THE MEANS TEST IN CHAPTER 13 CASES

Recall earlier in this chapter that application of the Means Test in Chapter 7 cases is to determine the debtor's eligibility under this section of the Bankruptcy Code to discharge his or her debt. When applied to Chapter 13 cases, the Means Test does not determine eligibility; rather, it determines how much the debtor will pay unsecured creditors and the duration of the repayment plan. If the debtor's annual gross income is more than the median income for a household of the debtor's size, the debtor is required to file a five-year repayment plan unless all debts can be paid off in less than that time. If the debtor's annual gross income is less that the median income, the repayment plan is three years.

The Chapter 13 Means Test is used to calculate how much of the debtor's disposable income is available to pay unsecured creditors. The Means

(*Continued*)

Test takes into account the debtor's average gross income received six months prior to the bankruptcy filing. If the debtor's annual gross income is less than the median income for the same size household, the presumption is that the debtor is unable to pay unsecured debts. If the debtor's gross income is more than the median income, the Means Test allows the debtor to deduct necessary expenses from monthly gross income. This net figure determines how much of the debtor's monthly disposable income is available for payment of unsecured debts.

The results of the Means Test when applied to Chapter 13 repayment plans may sometimes have harsh consequences for the debtor. If changes in the debtor's projected income and expenses are not taken into account, the repayment plan may be unrealistic, setting the debtor up for failure. In the case of *Jan Hamilton, Trustee vs. Stephanie Kay Lanning*, 560 U.S. 505, 130 S.Ct. 2466, 177 L.Ed.2d 23 (2010), the United States Supreme Court held that bankruptcy court judges do not have to take a mechanical approach to the Means Test in Chapter 13 cases. Instead, bankruptcy trustees should take a forward-looking approach and consider the realities of the debtor's income. In this case, the debtor received a one-time buyout plan from her employer during the six-month period prior to filing for bankruptcy. The inclusion of this payment in calculating her monthly disposable income for the Chapter 13 repayment plan did not accurately reflect the debtor's future income. In this scenario, her disposable income was largely inflated, and any payments to creditors based on this figure would be unaffordable. Although the trustee viewed this case as a mechanical calculation under the Means Test, the Supreme Court held that changes to the debtor's future income and expenses should be considered when determining a repayment plan.

Remember our friends Sandra and Karl Wickes from the beginning of the chapter? They, like so many Americans, feel compelled to spend their earnings on lavish things and memberships to country clubs. It seems that there is enormous pressure for folks in higher-income strata to maintain a certain image. Often, this is accomplished by overspending on what some may refer to as the "outer trappings of wealth." Despite the significant changes in the Bankruptcy Code in 2005, including the enactment of the BAPCPA, many people are under the impression that they can simply file a Chapter 7 case to wipe out their unsecured debt. As you now know, it is not quite that simple. Both of the Wickeses are still employed despite their enormous debt. Due to their existing income, a presumption of abuse may arise if they attempt to file under Chapter 7. As you can see after reading this chapter, it is almost certain that the Wickeses will need to take the Means Test. They should be prepared for the likelihood that they will have no other option but to file under Chapter 13.

CHAPTER **SUMMARY**

Congress's intention in implementing the Bankruptcy Code and the BAPCPA is to prevent individuals who are perfectly capable of paying their debts from liquidating their obligations while their creditors are left unpaid. The law now requires debtors to pass a Means Test, which is a formula designed to determine whether debtors have income and the ability to restructure their debt and pay off their creditors. The Means Test consists of a series of financially related questions and formulas designed to determine whether debtors qualify for Chapter 7. For Chapters 13 filers, the Means Test determines the debtors' repayment plan.

The United States trustees, panel trustees, bankruptcy administrators, creditors, or other parties in interest may motion to have the case dismissed or converted to Chapter 11 or Chapter 13 if the court finds that granting relief under Chapter 7 would be considered abuse. There are three possible outcomes upon completion of the Means Test: no

presumption of abuse, a presumption of abuse, or presumption of abuse is temporarily inapplicable. When applied to Chapter 13 cases, the Means Test does not determine eligibility; rather, it determines how much the debtor will pay unsecured creditors and the duration of the repayment plan. If the debtor's annual gross income is more than the median income for a household of the debtor's size, the debtor is required to file a five-year repayment plan unless all debts can be paid off in less than that time.

CONCEPT REVIEW AND REINFORCEMENT

KEY **TERMS**

Affidavit of Special Circumstances
Bankruptcy Abuse Prevention and
   Consumer Protection Act of 2005
   (BAPCPA)

economic unit approach
heads-on-beds approach
income tax–dependent approach
Local Standards

Means Test
National Standards
necessary expense test

REVIEWING **KEY CONCEPTS**

1. Explain the statement, "Relief under Chapter 7 is not automatic."
2. Explain how a debtor could abuse the bankruptcy system.
3. Define the Means Test and explain its purpose.
4. Name the official bankruptcy form used to calculate the Chapter 7 Means Test.
5. Name the official bankruptcy form used to calculate the Chapter 13 Means Test.
6. If the Bankruptcy Code does not define bad faith, who does?

7. What is an Affidavit of Special Circumstances?
8. What provisions has the Bankruptcy Code made regarding application of the Means Test to reservists and members of the National Guard?
9. List the various types of income that must be included in the Means Test calculation.
10. Define National Standards and Local Standards and explain their significance in the Means Test.

BUILDING YOUR PARALEGAL SKILLS

CASE FOR **REVIEW**

Jan Hamilton, Trustee vs. Stephanie Kay Lanning, 560 U.S. 505, 130 S.Ct. 2466, 177 L.Ed.2d 23 (2010)

BUILDING A PROFESSIONAL PORTFOLIO

PORTFOLIO **EXERCISES**

Your local paralegal association is aware that you are employed by a bankruptcy attorney. The association is hosting a conference at which members will present topics in their area of the law. The head of the association has asked you to provide the group with a short presentation on the Means Test and how it differs for debtors in Chapter 7 and Chapter 13 cases. Prepare an outline that you can use as a handout at the association meeting.

chapter 6

CHAPTER 7 BANKRUPTCY: LIQUIDATION

LEARNING OBJECTIVES

After studying this chapter, you should be able to:

1. Explain the purpose of Chapter 7 liquidation.

2. Describe what happens at the first meeting of the creditors.

3. Summarize the Chapter 7 process.

4. Identify the various types of claims and their order of priority.

5. Define voidable preferences and fraudulent conveyances.

Nasim Pradhan graduated at the top of her law school class and landed a job as an associate attorney in a ritzy law firm in San Francisco. She recently married her high school sweetheart, Praveen Pradhan, who was a vice president at a local insurance company. The Pradhans earned a combined $267,000 per year. A six-figure, combined income was a new phenomenon to both of them. The Pradhans spent lots of money on what some wise folks might refer to as the "outer trappings of wealth." However, like so many Americans, they did not understand that true wealth is about increasing your net worth, not accumulating expensive things and running up debt in the process. They did little to save and prepare for hard times. Nasim had friends who had money in their family lineage for years and they always warned her not to go overboard with the spending because it would make her appear ostentatious and "nouveau riche."

A year or so after joining her law firm, Nasim was informed that the firm lost a huge client. Due to the economy, the client shopped around for less expensive representation. As a result, Nasim lost her job and found it very difficult to find work as an attorney. All the firms she applied to informed her that they were looking for paralegals and not attorneys at this time. With 50% of their income missing, it did not take long before the Pradhans' mortgage payments, car payments, and home equity line of credit became difficult to keep up with. The Pradhans made an appointment with a local bankruptcy attorney to discuss options for starting over with their financial life. Read on to find out whether the Pradhans, currently a family of two, will qualify for Chapter 7 liquidation under the Bankruptcy Code.

Introduction

Chapter 7 liquidation is what most people think of when they hear that someone has gone bankrupt. The legal result of a discharge in Chapter 7 is discharge of the debtor's obligations to his or her creditors and the chance for a fresh start. According to the U.S. Courts website, a total of 1,170,324 bankruptcy cases were filed during the 12-month period ending March 31, 2013; 804,885 of these cases were Chapter 7 bankruptcies. For the paralegal working for a bankruptcy attorney, voluntary Chapter 7 cases are the most common types of cases a busy practice encounters. This chapter provides the reader with the foundation of a voluntary Chapter 7 liquidation proceeding.

Introduction to Chapter 7 Liquidation

Chapter 7 is the most common type of bankruptcy filed in the United States. A Chapter 7 bankruptcy is often referred to as a **liquidation bankruptcy**, **straight bankruptcy**, **total bankruptcy**, **complete bankruptcy**, or a **consumer bankruptcy**. Clients most often file for a Chapter 7 bankruptcy when they are seeking relief for staggering debt due to insurmountable medical expenses, excessive credit debt, extended periods of unemployment, and divorce. In a Chapter 7 liquidation proceeding, the debtor seeks a discharge of his or her debt. The effect of a discharge is that the debtor is released from liability for certain debts incurred, giving the debtor's creditors no further legal recourse for the collection of those obligations. Filing a Chapter 7 petition allows the debtor to keep any assets that are exempt from bankruptcy proceedings under the law.

In a Chapter 7 proceeding, a bankruptcy trustee is appointed and is responsible for gathering the debtor's assets, selling them, and then distributing the proceeds to the creditors. The debtor's nonexempt property is **liquidated** by the trustee, who sells it and pays the administration expenses associated with the bankruptcy case. The net proceeds of the liquidation sales are then distributed to the creditors.

Most Chapter 7 liquidations are considered **no-asset cases**. Most of the debtor's assets are exempt from the proceedings, which leaves no nonexempt property for the trustee to sell. In other cases, the value of the nonexempt property is so minimal that it is not worth the trustee's time or effort to administer. The debtor then attends a 341 hearing, commonly referred to as the first meeting of the creditors, where the trustee questions her or him. Creditors may also be in attendance at this meeting and are given the opportunity to ask the debtor any questions regarding the bankruptcy petition, schedules, and statements filed. If all goes well for the debtor, it will take 60 days from the date of the first meeting of the creditors for the Bankruptcy Court to discharge the debtor's obligations that are considered dischargeable.

liquidation bankruptcy
A term used to define a Chapter 7 bankruptcy.

straight bankruptcy
A term used to define a Chapter 7 bankruptcy.

total bankruptcy
A term used to define a Chapter 7 bankruptcy.

complete bankruptcy
A term used to define a Chapter 7 bankruptcy.

consumer bankruptcy
A term used to define a Chapter 7 bankruptcy.

liquidated
The legal process by which the trustee sells nonexempt property and pays the administration expenses associated with the bankruptcy case.

no-asset case
A bankruptcy case in which most of the debtor's assets are exempt from the proceedings, leaving no nonexempt property for the trustee to sell.

The Chapter 7 Process

WHO MAY FILE FOR CHAPTER 7

According to 11 U.S.C § 101(41), any person—an individual; partnership; corporation or other form of business entity that resides or has a domicile, place of business, or property in the United States; or municipality—may file for Chapter 7 liquidation bankruptcy. Exceptions are outlined in 11 U.S.C. § 109(b) and include entities such as railroads and banks, whose insolvency issues are governed under laws that fall outside the Bankruptcy Code.

PRE-PETITION CREDIT COUNSELING

credit counseling course
A mandatory course that provides debtors with alternatives to bankruptcy and explores the possibility of working out a payment plan with creditors instead.

Debtors who wish to file for Chapter 7 protection must take a pre-petition **credit counseling course** from a service the U.S. Trustee Program approves within the 180-day period prior to filing for bankruptcy. The goal of the credit counseling course is to provide debtors with alternatives to bankruptcy and explore the possibility of working out a payment plan with creditors instead. These services are in person, on the phone, or available on the Internet at low cost to potential filers. A list of approved providers is available on the U.S. Trustee Program's website. For legal professionals who work in the states of Alabama and North Carolina, it is important to note that these bankruptcy courts do not operate under the U.S. Trustee Program. Instead, these states have bankruptcy administrators who have lists of approved credit counseling course providers. When the debtor has completed the course, he or she is provided with a certificate of credit counseling completion, which must be filed along with the debtor's Chapter 7 petition. A list of approved credit counseling agencies broken down by state and judicial district may be found on the Department of Justice website.

The Chapter 7 Petition

bankruptcy petition
The initiating document that is filed along with a filing fee in the bankruptcy court of the federal district where the debtor is domiciled or resides with the intent to remain permanently. The petition includes Schedules and the Statement of Financial Affairs, among other documents, which includes information regarding the debtor's assets, liabilities, expenses, and a list of creditors to whom debts are due.

A Chapter 7 bankruptcy begins with filing a **bankruptcy petition**. The details of preparing and filing petitions, schedules, and other forms is addressed in Chapter 15 of this book. For purposes of this chapter, however, a bankruptcy petition is a document filed in the bankruptcy court of the federal district where the debtor resides. If the debtor is a business, the petition is filed in the federal district that constitutes the debtor's principal place of business. The bankruptcy petition and its accompanying schedules, statement of financial affairs, statement of intention, and creditor matrix provides the bankruptcy court with the basic information necessary to commence the bankruptcy case.

APPOINTMENT OF A TRUSTEE

trustee
An individual typically appointed in a Chapter 11 case when the bankruptcy court finds that the current management has engaged in some type of fraud, dishonesty, incompetence, or gross mismanagement.

The U.S. trustee appoints a disinterested person called a **trustee** from a panel of attorneys who takes on the responsibility of liquidating the debtor's nonexempt property and distributing the proceeds to the creditors. This individual serves as an interim trustee and remains as a permanent trustee unless the creditors choose another person at the 341 hearing. The trustee is entitled to reasonable compensation that is subject to the limits in 11 U.S.C. § 326(a) and the approval of the bankruptcy court. The creditors also have the power to elect a new trustee if the current trustee is removed, fails to qualify, dies, or resigns. The duties of the Chapter 7 trustee are found in 11 U.S.C. § 704 and include:

1. Collecting the debtor's property
2. Selling the debtor's property for cash
3. Reviewing documents filed by an individual debtor to determine whether a presumption of abuse applies
4. Maintaining an accounting for the property received
5. Investigating the debtor's financial affairs
6. Reviewing proofs of claim filed by creditors

7. Objecting to a discharge when appropriate.
8. Providing information regarding the bankruptcy estate to any parties in interest.
9. Filing business reports if the debtor is in operation.
10. Preparing and filing a final report and accounting with the bankruptcy court and the U.S. trustee.

TRUSTEE COMPENSATION

Bankruptcy Code 11 U.S.C. § 327 addresses the issue of trustee compensation. Specifically, "professional persons employed under 11 U.S.C. § 327 of the Bankruptcy Code are entitled to reasonable compensation for actual, necessary services rendered."

The Chapter 7 trustee (the panel trustee) is compensated for administering the Chapter 7 bankruptcy case. He or she is appointed to review the bankruptcy petition and other documents debtor files, verify the information in these filings, conduct the 341 hearing, collect and liquidate the debtor's nonexempt assets, and distribute any cash received to creditors in their order of priority.

The panel trustee receives an **administrative fee** of $60.00 per bankruptcy case and is paid out of the debtor's filing fee. In addition, the Code provides that the panel trustee may also earn a commission based on the total disbursements made to interested parties of the estate, except for any payments to the debtor.

The basis for compensation of Chapter 7 trustees is found in 11 U.S.C. § 326(a), and the commission rate is based on the following calculations.

1. 25% on the first $5,000 or less
2. 10% on any amount in excess of $5,000 but not in excess of $50,000
3. 5% on any amount in excess of $50,000 but not in excess of $1,000,000
4. reasonable compensation not to exceed 3% of such moneys in excess of $1,000,000

When the Chapter 7 trustee has completed work on the bankruptcy estate, he or she submits an application to the court as well as notice to all other interested parties in the case. The court reviews the trustee's bill based on the reasonable-compensation standard in 11 U.S.C. § 327 and hears any objections. If no objections are raised, the trustee will be paid the maximum compensation allowed under bankruptcy law.

The Bankruptcy Estate

The filing of a Chapter 7 petition creates a **bankruptcy estate**, which consists of all legal and equitable interests a debtor might own in property at the time of the filing of the Chapter 7 petition. It also includes any property the debtor receives within 180 days of the filing date of the petition. Under 11 U.S.C. § 541(b), the bankruptcy estate does not include the following:

1. Any power the debtor may exercise solely for the benefit of an entity other than the debtor
2. Any interest of the debtor as a lessee under a lease of nonresidential real property that has terminated

bankruptcy estate
All the legal and equitable interests a debtor may own in property at the time he or she files a Chapter 7 petition. It also includes any property the debtor receives within 180 days of the filing date of the petition.

3. Any eligibility of the debtor to participate in programs authorized under the Higher Education Act of 1965
4. Specific interests of the debtor in liquid or gaseous hydrocarbons
5. Specific funds placed in an education individual retirement account
6. Specific funds used to purchase a tuition credit or certificate programs
7. Any amount withheld by an employer from the wages of employees for payment as contributions
8. Specific assets pledged as collateral for a loan
9. Any interest in cash or cash equivalents that constitute proceeds of a sale by the debtor of a money order

Exempt Property

exempt property
Property that is exempt from seizure by creditors.

nonexempt property
Property that becomes part of the bankruptcy estate and may be sold by the bankruptcy trustee to raise funds to pay back creditors.

Exempt property is the term used to define property that is exempt from seizure by creditors and the trustee, except in rare circumstances. **Nonexempt property**, however, is subject to seizure. The previous section listed the property interests that are excluded from the bankruptcy estate; this section focuses on property interests that cannot be seized or sold to satisfy creditor claims. The purpose of the exemptions is to leave the debtor with a minimum amount of essential real and personal property to make a fresh start. The Bankruptcy Code allows the debtor to choose between the federal exemptions provided in 11 U.S.C. 522(d) or those allowed under state law. The debtor's state however, may have opted out of the federal list of exemptions. If so, the debtor is limited to the exemptions allowed under state law. Most states have chosen to opt out of the federal exemptions. State bankruptcy exemptions are found in the statutory codes of that particular jurisdiction.

Adjustments to the federal exemptions were made on April 1, 2013, and apply to all bankruptcy petitions filed on or after that date. The exemption amount is calculated based on the fair market value of the property as of the date of the bankruptcy petition, subtracting the amount of any liens or security interests remaining. The exemption amounts pursuant to 11 U.S.C. § 522(d) include those listed in Table 6.1.

Spouses applying for bankruptcy in a joint petition are allowed to double their exemptions. Spouses filing jointly, however, must choose the same set of exemptions if they live in a state that allows them to choose between the federal and state exemptions. Exemptions are listed in Schedule C and are part of the debtor's Schedules and Statements of Financial Affairs. The property listed in the debtor's Schedule C is exempt unless the trustee or any creditor objects to the claimed exemption in a timely fashion pursuant to the Federal Rules of Bankruptcy 4003(b):

(b) Objections to claim of exemptions. A party in interest may file an objection to the list of property claimed as exempt only within 30 days after the meeting of creditors held under § 341(a) is concluded or within 30 days after any amendment to the list or supplemental schedules is filed, whichever is later....

If no objections are filed within the timeframe of the Federal Rules of Bankruptcy, all of the debtor's property claimed under the exemptions will be exempt.

TABLE 6.1 Exemption Amounts Pursuant to 11 U.S.C. § 522(d)

EXEMPTION	DESCRIPTION
Homestead Exemption 11 U.S.C. 522(d)(1); (d)(5)	Up to $22,975 of real property or personal property that the debtor or a dependent of the debtor uses as a residence, in a cooperative that owns property that the debtor or a dependent of the debtor uses as a residence, or in a burial plot for the debtor or a dependent of the debtor.
Motor Vehicle Exemption 11 U.S.C. 522(d)(2)	Up to $3,675 in value for one vehicle
Household Goods Exemption 11 U.S.C. 522(d)(3)	Up to $575 in value in any particular item or $11,525 in total value, in household furnishings, household goods, wearing apparel, appliances, books, animals, crops, or musical instruments, that are held primarily for the personal, family, or household use of the debtor or a dependent of the debtor
Jewelry Exemption 11 U.S.C. 522(d)(4)	Up to $1,550 in jewelry held primarily for the personal, family, or household use of the debtor or a dependent of the debtor
Wildcard Exemption 11 U.S.C. 522(d)(5)	As the name suggests, this exemption may be applied to any property the debtor owns in the amount of $1,225 plus $11,500 of any unused portion of the debtor's homestead exemption to exempt any type of property
Tools of the Trade Exemption 11 U.S.C. 522(d)(6)	Up to $2,300 in any implements, professional books, or tools of the trade of the debtor or the trade of a dependent of the debtor
Unmatured Life Insurance Exemption 11 US.C. 522(d)(7)	Unlimited
Cash Value/Interests in Unmatured Life Insurance Contracts Exemption 11 U.S.C. 522(d)(8)	Up to $12,250, less any amount of property of the estate transferred in the manner specified in section 542(d) of this title, in any accrued dividend or interest under, or loan value of, any unmatured life insurance contract the debtor owns under which the insured is the debtor or an individual of whom the debtor is a dependent
Prescribed Health Aids Exemption 11 U.S.C. 522(d)(9)	Unlimited. Professionally prescribed health aids for the debtor or a dependent of the debtor
Benefits and Domestic Support Exemptions 11 U.S.C. 522(d)(10)(A)	Unlimited. Social security benefit, unemployment compensation, or a local public assistance benefit, veterans' benefit, disability, illness, or unemployment benefit, alimony, support, or separate maintenance, to the extent reasonably necessary for the support of the debtor and any dependent of the debtor
Retirement Funds Exemption 11 U.S.C. 522(b)(3)(C)	Unlimited if tax exempt under Internal Revenue Code
Personal Bodily Injury Exemptions 11 U.S.C. 522(d)(11)(D)	Up to $22,975 on account of personal bodily injury, not including pain and suffering or compensation for actual pecuniary loss, of the debtor or an individual of whom the debtor is a dependent
Crime Victim's Award Exemption 11 U.S.C. 522(d)(11)(A)	Unlimited. Award under a crime victim's reparation law
Wrongful Death Exemption 11 U.S.C. 522(d)(11)(B)	Unlimited. Payment on account of the wrongful death of an individual of whom the debtor was a dependent, to the extent reasonably necessary for the support of the debtor and any dependent of the debtor
Insurance Proceeds Exemption 11 U.S.C. 22(d)(10)(C) 11 U.S.C. 22(d)(11)(C)	Unlimited. Payment under a life insurance contract that insured the life of an individual of whom the debtor was a dependent on the date of such individual's death, to the extent reasonably necessary for the support of the debtor and any dependent of the debtor
Loss of Future Earnings Payment Exemption 11 U.S.C. 522(d)(11)(E)	Unlimited. Payment in compensation of loss of future earnings of the debtor or an individual of whom the debtor is or was a dependent, to the extent reasonably necessary for the support of the debtor and any dependent of the debtor

Claims and Priority of Distribution

The Bankruptcy Code defines a claim as "[a] right to payment, whether or not such right is reduced to judgment, liquidated, unliquidated, fixed, contingent, matured, unmatured, disputed, undisputed, legal, equitable, secured or unsecured...." 11 U.S.C. § 101(5). In simpler terms, a **claim** is the creditor's right to receive payment for a debt the debtor owes on the date of the bankruptcy filing.

After a debtor files for bankruptcy, the creditors listed on the bankruptcy petition receive notice of the filing and Proof of Claim. A **Proof of Claim** (B10 (Official Form 10)) is a form the creditor uses to indicate the amount of the debt the debtor owes on the date of the bankruptcy filing. The creditor must file the form with the clerk of the same bankruptcy court in which the bankruptcy case was filed. In a no asset case, there is nothing to distribute, so the creditor is instructed not to file a claim until further notice from the court.

TYPES OF CLAIMS

Claims are categorized in order of priority according to the Bankruptcy Code. A **priority claim** is a debt that takes precedence over others because it is within the public interest to do so, or the money is owed to the government. An example of a priority claim would be child support or alimony payments. A **nonpriority claim** is an unsecured debt that does not take precedence over other debts, for example, credit card debt or medical bills. They include **secured claims**, **priority unsecured claims**, and **nonpriority unsecured claims**. The debtor is required to file a list of claims in the debtor's Schedules and Statement of Financial Affairs. Creditors, however, must file what is known as a Proof of Claim with the court within 90 days of the first date set for the 341 meeting of creditors. Here the creditor attaches actual evidence of the amount the debtor owes. This can include contracts, invoices, receipts, or any other documentation of the debt. An exception to this rule is when the debtor has filed a no asset case and there is literally nothing to distribute. Any creditor or party in interest has the right to object to a claim under 11 U.S.C. § 502(a).

SECURED CLAIMS

A **secured claim** is a loan granted to the debtor in exchange for a lien on the property. Secured claims receive top priority in repayment of debts in a bankruptcy proceeding; they are first in line. The real or personal property acts as collateral on the loan. If the debtor cannot pay the loan, the secured creditor has the right to repossess the property and sell it to satisfy the debt. If the property is worth less than the debt, the portion of the debt covered by collateral is categorized as a secured claim, and the remaining balance is categorized as an unsecured claim.

NONPRIORITY UNSECURED CLAIMS

Nonpriority unsecured claims have no collateral securing the creditor's interest and are not entitled to priority under 11 U.S.C. § 507. Creditors with this type of claim may receive a pro rata share after all the debtor's priority claims have been satisfied. In many cases, nothing is left after the secured claims and priority unsecured claims are paid. Examples of nonpriority unsecured claims include credit card debt, medical debt, student loans, and personal loans.

---

nonpriority unsecured claims
Creditor claims in which creditors are not entitled to priority and no collateral secures their interest.

secured claim
A loan granted to the debtor in exchange for a lien on the property. Secured claims receive top priority in repayment of debts in a bankruptcy proceeding.

priority unsecured claims
Claims that take precedence over the claims of other creditors.

PRIORITY UNSECURED CLAIMS

Whereas creditors holding unsecured claims typically receive the lowest priority, some receive priority status over other creditors' unsecured claims. Creditors in this position have what is referred to as a priority claim. Bankruptcy Code 11 U.S.C. § 507 has established the following ten priority unsecured claims and requires each category of creditors to be paid in full before the next category may be considered for payment.

1. Any domestic support obligations, such as alimony and child support
2. Administrative expenses
3. Unsecured claims for debts related to the debtor's regular business expenses that were incurred after an involuntary case was initiated and prior to either the appointment of a trustee or an order for relief from the bankruptcy court.
4. Claims for payment of employees' wages, salaries, or commissions, including sick, vacation, and severance compensation. This applies to earnings by an employee, a corporation with a sole employee, or an independent contractor (if, during the 12 months prior, the debtor was responsible for 75% of the corporation or independent contractor's income) within 180 days of either the debtor's business closing or petition filing. The maximum payment is $11,725 per person.
5. Unsecured claims for contributions to employee benefit plans, including medical and life insurance, must be paid within 180 days of the petition filing or close of business. This figure is the number of employees multiplied by $11,725, less the amount that was paid to employees for the fourth priority.
6. Unsecured claims against the debtor of up to $5,775 per person must be paid to persons with claims who produce or raise grain or fish.
7. Claims for deposits related to the personal or family purchase, lease, or rental of property; services; or goods that were not supplied or completed, to a maximum of $2,600 per person.
8. Claims of taxes or other governmental revenues
9. Unsecured claims based on any commitment by the debtor to a federal depository institutions regulatory agency (or predecessor to such agency) to maintain the capital of an insured depository institution.
10. Claims for death or personal injury resulting from the operation of a motor vehicle or vessel if such operation was unlawful because the debtor was intoxicated from using alcohol, a drug, or another substance.

The Automatic Stay

Filing a Chapter 7 petition protects the debtor from all collection efforts against him or her or his or her property unless the creditor has obtained permission from the bankruptcy court. This is known as the Automatic Stay and was covered extensively in the previous chapter.

First Meeting of the Creditors

The primary objective of the Chapter 7 debtor is to obtain a discharge of his or her debts. A trustee is appointed in the Chapter 7 case to collect the debtor's non-exempt property, liquidate the assets by converting them to cash, and paying the unsecured creditors in the order of priority. The debtor is required to appear at a

first meeting of the creditors or **341 hearing** within 40 days after the bankruptcy petition is filed. Here, the trustee reviews the debtor's petition, schedules, and statements and provides the creditors, present at the hearing, the opportunity to ask the debtor questions about his or her case. The trustee puts the debtor under oath so that he or she may answer questions posed by the trustee and creditors. Spouses who file jointly must appear together and submit to questioning at the meeting of the creditors. The trustee may schedule subsequent meetings if additional time is needed to liquidate the assets of the bankruptcy estate or allow the debtor time to gather any relevant documentation or information.

Questions Asked at 341 Meeting of Creditors

Following is a list of the first 10 questions the trustee may ask the debtor during the 341 hearing. Follow-up questions are available on the U.S. Department of Justice website.

1. State your name for the record. Is the address on the petition your current address?
2. Please provide your picture ID and Social Security number card for review.
3. Did you sign the petition, schedules, statements, and related documents and is the signature your own? Did you read the petition, schedules, statements, and related documents before you signed them?
4. Are you personally familiar with the information contained in the petition, schedules, statements, and related documents? To the best of your knowledge, is the information contained in the petition, schedules, statements, and related documents true and correct? Are there any errors or omissions to bring to my attention at this time?
5. Are all your assets identified on the schedules? Have you listed all your creditors on the schedules?
6. Have you previously filed for bankruptcy? (If so, the trustee must obtain the case number and the discharge information to determine the debtor's discharge eligibility.)
7. What is your current employer's address?
8. Is the copy of the tax return you provided a true copy of the most recent tax return you filed?
9. Do you have a domestic support obligation? To whom? Please provide to me the claimant's address and telephone number, but do not state it on the record.
10. Have you read the Bankruptcy Information Sheet the United States Trustee provided?

Source: United States Department of Justice website

Voidable Preferences and Fraudulent Conveyances

It is also the trustee's responsibility to determine whether the debtor, prior to filing for bankruptcy, engaged in any suspicious transactions such as voidable preferences or fraudulent conveyances. A **voidable preference** occurs when the debtor transfers assets to a creditor prior to filing for bankruptcy. Here, the debtor pays a preferred or favored creditor in full, and the rest of the creditors must divide a pro rata share after a bankruptcy case has been filed. Under the Bankruptcy Code, a trustee who can establish that such voidable preferences were made has the power to recover the money from the preferred creditor. The elements of a transfer to a preferred creditor are as follows:

1. To or for the benefit of a creditor
2. For or on account of an antecedent debt (a debt owed prior to the time of the transfer)
3. Made while the debtor was insolvent
4. Within 90 days before petition date or, if the creditor was an insider who had reasonable cause to believe that the debtor was insolvent at the time of the transfer, within one year before the petition date
5. That increases the amount the creditor would have received in a liquidation proceeding

A **fraudulent conveyance** occurs when the debtor transfers assets to a third party to prevent creditors from satisfying their claims after the debtor files for bankruptcy. The trustee has the power under the Bankruptcy Code to set aside or avoid certain transfers of the debtor's assets that place creditors at a disadvantage. When interviewing the bankruptcy client, the paralegal should make careful note of any suspicious transfers and alert the attorney for further investigation.

There are two types of fraudulent conveyances: actual and constructive fraud. **Actual fraud** involves (1) making a transfer within one year before the date of the filing of a bankruptcy petition (2) with intent to hinder or defraud a creditor. According to 11 U.S.C. § 727, a Chapter 7 debtor cannot receive a discharge if he or she has transferred property with the intent to hinder, delay, or defraud a creditor in the one year before filing. In **constructive fraud**, the debtor transfers assets for grossly inadequate consideration. For example, the client sells his Harley-Davidson motorcycle, worth $12,000, to his brother for $1.00. Bankruptcy Code 11 U.S.C. § 548 empowers the trustee to recover transfers made for grossly inadequate consideration in the two years prior to filing for bankruptcy. It is also important to check state law regarding fraudulent transfers because some states allow a look-back period beyond the two years the Bankruptcy Code requires.

fraudulent conveyance
When a debtor transfers assets to a third party to prevent creditors from satisfying their claims after the debtor files for bankruptcy. The trustee has the power under the Bankruptcy Code to set aside or void certain transfers of the debtor's assets that place creditors at a disadvantage.

actual fraud
A fraudulent transfer made within one year before the date of the filing of a bankruptcy petition and with the intent to hinder or defraud a creditor.

constructive fraud
A fraudulent transfer by which the debtor transfers assets for grossly inadequate consideration.

Predischarge Debtor Education

In addition to taking a credit counseling course before filing for Chapter 7, debtors must also take a predischarge **debtor education course** from a provider approved by the U.S. Trustee Program or bankruptcy administrator in Alabama and North Carolina. Clients filing for Chapter 7 relief must complete the debtor education course within 60 days of the initial date set for the meeting of creditors. The course focuses on creating a budget, managing money, and using credit wisely. When the debtor has completed the course, which runs approximately two hours, he or she must obtain a certificate of completion before the case may proceed to a discharge of the debtor's obligations.

Dismissal or Conversion

If the trustee determines that the debtor does not qualify for Chapter 7, he or she may recommend that the debtor convert the Chapter 7 case to a Chapter 13. This might occur when the debtor has failed to pass the Means Test, indicating that the debtor has sufficient income to repay his or her creditors.

If the debtor filed for bankruptcy in bad faith, failed to comply with the requirements of the Bankruptcy Code, or failed to file the necessary forms and information, the bankruptcy court can dismiss the debtor's case. A **dismissal** means that the debtor's bankruptcy case has been thrown out of court, and the debtor is now left with his or her debts. A debtor may also request a voluntary dismissal if circumstances exist that cause the creditor to withdraw the case.

Discharge

If the trustee determines that the debtor is eligible for Chapter 7 liquidation, the case may now proceed to discharge. A **discharge** releases the debtor from liability for certain debts and prohibits the creditor from pursuing any legal action to collect those debts. Some debts, as discussed earlier, cannot be discharged in bankruptcy. Upon discharge, secured creditors may seize any collateral securing the respective debt and sell it to recover some of its cost. Debtors who want to keep property secured under a loan, such as a car, may reaffirm the debt before the discharge takes place. The legal effect of a **reaffirmation** is to assert that the debtor will resume the responsibility to pay off the loan. The creditor agrees not to seize the property as long as the debtor continues to make payments. For a quick review, Exhibit 6.1 illustrates the basic steps in the Chapter 7 bankruptcy process.

dismissal
The bankruptcy court has closed the case, and the debtor does not obtain the benefit of a fresh start. The debtor's obligations are still due, and the court will take no further action on the case.

discharge
A document a bankruptcy judge issues that releases the debtor from liability and prohibits the creditor from pursuing any legal action to collect those debts.

reaffirmation
The debtor agrees to resume the responsibility to pay off the loan. The creditor agrees not to seize the property as long as the debtor continues to make payments.

EXHIBIT 6.1 How Cases Move through Federal Courts: Chapter 7 Bankruptcy Courts

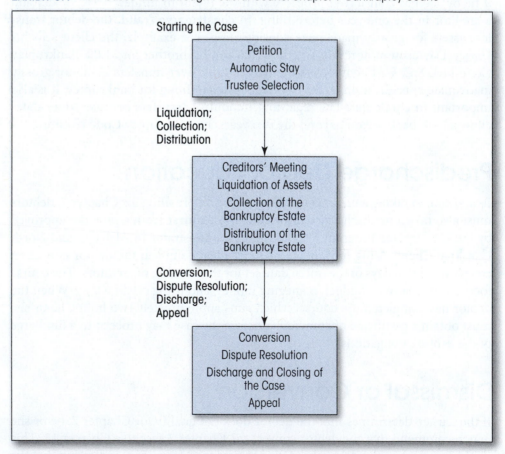

Source: Federal Judicial Center (http://www.fjc.gov/federal/courts.nsf/autoframe?OpenForm&nav=menu4c&page=/federal/courts.nsf/page/82AAB7E9ED41487485256A300066E531?opendocument)

Assuming all goes well for the debtor, the bankruptcy court will close the debtor's case within three to six months of the discharge date. The debtor has now achieved the ultimate goal of a Chapter 7 liquidation case—a fresh start.

After reading this chapter, you should have a solid grasp of how a Chapter 7 case works to help provide a debtor with relief from most of his or her unsecured debts. We discussed the process of filing a Chapter 7 liquidation case and discussed the various items of property the debtor owes that might qualify as exempt. In the example at the beginning of the chapter, recall that the Pradhans, a recently married family of two, had a sudden change in financial circumstances. Many Americans feel secure in their jobs and forget that hard times can be just a layoff or illness away for most of us. They do little to prepare financially for this unfortunate reality. Depending on which state the Pradhans are from, they may qualify for Chapter 7 with Nasim's lost income. They may be able to claim an exemption for much of their property, including any equity they might have in their home, necessary items such as household furnishings, sensible vehicles, and tools of the trade. Unfortunately, despite the Pradhans' former $200,000-plus double income, they appear to have accumulated more debt than wealth. They hope the bankruptcy attorney they plan to visit will have some good news for them about filing for Chapter 7 bankruptcy. Their attorney will need to look at their present income to see whether they quality for a Chapter 7 case. Once again, depending on the state the Pradhans are from, they might still have enough income to limit their choice to a Chapter 13 filing.

CHAPTER **SUMMARY**

A Chapter 7 bankruptcy filing is the most common type of bankruptcy filed in the United States. It begins with filing a bankruptcy petition. In a Chapter 7 liquidation proceeding, the debtor seeks a discharge of his or her debt. A discharge releases the debtor from liability for certain debts, giving the debtor's creditors no further legal recourse for the collection of those obligations.

Filing a Chapter 7 petition allows the debtor to keep any assets that are exempt from bankruptcy proceedings under the law. If the debtor is eligible for Chapter 7, the debtor then attends a 341 hearing, commonly referred to as the first meeting of the creditors, where he or she is questioned by the trustee. Creditors may also be in attendance at this meeting and are provided with the opportunity to ask the debtor any questions regarding the bankruptcy petition, schedules, and statements filed. If all goes well for the debtor, his or her case will be discharged, and the bankruptcy court releases the debtor from liability for certain debts and prohibits the creditor from pursuing any legal action to collect those debts

CONCEPT REVIEW AND REINFORCEMENT

KEY **TERMS**

actual fraud	dismissal	nonpriority unsecured
bankruptcy estate	exempt property	claims
bankruptcy petition	first meeting of the	priority unsecured claims
complete bankruptcy	creditors (341 hearing)	reaffirmation
constructive fraud	fraudulent conveyances	secured claims
consumer bankruptcy	liquidated	straight bankruptcy
credit counseling	liquidation bankruptcy	total bankruptcy
course	no-asset case	trustee
discharge	nonexempt property	voidable preferences

REVIEWING **KEY CONCEPTS**

1. What is the client's goal when filing for bankruptcy under Chapter 7?
2. Explain the difference between the pre-petition credit counseling course and predischarge debtor education course.
3. What is a bankruptcy petition and what is its purpose?
4. Explain the statement, "Relief under a Chapter 7 liquidation case is not automatic."
5. Research the exemption amounts available in your state, if any, and compare to those provided in the Bankruptcy Code. Does your state allow a bankruptcy client to choose between the federal or state exemptions? Which benefit clients in your state, the federal or state exemptions?
6. Define secured claims, priority unsecured claims, and nonpriority unsecured claims.
7. What happens at the first meeting of the creditors? Does the debtor have to attend this meeting?
8. Define voidable preferences and fraudulent conveyances.
9. What is the difference between a discharge and a dismissal in a Chapter 7 case?
10. Explain a reaffirmation.

BUILDING YOUR PARALEGAL SKILLS

CASE FOR **REVIEW**

In re Sophie Serrato, Debtor, No. 90-54408-MM/*Decker vs. Voisenat*, Chapter 7 Adversary No. 92-5396 (Bankr.N.D. Cal. Sept. 30, 1997)

BUILDING A PROFESSIONAL PORTFOLIO

PORTFOLIO **EXERCISES**

You work for the bankruptcy firm of Pilcher and Byrd. Attorney Janice Pilcher asks you to prepare a handout informing clients of the requirements to take a pre-petition credit counseling course and a predischarge debtor education course. Be sure to draft this document on behalf of Attorney Pilcher and include a section for her signature. For the client's convenience, include a list of approved providers for your state's bankruptcy court district along with cost and contact information.

chapter 7

CHAPTER 13 BANKRUPTCY: DEBT RESTRUCTURING FOR INDIVIDUALS

Miguel Matos thought he had it all. After working for many years as a paralegal in a top law firm handling bankruptcy cases, he earned his way up to a very comfortable salary. Miguel and his wife bought a very large home and owned two luxury cars. They also purchased a second home, a small condominium in Vermont to use during the summer and fall months and to rent to skiers in the winter. Miguel's two homes and his vehicles were financed and the value of both cars and both homes fell below the balance on their respective loans.

After the effects of the suffering economy took their toll on his employer, Miguel was forced to take a pay reduction. It was either that or lose his job entirely. The reduction in pay made it hard for Miguel and his wife to keep up with the mortgage payments on both homes and the car payments on both vehicles. They were struggling with credit card debt as well. Miguel and his wife both went for a consultation with a bankruptcy attorney. The attorney advised them that between the two of them, despite having trouble paying their bills, they both earned too much money to qualify for a Chapter 7 bankruptcy. They both decided to file for a Chapter 13 bankruptcy, which would require them to pay back at least a portion of their debts. What can the Matoses expect throughout the Chapter 13 process? What possible benefits could the Matos couple take advantage of in a Chapter 13 case? Read on and find out.

LEARNING OBJECTIVES

After studying this chapter, you should be able to:

1. Explain how a Chapter 13 bankruptcy filing works.

2. Recognize the differences between a Chapter 13 case and a Chapter 7 case.

3. Summarize the benefits and drawbacks associated with filing a Chapter 13 case.

4. Describe how a repayment plan should be proposed to the court.

Introduction

Although Chapter 7 is more widely recognized, the change in bankruptcy law has resulted in an increase of Chapter 13 filings. Reorganizations are typically thought to be reserved for businesses trying to reorganize their debt to be more manageable, to get their business on the road to financial recovery, and to shield themselves from creditors' claims. As we discuss in more detail in the pages that follow, Chapter 13 is a reorganization chapter much like Chapter 11. However, Chapter 13 is reserved for the individual who has the ability to repay at least some of his or her debt.

Much like Chapter 7, the desired result of a Chapter 13 filing is for the debtor's obligations to his or her creditors to be wiped out and for the debtor to be given a fresh start. Chapter 13 cases are the second most prevalent type of bankruptcy case filed in the United States. For the paralegal, Chapter 7 cases are the most common type of filing a busy practice encounters. This chapter provides the reader with a basic understanding of a Chapter 13 reorganization proceeding for an individual with regular income. Many individuals file for Chapter 13 because they are not eligible to file for a Chapter 7 liquidation. However, a growing number of individual filers are choosing Chapter 13 because they would like to use a repayment plan to assist them with making mortgage, car, and student loan payments more manageable. We will discuss other, less-known benefits available to a debtor under this chapter of the Bankruptcy Code while detailing the inception and life cycle of a repayment plan.

Introduction to Chapter 13: Reorganization

disposable income
Income remaining after the debtor pays for certain expenses the Bankruptcy Code allows such as mortgage payments, health insurance payments, medical bills, and food bills.

Sometimes referred to as the wage earner plan, Chapter 13 is available for individuals who have regular income and who have sufficient disposable income each month to repay a significant portion of their debts. A debtor's **disposable income** is the income left over each month after the debtor pays for certain expenses allowed by the Bankruptcy Code, such as mortgage payments, health insurance payments, medical bills, and food bills. There are many reasons an individual might file for Chapter 13 bankruptcy protection, some by choice and some by design. These reasons, as well as a breakdown of the mechanics of a Chapter 13 filing, are discussed at great length in this chapter.

Advantages of a Chapter 13 Bankruptcy Filing

THE AUTOMATIC STAY

Filing for a Chapter 13 bankruptcy has the same power that Chapter 7 has to invoke the powers and protection of the Automatic Stay, thus protecting the debtor from the collections efforts of his or her creditors. Filing the bankruptcy petition immediately stops all attempts by creditors to collect their debts from the debtor. The debt collections efforts that must cease include wage executions and garnishments, foreclosure cases, collections cases regardless of whether litigation has been filed, and repossessions.

THE ABILITY TO KEEP ASSETS

Some debtors must file for bankruptcy under Chapter 13 because the Means Test reveals that their income levels and the amount of disposable income disqualify them from filing for Chapter 7 liquidation. The fact that some individuals actually choose to file for a Chapter 13 bankruptcy is worthy of discussion.

Chapter 13 filers, including individuals with only **consumer debt**, or debt not related to business, can keep both their exempt and their nonexempt property. This becomes especially important for debtors who intend to keep their homes as well as other property while making their monthly payments more manageable by including those payments on their payment plan. This advantage of Chapter 13 allows the debtor a way out of a foreclosure by allowing the debtor a chance to catch up on his or her mortgage payments by paying missed monthly mortgage payments through the repayment plan. Chapter 13, however, cannot be used to amend the terms of the debtor's original mortgage document and note with his or her lender. The debtor is still responsible for mortgage payments that are currently due.

Chapter 13 also offers debtors a way to avert repossession of their vehicle. Furthermore, debtors in this situation do not have to sign a **reaffirmation agreement**, as they would have to do in a Chapter 7 case.

consumer debt
Non–business related debt.

reaffirmation agreement
A contract between the debtor and creditor by which the debtor reassumes the responsibility of paying off the loan.

CULTURAL, RELIGIOUS, AND REGIONAL DIFFERENCES

Many debtors choose Chapter 13 for cultural or religious reasons, especially when the repayment of one's debts is considered an important obligation. It is interesting that more Chapter 13 cases are filed in the southern states than in northern states for various reasons. According to United States Department of Justice statistics, for example, between 1989 and 1999, Tennessee displayed Chapter 13 consumer-case filing percentages ranging between 55.5% and 65.9%, whereas Massachusetts ranged between 12.5% and 17.6%.

It is also good for the economy when creditors receive at least a portion of debts owed to them. This is in sharp contrast to Chapter 7, which allows debtors to discharge their unsecured debt, with no requirement to pay anything to creditors. Chapter 7 certainly does have its place in our society. It is valuable for individuals and businesses struggling with insurmountable debt for whatever reason and have zero to little means to repay their debts. The Bankruptcy Abuse Prevention and Consumer Protection Act of 2005 made a very solid attempt at balancing the equities with regard to individuals' income and their ability to repay some or all of their debts.

RECOVERING DEBTORS' CREDIT SCORE

Critics of BAPCPA oppose the amendments because the injustice of forcing individuals to take a Means Test and compelling them to repay a good portion of their debt if they can afford to do so. However, it is beneficial for the debtor to repay at least some portion of his or her debts because it is a faster route to a healthier credit score than filing a Chapter 7 case. Recovery of a credit score is much faster for Chapter 13 debtors than it is for Chapter 7 cases because a Chapter 13 bankruptcy mark is removed from a debtor's credit report within seven years from the date of the bankruptcy petition filing. A Chapter 7 bankruptcy stays on the debtor's credit report for ten years.

Many debtors are preoccupied with the understandable fear that by filing for either a Chapter 7 or Chapter 13 bankruptcy case, their credit score will drop. After all, there is truth behind this fear, and the debtor has undoubtedly been bombarded with about as many opinions on this subject from their great Aunt Matilda as from their best friend from high school. The consensus across the nation appears to be that filing any type of bankruptcy will damage one's credit score. Again, this belief is correct, at least temporarily.

Many individual debtors contemplating bankruptcy are likely to have very poor credit scores, but the minor damage done to a debtor's credit score pales in comparison to the rehabilitation the debtor's credit score will receive after a successful bankruptcy case. Many debtors see an increase in their credit scores of 50 to 100 points within a year after paying off their debts or having the bankruptcy court discharge them.

REDUCTION IN NONDISCHARGEABLE DEBT

The Chapter 13 filer can also take advantage of this chapter to allow a reduction in some of his or her debt that is nondischargeable under Chapter 7 and Chapter 13. Student loan payments, although not dischargeable in any bankruptcy filing, can be reduced to a more manageable level in a Chapter 13 plan. The Automatic Stay will shield the debtor from collections efforts with regard to student loans. Even though this type of debt will remain after the Chapter 13 case ends, it will allow the debtor some time to make payments on the loan(s) that he or she can afford.

Disadvantages of a Chapter 13 Bankruptcy Filing

LONG TERM COMMITMENT

An individual filing bankruptcy under Chapter 13 must consider some drawbacks. Primarily, a Chapter 13 plan requires a long commitment; the average life span of a Chapter 13 case lasts from three to five years. This bankruptcy option does not provide a quick way for the debtor to discharge most of his or her unsecured debts. All of the debtor's remaining disposable income must be turned over to the trustee to be distributed to the creditors according to the plan. The debtor, under this plan, is subject to continuous court scrutiny and is not allowed to incur any further debt without first obtaining permission from the court. Furthermore, it requires regular income, which many debtors facing the decision to file bankruptcy may not have.

LOW SUCCESS RATE

Unfortunately, Chapter 13 cases have a low success rate. It has been estimated that between 75% and 90% of Chapter 13 cases fail compared with a nearly 100% success rate for Chapter 7 cases. The reasons for this low Chapter 13 success rate seem varied and difficult to ascertain. Reorganization plan payments at the beginning of the Chapter 13 case for many filers appear to be affordable. Factors such as unexpected health issues, job loss, and the ever-increasing cost of living, singularly or combined, may make a once affordable repayment plan unrealistic. Options are available to some Chapter 13 filers who may be struggling to stay current on a repayment plan. The debtor can petition the court for extended time to catch up on plan payments while recovering from a minor economic set back. If the plan payments have become entirely unaffordable due to a host of possible circumstances, the debtor may seek a modification from the court. This requires the debtor to propose a new repayment plan that includes documentation proving the inability to pay payments on the old plan. The court must approve the newly proposed repayment plan.

The Means Test in Chapter 13 Cases

Recall in the previous chapter that application of the Means Test in Chapter 7 cases is to determine the debtor's eligibility under this section of the Bankruptcy Code to discharge his or her debt. When applied to Chapter 13 cases, the Means Test does not determine eligibility; rather, it determines how much the debtor will pay unsecured creditors and the duration of the repayment plan. If the debtor's annual gross income is more than the median income for a household of the debtor's size, the debtor is required to file a five-year repayment plan unless all debts can be paid off in fewer than five years. If the debtor's annual gross income is less than the median income, the repayment plan is three years.

The Chapter 13 Means Test is used to calculate how much of the debtor's disposable income is available to pay unsecured creditors. The Means Test takes into account the debtor's average gross income received six months prior to the bankruptcy filing. If the debtor's annual gross income is less than the median income for the size of the household, the presumption is that the debtor is unable to pay unsecured debts. If the debtor's gross income is more than the median income, the Means Test allows the debtor to deduct necessary expenses from monthly gross income. This net figure determines how much of the debtor's monthly disposable income is available for payment of unsecured debts.

The results of the Means Test, when applied to Chapter 13 repayment plans, may sometimes have harsh consequences for the debtor. If changes in the debtor's projected income and expenses are not taken into account, the repayment plan may be unrealistic, setting the debtor up for failure. In the case of *Jan Hamilton, Trustee vs. Stephanie Kay Lanning*, 560 U.S. 505, 130 S.Ct. 2466, 177 L.Ed.2d 23 (2010), the United States Supreme Court held that bankruptcy court judges do not have to take a mechanical approach to the Means Test in Chapter 13 cases. Instead, bankruptcy trustees should take a "forward-looking" approach and consider the realities of the debtor's income. In this case, the debtor received a one-time buyout plan from her employer during the six-month period prior to filing for bankruptcy. The inclusion of this payment in calculating her monthly disposable income for the Chapter 13 repayment plan did not reflect the debtor's future income accurately. In this scenario, her disposable income was largely over-inflated, and any payments to creditors based on this figure would be unaffordable. The trustee viewed this case as a mechanical calculation under the Means Test, and the Supreme Court held that changes to the debtor's future income and expenses should be considered when determining a repayment plan.

The Chapter 13 Process

WHO MAY QUALIFY FOR CHAPTER 13

Only individuals whose debt does not exceed a certain amount are eligible to file for bankruptcy protection under Chapter 13. Sole proprietors, partnerships, and corporations are not considered individuals under the Bankruptcy Code.

CO-DEBTORS

co-debtors
People, in addition to the debtor, who are potentially liable for one or more of the debts listed in the bankruptcy schedules.

Cosigners, also known as **co-debtors**, are individuals who were kind enough to cosign on a loan with the debtor prior to the debtor's bankruptcy case. It is in the interest of co-debtors for the debtor to make timely payments under the Chapter 13 plan. Unlike Chapter 7, under which the co-debtor will quite often be responsible for the debt, the Chapter 13 debtor will most likely have included the shared debt on his or her repayment plan. In addition, unlike Chapter 7, Chapter 13 extends the same protection of the Automatic Stay to the co-debtor. However, if the bankruptcy debtor converts his or her case to a Chapter 7 or if the Bankruptcy Court dismisses the Chapter 13 case for whatever reason, the co-debtor will be exposed, once again, to a creditor's claim.

PRE-PETITION CREDIT COUNSELING AND DEBTOR EDUCATION COURSE

pre-petition certificate
Documentary proof of the debtor's completion of the credit counseling requirement.

Individuals filing for Chapter 13 must complete credit counseling from an approved credit counseling agency within 180 days of filing the petition and provide proof of completing this requirement, usually by including what is known as a **pre-petition certificate** provided by the credit counseling agency. As with Chapter 7 filings, the debtor must also complete a debtor education course again toward the end of the bankruptcy case prior to receiving a discharge of debt.

The Chapter 13 Petition

After the debtor has received sufficient legal counsel and determined that there is enough disposable income each month to make a Chapter 13 reorganization plan work, it is time to file the petition and other necessary paperwork to start the Chapter 13 case. To commence a Chapter 13 case, the debtor must complete the petition, schedules A to J, and Statement of Financial Affairs and create a list of all creditors. These items are usually filed electronically.

THE AUTOMATIC STAY

After the case is filed, the Automatic Stay immediately protects the debtor, and all attempts by creditors, including wage garnishments and executions, foreclosures, and lawsuits for debt collection, must stop at least temporarily. The Automatic Stay is likened to an injunction the bankruptcy court imposes. The bankruptcy clerk sends out a notice to all the creditors the debtor has indicated in schedules D, E, and F and in the list of creditors provided. When the creditors receive notice of the bankruptcy filing, all their debt collection efforts usually cease. It is uncommon for a creditor to continue debt collection in spite of receiving a notification that one of its debtors has filed for bankruptcy protection. The power of the Bankruptcy Code to stay collections efforts by creditors is extremely powerful and is outlined in 11 U.S.C. § 362(a).

The bankruptcy attorney, if the debtor has retained counsel, does not send notice to the creditors of the bankruptcy filing. Rather, the bankruptcy court mails Official Form B9I to each creditor, providing notice that the debtor has filed for bankruptcy. This form also provides information regarding upcoming dates and whether the debtor has completed a repayment plan. The reverse side of the form contains various procedural guidelines and instructions to creditors and information with regard to making proofs of claim. It also informs the creditors of the restrictions the Automatic Stay imposes. This form is included at the end of the chapter.

APPOINTMENT OF A TRUSTEE

In a Chapter 13 case, much like in a Chapter 7 case, a bankruptcy trustee is appointed. The bankruptcy trustee is responsible for distributing the proceeds collected from the debtor to the creditors according to the repayment plan. It is the trustee's job to review all documents and information the debtor provides; these documents include the petition, schedules, repayment plan, monthly expenses, tax returns, and pay stubs. The trustee must verify that the income the debtor reports is accurate and adequate to sustain the repayment plan the debtor proposed. The trustee also reviews the debtor's proposed repayment plan to ensure that it is fair and equitable to all the creditors. If the trustee finds any issue with the debtor's documents, in particular with the debtor's repayment plan, the trustee will either request more information from the debtor prior to approving the repayment plan or file an objection with the bankruptcy court, which will prompt the court to schedule a hearing.

THE REPAYMENT PLAN

Chapter 13 debtors must submit a plan indicating how they intend to pay the creditors over a three- to five-year period. If the debtor's **repayment plan** is not filed with the petition and schedules, it should be filed with the court at least 15 days after filing the petition. This gives the Chapter 13 trustee something to analyze and work with prior to the **meeting of the creditors**.

> **repayment plan**
> The debtor's proposal for how the money the debtor owes to the creditors will be paid back and the monthly amount of such payments.

Most Chapter 13 plans may be confirmed the first time, especially if the debtor is represented by an experienced bankruptcy attorney who works with the trustee to construct a realistic plan.

However, the plan the debtor proposes might also be rejected by the court or objected to by creditors. Often the debtor proposes to pay less to the creditor than the bankruptcy court would require. Therefore, some plans must be rewritten before receiving final approval from the court. The debtor is often advised by his or her attorney that he or she must begin making payments on the proposed plan as soon as possible even though it has not yet been approved by the court. There is no official form for the debtor to use in connection with making his or her repayment plan. The repayment plan must allow for payments to be made to creditors according to their rank.

Not every creditor is expected to be paid in full. If that were the case, Chapter 13 bankruptcy would be unnecessary. After all, the reason the debtor is filing for bankruptcy is the inability to pay back all or at least a good portion of his or her debts. There are three classifications of creditors, and each classification must be provided a certain level of treatment in the debtor's repayment plan for the court, trustee, and creditors to accept it.

MEETING OF THE CREDITORS

Approximately 30 days after the petition is filed, the court schedules the **meeting of the creditors**, or the **341 hearing.** The debtor must attend this meeting or face the possibility that the court will dismiss his or her case. If the debtor has filed jointly with his or her spouse, both debtors must be present. At this meeting, the

> **meeting of the creditors (341 Hearing)**
> The first court appearance the debtor makes in a bankruptcy case. This meeting may also be referred to as the **341 meeting,** named after the Bankruptcy Code section where it is found. The debtor must attend this meeting or face the possibility that the court will dismiss his or her case.

Chapter 13 trustee places the debtor under oath and questions him or her regarding the financial situation. The trustee is primarily concerned with the issue of whether the debtor has sufficient disposable income to support a repayment plan. The trustee may also question the debtor or raise objections if the debtor's plan does not adequately provide regular payments to satisfy a priority creditor's claim completely.

The creditors present at the meeting may question the debtor regarding the proposed repayment plan. The creditors may also question the debtor's financial situation and the amount the debtor designates to pay the creditor regularly. Remember that although the trustee might end up approving the Chapter 13 debtor's plan, one or more of the creditors may still object. If so, the objection will need to be heard, and the court cannot confirm the plan until the creditor's objection is resolved.

Generally, most of the unsecured creditors will not attend this meeting. The creditors that are most likely to be present are the secured creditors. Secured creditors want to know whether the debtor plans to surrender the property to foreclosure or repossession or intends to keep the secured property (most likely a home or a car) and pay the arrearage in full through the Chapter 13 plan.

Although this text discusses the different types of creditors in the other chapters of this book, it is necessary to introduce them here in the context of the debtor's repayment plan. The three classifications of creditors, in descending order, are as follows:

- Secured creditors
- Priority creditors
- Nonpriority or general unsecured creditors

SECURED CREDITORS

secured creditors
Creditors that have a claim against the debtor, and property is secured as collateral in exchange for extension of credit.

collateral
An asset or specific property pledged in exchange for a secured loan.

Secured creditors, such as mortgage companies and car finance companies, whose loans are secured by a certain item of **collateral** such as a house or a car, are entitled to be paid in full by the end of the Chapter 13 plan. The repayment plan the debtor proposes should reflect regular monthly or biweekly payments sufficient to satisfy any arrearage owed to the secured creditor. When the debtor has chosen Chapter 13 as a way to save a home, and 15 years are still left on a mortgage, the debtor is not expected to pay the mortgage balance in full. The arrearage must be paid in full by the end of the plan. The debtor must continue, throughout the repayment plan period, to make the regularly mortgage payments that are due monthly. This type of debt is referred to as an ongoing debt. The same rules apply to car loans. Unless the car loan payment schedule is set to be finished prior to the end of the Chapter 13 plan, the balance does not have to be paid in full; however, any arrearage due must be paid in full by the end of the plan.

PRIORITY CREDITORS

priority creditor
A creditor to whom the debtor pledges no type of collateral to satisfy the loan if the debtor defaults on payment; an unsecured creditor whose claims take precedence over the claims of other unsecured creditors.

The next category of creditor that must be provided for in the repayment plan is the **priority creditor**. The debtor does not pledge any type of collateral to this type of creditor to satisfy the loan if the debtor defaults on payment. However, priority creditors are literally given priority over other unsecured creditors when there is a liquidation of the debtor's assets in a Chapter 7 case. Examples of a priority creditor may include government tax obligations or a spouse who is owed alimony or child support. In a Chapter 13 case, priority creditors are given priority over other unsecured creditors, but in a different way. Priority creditors in a Chapter 13 plan must be paid in full by the end of the debtor's repayment plan. Assume, for instance, that the debtor has an obligation to pay his ex-wife child support of $86.00 per week and has missed about 12 weeks of payments. He will have an arrearage of $1032. The creditor in this case would be his ex-wife, and she will need to be paid in full on the arrearage by the end of the repayment plan.

NONPRIORITY OR GENERAL UNSECURED CREDITORS

The next category of creditors that must be given consideration on the debtor's repayment plan are referred to as **unsecured, nonpriority creditors**, or **general unsecured creditors**. These creditors are not required to be paid in full but the debtor must show good faith and his or her best efforts to include this class of creditor while formulating the repayment plan. Examples of creditors that fall into this category are credit card companies, doctors, the divorce lawyer, and student loans. The test for whether the debtor acted in the unsecured creditors' interests is based on whether the creditor would have received as much from a Chapter 7 liquidation as they would be expected to receive from the proposed repayment plan.

As previously discussed, many individuals file for Chapter 13 because they are not eligible to file for a Chapter 7 liquidation. However, a growing number of individual filers are opting for it because it allows the debtor to restructure his or her debt to more manageable payments and to keep items of personal as well as real property.

CONFIRMATION OF PLAN

After the meeting of the creditors, the bankruptcy court schedules a **confirmation hearing**. The court must schedule this hearing no later than 45 days after the meeting of the creditors. At the confirmation hearing, the bankruptcy court judge determine whether to accept the debtor's repayment plan. The bankruptcy judge also hears objections the trustee and any of the creditors raise regarding the amounts paid or the feasibility of the plan the debtor has proposed. The debtor may or may not be required to attend. Some jurisdictions allow the debtor's attorney to be present and argue on behalf of the debtor; others require the debtor to be present regardless of attorney representation.

confirmation hearing
A hearing at which the bankruptcy court judge determines whether to accept the debtor's repayment plan.

If no resolution regarding the repayment plan is reached, the judge will not make a ruling. Instead, the judge will order the debtor to redraft the repayment plan to make the plan more compliant with the Bankruptcy Code. A second confirmation hearing will be scheduled to review the changes the debtor makes to the repayment plan. It is not uncommon for a debtor to propose a repayment plan several times before the court finally approves it. The court then may approve the repayment plan, dismiss the case, or convert it to a Chapter 7.

For a quick review, Exhibit 7.1 illustrates the basic steps in the Chapter 13 bankruptcy process.

Cramdown

Another interesting benefit available to a Chapter 13 debtor is the ability to propose to the court that the amount owed on a debt such as a car loan should be reduced to the dollar amount that represents the value of the vehicle. This is a court-ordered modification made to a loan that is crammed down the creditors'

EXHIBIT 7.1 How Cases Move through Federal Courts: Chapter 13 Bankruptcy Cases

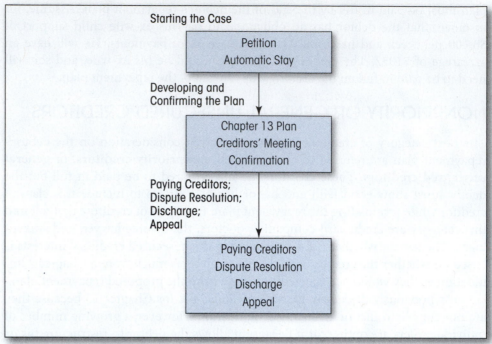

Source: Federal Judicial Center (http://www.fjc.gov/federal/courts.nsf/autoframe?OpenForm&nav=menu4c&page=/federal/courts.nsf/page/270?opendocument)

cramdown
Court-ordered modifications made to loans that are crammed down the creditors' throats.

throats by a judge forcing the creditor to accept these new terms. This is called a **cramdown** and is available to Chapter 13 debtors. Under Chapter 13, a secured loan may be restructured to reflect the current market value of the property. In the case of a motor vehicle, the debtor's vehicle must have been purchased not fewer than 910 days prior to filing for bankruptcy.

For example, assume the debtor purchased a brand-new vehicle three years ago for $17,500, and the vehicle is now worth $10,500. Motor vehicles, unless they are vintage collectors' items in mint condition, depreciate at an alarming rate. The debtor still owes $12,500 toward the remainder of the loan. The portion of the loan that is secured equals the market value of the vehicle in its present condition and the unsecured portion is the difference between what the debtor still owes toward the balance of the loan and the current fair value of the vehicle. In this example, the unsecured portion of the debt on the vehicle is $2,000. The debtor, in his or her repayment plan proposal, will outline how he or she intends to repay the value of the vehicle over the three- to five-year Chapter 13 plan.

The bankruptcy court will determine a fair interest rate to apply to the remainder of the cramdown loan. The remainder of the loan or the unsecured portion of the loan will be treated in the same manner as the debtor's other debts. Therefore, the creditor will receive little or no payment on the unsecured portion. However, one very important restriction should be mentioned with regard to vehicle cramdowns. The debtor must have purchased the vehicle at least two and a half years prior to filing for Chapter 13 bankruptcy. The provision of the Bankruptcy Code that gives the court the power to force a secured creditor to accept an amount equal to the present-day value of the collateral securing its loan is found in 11 U.S.C § 1325 (a)(5)(B)(iii).

A debtor is not allowed to cram down the loan balance on his or her primary residence. He or she can cram down the unsecured portion of the loan on his or her investment properties in much the same way as he or she could cram down an auto loan. The remaining principal of the mortgage on an investment property is reduced to the home's current market value, and the bankruptcy court reduces the interest rate. Much like the remaining unsecured debt in the car loan example, the unsecured portion of this debt is treated in the same fashion as the debtor's other unsecured debt and may receive some or no payment through the debtor's repayment plan.

Lien Stripping

Although a Chapter 13 debtor is not allowed to cram down the mortgage balance on a primary residence, the debtor has another option. If there is a second or even a third mortgage or a home equity line of credit on the debtor's property, the secondary loan or loans may be eligible to be stripped away from the primary loan on the property. This is known as **lien stripping**. Lien stripping works only if the debtor's home has insufficient value to secure the secondary loans on the property. If there is just enough or not enough value in the debtor's home to secure all or some of the primary loan on the property, the secondary loans are presumed unsecured, and the bankruptcy court will strip away the secondary loans. The court will treat those loans (liens) as unsecured debt that will receive little or no payment from the debtor's repayment plan.

Lien stripping is no simple matter; the debtor cannot be afforded this benefit simply by adding language to the repayment plan that asserts that the junior loan on a primary residence should be stripped because the value of the collateral (the home) is not sufficient to secure the junior loan. Some debtors have submitted repayment plans that simply omit any payment to a lender creditor on a secondary loan.

The debtor must file for an adversary hearing with the court to properly assert that a secondary lien should be stripped away from a primary lien. An adversary proceeding is a separate lawsuit filed within a bankruptcy case, and the judge must resolve it before the case can proceed to discharge. An adversary proceeding in a bankruptcy case is treated much like a civil lawsuit. The lender has an opportunity to object to the debtor's assertions regarding value of the collateral and to present a defense by offering evidence about the value of the collateral.

To invoke either the cramdown or lien-stripping benefits in a Chapter 13 filing, the debtor files and properly serves the lender in question with a **motion to value the collateral**. Upon hearing the motion, the bankruptcy court determines the value of the collateral, compares it to the amount of the secured creditor's claim, and makes a determination regarding the unsecured portion of the creditor's claim. Bankruptcy Code 11 U.S.C. § 506 (a)(b) provides guidelines for the court when making a ruling on the value of both the collateral and the unsecured portion of a creditor's claim.

Remember the Matos couple from the beginning of this chapter? They may have been disappointed, at least initially, to hear that they had no other choice but to file a Chapter 13 case. However, after discussing their financial situation with a bankruptcy attorney, they should now be aware of the several benefits available to them under Chapter 13 of the Bankruptcy Code. The Matos couple has a

lien stripping
If the debtor has a second or even a third mortgage or a home equity line of credit on his or her property, that secondary loan may be eligible to be stripped away from the primary loan on the property. A benefit usually available only to Chapter 13 debtors with regard to the primary residence.

motion to value the collateral
A motion that a debtor who wishes to invoke either the cramdown or lien-stripping benefits of a Chapter 13 filing must file. Here, the bankruptcy court determines the value of the collateral, compares it with the amount of the secured creditor's claim, and makes a determination regarding the unsecured portion of the creditor's claim.

secondary rental home in Vermont with an outstanding mortgage balance that is higher than the current value of the home. They also have two financed vehicles on which the value has dropped below the current loan balance on each. As you and, hopefully, the Matos couple now know, they should be able to cram down the current balance on their secondary home and both cars to their current market value. By doing this, they will make the payments on all three secured debts more manageable. Further, although they won't be able to cram down the balance on their primary residence, they will be able to add that monthly payment to their repayment plan, making it more manageable at least during the life of their Chapter 13 case. Many debtors don't choose to file Chapter 13. However, many soon discover the ability Chapter 13 has to help them retain some or all of their assets.

CHAPTER **SUMMARY**

Sometimes referred to as the wage earner plan, Chapter 13 is available for individuals who have regular income and sufficient disposable income each month to repay a significant portion of their debts. Only individuals are eligible to file for bankruptcy protection under Chapter 13. Partnerships and corporations are not considered individuals under the Bankruptcy Code.

In a Chapter 13 filing, the debtor fills out the voluntary petition and the schedules containing his or her assets and debts. The debtor then proposes a repayment plan to the court. The repayment plan is the debtor's proposal of how the creditors will be paid and the monthly amount of such payments. A bankruptcy trustee is appointed and is responsible for distributing the proceeds collected from the debtor to the creditors according to the repayment plan. Remember that while the trustee may end up approving the Chapter 13 debtor's plan, one or more of the creditors may still object.

Filing for a Chapter 13 bankruptcy invokes the powers and protection of the Automatic Stay, thus protecting the debtor from the creditors' collections efforts. In some cases, the reorganization plan payments at the beginning of the Chapter 13 case appear affordable to the debtor. Yet, factors such as unexpected health issues, job loss, and the ever-increasing cost of living, singularly or combined, can make a once reasonable plan now unaffordable.

After the meeting of the creditors, the bankruptcy court schedules a confirmation hearing, at which the bankruptcy court judge determines whether to accept the debtor's repayment plan. The repayment plan may require some revisions, so it is not uncommon for the court to schedule another confirmation hearing. The court may then approve the repayment plan, dismiss the case, or convert it to a Chapter 7.

CONCEPT REVIEW AND REINFORCEMENT

KEY **TERMS**

co-debtors
collateral
confirmation hearing
consumer debt
cramdown

disposable income
lien stripping
meeting of the creditors
    (341 hearing)
motion to value the collateral

pre-petition certificate
priority creditor
reaffirmation agreement
repayment plan
secured creditors

REVIEWING **KEY CONCEPTS**

1. Identify some of the advantages and disadvantages of filing a Chapter 13 bankruptcy.
2. Explain how the Means Test applies in Chapter 13 cases.
3. Discuss the importance of the United State Supreme Court ruling in *Jan Hamilton, Trustee vs. Stephanie Kay Lanning*, 560 U.S. 505, 130 S.Ct. 2466, 177 L.Ed.2d 23 (2010).

4. Summarize the Chapter 13 process.
5. How are priority creditors treated in a debtor's repayment plan?
6. How are secured creditors treated in a debtor's repayment plan?
7. How are unsecured nonpriority creditors treated in a debtor's repayment plan?

8. What is a cramdown and how does this concept in Chapter 13 bankruptcy cases help the debtor?
9. Explain the concept of lien stripping.
10. What is the purpose of a motion to value the collateral?

BUILDING YOUR PARALEGAL SKILLS

CASE FOR **REVIEW**

In re Williams, 488 B.R. 492 (Bankr. M.D.Ga. Mar. 15, 2013)

BUILDING A PROFESSIONAL PORTFOLIO

PORTFOLIO **EXERCISE**

You work for the law offices of Marie Barbagallo, LLC, and your firm represents the debtor Jane Conway. Jane Conway is an individual debtor with primarily consumer debts. She is quite interested in filing for Chapter 13 because she has regular income and would like to keep both her car and home. Ms. Conway has owned her vehicle for three years, and its value is $9,500. She still owes $12,000 on the loan. Attorney Barbagallo would like to advise Ms. Conway on her options under Chapter 13 to help make her car payments more manageable. Based on what you have learned from reading this chapter and any outside research, draft an intraoffice memorandum to Attorney Barbagallo outlining the options Ms. Conway will have to cram down her car loan.

chapter 8

CHAPTER 11 BANKRUPTCY: REORGANIZATION

LEARNING OBJECTIVES

After studying this chapter, you should be able to:

1. Describe the main purpose of a Chapter 11 bankruptcy.

2. Identify the parties in a Chapter 11 case.

3. Distinguish between a Chapter 7 and a Chapter 11 case.

4. Summarize the Chapter 11 process.

5. Explain the Chapter 11 plan of reorganization and its requirements.

After gathering with her friends at her favorite restaurant, Shelby's Bar & Grille, Ashmi heard on the news the next morning that the restaurant filed for Chapter 11 bankruptcy! Ashmi is devastated because she really loves this restaurant's Paleo Diet menu selections. Immediately, she called her friends to inform them that they needed to find a new Saturday hangout since Shelby's was closing. What Ashmi doesn't seem to understand is that her favorite restaurant may not be closing right away, if at all. Read on and find out how Ashmi's favorite restaurant can file for bankruptcy and still stay in business.

Introduction

Unlike Chapter 7, which allows debtors to liquidate their debt, Chapter 11 of the Bankruptcy Code deals with the reorganization of debt and allows debtors to restructure their debt and pay back their creditors. Most Chapter 11 cases are filed by businesses; however, individuals may also file for relief under this section of the Bankruptcy Code. This chapter provides an introduction to Chapter 11. Although most paralegals working in this field concentrate on consumer bankruptcies under Chapter 7 and Chapter 13, it is important to be aware of the basic framework of a Chapter 11 case. The paralegal's supervising attorney may be representing creditors on the creditors' committee who actually participate in the restructuring process.

Introduction to Chapter 11 Reorganization

In 2013, *The Economic Times* reported that although U.S. companies were starting to see signs of economic recovery, companies in India were not rebounding as quickly. A proposed solution to this problem is for India to adopt a Chapter 11 reorganization structure much like that of the United States, by which large and small businesses that are experiencing financial difficulties may keep their doors open by reorganizing or restructuring their debt under Chapter 11 of the Bankruptcy Code.

The purpose behind a Chapter 11 bankruptcy is to allow the debtor to stay in business by reaching a compromise with its creditors for the repayment of debts that will accommodate their unique relationship and circumstances. For this reason, the requirements of reaching a reorganization under the Bankruptcy Code are not a one-size-fits-all proposition but, rather, are flexible enough to accommodate the varying needs of the particular debtor–creditor relationship. The business is rehabilitated by restructuring its debt. Some businesses may also choose to file for Chapter 11 when they plan to liquidate the business over an extended period or sell the business as a going concern.

WHO MAY FILE FOR CHAPTER 11

The majority of the debtors who file for Chapter 11 protection are businesses such as corporations and partnerships. Businesses are not eligible to file for Chapter 13 protection. It is important to note, however, that banks, insurance companies, and savings and loans are not eligible to file under this chapter of the Bankruptcy Code. Railroads may also file for Chapter 11, but these filings are rare and are addressed in a special section of the Bankruptcy Code. Individual filings for relief under this section of the Bankruptcy Code, whether engaged in business or not, are also rare.

Individuals may also file for bankruptcy protection under Chapter 11. Individuals who wish to reorganize their debt generally file for Chapter 13, but if the debtor's debt limits exceed $1,149,525 in secured debt and $383,175 in unsecured debt, he or she must file for Chapter 11. Bankruptcy Code 11 U.S.C. § 104 (a) required these limits to be reassessed with the new three-year period beginning on April 1, 2013. The practical effect of this increase is that more individuals will qualify for Chapter 13.

Although the average individual debtor might not qualify for Chapter 11, this form of relief may be perfect for high-wage earners, small-business owners, or professionals who wish to continue their practices and reorganize their debt at the same time. Regardless of the relief sought under the various chapters in the Bankruptcy Code, all individual debtors must receive credit counseling from an approved agency within 180 days before filing. In addition, individuals cannot file for any chapter under the Bankruptcy Code if a prior bankruptcy petition was voluntarily dismissed after creditors sought relief from the bankruptcy court to recover property on which they hold liens or was dismissed because the debtor willfully failed to obey court orders or failed to appear before the court when required to do so.

SMALL-BUSINESS DEBTOR

A small business may also seek Chapter 11 protection if it meets certain qualifications under 11 U.S.C. 101(51D). If the debtor qualifies as a small business, the Chapter 11 process is streamlined, and certain formalities are not observed so the case can be fast tracked through the bankruptcy court process.

Under Bankruptcy Code Section 101(51D), a "small business debtor" must be engaged in commercial or business activities (other than primarily owning or operating real property) and have a total debt of not more than $2,490,925.

Another requirement is that the U.S. trustee has chosen not to appoint a creditors' committee or the bankruptcy court has dispensed with it because it is insufficiently active and representative to provide oversight of the debtor. The debtor is required to attach financial documents such as balance sheets, cash-flow statements, statement of operations, and recently filed tax returns to the bankruptcy petition.

The small-business debtor is subject to greater oversight by the U.S. trustee and must provide the trustee with additional documents about the finances and business operation during the pendency of the case. The small-business debtor also has less time to file a reorganization plan, namely, 180 days. After the 180 days have expired, any creditor or party in interest may file its own reorganization plan within 300 days. The bankruptcy court can also shorten or extend this time frame if one of the parties argues that there is cause to do so.

THE DIFFERENCES BETWEEN CHAPTER 7 AND CHAPTER 11

A Chapter 7 bankruptcy is a liquidation. Debtors relinquish their assets to the trustee who then sells those assets and, with the remaining proceeds, pays off creditors. After this process is completed, debtors receive a full discharge of the remaining outstanding debts. A business may choose to file for Chapter 7 if it intends to go out of business, whereas others may be forced into a Chapter 7 bankruptcy by its creditors. A business that wishes to continue providing goods or services in the marketplace has the right to file for Chapter 11 if it has done so voluntarily. If its creditors have forced it into a Chapter 7, it also has the right to convert the Chapter 7 liquidation bankruptcy to a Chapter 11 reorganization. The main purpose of filing for Chapter 11 is to allow the business debtor to continue to function, carry on its business, and restructure its debt.

Although some businesses successfully emerge from Chapter 11 bankruptcy with renewed economic stability, others are not as fortunate and find that despite their best efforts, they can no longer stay in business.

Creditors can force a business into a Chapter 7 or Chapter 11 bankruptcy if the business debtor cannot pay its debts. After a business files for Chapter 11, the Automatic Stay goes into effect, and creditors can no longer pursue the obligations owed to them through other legal means such as debt collection processes, foreclosure, or recovering collateral.

THE SIMILARITIES AND DIFFERENCES BETWEEN CHAPTER 11 AND CHAPTER 13

The main similarity between the two chapters is that whether a business files for Chapter 11 or 13, the goal is to preserve the business as a going concern by reorganizing its obligations with a plan to pay back its creditors. Both also offer the advantage of the Automatic Stay to hold off creditors while the business engages in the restructuring process. One of the differences between the two chapters is who has control over the bankruptcy estate. Although the assets in a Chapter 13 case are under the control of the trustee, the Chapter 11 assets are under the control of the debtor in possession (DIP). The debtor in possession is typically an officer or director of the business that has filed for Chapter 11. Another difference is that although a Chapter 13 repayment plan does not require the approval of creditors, a

Chapter 11 does. Debtors in a Chapter 11 must deal with the creditors' committee, which is explained later in this chapter.

One of the main differences between Chapter 11 and 13 is the debt limits previously described and the legal fees and expenses involved. Many Chapter 11 bankruptcies deal with issues far more complicated than those involved in a Chapter 13 case. Legal fees can run in the tens of thousands to millions of dollars in very complex cases. For example, the *Wall Street Journal* reported on June 3, 2012, that the law firm of Weil, Gotshal & Manges received $389 million in legal fees and expenses for its representation of Lehman Brothers in the largest bankruptcy filed in the history of the United States. Weil, Gotshal & Manges was not the only law firm involved in representing Lehman Brothers; other firms handled various aspects of the case. The total cost in legal fees and expenses in this case was over $1.4 billion. This does not sit well with laid-off employees or unpaid creditors who are often infuriated when their interests are pushed aside while large fees are doled out to lawyers.

The Department of Justice U.S. Trustee Program responded in June 2013 by issuing new guidelines for overhauling the guidelines for legal fees in Chapter 11 cases. The new guidelines, which went into effect on November 1, 2013, apply to Chapter 11 cases with $50 million or more in assets and $50 million or more in liabilities aggregated for jointly administered cases. The new guidelines provide for more disclosure regarding legal fees and expenses and more scrutiny from the U.S. trustee. The bankruptcy court may also appoint a fee examiner, whose sole purpose is to review invoices law firms file and determine whether the fees are reasonable. One such examiner was appointed by the bankruptcy court to scrutinize the legal fees in the Chapter 9 municipal bankruptcy of the city of Detroit.

The Prepackaged Chapter 11

The **prepackaged bankruptcy** in Chapter 11, or **prepack**, is a reorganization that has been prenegotiated between the debtor and its creditors. It is an especially attractive strategy for debtors who have a small group of creditors as opposed to a large number that might have different claims against the debtor. Prior to filing the Chapter 11 petition, the respective parties have already determined how the debts will be paid, in what amounts, and under what terms. Bankruptcy Code 11 U.S.C. § 1126(b) permits the bankruptcy courts to accept votes on a plan that was solicited before the commencement of the case, provided the debtor gives creditors an adequate disclosure statement.

prepackaged bankruptcy or prepack
A Chapter 11 reorganization that has been prenegotiated between the debtor and its creditors.

A prepack has many advantages, especially when the debtor has a small number of creditors. Debtors and creditors that engage in this process and reach a consensus will save legal and accounting fees. In addition to cutting costs, prepacks also minimize the duration of the bankruptcy proceedings. The debtor benefits because it can resume business operations with the confidence that the issues with creditors have been resolved, in essence giving the Chapter 11 business a fresh start. There are also some disadvantages with a prepack. After the debtor has approached the creditors regarding a possible pre-petition negotiation, the business community becomes aware of the debtor's financial problems. Furthermore, creditors who are not so willing to negotiate may pursue a collection action against the debtor in anticipation of the bankruptcy filing. A competent bankruptcy attorney can assist the debtor in weighing the advantages and disadvantages of pursuing a prepack.

Chapter 11 Petitions, Schedules, and Statements

Although creditors may force a debtor into a Chapter 11 bankruptcy by filing an involuntary petition by which the creditors force the debtor into bankruptcy, it is more common for the debtor to do so on a voluntary basis. According to 11 U.S.C. § 301, filing a voluntary petition acts as an immediate order for relief, signifying that the debtor is now under the control of the bankruptcy court.

> **11 U.S.C. § 301 (2011) Voluntary cases**
>
> (a) A voluntary case under a chapter of this title is commenced by the filing with the bankruptcy court of a petition under such chapter by an entity that may be a debtor under such chapter.
>
> (b) The commencement of a voluntary case under a chapter of this title constitutes an order for relief under such chapter.

The Chapter 11 petition must include the names and addresses of each of the debtor's creditors and a list of creditors holding the 20 largest unsecured claims against the debtor. The debtor is also required to file the following documents along with the petition; failure to file these documents may be grounds for dismissal of the debtor's bankruptcy petition.

- A certificate indicating that the debtor has received credit counseling during the 180-day period before filing the petition
- A debt repayment plan developed during that credit counseling, if any
- A court determination excusing the debtor from the required credit counseling

Within 15 days of filing the voluntary petition, the debtor must file the following schedules, statements, and other forms with the bankruptcy court:

- Schedules of assets and liabilities
- Schedules of current income and expenditures
- Schedule of executory contracts and unexpired leases
- Statement of financial affairs

After the Chapter 11 petition is filed, the Automatic Stay goes into effect. Because the purpose of Chapter 11 is to reorganize, this process can take from six months to two years, depending on the complexities of the case. For creditors, a prolonged negotiation process results in a decline in value of the secured creditors' collateral. After the bankruptcy petition is filed, a bankruptcy judge and a U.S. trustee are assigned to the debtor's case. The U.S. trustee is responsible for overseeing the overall progress of the case and reviews all financial documents, including the disclosure statement and reorganization plan. The debtor is now considered a debtor in possession and serves in this role during the course of the reorganization process until:

- A trustee is appointed in the Chapter 11 case.
- The reorganization plan is approved and confirmed.
- The Chapter 11 case is dismissed.
- The Chapter 11 case is converted to a Chapter 7.

The Chapter 11 Parties

DEBTOR IN POSSESSION

A typical Chapter 11 case does not include a trustee as does a Chapter 7. Instead, there is a **debtor in possession,** or **DIP**. The debtor in possession is typically an officer or director of the business and has all the powers of the trustee. In essence, the DIP continues operating the business without having to seek court approval unless the court steps in and orders the appointment of a trustee to take the place of the debtor in possession. The DIP may exercise all the rights and powers of a trustee under 11 U.S.C. § 1107(a).

debtor in possession (DIP)
An individual or business that files for Chapter 11 relief while it still has control over its assets and continues operating without having to seek court approval.

CREDITORS' COMMITTEE

The **creditors' committee** is appointed by the United States trustee, who is appointed by the federal government, unlike private case or panel trustees. The purpose of the creditors' committee is to negotiate a **plan of reorganization** with the business, or debtor, under the supervision of the U.S. trustee. During these negotiations, the parties determine the best way for the business debtor to remain viable by selling off assets, cutting expenses, and reaching a compromise with creditors about paying back debts. Claims owed to the creditors are restructuring by possibly reducing the amount of the debt and changing maturity dates so the business debtor's obligations are more manageable.

creditors' committee
A group appointed by the United States trustee that represents creditors that have claims against a business in a bankruptcy proceeding. The creditors' committee is divided between secured and unsecured creditors.

The claims of secured creditors are secured by assets, so if the debtor's attempt to reorganize under Chapter 11 is unsuccessful and must liquidate the business, the secured creditor is in a better position because it can recoup some of its debt through the liquidation of the collateral asset. The unsecured creditor, however, is in no such position. Therefore, the Bankruptcy Code allows unsecured creditors to participate in the Chapter 11 process.

plan of reorganization or Chapter 11 plan
A process by which the debtor creates a plan designed to restructure the financial claims owed to the creditor so that the debtor's business may remain viable and stand on its own without the legal protections of a Chapter 11 filing.

The U.S. trustee has the authority to appoint a committee of unsecured creditors shortly after the voluntary petition is filed or shortly after the court enters an order for relief in an involuntary Chapter 11 case. This committee typically consists of the seven largest unsecured claims against the debtor that are actually willing to serve on the committee. The Bankruptcy Code, however, does not allow the Internal Revenue Service or any other governmental agency, such as a state department of revenue services or local tax collector, to serve on the committee.

The U.S. trustee may have to appoint separate creditors' committees to represent the specific interests of creditors. When very large businesses file for Chapter 11 protection, more than one creditors' committee may have to be appointed to represent their specific concerns. Creditors' committees may hire financial advisors, attorneys, accountants, appraisers, and other professionals to contribute to the negotiation process. The debtor's bankruptcy estate bears the expenses for these professional advisors.

The powers of creditors' committees are extensive and found in 11 U.S.C. §§ 1102 and 1103. Note that 11 U.S.C. § 1102 is titled, "Creditors' and Equity Security Holders' Committees." An **equity security holder** owns an ownership interest in the business—for example, an interest of a limited partner in a limited partnership— or shares in a corporation. The equity security holder has the right to vote on the reorganization plan and file a proof of interest against the Chapter 11 bankruptcy estate much like a creditor may file the equivalent, called a proof of claim. In this environment, the creditors negotiate with each other regarding the payment of claims.

equity security holder
One who holds an ownership interest in a business.

institutional creditors
Creditors such as banks or other lending institutions that may wish to liquidate the business to satisfy their claims.

trade creditors
Creditors that supply goods or services to the debtor's business and give the business a grace period to pay its debt.

Tensions often arise between institutional and trade creditors. **Institutional creditors** include banks that may wish to liquidate the business to satisfy their claims. **Trade creditors** are creditors who supply goods or services to the debtor's business and give the business a grace period to pay its debt. Negotiations can get quite heated as each creditor seeks to minimize its losses. Institutional creditors may seek to liquidate the assets of the business debtor to recover on loans; trade creditors may be more interested in the preservation of the business not only to recover its current debt but also to continue the business relationship. These contractual relationships can be a vital factor in the continuation of the business and might need to be resumed to ensure the survival of the enterprise.

First Day Motions

first day motions
A series of pleadings the debtor files on the first day the Chapter 11 petition is filed to obtain court approval to engage in activities that are not allowed under the Bankruptcy Code.

When the Chapter 11 petition is filed, the debtor files a series of pleadings to obtain court approval to engage in activities that are not allowed under the Bankruptcy Code. These pleadings are called **first day motions** because the debtor files them literally on the first day of the filing. An example of a first day motion might include a motion to employ counsel. The bankruptcy court must approve the employment of attorneys by a debtor filing for Chapter 11 protection before fees may be paid out of the bankruptcy estate. If the creditor files an objection to any of the first day motions, the matter will have to be decided by the bankruptcy judge. The court will typically grant these motions when the debtor can establish that approval of the motion is necessary to preserve the business as a going concern. The debtor and creditor may also reach an agreement called a stipulation, which dispenses with the need to argue the issue before the judge.

MOTION TO USE CASH COLLATERAL OR OBTAIN DIP FINANCING

motion to use cash collateral or obtain DIP financing
Motion filed by the debtor upon filing a Chapter 11 petition, asking the court to allow the debtor to use income he or she generates, or to obtain loans, to pay certain expenses so the business may continue as a going concern.

cash collateral
Income generated by the debtor during the course of a Chapter 11 bankruptcy case.

One of the most important first day motions filed is called the **motion to use cash collateral or obtain DIP financing**. After the Chapter 11 petition is filed, any income a debtor generates is subject to a creditors' lien. For example, if the debtor owns several restaurants and continues selling prepared foods to customers, it generates cash on a daily basis. The money collected is known as **cash collateral**.

The debtor will need to access the cash pay its obligations, which may include bank loans secured by a bank lien against the debtor's cash and accounts receivables. From the debtor's perspective, it needs the cash to continue its business operations as it goes through the reorganization process. The debtor needs to continue paying its postpetition obligations, such as employee salaries, health insurance, and benefits, to retain a workforce that can support the business entity as a going concern. Otherwise, there will be a mass exodus of workers and an inability to hire others because of fear of not being compensated. The debtor may also need to pay critical vendors and suppliers of the business who provide goods and services essential to its day-to-day operations.

The business debtor may need financing during the course of the administration of the Chapter 11 estate. For instance, the bankruptcy court may grant a new creditor, which has extended financing to the business during the administration of a Chapter 11, priority over other creditors to encourage the infusion of cash into the business so it remains viable. The court may also create liens in new property acquired by the business on behalf of the debtor as a basis for collateral to secure the repayment of a new loan.

DIP financing is new debt obtained by a business in the process of a reorganization under Chapter 11; it has priority over existing debt, equity, and security claims. DIP financing allows businesses filing for Chapter 11 to obtain loans to continue its day-to-day operations during the reorganization process. Therefore, it is essential for a debtor to file a motion early on in the Chapter 11 case to obtain a court order to use cash collateral to pay its bills.

In September 2013, the U.S. Bankruptcy Court for the District of Delaware granted Furniture Brands International's first day motion in the company's voluntary Chapter 11 case. Furniture Brands is in the business of designing, manufacturing, sourcing, and retailing home furnishings and is the maker of some famous furniture brands such as Thomasville, Broyhill, Lane, and Drexel Heritage. The company suffered financially during the collapse of the housing market and filed for Chapter 11 reorganization. The bankruptcy court approved $140 million DIP financing, which allowed the business to continue conducting its daily operations without interruption. With DIP financing, the company can pay employee wages and benefits, pay its suppliers, and continue providing services to its customers without delay.

DIP financing
New debt obtained by a business in the process of a reorganization under Chapter 11; it has priority over existing debt, equity, and security claims. DIP financing allows businesses filing for Chapter 11 to obtain loans to continue its day-to-day operations during the reorganization process.

Meeting of Creditors

Under 11 U.S.C. § 341, a **meeting of the creditors'** must take place in a Chapter 11 case 20 to 40 days after the voluntary petition is filed. This meeting may also be referred to as the **341 meeting**, named after its Bankruptcy Code section. It is the job of the bankruptcy court clerk to send notices to all interested parties to attend this meeting. Creditors must also attend. At this meeting, the creditors can assess the debtor's financial status and determine whether payment of their respective debts is possible and under what circumstance. The bankruptcy judge, however, is not present at the meeting, which is held by the U.S. trustee. The goal of the 341 meeting of creditors is to facilitate a negotiated agreement between the debtor and its creditors without the imposition of orders by the bankruptcy court judge.

In Chapter 11 cases dealing with small businesses with debts under $2 million, unsecured creditors may be unwilling to serve on the creditors' committee. Here, the bankruptcy judge may decide to do away with the creditors' committee and, instead, supervise the case in a series of status conferences.

meeting of the creditors (341 meeting)
The first court appearance the debtor makes in a bankruptcy case. This meeting may also be referred to as the **341 meeting,** named after the Bankruptcy Code section where it is found. The debtor must attend this meeting or face the possibility that the court will dismiss his or her case.

Appointment of Trustees and Examiners

Reorganization of a business under Chapter 11 requires stability so that day-to-day business operations can be conducted without disruption. This is why a debtor in possession, rather than a trustee, is allowed under the Bankruptcy Code to operate the business entity without having to seek court approval. A **trustee** is typically appointed in a Chapter 11 case when the bankruptcy court finds that the current management has engaged in some type of fraud, dishonesty, incompetence, or gross mismanagement. An **examiner**, on the other hand, is appointed when an interested party asks the court to appoint someone to investigate allegations of fraud, dishonesty, misconduct, or irregularity in managing the affairs of the debtor either by current or former management of the debtor.

trustee
An individual typically appointed in a Chapter 11 case when the bankruptcy court finds that the current management has engaged in some type of fraud, dishonesty, incompetence, or gross mismanagement.

examiner
An individual appointed in cases when an interested party asks the court to appoint someone to investigate allegations of fraud, dishonesty, misconduct, or irregularity in managing the affairs of the debtor either by current or former management of the debtor.

Whereas appointment of a trustee results in that trustee replacing the debtor in possession, the appointment of an examiner does not. The examiner conducts an investigation and files a report of his or her findings with creditors and the court.

Appointment of a trustee or examiner in a Chapter 11 case is accomplished by filing a motion before the court. This motion may be filed by any interested party in the case, which would include the U.S. trustee, the creditors' committee, or any other creditor. The bankruptcy court may for example, appoint a trustee for cause or if it is in the best interest of the creditors. The bankruptcy court may also appoint a trustee or examiner when dismissal or conversion of the Chapter 11 is in the best interest of the creditors and the estate. The statutory authority to appoint either a trustee or examiner is found in 11 U.S.C. § 1104.

Plan of Reorganization

The primary reason for filing a Chapter 11 bankruptcy case is to obtain a **plan of reorganization** or **Chapter 11 plan** so the business may continue as a going concern. The purpose of the plan of reorganization is to restructure the financial claims owed to the creditor so that the debtor's business may remain viable and stand on its own without the legal protections of a Chapter 11 filing.

The debtor has the exclusive right to propose a plan of reorganization during the first 120 days after the Chapter 11 has been filed. This is known as the **exclusivity period**. After the exclusivity period has lapsed, creditors are free to file their own reorganization plans. Plans filed by creditors may not be as favorable to the debtor, so it is in the debtor's best interest to propose a plan during the exclusivity period that has been at least crafted with the debtor's interests in mind. The exclusivity period may be extended by order of the bankruptcy court judge.

REQUIREMENTS OF A CHAPTER 11 PLAN

The plan of reorganization must contain the requirements established in 11 U.S.C. § 1123(a), known as the mandatory provisions. Some of the mandatory requirements of the Chapter 11 plan of reorganization stipulate that:

1. Creditors and equity security holders must be divided into different classes in order of priority of claims against the debtor.
2. Specification must be made regarding treatment of each of the creditor claims under the plan. Although classes of creditors may be treated differently, every creditor in the same class must be treated equally.
3. The treatment and explanation must be made to all impaired classes. An impaired class is a group of creditors with similar claims whose debt, under the proposed plan, will not be paid in full.
4. Adequate means for the plan's implementation must be made.

In addition, 11 U.S.C. § 1123(b) gives the debtor the discretion to include other elements in its reorganization plan such as changes made to executory contracts or unexpired leases. An **executory contract** is a contract that has not been fully executed. The parties are still required to perform under the terms of the agreement. A business may still have pending agreements with employees, independent contractors, unions, or suppliers of goods and services. An **unexpired lease** is a

exclusivity period
The debtor's exclusive right to propose a plan of reorganization during the first 120 days after the Chapter 11 has been filed.

executory contract
A contract under which insufficient or incomplete performance has occurred on either side of the contract.

unexpired lease
A lease that is still in effect.

lease that is still in effect. A business could be leasing a building, office space, or equipment. Renegotiating these obligations may provide the debtor with more cash on hand to pay creditors.

ADEQUATE INFORMATION AND THE DISCLOSURE STATEMENT

The **disclosure statement** is a document filed in a Chapter 11 bankruptcy case that provides a detailed description to the bankruptcy court of how the debtor intends to reorganize and restructure so that it can stay in business and pay its creditors. The disclosure statement must supply creditors with **adequate information** to enable them to evaluate the debtor's reorganization and make an informed decision about whether to accept the debtor's proposed plan. Adequate information is defined in 11 U.S.C. § 1125(a)(1):

> **11 U.S.C. § 1125 (2011): Postpetition disclosure and solicitation**
>
> (a)(1) "[A]dequate information" means information of a kind, and in sufficient detail, as far as is reasonably practicable in light of the nature and history of the debtor and the condition of the debtor's books and records, including a discussion of the potential material Federal tax consequences of the plan to the debtor, any successor to the debtor, and a hypothetical investor typical of the holders of claims or interests in the case, that would enable such a hypothetical investor of the relevant class to make an informed judgment about the plan, but adequate information need not include such information about any other possible or proposed plan and in determining whether a disclosure statement provides adequate information, the court shall consider the complexity of the case, the benefit of additional information to creditors and other parties in interest, and the cost of providing additional information....

The bankruptcy court has broad discretion to determine the adequacy of the information provided in the disclosure statement. Adequate information, therefore, is determined on a case-by-case basis. Although each disclosure statement is tailored to the specific circumstances of the debtor's case, the typical provisions of this document must include the following information, enumerated by the bankruptcy court in *In re Scioto Valley Mortgage Co.*, 88 B.R. 168, 170 (Bankr. S.D. Oh. Jun. 23, 1988).

1. The circumstances that gave rise to the necessity to file the bankruptcy petition
2. A discussion of available assets and their value
3. A summary of what the debtor anticipates doing going forward
4. Where the information used in the disclosure statement came from
5. A disclaimer stating that no statements or information regarding the debtor, its assets, or securities are authorized other than those included in the disclosure statement
6. The debtor's condition during its bankruptcy proceeding
7. Claim information
8. An analysis showing what creditors would receive from the debtor if it liquidated under Chapter 7
9. The accounting and valuation methods used in the disclosure statement

disclosure agreement or disclosure statement
A document that lists all the mandatory disclosures required by 11 U.S.C. § 527, Section 527. It includes information such as the financial details of the debtor's business, enough to allow the creditors to determine how their interests will be affected.

adequate information
In a Chapter 11 bankruptcy, the debtor must supply creditors with enough data to enable them to evaluate the debtor's reorganization and make an informed decision about whether to accept the debtor's proposed plan.

10. Information regarding the debtor's management going forward
11. A summary of the plan of liquidation or reorganization
12. A summary of the administrative expenses, including bankruptcy professional fees
13. A review of the debtor's accounts receivables
14. Financial information necessary to allow a creditor to decide whether to approve or reject the plan
15. Information regarding the risks the creditors are taking
16. The amount expected for recovery through avoidance actions
17. A discussion of nonbankruptcy litigation
18. Tax consequences of the plan
19. The debtor's relationship with any affiliates

The bankruptcy court has the task of reviewing the disclosure statement and approving it before moving on to the next phase of the Chapter 11 case. The adequacy of the information may face some objections by creditors who typically file those objections with the bankruptcy court. It is up to the bankruptcy court judge to hear these objections and determine whether they have enough validity to reject the proposed reorganization plan and deny confirmation of the plan.

Confirmation

confirmation
The bankruptcy court's process of approving the debtor's reorganization plan.

cramdown
A reorganization plan that is involuntarily imposed on a creditor or class of creditors over those creditors' objections when the court determines that it is more equitable to all parties involved including the debtor and the remaining creditors.

impaired class
A class of creditors that will not receive the full value of their claims.

After the bankruptcy court approves the debtor's reorganization plan, the next step in the process is **confirmation** of the plan. There are two ways to obtain confirmation of the reorganization plan, either consensually or through what is known as a **cramdown** plan. The plan of reorganization must also include a classification of the claims against the Chapter 11 bankruptcy estate and indicate how each of the claims will be treated under the plan. The creditors whose claims are impaired must vote on the plan. An **impaired class** is one whose the creditors will not receive the full value of their claims. When the disclosure statement is approved, the creditor ballots are calculated. A confirmation is scheduled with the bankruptcy court, which determines whether the plan should be confirmed or rejected.

The bankruptcy court and the creditors in every impaired class must approve the debtor's reorganization plan. Before the confirmation hearing, each class of creditor casts its vote for the plan through a mail-in ballot. The vote, however, does not have to be unanimous. A Chapter 11 plan can be confirmed only if at least one class of impaired creditors votes to accept the plan.

If creditors oppose the reorganization plan, the debtor may force its plan on the creditors by seeking confirmation under the cramdown provisions of the Bankruptcy Code. In this situation, the debtor is asking the bankruptcy court to "cram" the plan "down the creditors' throats" over their objections.

Discharge

discharge
A document a bankruptcy judge issues that releases the debtor from liability and prohibits the creditor from pursuing any legal action to collect those debts.

After the debtor's reorganization plan is approved and confirmed, the bankruptcy court grants the debtor a discharge. This **discharge** releases the debtor from debts that are legally dischargeable under the Bankruptcy Code. Debts that are not part of the reorganization plan are discharged, obligating the debtor to pay the debts enumerated in the plan.

If the reorganization plan is not approved, the bankruptcy court may dismiss the case. If dismissed, the debts are still owed to its creditors. The bankruptcy court may also dismiss a Chapter 11 case if the debtor fails to comply with the requirements of the Bankruptcy Code. On November 8, 2013, Bankruptcy Court Judge Robert D. Drain of the United States Bankruptcy Court for the Southern District of New York dismissed rapper DMX's Chapter 11 bankruptcy petition. DMX, or Earl Simmons as he was known before the bankruptcy court, owes approximately $1.8 million to creditors for unpaid goods, services, contractual disputes, and child support. The U.S. trustee initially requested the case to be converted to a Chapter 7, by which Simmons's assets would be sold off and the proceeds used to pay creditors. Instead, the court dismissed the case against Simmons for failure to appear at a meeting of the creditors, failure to comply with the Trustee's request for information, filing court papers that were in disarray and factually inconsistent, and failure to give the court trustworthy information. Judge Drain's ruling also prohibits Simmons from re-filing for bankruptcy for a period of 18 months.

If the debtor is unable to meet its obligations under the plan for reorganization, the creditors can either file a lawsuit against the debtor to seek payment of the monies owed or request the court to convert the case to a Chapter 7 liquidation. The debtor also may request a conversion to Chapter 7 if it finds that it cannot meet its obligations under the plan.

For a quick review, Exhibit 8.1 illustrates the basic steps in the Chapter 11 bankruptcy process.

EXHIBIT 8.1 How Cases Move Through Federal Courts—Chapter 11 Bankruptcy Cases

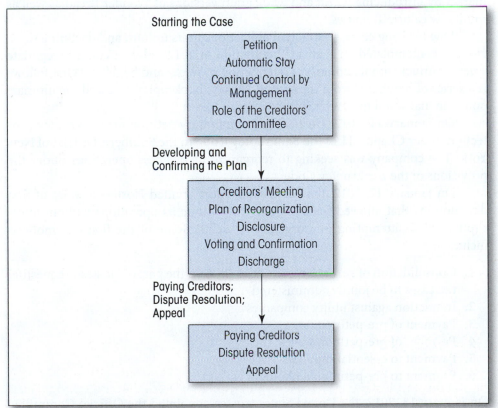

Source: Federal Judicial Center (http://www.fjc.gov/federal/courts.nsf/autoframe?OpenForm&nav=menu4c&page=/federal/courts.nsf/page/82AAB7E9ED41487485256A300066E531?opendocument)

The Hostess Bankruptcy Case

Most readers are familiar with Hostess brand products such as the popular cream-filled snack cakes known as Suzy Q's®, SNO BALLS®, and Ding Dongs® and its most famous confectionery, Twinkies®, which were invented during the Great Depression as an inexpensive treat. Since its inception, Hostess grew by purchasing one company after another. Along with this expansion, Hostess inherited multiemployer pension plans and numerous collective bargaining agreements that prohibited it from streamlining its delivery and production process.

Hostess first filed for Chapter 11 in 2004. The low-carbohydrate diet craze led by the Atkins diet and similar weight-loss fads resulted in declining sales for Twinkies and other Hostess brands such as Wonder Bread®. The initial reason for the bankruptcy filing included dwindling sales, high debt, and union contractual obligations. During this 2004 restructuring of the snack-cake giant, two unions, the Teamsters and the Bakery, Confectionery, Tobacco Workers and Grain Millers International Union, made concessions to help save the company and relinquished $110 million in annual employee wages and benefits. However, portions of the labor union contracts failed to address other issues. The company held on to more debt that it could handle, hoping that its financial picture would improve.

Unfortunately, it did not. The American consuming public, which once gobbled up the tasty snack treats, was losing its taste for sugary junk foods and, instead, shopped for healthier alternatives. Hostess was unable to produce products that would appeal to a more health-conscious public, and sales dropped. Over the years, Hostess unsuccessfully attempted to break into the health-conscious market by introducing wheat and wholegrain versions of Wonder Bread as well as mini–low calorie Twinkies.

Due to rising costs, contractual obligations to its unions, and declining sales, Hostess contemplated a Chapter 7 liquidation in 2012 unless it could renegotiate a new contract with its unions for a reduction in wages and benefits. What follows is a series of highlights from the second Hostess bankruptcy case and the ultimate outcome that saved the Twinkie from extinction.

On January 11, 2012, Hostess filed a voluntary petition for bankruptcy protection under Chapter 11 of the Bankruptcy Code in the Southern District of New York. The company was seeking to reorganize its business operations under the provisions of the Bankruptcy Code.

On January 12, 2012, the bankruptcy court granted Hostess a series of first day motions that allowed the company to continue its operations without interruption while attempting to reorganize its debts. Some of the first day motions included:

1. Consolidation of six bankruptcy cases filed on the part of Hostess, requesting the cases to be jointly administered
2. Injunction against utility companies
3. Payment of pre-petition taxes
4. Payment of pre-petition wages
5. Payment to essential suppliers
6. Payment to pre-petition lienholders

On January 18, 2012, the United States trustee appointed the Official Committee of Unsecured Creditors of Hostess Brands, Inc. The 10 largest unsecured creditors as well as the amount of the Debt Hostess Owed

Bakery and Confectionary Union and Industry International Pension Fund	$944,158,000
Central States, Southeast and Southwest Areas Pension Plan	$11,817,000
Cereal Food Processors	$8,530,000
Twin Cities Bakery Drivers Pension Fund	$8,357,000
Western Conference of Teamsters Pension Plan	$6,997,000
New England Teamsters & Trucking Industry Pension Fund	$4,768,000
Automotive Industries Pension Plan	$4,158,000
Bakery Drivers and Salesman Local 550 and Industry Pension Fund	$2,268,000
Cargill, Inc.	$1,924,000
Bakery Drivers and Salesmen Local 194 and Industry Pension Fund	$1,846,000

HOSTESS'S PLAN OF REORGANIZATION

Hostess's reorganization plan depended on the company's ability to obtain concessions from the labor unions according to the various collective bargaining agreements. Hostess proposed modifying these agreements with lower wages and benefits and relaxed work rules. Hostess also sought to modernize its distribution system, which it claimed could not be streamlined unless it could bypass certain provisions in the collective bargaining agreements. Hostess also wished to withdraw from the multiemployer pension plans, claiming that it was hindered by huge costs in pensions when former employers were no longer making contributions to the plan. The company also hoped to secure new additional capital investments to pay for its modernization and restructure its debt.

On February 3, 2013, the bankruptcy court authorized Hostess to obtain postpetition financing and use cash collateral. Silver Point Capital and Monarch Alternative Capital, two of Hostess's hedge fund lenders, provided DIP financing for $75 million. Silver Point and Monarch were the only lenders to step in and assist Hostess during the restructuring process. As a result, both companies received priority in the line of secured creditors and were the first to be paid out of the bankruptcy estate.

On October 10, 2012, Hostess completed its reorganization plan, a portion of which called for an 8% cut in employee wages and a 17% cut in health and welfare benefits. It also called for a two-year cessation of payments to multiemployer pension plans.

Unfortunately for Hostess, its reorganization was never confirmed by the bankruptcy court. The company made news headlines when several unsecured creditors informed the court that Hostess corporate executives received an 80% increase in salaries. The unions were outraged. Hostess, however, maintained that it could not survive as a going concern unless the unions agreed to its proposed cuts. If Hostess could not reorganize its affairs, it would be forced to into liquidation.

Although the Teamsters, which represented the company's estimated 7,500 drivers, agreed to the concessions, the bakers, represented by the Bakery, Confectionery, Tobacco Workers and Grain Millers International Union, did not.

In November 2012, the Bakery, Confectionery, Tobacco Workers and Grain Millers International Union, whose 5,680 workers accounted for approximately 30% of Hostess's workforce, went on strike. The strike resulted in disruption of operations and many closed bakeries. On November 14, 2012, management issued an ultimatum, warning the striking employees that if they did not return to work by 5:00 p.m. on November 15, it would be forced to liquidate the company. The union did not relent, and Hostess kept its promise. On November 27, 2012, the bankruptcy court approved Hostess's motion to wind down its affairs.

WHO WILL SAVE THE TWINKIE?

News of Hostess's impending shutdown resulted in consumers flocking to grocery stores to stock up the various Hostess brand products in case they would forever lose their beloved snack cakes. Internet sales were just as brisk, with numerous sales of Twinkies, Ding Dongs, and Ho Hos on eBay, Amazon, and Craigslist.

Section 363 sale
A procedure that allows a bankruptcy trustee or debtor in possession to sell the bankruptcy estate's assets free and clear of any interest in such property.

The Hostess bankruptcy remained as a Chapter 11, selling the company off in pieces under a **Section 363 sale**. A Section 363 sale allows a bankruptcy trustee or debtor in possession to sell the bankruptcy estate's assets free and clear of any interest in such property. In the Hostess case, the various divisions that made up the entire company were sold off to the highest bidder. The theory behind this practice is that selling the various divisions as a whole would result in more money going into the bankruptcy estate for the benefit of the creditors than would selling the dismantled parts. For example, a buyer could purchase Hostess's bread division, which would include its factory, supplies, trucks, distribution routes, and trademarks as opposed to numerous buyers purchasing pieces and parts. Ultimately, the various Hostess brands were sold off at auction to the following bidders for a total of $829.5 million.

Target Brand	Lead Bidder	Bid
BeefSteak Bread Brand	Grupo Bimbo	$31.9 million
Bread Brands	Flowers Foods	$360 million
Snack Cake Brands	Apollo Global Management	$410 million
Drake's Brand	McKee Foods Corporation	$27.5 million

In the end, Apollo Global Management's purchase of Hostess's snack cake brands saw to it that Twinkies were back on store shelves by July 15, 2013. Now all junk food lovers can breathe a sigh of relief knowing that all is well in the world of snack cakes!

Just think how delighted Ashmi would have been to learn that her favorite restaurant, Shelby's Bar & Grill, is probably not going anywhere, at least for now. Because the restructuring of a business's debt under Chapter 11 requires stability, Chapter 11 of the Bankruptcy Code allows a senior official or manager of the business debtor to assume a role similar to the Chapter 13 trustee. The role this person plays is why a business debtor in a Chapter 11 case is referred to as the debtor in possession (DIP). Ashmi's favorite restaurant will most likely stay open and will continue to operate its business while restructuring its debts. Ashmi, like many Americans, may not realize that many of the businesses we patronize each day may have filed Chapter 11 at one point or another. The hope is that the business, by filing Chapter 11, will successfully restructure its debt and remain open and become financially stronger than before.

CHAPTER **SUMMARY**

The purpose behind a Chapter 11 bankruptcy is to allow the debtor to stay in business by reaching a compromise with its creditors for the repayment of debts that will accommodate their unique relationship and circumstances. For this reason, the requirements for reaching reorganization under the Bankruptcy Code are not a one-size-fits-all proposition but, rather, flexible enough to accommodate the varying needs of the particular debtor–creditor relationship.

The Automatic Stay immediately goes into effect when the Chapter 11 bankruptcy petition is filed. This gives the debtor some breathing room to regroup by suspending collections, judgments, repossessions, and foreclosures and allows the reorganization process to take place without these impending threats.

A meeting of the creditors, or 341 meeting, affords creditors the opportunity to assess the debtor's financial status and determine whether payment of their respective debts is possible and under what circumstance. The creditors' goal of the 341 meeting is to facilitate a negotiated agreement between the debtor and its creditors without the imposition of orders by the bankruptcy court judge. It is hoped that these negotiations result in a plan of reorganization for the debtor.

The plan of reorganization must contain the requirements established in 11 U.S.C. § 1123(a), known as the mandatory provisions. After the bankruptcy court approves the debtor's reorganization plan, the next step in the process is confirmation of the plan. There are two ways to obtain confirmation of the reorganization plan, consensually or through what is known as a cramdown plan.

After the debtor's reorganization plan is approved and confirmed, the bankruptcy court grants the debtor a discharge. If the reorganization plan is not approved, the bankruptcy court may dismiss the case. If the case is dismissed, the debts are still owed to its creditors. The bankruptcy court may also dismiss a Chapter 11 case if the debtor fails to comply with the requirements of the Bankruptcy Code.

If the debtor cannot meet its obligations under the plan of reorganization, the creditors can either file a lawsuit against the debtor to seek payment or request the court to convert the case to a Chapter 7 liquidation. The debtor may also request a conversion to Chapter 7 if it finds that it cannot meet its obligations under the plan.

CONCEPT REVIEW AND REINFORCEMENT

KEY **TERMS**

adequate information	disclosure agreement or disclosure	meeting of the creditors
cash collateral	statement	(341 meeting)
Chapter 11 plan	equity security holder	motion to use cash collateral
confirmation	examiner	or obtain DIP financing
cramdown	exclusivity period	plan of reorganization
creditors' committee	executory contract	prepackaged bankruptcy (prepack)
debtor in possession	first day motions	Section 363 sale
(DIP)	impaired class	trade creditors
DIP financing	institutional	trustee
discharge	creditors	unexpired lease

REVIEWING **KEY CONCEPTS**

1. What is the main purpose of filing for bankruptcy under Chapter 11?
2. Who may qualify for Chapter 11 protection?
3. What is the main difference between a Chapter 7 bankruptcy and a Chapter 11 bankruptcy?
4. What is a prepackaged bankruptcy and what are its advantages?
5. Briefly describe the parties in a Chapter 11 case.
6. Describe one of the most important first day motions filed in a Chapter 11 case.
7. What is the goal of the 341 meeting?
8. Define plan of reorganization and describe its requirements under the Bankruptcy Code.
9. List the two ways of obtaining confirmation of a plan of reorganization.
10. What happens in a Section 363 sale?

BUILDING YOUR PARALEGAL SKILLS

CASE FOR **REVIEW**

Radlax Gateway Hotel, LLC, et al., v. Amalgamated Bank, 132 S. Ct. 2065 (2012)

Research Assignment

Did They Survive? Popular Businesses Who Filed for Chapter 11

Using an Internet search engine such as Google or Bing, research one of the following companies found in any U.S. mall, at one time or another, that has filed for Chapter 11 and answer the questions that follow.

- Abercrombie & Fitch
- Blockbuster LLC
- Borders Group

- Chuck E. Cheese
- Circuit City
- Eddie Bauer
- Friendly's
- Sbarro
- Mandee
- Mrs. Field's

1. Why did the company file for Chapter 11 protection?
2. Briefly describe the company's reorganization plan.
3. Did the company survive because of the organization? If no, give the reason the reorganization was unsuccessful.

BUILDING A PROFESSIONAL PORTFOLIO

PORTFOLIO **EXERCISES**

Many legal experts and practitioners propose simplifying the Bankruptcy Code's definition of the small-business debtor. The main criticism is that changes to the law intended to make the Chapter 11 process easier for small-business debtors have in reality made the process more difficult. Conduct Internet research on the topic and determine what the problems are with the current system and why small-business debtors do not fare very well. Prepare a memo for your supervising attorney about the difficulties encountered when filing as a small-business debtor under Chapter 11, so that he or she may advise clients accordingly. Research alternative solutions for the small-business debtor and include it in your memo.

chapter 9

BANKRUPTCY CREDITORS: RIGHTS, RESTRICTIONS, AND RESPONSIBILITIES

Norma just received her degree in business administration last year, graduating at the top of her class at State University. Norma chose to go to a state college because she did not want to pay exorbitant tuition at a private university. Norma had a knack for making jewelry in her spare time and, with her degree in business administration, she now had the skills it took to market and run her own business. Norma attempted to find a job working for someone else but, due to the economy, her prospects were bleak. Norma decided to open her own business called Norma's Fantastic Gems.

It took Norma quite some time the first year to turn a profit after all her start-up costs and business taxes were paid. Things were running smoothly at the beginning of her second year in business; however, Norma's third year was not so profitable, and her accounts suffered. She had no choice but to turn over her delinquent accounts to a collection agency. Norma's bills just kept piling up. Very soon, Norma received notices that several of her customers had filed for bankruptcy. What can Norma do at this point? What type of creditor is Norma? Does she have any rights against her debtors? Read on and find out.

LEARNING OBJECTIVES

After studying this chapter, you should be able to:

1. Understand how the trustee provides for a creditor in a liquidation or reorganization case, depending on the creditor's status.

2. Summarize the rights of creditors to seek relief from the Automatic Stay.

3. Describe the differences between secured and unsecured creditors.

4. Explain how the trustee handles executory contracts and unexpired leases.

5. Identify the various reasons a debtor may enter into a reaffirmation agreement with a creditor.

Introduction

The image that often comes to mind when we mention the word *creditor* is one of a "corporate America," billion-dollar giant. Although many creditors are powerful credit card companies, large hospitals, and for-profit companies, the truth is that creditors may also include those whom we least expect. A creditor can be:

- A small business whose survival depends on its ability to collect revenue for goods and services supplied to its customers.

- A minimum-wage earner who depends on a paycheck, working for a fast food restaurant that has filed for Chapter 11.
- A single parent, raising three children, who has not seen a dime of child support or alimony in months.

This chapter discusses the most common types of creditors paralegals encounter in a bankruptcy practice. We also discuss the classifications of creditors, creditors' rights, and the amounts they may receive in a bankruptcy case. We review creditors' responsibility to provide proof of their claims and explore creditors' responses to the Automatic Stay and their rights in potentially overcoming this protection afforded to the debtor.

Types of Creditors

secured creditors
Creditors that have a claim against the debtor, and property is secured as collateral in exchange for extension of credit.

unsecured creditor
A type of creditor whose debt is not secured by collateral.

Secured creditors' loans are secured by collateral such as a house or a car and include mortgage lenders and car financing companies. **Unsecured creditors**, creditors whose loans are not secured by collateral, are also reviewed. Unsecured creditors fall into two categories: **priority** and **nonpriority**. Priority unsecured creditors include mothers or fathers who are owed child support from the noncustodial parent and employees who are owed back wages. Priority unsecured creditors are paid before nonpriority creditors in a liquidation, and nonpriority creditors take what is left, if anything.

SECURED CREDITORS

Most people who consider filing for bankruptcy are prompted by the threat of losing a home or a vehicle to the foreclosure or repossession process. Secured creditors enjoy an exclusive category in the bankruptcy process. For example, a mortgage or car loan is an example of a secured claim. Their claims are provided with greater protection than are the claims of both types of unsecured creditors because the secured creditor's loan is protected by the value attached to a specific article of property owned or possessed by the debtor. The property that secures the loan can be a house, condominium, car, or household item bought on credit for which the debtor voluntarily entered into a secured agreement with the creditor.

The need for secured loans has, at times, been a topic for debate. Those opposed to secured loans argue that the terms of the loans along with the right of the creditor to repossess or foreclose on the collateral cause undue hardship for the debtor. Proponents of secured loans point out that secured loans on cars, household goods, and homes provide the debtor with several advantages, including more lenient purchase terms, lower prices, and lower interest rates. These types of loans also benefit the creditor in that they lower the risk of nonpayment on the loan. After all, to be able to provide benefits to the borrower, there has to be a little "quid pro quo" for the lender as well, correct? When you think about this for a moment, it makes sense. Consider the interest rates on most unsecured credit cards compared with the interest rates on mortgage loans and car loans as of late.

collateral
An asset or specific property pledged in exchange for a secured loan.

With a secured loan, the debtor pledges an asset or specific item of property as **collateral** for the loan. The debtor does this by signing a promissory note, a deed of trust or mortgage deed, or both prior to receiving the loan to buy the car or home. The debtor is agreeing, by pledging the collateral in exchange for the loan, that the lender may take ownership or possession of the collateral either by repossession or a formal court proceeding known as foreclosure. The determining factor of whether the creditor exercises its right to acquire the collateral by repossession or foreclosure depends on the type of property that is defined as collateral. If the collateral is an article of personal property such as a car, household furnishings, or jewelry, the creditor acquires the collateral by repossession. If the collateral is a parcel of real property such as a house, building lot, or condominium, the creditor acquires the property by court-mandated and ordered foreclosure. Foreclosure procedures vary from state to state and are creatures of state law.

If a debtor defaults on a car loan, the creditor does not have to go through a lengthy court process to retrieve the vehicle to secure its loan. The creditor may engage in self-help and simply take the item of personal property (such as a car) if it is accessible and not blocked by someone else's property. The creditor often accomplishes this task by hiring a third party, sometimes colloquially referred to as the "repo" man or woman, who may take the property subject to some general rules. The party physically repossessing the vehicle must do so peacefully, without damaging garage doors, locks, or the property of another. He or she may not yell at or harass the debtor in any way.

A **mortgage** is a loan to finance the purchase of real estate, payable over a period of years and at a rate of interest. The debt is secured by the real estate, so if the borrower defaults on the mortgage, the lender may take possession of the property through a process called foreclosure. A **deed of trust** is a legal arrangement by which a lender, such as a bank, provides a borrower with the money to purchase real estate. The borrower executes a promissory note, transferring the legal interest (the right to manage and control) to a trustee, usually a title company, which holds it for the benefit of the lender. The borrower retains an equitable interest (right of enjoyment) in the property. If the borrower defaults on payments, the trustee has a right to sell the property.

If a debtor defaults on a mortgage loan on a parcel of real property, the creditor, often a bank or mortgage company, must commence a legal proceeding against the debtor called a **foreclosure**. Unlike a repossession case, the creditor seeking a foreclosure is required to provide adequate notice to the debtor that it is bringing the foreclosure action in civil court. The debtor is entitled to his or her day in court to defend his or her position with regard to the defaulted loan and negotiate with the creditor to reinstate the loan and keep the collateral. The foreclosure process can take anywhere from three to six months. In the beginning of the foreclosure process, the creditor deals directly with the debtor to reach an agreement or resolution with regard to the loan. If no resolution is reached, the case proceeds in court, and a date for a public auction is set. If the public auction is not successful, the secured creditor (bank) becomes the owner of the property. Bank-owned properties are referred to as **REO (real estate owned) properties**.

Another important factor to consider with respect to foreclosure is that the secured creditor in this case is acquiring title to the real property. This requires court intervention, often with the appointment of a foreclosure attorney (referred to in some states as a committee) to help establish good title.

JUDICIAL VERSUS NONJUDICIAL FORECLOSURES

Twenty-five states require lenders to obtain a court order before foreclosing on a property. This is called a **judicial foreclosure**. The other twenty five allow what is known as a **nonjudicial foreclosure**. These jurisdictions allow lenders to foreclose

mortgage
A loan to finance the purchase of real estate, payable over a period of years and at a rate of interest.

deed of trust
A legal arrangement wherein a lender, such as a bank, provides a borrower with the money to purchase real estate.

foreclosure
A legal proceeding a lender, usually a bank or mortgage trust company, files against a debtor who defaults on a mortgage loan on a parcel of real property. The lender seeks to force the sale of real property secured by a mortgage to recover the money and interest due, plus the legal costs of the foreclosure, when the borrower failed to make payments.

REO (real estate owned) properties
Bank-owned properties.

on property without first getting a court order. They are also only available for deeds of trust that include power-of-sale clauses and not traditional mortgages. A deed of trust is created when the lender gives the borrower money to purchase real estate in exchange for one or several promissory notes.

Nonjudicial foreclosures, however, are highly regulated and include strict notice requirements and statutory waiting periods before the property is auctioned. A nonjudicial foreclosure is not automatic, and the borrower has the opportunity to seek other remedies to avoid foreclosure. If the borrower cannot cure the default, the trustee may proceed with the foreclosure.

The borrower then transfers the property to a trustee, generally a title company, who has the legal authority to assume control over the real estate if the borrower defaults. It is the power-of-sale clause in the deed of trust that allows a foreclosure without court intervention. Nonjudicial procedures vary from state to state, so it is important to know state law.

A mortgage or a deed of trust is not the only way a debtor can obtain a secured loan. Some banks will lend money for a loan or business loan if the debtor pledges some sort of collateral, whether that collateral is a home, car, bank account, or some type of investment. It is almost never advisable for a debtor to obtain a secured loan or credit card from a lending institution unless the debtor has no other choice. Often, a debtor's credit is too poor to obtain an unsecured loan. The lender, in this case, often looks for the borrower or debtor to assume a certain amount of risk in the loan.

As we discuss in greater detail in later chapters, the secured creditors are scheduled on Schedule D of the official bankruptcy forms. In Schedule D, the debtor must indicate the name of the secured creditor, the amount of the claim, the present value of the collateral, and the deficiency or unsecured portion of the debt. Exhibit 9.1 is an example of how this type of debt is scheduled using Schedule D from the "Official Bankruptcy Forms" section of the U.S. Bankruptcy Court website. The unsecured portion of the debt will be treated in the same manner as other unsecured debts in the bankruptcy estate.

UNSECURED CREDITORS

unsecured priority creditor
A creditor given priority over non-priority secured debtors in a bankruptcy liquidation or reorganization. Examples include custodial parents owed child support payments and employees owed back wages.

Unsecured creditors are entities to whom the debtor owes a debt; no security agreement is signed, and the debtor pledges no collateral to secure the debt. Within this group of unsecured creditors, there are two types: **unsecured priority creditors**, also known as priority creditors, and **unsecured nonpriority creditors**, sometimes referred to as general unsecured creditors. Examples of unsecured priority creditors include child support recipients, alimony recipients, and an employee who is owed back wages by an employer who has filed for bankruptcy.

UNSECURED PRIORITY CREDITORS

unsecured nonpriority creditor
A creditor that does not receive any priority treatment in bankruptcy liquidation or reorganization.

This class of creditors is aptly named because they are, indeed, given priority over any nonpriority unsecured creditors a debtor may have in liquidation or reorganization bankruptcy. The reason the Bankruptcy Code provides certain creditors with priority status seems to stem from the fact that paying certain debts first or in full in a bankruptcy case simply contributes to the common good. In other words,

EXHIBIT 9.1 B 6D (Official Form 6D) (12/07)

B 6D (Official Form 6D) (12/07)

B6D - Official Form 6D
Schedule D : Creditors Holding Secured Claims

In re Sam Smith, Debra Smith   ,   Case No. _____
           Debtor   **(If known)**

SCHEDULE D - CREDITORS HOLDING SECURED CLAIMS

    State the name, mailing address, including zip code, and last four digits of any account number of all entities holding claims secured by property of the debtor as of the date of filing of the petition. The complete account number of any account the debtor has with the creditor is useful to the trustee and the creditor and may be provided if the debtor chooses to do so. List creditors holding all types of secured interests such as judgment liens, garnishments, statutory liens, mortgages, deeds of trust, and other security interests.

    List creditors in alphabetical order to the extent practicable. If a minor child is the creditor, state the child's initials and the name and address of the child's parent or guardian, such as "A.B., a minor child, by John Doe, guardian." Do not disclose the child's name. See, 11 U.S.C. §112 and Fed. R. Bankr. P. 1007(m). If all secured creditors will not fit on this page, use the continuation sheet provided.

    If any entity other than a spouse in a joint case may be jointly liable on a claim, place an "X" in the column labeled "Codebtor," include the entity on the appropriate schedule of creditors, and complete Schedule H – Codebtors. If a joint petition is filed, state whether the husband, wife, both of them, or the marital community may be liable on each claim by placing an "H," "W," "J," or "C" in the column labeled "Husband, Wife, Joint, or Community."

    If the claim is contingent, place an "X" in the column labeled "Contingent." If the claim is unliquidated, place an "X" in the column labeled "Unliquidated." If the claim is disputed, place an "X" in the column labeled "Disputed." (You may need to place an "X" in more than one of these three columns.)

    Total the columns labeled "Amount of Claim Without Deducting Value of Collateral" and "Unsecured Portion, if Any" in the boxes labeled "Total(s)" on the last sheet of the completed schedule. Report the total from the column labeled "Amount of Claim Without Deducting Value of Collateral" also on the Summary of Schedules and, if the debtor is an individual with primarily consumer debts, report the total from the column labeled "Unsecured Portion, if Any" on the Statistical Summary of Certain Liabilities and Related Data.

☐   Check this box if debtor has no creditors holding secured claims to report on this Schedule D.

CREDITOR'S NAME AND MAILING ADDRESS INCLUDING ZIP CODE AND AN ACCOUNT NUMBER (*See Instructions Above.*)	CODEBTOR	HUSBAND, WIFE, JOINT, OR COMMUNITY	DATE CLAIM WAS INCURRED, NATURE OF LIEN, AND DESCRIPTION AND VALUE OF PROPERTY SUBJECT TO LIEN	CONTINGENT	UNLIQUIDATED	DISPUTED	AMOUNT OF CLAIM WITHOUT DEDUCTING VALUE OF COLLATERAL	UNSECURED PORTION, IF ANY
ACCOUNT NO. 56565445 Acme Car Loans 123 Get Me a Loan Drive Anywhere, NJ 07000	X	H	May 24, 2015 Car Loan 2011 Acme Truck VALUE $11,500				$ 14,500	$ 3,000
ACCOUNT NO. 5555656544 Car Finance Company 156 Anyavenue Drive Anywhere, YS 12456		W	March 8, 2014 Car Loan 2013 Bundai Delantra VALUE $12,000				$ 10563	
ACCOUNT NO. 12569878 The Car Loan Store 145 I Need That Car Drive Anytown, YS 12345		J	April 2, 2010 Car Loan 2011 BWM VDrive VALUE $18,000				20,000	$ 2,000

   _1_ continuation sheets
        attached

Subtotal ▶ (Total of this page)	$ 45,063	$ 5,000
Total ▶ (Use only on last page)	$	$
	(Report also on Summary of Schedules.)	(If applicable, report also on Statistical Summary of Certain Liabilities and Related Data.)

(Continued)

EXHIBIT 9.1 Continued

B 6D (Official Form 6D) (12/07) – Cont.   2

In re _Sam Smith, Debra Smith_____,   **Case No.** _____
         Debtor   **(if known)**

SCHEDULE D - CREDITORS HOLDING SECURED CLAIMS
(Continuation Sheet)

CREDITOR'S NAME AND MAILING ADDRESS INCLUDING ZIP CODE AND AN ACCOUNT NUMBER (*See Instructions Above.*)	CODEBTOR	HUSBAND, WIFE, JOINT, OR COMMUNITY	DATE CLAIM WAS INCURRED, NATURE OF LIEN, AND DESCRIPTION AND VALUE OF PROPERTY SUBJECT TO LIEN	CONTINGENT	UNLIQUIDATED	DISPUTED	AMOUNT OF CLAIM WITHOUT DEDUCTING VALUE OF COLLATERAL	UNSECURED PORTION, IF ANY
ACCOUNT NO. 23636565 Mortgage Finance Company 45 Any Old Street Anyoldtown, YS 12345		J	August 2, 2005 Mortgage Loan 67 Harris Street Anytown, YS 12345 VALUE $156,000				$ 125,000	
ACCOUNT NO.			 VALUE $					
ACCOUNT NO.			 VALUE $					
ACCOUNT NO.			 VALUE $					
ACCOUNT NO.			 VALUE $					

Sheet no. __1__ of __1__ continuation sheets attached to Schedule of Creditors Holding Secured Claims

Subtotal (s) ▶
(Total(s) of this page)

$ 125,000	$

Total(s) ▶
(Use only on last page)

$ 170,063	$ 5,000
(Report also on Summary of Schedules.)	(If applicable, report also on Statistical Summary of Certain Liabilities and Related Data.)

as we lawyers sometimes like to say, certain laws or rules promote good public policy. It just makes sense, and no one seems to argue with the fact that certain debts should be given priority over others. Examples include the payment of back child support to the custodial parent of the debtor's children or the payment of back wages or contributions owed to an employee of the debtor. We discuss the various types of priority creditors in more detail later.

In the relatively rare event that the bankruptcy trustee in a Chapter 7 case liquidates any nonexempt assets the debtor might have, the priority creditors must be paid prior to any unsecured creditor and in rank order as determined by 11 U.S.C. § 507. In most liquidation cases, there are usually no funds left, after paying the priority creditors, to disburse to the nonpriority creditors. In a Chapter 11 reorganization case, generally, all priority creditors must be paid in full by the end of the reorganization plan. This puts this type of creditor at an advantage over the general unsecured creditors in either type of bankruptcy filing.

According to 11 U.S.C. § 507, the ten kinds of **priority creditors** an individual or business debtor may have are ranked in the following order:

priority creditor
A creditor to whom the debtor pledges no type of collateral to satisfy the loan if the debtor defaults on payment; an unsecured creditor whose claims take precedence over the claims of other unsecured creditors.

1. Domestic support obligations such as alimony and child support.
2. Administrative expenses associated with the bankruptcy case.
3. Unsecured claims for debts related to the debtor's regular business expenses, that were incurred after an involuntary case was initiated and prior to either the appointment of a trustee or an order for relief from the bankruptcy court.
4. Claims for payment of employees' wages, salaries, or commissions, including sick, vacation, and severance compensation. This applies to earnings by an employee, a corporation with a sole employee, or an independent contractor within either 180 days of the debtor's business closing or petition filing. The maximum payment is $11,725 per person.
5. Unsecured claims for contributions to employee benefit plans, including medical and life insurance, which must be paid within 180 days of the petition filing or close of business. This figure is the number of employees multiplied by $11,725, less the amount that was paid to employees for the fourth priority.
6. Unsecured claims of up to $5,775 per person to persons who produce or raise grain or fish.
7. Deposits related to the personal or family purchase, lease, or rental of property, services, or goods that were not supplied or completed, to a maximum of $2,600 per person.
8. Taxes or claims from other governmental entities.
9. Unsecured claims based on any commitment by the debtor to a federal depository institution regulatory agency (or predecessor to such agency) to maintain the capital of an insured depository institution.
10. Claims for death or personal injury resulting from the operation of a motor vehicle or vessel if such operation was unlawful because the debtor was intoxicated from using alcohol, a drug, or another substance.

When a debtor has priority debts, the debtor, or the paralegal for the debtor's attorney, schedules this information in Schedule E of the official bankruptcy forms found on the Bankruptcy Court's website. Schedule E consists of two parts. The first part consists of a list of potential priority creditors, some of whom were mentioned in the preceding list. The second part details the claims of the creditors listed in the first part of Schedule E. After determining how many such creditors the debtor may have, the paralegal would then simply check the box next to all the appropriate creditors. For example, if the debtor owed money to an ex-spouse for child support, the first half of the form would look like this:

B6E (Official Form 6E) (04/13)

B6E - Official Form 6E
Schedule E : Creditors Holding Unsecured Priority Claims

In re Sam Smith, Debra Smith   ,   Case No. _____
            Debtor   *(if known)*

SCHEDULE E - CREDITORS HOLDING UNSECURED PRIORITY CLAIMS

A complete list of claims entitled to priority, listed separately by type of priority, is to be set forth on the sheets provided. Only holders of unsecured claims entitled to priority should be listed in this schedule. In the boxes provided on the attached sheets, state the name, mailing address, including zip code, and last four digits of the account number, if any, of all entities holding priority claims against the debtor or the property of the debtor, as of the date of the filing of the petition. Use a separate continuation sheet for each type of priority and label each with the type of priority.

The complete account number of any account the debtor has with the creditor is useful to the trustee and the creditor and may be provided if the debtor chooses to do so. If a minor child is a creditor, state the child's initials and the name and address of the child's parent or guardian, such as "A.B., a minor child, by John Doe, guardian." Do not disclose the child's name. See, 11 U.S.C. §112 and Fed. R. Bankr. P. 1007(m).

If any entity other than a spouse in a joint case may be jointly liable on a claim, place an "X" in the column labeled "Codebtor," include the entity on the appropriate schedule of creditors, and complete Schedule H-Codebtors. If a joint petition is filed, state whether the husband, wife, both of them, or the marital community may be liable on each claim by placing an "H," "W," "J," or "C" in the column labeled "Husband, Wife, Joint, or Community." If the claim is contingent, place an "X" in the column labeled "Contingent." If the claim is unliquidated, place an "X" in the column labeled "Unliquidated." If the claim is disputed, place an "X" in the column labeled "Disputed." (You may need to place an "X" in more than one of these three columns.)

Report the total of claims listed on each sheet in the box labeled "Subtotals" on each sheet. Report the total of all claims listed on this Schedule E in the box labeled "Total" on the last sheet of the completed schedule. Report this total also on the Summary of Schedules.

Report the total of amounts entitled to priority listed on each sheet in the box labeled "Subtotals" on each sheet. Report the total of all amounts entitled to priority listed on this Schedule E in the box labeled "Totals" on the last sheet of the completed schedule. Individual debtors with primarily consumer debts report this total also on the Statistical Summary of Certain Liabilities and Related Data.

Report the total of amounts <u>not</u> entitled to priority listed on each sheet in the box labeled "Subtotals" on each sheet. Report the total of all amounts not entitled to priority listed on this Schedule E in the box labeled "Totals" on the last sheet of the completed schedule. Individual debtors with primarily consumer debts report this total also on the Statistical Summary of Certain Liabilities and Related Data.

☐   Check this box if debtor has no creditors holding unsecured priority claims to report on this Schedule E.

TYPES OF PRIORITY CLAIMS (Check the appropriate box(es) below if claims in that category are listed on the attached sheets.)

☑ **Domestic Support Obligations**

Claims for domestic support that are owed to or recoverable by a spouse, former spouse, or child of the debtor, or the parent, legal guardian, or responsible relative of such a child, or a governmental unit to whom such a domestic support claim has been assigned to the extent provided in 11 U.S.C. § 507(a)(1).

☐ **Extensions of credit in an involuntary case**

Claims arising in the ordinary course of the debtor's business or financial affairs after the commencement of the case but before the earlier of the appointment of a trustee or the order for relief. 11 U.S.C. § 507(a)(3).

Amount subject to adjustment on 4/01/16, and every three years thereafter with respect to cases commenced on or after the date of adjustment.

B6E (Official Form 6E) (04/13) – Cont.

☐ **Wages, salaries, and commissions**

Wages, salaries, and commissions, including vacation, severance, and sick leave pay owing to employees and commissions owing to qualifying independent sales representatives up to $12,475* per person earned within 180 days immediately preceding the filing of the original petition, or the cessation of business, whichever occurred first, to the extent provided in 11 U.S.C. § 507(a)(4).

☐ **Contributions to employee benefit plans**

Money owed to employee benefit plans for services rendered within 180 days immediately preceding the filing of the original petition, or the cessation of business, whichever occurred first, to the extent provided in 11 U.S.C. § 507(a)(5).

In re _____ ,   Case No. _____
                                    Debtor   *(if known)*

☐ **Certain farmers and fishermen**

Claims of certain farmers and fishermen, up to $6,150* per farmer or fisherman, against the debtor, as provided in 11 U.S.C. § 507(a)(6).

☐ **Deposits by individuals**

Claims of individuals up to $2,775* for deposits for the purchase, lease, or rental of property or services for personal, family, or household use, that were not delivered or provided. 11 U.S.C. § 507(a)(7).

☐ **Taxes and Certain Other Debts Owed to Governmental Units**

Taxes, customs duties, and penalties owing to federal, state, and local governmental units as set forth in 11 U.S.C. § 507(a)(8).

☐ **Commitments to Maintain the Capital of an Insured Depository Institution**

Claims based on commitments to the FDIC, RTC, Director of the Office of Thrift Supervision, Comptroller of the Currency, or Board of Governors of the Federal Reserve System, or their predecessors or successors, to maintain the capital of an insured depository institution. 11 U.S.C. § 507 (a)(9).

☐ **Claims for Death or Personal Injury While Debtor Was Intoxicated**

Claims for death or personal injury resulting from the operation of a motor vehicle or vessel while the debtor was intoxicated from using alcohol, a drug, or another substance. 11 U.S.C. § 507(a)(10).

* Amounts are subject to adjustment on 4/01/16, and every three years thereafter with respect to cases commenced on or after the date of adjustment.*

Let's say that the ex-wife creditor is claiming that Sam Smith owes her $1,200, and Mr. Smith claims he owes her only $900 and disputes the remainder of her claim; the second half of Schedule E would look like this:

B6E (Official Form 6E) (04/13) – Cont.

In re _Sam Smith, Debra Smith_____ ,   Case No. _____
               Debtor   *(if known)*

SCHEDULE E - CREDITORS HOLDING UNSECURED PRIORITY CLAIMS
(Continuation Sheet)

Type of Priority for Claims Listed on This Sheet

CREDITOR'S NAME, MAILING ADDRESS INCLUDING ZIP CODE, AND ACCOUNT NUMBER *(See instructions above.)*	CODEBTOR	HUSBAND, WIFE, JOINT, OR COMMUNITY	DATE CLAIM WAS INCURRED AND CONSIDERATION FOR CLAIM	CONTINGENT	UNLIQUIDATED	DISPUTED	AMOUNT OF CLAIM	AMOUNT ENTITLED TO PRIORITY	AMOUNT NOT ENTITLED TO PRIORITY, IF ANY
Account No. Sally Smith 9 Creditor Way Anytown, NJ 07000		H	2/21/2014 Child Support			X	1,200.00	0.00	
Account No.									
Account No.									
Account No.									

Sheet no. ___ of ___ continuation sheets attached to Schedule of Creditors Holding Priority Claims

Subtotals ▶ (Totals of this page)	$ 1,200.00	$ 0.00
Total ▶ (Use only on last page of the completed Schedule E. Report also on the Summary of Schedules.)	$ 1,200.00	
Totals ▶ (Use only on last page of the completed Schedule E. If applicable, report also on the Statistical Summary of Certain Liabilities and Related Data.)		$ 0.00 $

The paralegal will fill out a separate Schedule E form for each type of priority creditor as indicated in the preceding examples. If a debtor has both alimony and child support claims, they will both be entered on one Schedule E form. If the same debtor also owes for back income taxes and for a former employee's back wages, the paralegal fills out two Schedule E forms. We discuss Schedule E and all the other schedules in greater detail in later chapters.

BANKRUPTCY ADMINISTRATIVE EXPENSE CLAIMS

Domestic support obligations are considered first priority claims. Next in the ranking of order of priority are bankruptcy administrative expenses, defined as costs related to the bankruptcy case. Examples of these costs include:

- Certain nonresidential real property lease expenses
- Costs and expenses of closing a health care business
- Costs, expenses, and taxes associated with the preservation of bankruptcy estate property
- Professional service fees (accounting and legal)
- Reasonable compensation for trustees
- Value of certain goods the debtor received within 20 days before the case was filed
- Witness fees and mileage

UNSECURED NON-PRIORITY CREDITORS

The final genre of creditors to be discussed is **unsecured nonpriority creditors**, sometimes referred to as general unsecured creditors. Unsecured nonpriority creditors do not receive any priority treatment in a bankruptcy liquidation or reorganization. In fact, most general unsecured creditors receive no payment in a liquidation case. In a reorganization case, they receive some payment but are not entitled to receive payment in full as priority creditors are. This class of debt consists, for example, of medical bills, credit card bills, bills for services rendered such as to plumbers, roofing contractors, and any other debt that is not secured by property. General unsecured debt that has spiraled out of control is one of the primary reasons individuals file for bankruptcy.

If a debtor has a credit card with VISTA, for example, with a balance of $11,000 incurred during the years of 2013 to 2014, and owes Smith's Plumbing, LLC, $2,000 for services rendered in July 2014 along with various other nonpriority debts, the paralegal schedules the unsecured creditors on Schedule F. See Exhibit 9.2 for an example of how a typical Schedule F might appear.

As with other types of creditors, it is extremely important for the debtor to relay a complete and accurate list to the paralegal of all unsecured creditors. During the client intake, the paralegal should emphasize with the client the importance of scheduling all debts in a bankruptcy case. If an unsecured creditor is not scheduled, the unscheduled creditor may obtain a judgment against the debtor-client while the bankruptcy case is pending. This would be so if the creditor can prove that he or she were intentionally or fraudulently omitted from being listed in Schedules D, E, or F, as the following case demonstrates.

EXHIBIT 9.2 B 6F (Official Form 6F) (12/07)

B6F - Official Form 6F - Schedule F: Creditors Holding
Unsecured Non-Priority Claims

B 6F (Official Form 6F) (12/07)

In re   Sam Smith   ,   Case No. _____
                    Debtor   **(if known)**

SCHEDULE F - CREDITORS HOLDING UNSECURED NONPRIORITY CLAIMS

State the name, mailing address, including zip code, and last four digits of any account number, of all entities holding unsecured claims without priority against the debtor or the property of the debtor, as of the date of filing of the petition. The complete account number of any account the debtor has with the creditor is useful to the trustee and the creditor and may be provided if the debtor chooses to do so. If a minor child is a creditor, state the child's initials and the name and address of the child's parent or guardian, such as "A.B., a minor child, by John Doe, guardian." Do not disclose the child's name. See, 11 U.S.C. §112 and Fed. R. Bankr. P. 1007(m). Do not include claims listed in Schedules D and E. If all creditors will not fit on this page, use the continuation sheet provided.

If any entity other than a spouse in a joint case may be jointly liable on a claim, place an "X" in the column labeled "Codebtor," include the entity on the appropriate schedule of creditors, and complete Schedule H - Codebtors. If a joint petition is filed, state whether the husband, wife, both of them, or the marital community may be liable on each claim by placing an "H," "W," "J," or "C" in the column labeled "Husband, Wife, Joint, or Community."

If the claim is contingent, place an "X" in the column labeled "Contingent." If the claim is unliquidated, place an "X" in the column labeled "Unliquidated." If the claim is disputed, place an "X" in the column labeled "Disputed." (You may need to place an "X" in more than one of these three columns.)

Report the total of all claims listed on this schedule in the box labeled "Total" on the last sheet of the completed schedule. Report this total also on the Summary of Schedules and, if the debtor is an individual with primarily consumer debts, report this total also on the Statistical Summary of Certain Liabilities and Related Data..

☐ Check this box if debtor has no creditors holding unsecured claims to report on this Schedule F.

CREDITOR'S NAME, MAILING ADDRESS INCLUDING ZIP CODE, AND ACCOUNT NUMBER *(See instructions above.)*	CODEBTOR	HUSBAND, WIFE, JOINT, OR COMMUNITY	DATE CLAIM WAS INCURRED AND CONSIDERATION FOR CLAIM. IF CLAIM IS SUBJECT TO SETOFF, SO STATE.	CONTINGENT	UNLIQUIDATED	DISPUTED	AMOUNT OF CLAIM
ACCOUNT NO. 1234656789 VISTA P.O. Box 12344 Wilminton, DE 19810		H	2013–2014 General Merchandise				11,000.00
ACCOUNT NO. 1256565 Smith's Plumbing, LLC 123 Anystreet Avenue Anytown, NJ 07635		J	July 2013 Plumbing services performed at residence				2,000.00
ACCOUNT NO. 123456 Dr. Feel Better 156 Anystreet Way Anytown, YS, 11111		W	2012–2013 Medical Bills				4,500.00
ACCOUNT NO. 23696314 Spears Department Store 125 Tower Way Anytown, KS 12345		W	2013–2014 General Merchandise				2,500.00

__1__ continuation sheets attached

Subtotal ▶ $ 20,000.00

Total ▶ $

(Use only on last page of the completed Schedule F.)
(Report also on Summary of Schedules and, if applicable, on the Statistical
Summary of Certain Liabilities and Related Data.)

EXHIBIT 9.2 Continued

B 6F (Official Form 6F) (12/07) - Cont.

In re _Sam Smith_____, **Case No.** _____

          Debtor   **(if known)**

SCHEDULE F - CREDITORS HOLDING UNSECURED NONPRIORITY CLAIMS

(Continuation Sheet)

CREDITOR'S NAME, MAILING ADDRESS INCLUDING ZIP CODE, AND ACCOUNT NUMBER (See instructions above.)	CODEBTOR	HUSBAND, WIFE, JOINT, OR COMMUNITY	DATE CLAIM WAS INCURRED AND CONSIDERATION FOR CLAIM. IF CLAIM IS SUBJECT TO SETOFF, SO STATE.	CONTINGENT	UNLIQUIDATED	DISPUTED	AMOUNT OF CLAIM
ACCOUNT NO. 1234656789 Jolly Good Cruise Line Credit Card P.O. Box 125 Anytown, DE 12345		H	2014–2015 General Merchandise				4,000.00
ACCOUNT NO.							
ACCOUNT NO.							
ACCOUNT NO.							
ACCOUNT NO.							

Sheet no. _1_ of _1_ continuation sheets attached
to Schedule of Creditors Holding Unsecured
Nonpriority Claims

           Subtotal ➤ $ 4,000.00

           Total ➤ $ 24,000.00
(Use only on last page of the completed Schedule F.)
(Report also on Summary of Schedules and, if applicable on the Statistical
Summary of Certain Liabilities and Related Data.)

CASE **9.1** In Re William C. Ritchey and Donna M. Ritchey, Debtors, No. 10–36149 (Bankr. S.D. Tex Jun. 18, 2013)

Memorandum Opinion on Debtors' Motion to Reopen Their Chapter 7 Case

JEFF BOHM, United States Chief Bankruptcy Judge.

…The Court writes this Memorandum Opinion to clarify the current state of the law concerning a creditor's right to sue on an unscheduled debt after the debtor has received a discharge. The right to do so is not nearly as broad as a creditor, and its counsel, might think. Indeed, the post-discharge right to sue to recover an unscheduled, pre-petition debt is sufficiently narrow that it can be a painful trap for the unwary creditor. Such is the case here.

In 2009, William Ritchey contracted with Ductwork, Inc. (the Creditor) for custom duct work and signed a promissory note in the amount of $24,947.00…. Mr. Ritchey and his wife, Donna Ritchey (the Debtors), filed for Chapter 7 on July 23, 2010…. On October 26, 2010, the Debtors received a discharge of their debts…and the case was closed…. The Debtors did not own any non-exempt assets, and the Chapter 7 trustee (the Trustee) made no distributions to creditors. The Creditor's claim was not listed in the Debtors' Schedules, nor was the Creditor listed on the Creditors' Matrix….

On March 12, 2013—which was two and a half years after this Court discharged the Debtors—the Creditor filed a lawsuit in Texas state court seeking repayment of the unscheduled debt…. In the pleadings filed in state court, the Creditor alleged that because the debt was unscheduled and the Creditor did not learn of the bankruptcy until after the case was closed, the Creditor was unable to file a timely proof of claim and should therefore be able to sue and recover on the debt…. In response, the Debtors moved to reopen their Chapter 7 case, pursuant to 11 U.S.C. § 350(b), in this Court so that: (1) they may remove the state court suit to this Court in order to request dismissal of the suit; and (2) recover their attorneys' fees and costs for having to defend against the state court suit…

…This is a no-asset case…where the Debtors failed to list the Debt on their schedules…. The Creditor claims an exception from discharge for the unlisted Debt…an issue governed by § 523(a)(3) and the Robinson test. The Creditor is not prejudiced because no dividend was paid, and the administration of the bankruptcy system is not disturbed by the omission. The sole issue in dispute is the Debtors' intent in omitting the Debt. The Debtors, in their case in chief, have met their burden in showing that the omission was inadvertent; the Creditor has presented no evidence to advance its assertion of mal-intent on the part of the Debtors. Therefore, pursuant to the Robinson test, the Debt was discharged. And, because the Debt was discharged, the Creditor's filing of the State Court Petition and the prosecution of the State Court Lawsuit provide a sound basis for reopening the Debtors' Chapter 7 case because § 350(b) provides for a reopening of a case "to accord relief to the debtor or for other cause"—and here, the relief is the dismissal with prejudice of the State Court Lawsuit and the recovery of the Debtors' attorneys' fees and costs for having to defend against the lawsuit. The bankruptcy case will therefore be reopened. The Debtors may then proceed to remove the State Court Lawsuit—if the Creditor has not already dismissed it—and also seek their reasonable attorneys' fees and costs from the Creditor for violation of the Discharge Order.

Creditors' Proof of Claim

All creditors listed in Schedules D, E, and F will receive a notification from the clerk of the court that the debtor has filed for bankruptcy. According to 11 U.S.C. § 501, to be paid by the trustee in either a liquidation or reorganization bankruptcy, a creditor must file an Official Form B10 **Proof of Claim** form with the bankruptcy court where the case is pending. A Proof of Claim form contains the amount of debt owed to the creditor and the reason for the debt. The creditor must include evidence proving the debt such as an invoice, statement, or receipts. The creditor must file this form with the court no later than 90 days after the first meeting of the creditors. A government creditor, such as a municipality or the IRS, that is owed back taxes by the debtor, has 180 days from the first meeting of the creditors to file its proof of claim. Many creditors will not file a Proof of Claim in Chapter 7 cases in which there are no assets.

In some cases, the debtor needs or would like the creditor to file a Proof of Claim. For example, a debtor chooses to file bankruptcy under Chapter 13 to help save his or her home. The debtor's mortgage company must file a Proof of Claim with the court to receive payments from the trustee through the reorganization plan. If the creditor does not file a timely Proof of Claim, as is sometimes the case, the debtor or the trustee may file the Proof of Claim on behalf of the creditor. Exhibit 9.3 is an example of a typical Proof of Claim filed by an unsecured creditor.

Proof of Claim
A court form a creditor files that contains the amount of debt owed to the creditor and the reason for the debt. The creditor must include evidence proving the debt, such as an invoice, statement, or receipts.

Creditors' Right to Relief from Automatic Stay

As mentioned in Chapter 4 of this text, the Bankruptcy Code provides the debtor with powerful protection under the shield of the Automatic Stay. This power, under 11 U.S.C. 362, stops the collections efforts of nearly all creditors against the debtor. This includes wage garnishments, lawsuits, and collections efforts. Even secured creditors are stopped in their tracks, if only temporarily, immediately upon the filing of the bankruptcy petition. This includes foreclosure lawsuits by mortgage lenders as well as repossession efforts by vehicle finance companies.

Creditors do have the right, upon filing a **motion for relief from Automatic Stay** with the bankruptcy court and serving the debtor and the trustee with proper notice of the motion, to request relief from the Automatic Stay. (Motions for relief from Automatic Stay are discussed in detail in Chapter 18 of this text.) Most bankruptcy courts hold the creditor to very strict procedural standards when considering this type of motion and often dismiss the motion if the proper procedures are not followed. Given the unique nature of the reasons for requesting relief from the Automatic Stay, there is no specific form for the creditor to fill out when making this type of motion. The creditor's motion must include the balance owed to the creditor, the value and a description of the collateral securing the loan, and whether the debtor is in default on the loan. In addition, the creditor must state the grounds on which it is seeking relief from the Automatic Stay.

The majority of motions for relief from the Automatic Stay are filed by secured creditors, either mortgage companies and banks or companies that

motion for relief from Automatic Stay
A motion filed by a creditor in a bankruptcy case asking the Automatic Stay *to* be lifted so the creditor may proceed with legal proceedings or collection against the debtor.

EXHIBIT 9.3 Proof of Claim

B10 (Official Form 10) (04/13)

UNITED STATES BANKRUPTCY COURT Middle District of Anytown, USA	**PROOF OF CLAIM**

| Name of Debtor:

Otto Schuler | Case Number:

XP00000002 | |

NOTE: *Do not use this form to make a claim for an administrative expense that arises after the bankruptcy filing. You may file a request for payment of an administrative expense according to 11 U.S.C. § 503.*

Name of Creditor (the person or other entity to whom the debtor owes money or property):
VISTA CREDIT CARD SERVICES

COURT USE ONLY

Name and address where notices should be sent:

VISTA Card Services, Inc.
2 Want Credit? Way
Anytown, DE 00000

Telephone number: (555) 555-5555   email:

❏ Check this box if this claim amends a previously filed claim.

Court Claim Number:_____
   (*If known*)

Filed on:_____

Name and address where payment should be sent (if different from above):

Telephone number: email:

❏ Check this box if you are aware that anyone else has filed a proof of claim relating to this claim. Attach copy of statement giving particulars.

1. Amount of Claim as of Date Case Filed: $_____30,000.00_____

If all or part of the claim is secured, complete item 4.

If all or part of the claim is entitled to priority, complete item 5.

☑Check this box if the claim includes interest or other charges in addition to the principal amount of the claim. Attach a statement that itemizes interest or charges.

2. Basis for Claim: _Credit Card - See Attached Billing and Interest Statements_____
   (See instruction #2)

3. Last four digits of any number by which creditor identifies debtor: 0 0 0 0	**3a. Debtor may have scheduled account as:** _____ (See instruction #3a)	**3b. Uniform Claim Identifier (optional):** _ (See instruction #3b)

4. Secured Claim (See instruction #4)
Check the appropriate box if the claim is secured by a lien on property or a right of setoff, attach required redacted documents, and provide the requested information.

Nature of property or right of setoff: ❏Real Estate ❏Motor Vehicle ❏Other
Describe:

Value of Property: $_____

Annual Interest Rate_____% ❏Fixed or ❏Variable
(when case was filed)

Amount of arrearage and other charges, as of the time case was filed, included in secured claim, if any:

$_____

Basis for perfection: _____

Amount of Secured Claim: $_____

Amount Unsecured: $_____

5. Amount of Claim Entitled to Priority under 11 U.S.C. § 507 (a). If any part of the claim falls into one of the following categories, check the box specifying the priority and state the amount.

❏ Domestic support obligations under 11 U.S.C. § 507 (a)(1)(A) or (a)(1)(B).

❏ Wages, salaries, or commissions (up to $12,475*) earned within 180 days before the case was filed or the debtor's business ceased, whichever is earlier – 11 U.S.C. § 507 (a)(4).

❏ Contributions to an employee benefit plan – 11 U.S.C. § 507 (a)(5).

Amount entitled to priority:

❏ Up to $2,775* of deposits toward purchase, lease, or rental of property or services for personal, family, or household use – 11 U.S.C. § 507 (a)(7).

❏ Taxes or penalties owed to governmental units – 11 U.S.C. § 507 (a)(8).

❏ Other – Specify applicable paragraph of 11 U.S.C. § 507 (a)(__).

$_____

Amounts are subject to adjustment on 4/01/16 and every 3 years thereafter with respect to cases commenced on or after the date of adjustment.

6. Credits. The amount of all payments on this claim has been credited for the purpose of making this proof of claim. (See instruction #6)

EXHIBIT 9.3 Continued

B10 (Official Form 10) (04/13)   2

7. Documents: Attached are **redacted** copies of any documents that support the claim, such as promissory notes, purchase orders, invoices, itemized statements of running accounts, contracts, judgments, mortgages, security agreements, or, in the case of a claim based on an open-end or revolving consumer credit agreement, a statement providing the information required by FRBP 3001(c)(3)(A). If the claim is secured, box 4 has been completed, and **redacted** copies of documents providing evidence of perfection of a security interest are attached. If the claim is secured by the debtor's principal residence, the Mortgage Proof of Claim Attachment is being filed with this claim. *(See instruction #7, and the definition of "redacted".)*

DO NOT SEND ORIGINAL DOCUMENTS. ATTACHED DOCUMENTS MAY BE DESTROYED AFTER SCANNING.

If the documents are not available, please explain:

8. Signature: (See instruction #8)

Check the appropriate box.

☐ I am the creditor.   ☑ I am the creditor's authorized agent.   ☐ I am the trustee, or the debtor,   ☐ I am a guarantor, surety, indorser, or other codebtor.
                                                                                         or their authorized agent.   (See Bankruptcy Rule 3005.)
                                                                                         (See Bankruptcy Rule 3004.)

I declare under penalty of perjury that the information provided in this claim is true and correct to the best of my knowledge, information, and reasonable belief.

Print Name: George Dollar,
Title: President
Company: VISTA Credit Card Services, INC.
Address and telephone number (if different from notice address above):   (Signature)   (Date)
 2 Want Credit? Way
 Anytown, DE 00000

Telephone number: (555) 555-5555   email:
Penalty for presenting fraudulent claim: Fine of up to $500,000 or imprisonment for up to 5 years, or both. 18 U.S.C. §§ 152 and 3571.

INSTRUCTIONS FOR PROOF OF CLAIM FORM

The instructions and definitions below are general explanations of the law. In certain circumstances, such as bankruptcy cases not filed voluntarily by the debtor, exceptions to these general rules may apply.

Items to be completed in Proof of Claim form

Court, Name of Debtor, and Case Number:
Fill in the federal judicial district in which the bankruptcy case was filed (for example, Central District of California), the debtor's full name, and the case number. If the creditor received a notice of the case from the bankruptcy court, all of this information is at the top of the notice.

Creditor's Name and Address:
Fill in the name of the person or entity asserting a claim and the name and address of the person who should receive notices issued during the bankruptcy case. A separate space is provided for the payment address if it differs from the notice address. The creditor has a continuing obligation to keep the court informed of its current address. See Federal Rule of Bankruptcy Procedure (FRBP) 2002(g).

1. Amount of Claim as of Date Case Filed:
State the total amount owed to the creditor on the date of the bankruptcy filing. Follow the instructions concerning whether to complete items 4 and 5. Check the box if interest or other charges are included in the claim.

2. Basis for Claim:
State the type of debt or how it was incurred. Examples include goods sold, money loaned, services performed, personal injury/wrongful death, car loan, mortgage note, and credit card. If the claim is based on delivering health care goods or services, limit the disclosure of the goods or services so as to avoid embarrassment or the disclosure of confidential health care information. You may be required to provide additional disclosure if an interested party objects to the claim.

3. Last Four Digits of Any Number by Which Creditor Identifies Debtor:
State only the last four digits of the debtor's account or other number used by the creditor to identify the debtor.

3a. Debtor May Have Scheduled Account As:
Report a change in the creditor's name, a transferred claim, or any other information that clarifies a difference between this proof of claim and the claim as scheduled by the debtor.

3b. Uniform Claim Identifier:
If you use a uniform claim identifier, you may report it here. A uniform claim identifier is an optional 24-character identifier that certain large creditors use to facilitate electronic payment in chapter 13 cases.

4. Secured Claim:
Check whether the claim is fully or partially secured. Skip this section if the

claim is entirely unsecured. (See Definitions.)   If the claim is secured, check the box for the nature and value of property that secures the claim, attach copies of lien documentation, and state, as of the date of the bankruptcy filing, the annual interest rate (and whether it is fixed or variable), and the amount past due on the claim.

5. Amount of Claim Entitled to Priority Under 11 U.S.C. § 507 (a).
If any portion of the claim falls into any category shown, check the appropriate box(es) and state the amount entitled to priority. (See Definitions.) A claim may be partly priority and partly non-priority. For example, in some of the categories, the law limits the amount entitled to priority.

6. Credits:
An authorized signature on this proof of claim serves as an acknowledgment that when calculating the amount of the claim, the creditor gave the debtor credit for any payments received toward the debt.

7. Documents:
Attach redacted copies of any documents that show the debt exists and a lien secures the debt. You must also attach copies of documents that evidence perfection of any security interest and documents required by FRBP 3001(c) for claims based on an open-end or revolving consumer credit agreement or secured by a security interest in the debtor's principal residence. You may also attach a summary in addition to the documents themselves. FRBP 3001(c) and (d). If the claim is based on delivering health care goods or services, limit disclosing confidential health care information. Do not send original documents, as attachments may be destroyed after scanning.

8. Date and Signature:
The individual completing this proof of claim must sign and date it. FRBP 9011. If the claim is filed electronically, FRBP 5005(a)(2) authorizes courts to establish local rules specifying what constitutes a signature. If you sign this form, you declare under penalty of perjury that the information provided is true and correct to the best of your knowledge, information, and reasonable belief. Your signature is also a certification that the claim meets the requirements of FRBP 9011(b). Whether the claim is filed electronically or in person, if your name is on the signature line, you are responsible for the declaration. Print the name and title, if any, of the creditor or other person authorized to file this claim. State the filer's address and telephone number if it differs from the address given on the top of the form for purposes of receiving notices. If the claim is filed by an authorized agent, provide both the name of the individual filing the claim and the name of the agent. If the authorized agent is a servicer, identify the corporate servicer as the company. Criminal penalties apply for making a false statement on a proof of claim.

(Continued)

EXHIBIT 9.3 Continued

B10 (Official Form 10) (04/13)   3

_____DEFINITIONS_____   _____INFORMATION_____

Debtor
A debtor is the person, corporation, or other entity that has filed a bankruptcy case.

Creditor
A creditor is a person, corporation, or other entity to whom debtor owes a debt that was incurred before the date of the bankruptcy filing. See 11 U.S.C. §101 (10).

Claim
A claim is the creditor's right to receive payment for a debt owed by the debtor on the date of the bankruptcy filing. See 11 U.S.C. §101 (5). A claim may be secured or unsecured.

Proof of Claim
A proof of claim is a form used by the creditor to indicate the amount of the debt owed by the debtor on the date of the bankruptcy filing. The creditor must file the form with the clerk of the same bankruptcy court in which the bankruptcy case was filed.

Secured Claim Under 11 U.S.C. § 506 (a)
A secured claim is one backed by a lien on property of the debtor. The claim is secured so long as the creditor has the right to be paid from the property prior to other creditors. The amount of the secured claim cannot exceed the value of the property. Any amount owed to the creditor in excess of the value of the property is an unsecured claim. Examples of liens on property include a mortgage on real estate or a security interest in a car. A lien may be voluntarily granted by a debtor or may be obtained through a court proceeding. In some states, a court judgment is a lien.

A claim also may be secured if the creditor owes the debtor money (has a right to setoff).

Unsecured Claim
An unsecured claim is one that does not meet the requirements of a secured claim. A claim may be partly unsecured if the amount of the claim exceeds the value of the property on which the creditor has a lien.

Claim Entitled to Priority Under 11 U.S.C. § 507 (a)
Priority claims are certain categories of unsecured claims that are paid from the available money or property in a bankruptcy case before other unsecured claims.

Redacted
A document has been redacted when the person filing it has masked, edited out, or otherwise deleted, certain information. A creditor must show only the last four digits of any social-security, individual's tax-identification, or financial-account number, only the initials of a minor's name, and only the year of any person's date of birth. If the claim is based on the delivery of health care goods or services, limit the disclosure of the goods or services so as to avoid embarrassment or the disclosure of confidential health care information.

Evidence of Perfection
Evidence of perfection may include a mortgage, lien, certificate of title, financing statement, or other document showing that the lien has been filed or recorded.

Acknowledgment of Filing of Claim
To receive acknowledgment of your filing, you may either enclose a stamped self-addressed envelope and a copy of this proof of claim or you may access the court's PACER system (www.pacer.psc.uscourts.gov) for a small fee to view your filed proof of claim.

Offers to Purchase a Claim
Certain entities are in the business of purchasing claims for an amount less than the face value of the claims. One or more of these entities may contact the creditor and offer to purchase the claim. Some of the written communications from these entities may easily be confused with official court documentation or communications from the debtor. These entities do not represent the bankruptcy court or the debtor. The creditor has no obligation to sell its claim. However, if the creditor decides to sell its claim, any transfer of such claim is subject to FRBP 3001(e), any applicable provisions of the Bankruptcy Code (11 U.S.C. § 101 *et seq.*), and any applicable orders of the bankruptcy court.

---

are financing one or more of the debtor's vehicles. Bankruptcy Code 11 U.S.C. 362(d), states:

> (d) On request of a party in interest and after notice and a hearing, the court shall grant relief from the stay provided under subsection (a) of this section, such as by terminating, annulling, modifying, or conditioning such stay—
>
> **(1)** for cause, including the lack of adequate protection of an interest in property of such party in interest;
>
> **(2)** with respect to a stay of an act against property under subsection (a) of this section, if—
>
> > **(A)** the debtor does not have an equity in such property; and
> > **(B)** such property is not necessary to an effective reorganization

Under some very specific circumstances, a creditor may be able to convince the court that it should be allowed to continue with its debt collection efforts against the debtor. In some cases, the debtor and the creditor have reached an agreement by which the debtor voluntarily surrenders his or her home to the creditor. When this happens, most debtor attorneys will negotiate with the creditor to be certain that any loan deficiency in existence due to inadequate value of the collateral is not pursued against the debtor. Even though there is an agreement between the debtor and the creditor regarding the Automatic Stay, the creditor may not resume any collection, repossession, or foreclosure procedures until the bankruptcy court grants the creditor relief. This is a testament to just how powerful the protection of the Automatic Stay is to the debtor.

In other cases, the creditor may have reason to believe that the collateral (often a home) is no longer protected by hazard insurance due to the debtor's lack of payment, or the debtor, for whatever reason, has simply stopped making payments in his or her Chapter 13 plan toward the mortgage. The creditor may also be able to convince the court to lift the Automatic stay if it can show that the debtor has no equity in the home. This type of showing can be compelling to the court simply because if no equity exists, the collateral serves no purpose in the bankruptcy case because there is nothing to distribute to the unsecured creditors and no homestead exemption the debtor can claim. In any event, the creditor may not resume a foreclosure or repossession until its motion for relief from the Automatic Stay is lifted.

CREDITOR STRATEGIES AND THE AUTOMATIC STAY

Although the Automatic Stay functions as an injunction against creditor collection activity of the debtor's property, knowledge of the exceptions to the Automatic Stay is important. If the Automatic Stay does not prohibit a certain activity, a lift is not necessary.

If the Automatic Stay does apply, the creditor is required to file a motion with the court to lift it. A parent who is owed child support from the debtor is a good example of a creditor who may file a motion to lift the Automatic Stay. The grounds for relief must be clearly stated in the motion. The motion should also include affidavits that show cause for lifting the Automatic Stay and is served on the debtor and his or her attorney. A motion should also be filed in cases when the parties have stipulated to lifting the Automatic Stay.

The Automatic Stay terminates 30 days after the filing and service of the motion for relief from the Automatic Stay unless the bankruptcy court issues an order sustaining the stay. If there is no objection or action on behalf of the debtor, the creditor is now free to pursue collection efforts against the collateral in secured property. If a preliminary hearing is held on the motion to lift the stay, the bankruptcy court judge will decide whether a reasonable likelihood exists that the debtor could win on the merits of the motion. If the debtor cannot prove his or her case, the judge will grant the creditors relief from the Automatic Stay.

Ex parte relief may be obtained when a secured creditor believes it will suffer irreparable damage due to the debtor's fraud, waste, possible destruction of collateral, or failure to insure the collateral properly. Ex parte relief means that the creditor has rushed to the bankruptcy court on an emergency basis to obtain relief from the court without notice to the debtor.

Executory Contracts and Unexpired Leases

Bankruptcy Code 11 U.S.C. § 3659(a) empowers the trustee either to affirm or reject contracts and leases the debtor enters into that have not been completed. The generally accepted definition of an **executory contract** is one in which there has been insufficient or incomplete performance of the contract, thus rendering a material breach by either party. The trustee may deem it proper to reject a contract if he or she determines it is in the best interests of the debtor to do so. Such is the case with **unexpired leases** for real property, which comprise the largest number

executory contract
A contract under which insufficient or incomplete performance has occurred on either side of the contract.

unexpired lease
A lease that is still in effect.

of contracts that bankruptcy trustees reject. An unexpired lease is a lease that is still in effect. Examples of an unexpired lease include time share contracts or leases, residential leases and agreements, and leases of real estate to harvest timber, minerals, or oil.

The bankruptcy court treats the rejected contract as if it were breached prior to filing the petition, and any remaining balance owed to the other contracting party, e.g., the lessor, will be treated as a general unsecured claim in the bankruptcy case.

If, on the other hand, the debtor had engaged in a pre-petition contract with a vendor for the purchase of a commodity that increased in value exponentially since the date of the contract, the trustee will likely affirm that contract because the debtor could stand to profit from that contract going forward. This is often the case with business debtors. It is important to note that the trustee, unless granted an extension, has 60 days beyond the filing of the petition to make a decision whether to affirm or reject executory contracts, or the court will assume them to be rejected.

Reaffirmation Agreements

reaffirmation agreement
A contract between the debtor and creditor by which the debtor reassumes the responsibility of paying off the loan.

A debtor may strike an agreement with a creditor to waive the discharge of the debt in a bankruptcy proceeding. This is known as a **reaffirmation agreement**, and authority for such an agreement is found in 11 U.S.C. § 524(c). For example, Marian files for bankruptcy, and one of her debts is a car loan. Although the debt is listed on her bankruptcy petition, she does not want it to be discharged. Instead, she wants to keep her car by continuing her monthly payments. To achieve her objective, Marian may enter a reaffirmation agreement with the creditor before the discharge is entered. Marian and her creditor must complete and sign a Form 240A Reaffirmation Agreement, which includes the nature of the debt, value of the collateral, and reason for reaffirmation. Form 240 must also be accompanied by a reaffirmation cover sheet. The debtor and creditor have to appear before a bankruptcy judge who determines whether it is in the best interest of the debtor to reaffirm the debt. The debtor has the right to rescind the reaffirmation agreement at any time prior to the entry of her discharge or within 60 days after the reaffirmation agreement is filed with the court, whichever occurs later. Reaffirmation agreements are voluntary, and not all creditors are amenable to this arrangement.

Bankruptcy clients should carefully consider the ramifications of entering into a reaffirmation agreement, especially if the debtor is unable to make good on the debt after the agreement is approved. A creditor who enters into a reaffirmation agreement retains all of its legal and equitable rights to collect the debt and may pursue the debtor in satisfaction of this obligation.

Remember Norma from the beginning of the chapter? She started her own jewelry business that really took off by its second year in business. By the third year, things started getting a little shaky for Norma's business. She had many delinquent accounts because many of her customers became unable to pay for one reason or another. The example at the beginning of the chapter helps illustrate that not all creditors are billion-dollar giants; many creditors are small businesses struggling for success in a tough economy. They can also be a single parent waiting for child support from the noncustodial parent.

Unfortunately for Norma, it appears that several of her clients have filed for bankruptcy. She knows this because, as a creditor, she is entitled to notice of her debtor's bankruptcy filings. Norma will then have a chance to file a Proof of Claim with the bankruptcy court. After reading this chapter, you might have surmised that Norma's business, in this case, would qualify as an unsecured nonpriority creditor. She will likely have a very difficult time collecting any money from her bankruptcy-protected clients. Even more unfortunate is the possibility that Norma's business might need to file bankruptcy as well.

CHAPTER **SUMMARY**

The paralegal working for an attorney who handles bankruptcy matters encounters several types of creditors. They include the secured creditor, the unsecured priority creditor, and the unsecured nonpriority creditor. It is the creditor's status that determines how the creditor is paid for debts owed. Secured creditors enjoy an exclusive category in the bankruptcy process. Their claims are provided with greater protection than are the claims of both types of unsecured creditors. This is so because the secured creditor's loan is protected by the value attached to a specific article of property the debtor owns or possesses.

The next genre of creditors is unsecured creditors. These are creditors that have loaned money to the debtor, but no security agreement is signed and no collateral is pledged by the debtor to secure the loan. Within the genre of unsecured creditors, there are two types: unsecured priority creditors and unsecured nonpriority creditors. Unsecured priority creditors are given priority over the unsecured nonpriority

creditors in liquidation or reorganization bankruptcy. Unsecured nonpriority creditors do not receive any priority treatment in a bankruptcy liquidation or reorganization. In fact, most general unsecured creditors receive no payment in a liquidation case. In a reorganization case, they receive some payment but are not entitled to receive payment in full as priority creditors are. All creditors listed in Schedules D, E, and F will receive a notification from the clerk of the court that the debtor has filed for bankruptcy.

According to 11 U.S.C. § 501, to be paid by the trustee in either a liquidation or reorganization bankruptcy, a creditor must file an Official Form B10 Proof of Claim with the bankruptcy court where the case is pending. Creditors do have the right, upon filing a motion for relief from Automatic Stay with the bankruptcy court and serving the debtor and the trustee with proper notice of the motion, to request relief from the Automatic Stay.

CONCEPT REVIEW AND REINFORCEMENT

KEY **TERMS**

collateral	motion for relief from	REO (real estate owned)
deed of Trust	Automatic Stay	properties
executory contract	priority creditor	secured creditor
foreclosure	Proof of Claim	unexpired lease
mortgage	reaffirmation agreement	unsecured creditor

REVIEWING **KEY CONCEPTS**

1. What are some of the advantages associated with an individual obtaining a secured loan versus an unsecured loan?
2. What are some of the reasons a secured creditor may seek relief from the Automatic Stay imposed by the court? Do only secured creditors have this right?
3. Explain the differences between foreclosure and repossession. In what ways are these two processes similar?
4. Provide examples of debt that would be classified as priority debt.
5. Why is it important for the debtor to relay a complete and accurate picture of his or her debt to the paralegal, the attorney, or both?

BUILDING YOUR PARALEGAL SKILLS

CASE FOR REVIEW

In Re Crites, 201 B.R. 277 (Bankr. D.Or. Sept. 26, 1996)

BUILDING A PROFESSIONAL PORTFOLIO

PORTFOLIO EXERCISES

1. You work for the law offices of Tammy Davis, LLC, and your firm represents the debtor Joe Smith. Smith is an individual debtor with primarily consumer debts. He is quite concerned about his low credit score and is afraid that filing bankruptcy under either Chapter 7 or Chapter 13 will drive his credit score even lower than it is. Based on what you have learned from reading this chapter and any outside research, draft a letter to the client on behalf of Attorney Davis, explaining how his credit score may be affected by filing for bankruptcy. Be sure your letter outlines the steps that Mr. Smith can take to improve his credit score after his case is complete or no longer subject to bankruptcy court proceedings. Be sure to mention the length of time his credit rating or credit score will be affected.

2. You work for the same firm as in the prior exercise. This time, your firm represents Neighborhood Loan Company, LLC, a moderately sized mortgage company. Neighborhood just had a consultation with your boss, Tammy Davis, Esq., regarding several notices it received indicating that some of its borrowers have filed for Chapter 7 bankruptcy. Attorney Davis would like you to prepare a motion for relief from automatic stay against one of Neighborhood's borrowers. Your attorney wants to file this motion soon so that Neighborhood can continue its foreclosure action against this particular borrower as soon as possible. The most significant factor in this case is that there is no equity in this particular borrower's home. The name of the case is *In Re Jones,* and it is pending in your local bankruptcy court.

chapter 10

VOIDABLE PREFERENCES AND FRAUDULENT TRANSFERS

After losing her job, Jane Schooner has been unable to pay thousands of dollars in overdue doctor bills. She plans to file for bankruptcy within the next few months. Ms. Schooner decides to repay the $1,500 loan she received from her father six months ago when she was low on cash. Jane paid off the mortgage on her home several years ago after receiving a large cash award from a personal injury case.

Jane heard a rumor that when she files bankruptcy, she may lose her home to help someone called the bankruptcy trustee pay her creditors. The thought of her home falling into the hands of strangers and being auctioned off to pay her bills is too devastating for her to think about. Jane decides that she will transfer her home, valued at $250,000, by way of a quitclaim deed to her younger sister for "one dollar and all my love and affection." She does this just months before filing bankruptcy. After all, this is Jane's home, and she should be able to do what she wants to do with it, correct?

Jane has no ill will toward the bankruptcy court or this person called the trustee; she just wants to keep the home in the family. After Jane files for bankruptcy and attends the first meeting of the creditors, she is stunned to learn that her father and sister are being sued by the trustee who is demanding that they turn the money and the house over to him! Can the trustee get away with this? Continue reading to find out.

LEARNING OBJECTIVES

After studying this chapter, you should be able to:

1. Recognize the power the Bankruptcy Code has with respect to pre-petition and postpetition transfers the debtor makes.

2. Summarize the right that the trustee has to reverse any unlawful transfer of property the debtor makes.

3. Describe the differences between preferences and fraudulent transfers.

4. Explain the process by which the trustee may pursue the transferee for the property or money that was transferred unlawfully.

5. Identify the defenses a transferee may assert against the trustee in a voidable transfer action.

Introduction

The Bankruptcy Code is a very powerful tool for debtors and creditors alike. Often, many of us only think of the Bankruptcy Code in terms of its ability to protect the debtor. The power of the code to stop creditors' collection efforts against a debtor, and its potential to cancel most of the debtor's debt, seems to get the most attention. Many do not realize its power to protect the creditors as well. The Bankruptcy Code is all about maintaining equity between the debtor and his or her creditors. It is also designed to treat creditors in the same category, such as general unsecured creditors, fairly. When a person files for bankruptcy, the code's power to preserve all of the parties' rights goes into effect.

This section discusses the power the Bankruptcy Code has to allow the trustee to bring an action to recover property the debtor may have unlawfully transferred either before or shortly after filing for bankruptcy. We define and discuss the different types of **voidable transfers** a debtor may make and why these transfers are voidable. In addition, we review the process by which the trustee goes about recovering a voidable transfer from a transferee. The types of voidable transfers discussed are known as **voidable preferences** and **fraudulent conveyance**. The paralegal's role with regard to voidable transfers and voidable transfer actions the trustee brings will be reviewed.

Preferences

A **voidable preference** occurs when a debtor, within 90 days of filing for bankruptcy, makes a payment or transfers property to one of his or her creditors in repayment of a debt. The bankruptcy code does not provide a definition for property. The bankruptcy and trial courts apply what seems to be the generally accepted definition of property: that which the debtor has an interest in or control of. This includes money as well as personal items and real estate. The first step in determining whether a preference exists is whether the property the debtor transferred would have been part of the bankruptcy estate if the debtor had not transferred it. Would that property have been available to the trustee to liquidate and proportionally distribute to the creditors if the transfer never occurred?

With regard to voidable preferences, it does not matter what the debtor's intentions were. This type of transfer can be voided even if it was an innocent transfer that the debtor made out of the kindness of his or her heart. The trustee may reverse an **involuntary transfer** if it occurred within 90 days of when the debtor filed for bankruptcy. Examples of involuntary transfers include repossessions, liens, or garnishments against the debtor.

Consider John Dogooder, an individual who is in arrears on his mortgage payments, credit card payments, and $1,200 to his doctor. He also owes ACME Painting $1,000 for a job ACME completed at his home the previous year. John has not filed for bankruptcy yet. John won a couple of thousand dollars after playing a scratch-off ticket from his state's lottery. He remembers how the owner of ACME Painting would always complain about how business was slow. He feels sorry for his painter, and a month and a half prior to filing for bankruptcy, John Dogooder paid off his balance to ACME Painting. After John files for bankruptcy and the initial meeting of the creditors is held, the trustee brings an action against ACME Painting to recover the $1,000, claiming that it was a voidable preference.

In this example, the payment that John Dogooder made to ACME Painting is considered a voidable preference because John paid ACME within 90 days of filing for bankruptcy. The money he paid to ACME should have been part of the bankruptcy estate and available to all of John's creditors to share proportionally. The litmus test in this situation seems to be whether the preferred creditor received more than it would have if the money had been available to all the creditors. In this case, all John's creditors were general unsecured creditors. As such, ACME Painting would have qualified as an unsecured creditor and surely

voidable preference or voidable transfer
A transfer the debtor makes to a creditor prior to filing for bankruptcy. Here, the debtor pays a preferred or favored creditor in full, and the rest of the creditors must divide a pro rata share after a bankruptcy case has been filed.

fraudulent conveyance
A transfer of assets to a third party for the purpose of preventing creditors from satisfying their claims.

involuntary transfer
A transfer that is not within the debtor's control, such as repossessions, liens, or garnishments against the debtor, that the trustee may reverse if it occurred within 90 days of when the debtor filed for bankruptcy.

would not have received the full $1,000 it was owed if the estate assets were distributed properly.

The purpose of the Bankruptcy Code's power to void preferences does not stem from an intention to punish any single creditor—or the debtor, for that matter. The policy behind the power of the Bankruptcy Code to void preferences serves, once again, to promote fairness among creditors in the same category and to prevent a creditor from aggressively pursuing the debtor once it fears a debtor may be filing for bankruptcy protection soon.

11 U.S.C. § 547 allows the trustee to void any such transaction occurring within the ninety day period pre-petition, for any creditor so long as the following elements are present. According to 11 U.S.C. § 547(b):

(b) Except as provided in subsections (c) and (i) of this section, the trustee may avoid any transfer of an interest of the debtor in property—

(1) to or for the benefit of a creditor;

(2) for or on account of an antecedent debt owed by the debtor before such transfer was made;

(3) made while the debtor was insolvent;

(4) made—

   (A) on or within 90 days before the date of the filing of the petition; or

   (B) between ninety days and one year before the date of the filing of the petition, if such creditor at the time of such transfer was an insider; and

(5) that enables such creditor to receive more than such creditor would receive if—

   (A) the case were a case under chapter 7 of this title;

   (B) the transfer had not been made; and

   (C) such creditor received payment of such debt to the extent provided by the provisions of this title.

Insiders

The trustee may void a transfer to a creditor up to one year pre-petition if the creditor qualifies as an **insider**. An insider is a person or entity that has a close relationship to the debtor. In the case of an individual debtor, an aunt, mother, brother, or father may be considered an insider. In the case of a corporate debtor, one or more of the corporation's directors, officers, or secretaries may qualify as an insider. The reason for the longer back period of one year pre-petition seems to be related to the amount of control the insider has over the debtor. This is in contrast to a typical creditor, such as a credit card company, which is dealing with the debtor from a distance. As such, it is presumed that the credit card company would not have the same degree of influence over the debtor as an insider would.

insider
A person or entity that has a close relationship to the debtor.

Creditors' Affirmative Defenses

A creditor may successfully defend itself against a trustee seeking to void a particular transfer if it can prove one of the following statutory defenses. Allowable amounts for preferential transfers as of 2014 are $600.00 or less for consumer cases and $5,000.00 for business cases and are adjusted annually for inflation. The following defenses are provided by 11 U.S.C. § 547(c) and state that a trustee may be unsuccessful in his or her attempts to avoid a transfer if one of the following defenses can be proven by the transferee:

contemporaneous exchange
A transfer in which the debtor received sufficient new value from the creditor in return for the exchange.

1. The transfer involved a **contemporaneous exchange** by which the debtor received sufficient new value from the creditor in return for the exchange. This means that the debtor received something of value in exchange for money.
2. The transfer was made during the ordinary course of business between the debtor and the creditor.

enabling loan
A loan by which a creditor records a security instrument for property it provided to the debtor.

3. The transfer resulted in an **enabling loan** by which a creditor records a security instrument for property it provided to the debtor.
4. The transfer resulted in subsequent new value provided to the debtor in exchange for a payment made by the debtor.
5. The transfer resulted in a floating inventory lien by which the creditor acquires a lien against all current and subsequent inventory of the debtor, which allows the debtor to maintain its business. This is a defense only to the extent that the creditor does not acquire a better position—more inventory securing the loan—after the debtor files his or her petition.

statutory lien
A lien created by operation of law such as a mechanic's lien or a tax lien.

6. The transfer resulted in a **statutory lien** such as a mechanic's lien or a tax lien.
7. The transfer was for the payment of alimony or child support.
8. The transfer or transfers were by an individual with consumer debt that resulted in a value less than $600.
9. The transfer, for a debtor that does not have primarily consumer debt, totaled less than $5,000.

In the following case, the Chapter 7 trustee filed a voidable preference action against one of the debtor's creditors. The creditor asserted that the alleged preferred payments that the debtor made were made in the ordinary course of business. The United States Court of Appeals from the Fifth Circuit disagreed.

CASE **10.1** In the Matter of Marvin E. Moye, Debtor.

Lowell T. Cage, Appellee, (Chapter 7 Trustee)
v.
Hardy Rawls Enterprises, L.L.C., Appellant. (Creditor)

486 Fed. Appx. 485 (2012)
United States Court of Appeals, Fifth Circuit.

Background

After creditor filed proof of claim against bankruptcy estate of debtors who were engaged in the used-car business, Chapter 7 bankruptcy trustee filed complaint against creditor to recover alleged preferential transfers by debtors. Both parties moved for summary judgment. The bankruptcy court ruled in favor of the trustee, and the United States District Court for the Southern District of Texas affirmed. Creditor appealed.

Holding

The Court of Appeals held that payments made to creditor were not made in the ordinary course of business and thus constituted avoidable preferences.

Affirmed.

...

Payments made by Chapter 7 debtors who were engaged in the used-car business to floor plan lender after they began to experience financial difficulties were not made in the "ordinary course of business" and thus constituted avoidable preferences. 11 U.S.C.A. § 547.

Brian Bakke Kilpatrick, Esq., Theresa D. Mobley, Cage, Hill & Niehaus, L.L.P., Houston, TX, for Appellee.

Ronald D. Hinds, Coppell, TX, for Appellant.

Appeal from the United States District Court for the Southern District of Texas (Houston) (4:10–CV–956).

Before WIENER, ELROD, and SOUTHWICK, Circuit Judges.

I. Facts and Proceedings

A. Background

In conducting their used car business, Debtors' purchases of automobiles for resale were financed by floor plan lenders, including Automotive Finance Corporation ("AFC"), Dealer Service Corporation ("DSC"), and HRE. In 2003, Debtors began to finance their retail sales of cars to customers in-house. In so doing, Debtors entered into installment contracts with their customers, creating liens on the vehicles in question and requiring payments of principal and interest at rates that averaged between 21 and 23 percent per annum. Debtors then sold assemblages or "pools" of such installment contracts to "pool participants" pursuant to master agreements. Debtors would collect customers' monthly payments and remit them to pool participants. The purchase prices for such pools equaled the aggregate principal balances on the retail customers' loans, so that the pool participants would receive principal, interest, and finance charges pursuant to the installment contracts. In the master agreements, Debtors guaranteed that they would replace installment contracts on which customers had defaulted with new installment contracts added to the pool. All together, the pool participants invested a total of approximately $9.7 million with the Debtors.

A review of Debtors' business and accounting records by the Trustee reveals that when such defaults occurred, Debtors would continue to pay the scheduled monthly installments to the pool participants, even though payments from defaulting customers were no longer being received. The Trustee's review also shows that, when such defaults caused Debtors to receive accelerated payments or to repossess vehicles, Debtors retained those payments and any revenue from resale, rather than applying such receipts to the pool participants' balances. That review also demonstrates that virtually all of the funds received by Debtors, whether from customers, floor plan lenders, or pool participants, were commingled without distinction in Debtors' bank accounts.

When they began to experience financial difficulties in June and July 2007, Debtors defaulted on payments owed to pool participants. Additionally, when the MRB Group, the largest group of pool participants, learned that about 30% of its pool's installment contracts were no longer secured because Debtors had repossessed and resold the vehicles, the MRB Group demanded an accounting from Debtors. As a result, Debtors and the MRB Group entered into a note sale agreement in August 2007, under which Debtors were required to sell the active installment contracts in the MRB Group's pool and deposit the proceeds in a trust account.

(Continued)

(Continued)

Debtors also obtained the consent of some of the other pool participants to sell the active installment contracts in their pools to a third party.

Debtors then reached an agreement with Mid–Atlantic Finance Co. Inc. under which Mid–Atlantic purchased active installment contracts of each customer's outstanding principal balance at a discounted price of 83 cents on the dollar. Under that agreement, Mid–Atlantic made payments to Debtors on August 17, September 4, September 27, and October 18, 2007 totaling $1.927 million. Except for funds designated for the MRB Group, payments received from Mid–Atlantic were deposited by Debtors into their general operating bank accounts.

Central to the preference issue in this case, debtors made eight payments to HRE between July 27 and October 15, 2007, totaling approximately $146,712.

B. Proceedings

The involuntary Chapter 7 bankruptcy petition against JMW was filed on October 31, 2007, and the Moyes filed a voluntary Chapter 7 petition a week later. For these cases, which are being administered jointly, the bankruptcy court appointed Cage to serve as Trustee and authorized his continued operation of the business for the benefit of the estate.

HRE filed a proof of claim for $1,756,012, of which $1,556,012 was designated as secured. The bankruptcy court disallowed HRE's claim after determining that it lacks a security interest in Debtors' inventory because it had failed to file UCC financing statements to perfect such interests. The district court affirmed that ruling on appeal, as did we.

. . .

In July of 2009, the Trustee filed a complaint against HRE to recover $143,167.37 of alleged preferential transfers by Debtors. The Trustee filed a motion for summary judgment on this claim, but the bankruptcy court denied it, concluding that a genuine issue of fact existed as to HRE's affirmative defense that the transfers in question had been made in the ordinary course of business. The bankruptcy court then recommended that the reference of the adversary proceeding be withdrawn and that the case proceed in the district court because a jury trial had been demanded.

After the district court took over the case, the Trustee and HRE filed opposing motions for summary judgment. In largely granting the Trustee's motion and denying HRE's motion, the district court ruled that the Trustee had proved that all but one of the payments in question were avoidable preferences and that HRE had failed to prove its affirmative defenses of "ordinary course of business" and "earmarking." The one payment that the district court held was not an avoidable preference was that of July 27, 2007, because it had occurred more than 90 days before the filing dates of the bankruptcy petitions, and HRE was not an insider. HRE timely appealed.

Fraudulent Transfers

The next type of transfer is made by the debtor with the actual or constructive intent to defraud his or her creditors. In other words, the debtor's intention with respect to the transfer is to prevent some or all of his or her creditors from receiving what they would have gotten if the transfer had not occurred. It is very difficult for a trustee to prove what the debtor's actual intent was with respect to a transfer. As such, the law allows the trustee to allege, by showing that certain criteria were present when the transfer was made, that the transfer was fraudulent and should be reversed. Consider Ms. Schooner from the beginning of the chapter. She conveyed her home to her sister for very little value and likely left herself with very little in the way of assets for the trustee to pay her creditors. Ms. Schooner did not seem to convey her house to her sister with the overt intention of defrauding her creditors. However, as we will discuss, the circumstances surrounding her transfer will likely be sufficient for the trustee to prove constructive fraud. If this is the case, the trustee may be successful with reversing the transfer Ms. Schooner made to her sister.

The trustee has the power, under 11 U.S.C § 548, to reverse a fraudulent transfer the debtor makes. According to 11 U.S.C. § 548(a):

(a) (1) The trustee may avoid any transfer (including any transfer to or for the benefit of an insider under an employment contract) of an interest of the debtor in property, or any obligation (including any obligation to or for the benefit of an insider under an employment contract) incurred by the debtor, that was made or incurred on or within 2 years before the date of the filing of the petition, if the debtor voluntarily or involuntarily

(A) made such transfer or incurred such obligation with actual intent to hinder, delay, or defraud any entity to which the debtor was or became, on or after the date that such transfer was made or such obligation was incurred, indebted; or

(B) (i) received less than a reasonably equivalent value in exchange for such transfer or obligation; and

(ii) (I) was insolvent on the date that such transfer was made or such obligation was incurred, or became insolvent as a result of such transfer or obligation;

(II) was engaged in business or a transaction, or was about to engage in business or a transaction, for which any property remaining with the debtor was an unreasonably small capital;

(III) intended to incur, or believed that the debtor would incur, debts that would be beyond the debtor's ability to pay as such debts matured; or

(IV) made such transfer to or for the benefit of an insider, or incurred such obligation to or for the benefit of an insider, under an employment contract and not in the ordinary course of business.

Actual Fraud

Under 11 U.S.C. § 548(a), as previously cited, a trustee can reverse a fraudulent transfer upon a showing that the debtor had the actual intent to defraud creditors as a result of the transfer. As mentioned earlier, this is often very difficult to prove. In a voidable transfer action or adversarial proceeding, to help prove **actual fraud**, the trustee may offer some of the following examples of circumstantial evidence.

actual fraud
A fraudulent transfer made within one year before the filing date of a bankruptcy petition and with the intent to hinder or defraud a creditor.

The court may make a finding of actual fraud if the trustee can show one or more of the following examples:

1. The transfer was made with little or no consideration.
2. The transfer was made to an insider with a particularly close relationship to the debtor.
3. The transfer was made in secret.
4. The transfer was made shortly before the debtor was named in a lawsuit by one or more of his or her creditors.
5. The transfer was made, and the debtor remained in control of the property after the transfer was made. (For example, the debtor transferred his house into his daughter's name shortly after incurring significant debt, and he regularly used the home or continued to live in it.)

The trustee must prove to the court that the debtor's actions with regard to the transfer or transfers were carried out with the intention to defraud the creditors. The transferee's role is irrelevant. Findings of actual fraud have been made when the trustee offered evidence showing that a debtor transferred assets shortly before filing for bankruptcy. Some examples include the transfer of title to real estate or personal property, such as a vehicle, just prior to filing the bankruptcy petition, with zero or little consideration received by the debtor or evidence that the debtor transferred assets in a bank account into another individual's name a week or so prior to filing the bankruptcy petition. To prove actual fraud, the evidence the trustee presents must persuade the court to find that no reasonable mind could conclude that the transfers were made for no other reason than to defraud the creditors.

Constructive Fraud

constructive fraud
A fraudulent transfer by which the debtor transfers assets for grossly inadequate consideration.

With **constructive fraud**, the trustee does not need to make a showing that the transfer of property by the debtor was done with the intent to defraud a creditor. The trustee must show that the transfer resulted in the debtor receiving nothing for the exchange or that the debtor received less than reasonable market value for the transferred asset.

According to 11 U.S.C. § 548(a)(1)(B):

The trustee may avoid any transfer (including any transfer to or for the benefit of an insider under an employment contract) of an interest of the debtor in property, or any obligation (including any obligation to or for the benefit of an insider under an employment contract) incurred by the debtor, that was made or incurred on or within 2 years before the date of the filing of the petition, if the debtor voluntarily or involuntarily—

...

(i) received less than a reasonably equivalent value in exchange for such transfer or obligation; and
(ii)   (I)   was insolvent on the date that such transfer was made or such obligation was incurred, or became insolvent as a result of such transfer or obligation;
        (II) was engaged in business or a transaction, or was about to engage in business or a transaction, for which any property remaining with the debtor was an unreasonably small capital;

(III) intended to incur, or believed that the debtor would incur, debts that would be beyond the debtor's ability to pay as such debts matured; or

(IV) made such transfer to or for the benefit of an insider, or incurred such obligation to or for the benefit of an insider, under an employment contract and not in the ordinary course of business.

As indicated in the preceding extract, after the transfer, the debtor must have been or will become unable to pay his or her debts because of the transfer. Problems could arise for the trustee when attempting to prove that the debtor received less than equivalent value for the transfer. In the case of Ms. Schooner at the beginning of the chapter, who transferred her house to her sister for "One dollar and love and affection," the trustee's burden of proof will be easy. However, many cases are not always this obvious. The courts have spoken to this issue and have held that "[I]n determining whether [the] debtor received 'reasonably equivalent value' in a transaction sought to be avoided under [the] Bankruptcy Code as constructively fraudulent, court should examine the totality of circumstances in order to determine whether the transaction conferred realizable commercial value to debtor that was reasonably equivalent to the realizable commercial value of the assets transferred; inquiry is to be performed from the vantage point of creditors rather than that of the debtor." See *Peltz v. Hatten*, 279 B.R. 710, 710, D.Del. 2002.

Postpetition Payments and Transfers

11 U.S.C. § 549 gives the trustee authority to void any transfer the debtor makes after he or she files for bankruptcy. The Bankruptcy Code requires the property transferred to belong to the bankruptcy estate. Such property includes "all legal or equitable interests of the debtor in property as of the commencement of the case." 11 U.S.C. § 541(a)(1). It also requires the transfer to be made postpetition and without the authority of the Bankruptcy Court. For example, consider the debtor who transfers his home, worth $300,000, to his brother for one dollar two weeks after filing his bankruptcy petition. The house is encumbered by a mortgage for $100,000. The debtor's brother pays off the mortgage. In an adversary proceeding, brought by the trustee, the sale of the home can be reversed, and the debtor's case will likely be dismissed.

If the debtor received authorization from the court prior to making a transfer, the transfer would not be voidable by the trustee. However, it must be noted that the debtor-defendant in a voidable transfer action would bear the burden of proof that he or she had the authority from the bankruptcy court to execute the transfer. In the case of a business debtor, any payments made in the ordinary course of business are not voidable. In the case of a real estate transfer, if the transferee can prove that he or she had no actual or constructive knowledge that the debtor-transferor filed for bankruptcy, the transferee may overcome the transfer. Further, the transferee would need to show that the property was purchased for fair market value.

Adversary Proceedings

As stated in earlier chapters, the trustee or creditor may initiate an **adversary proceeding**. 11 U.S.C. Sections 547, 548, and 549 authorize the trustee to bring an adversary proceeding against a debtor for preference, fraudulent conveyance, and postpetition transfer actions, respectively. By filing an adversary proceeding

adversary proceeding
A separate lawsuit filed within a bankruptcy case, which must be resolved by the judge before the case may proceed to discharge. An adversary proceeding in a bankruptcy case is treated much like a civil lawsuit would be treated.

against the debtor, the trustee may obtain the transferred property if the trustee can prove to the court that the transfer was made fraudulently. The burden of proof will fall on the trustee as the entity attempting to reverse a transfer or prevent the debtor from receiving his or her discharge.

An adversary proceeding in a bankruptcy case is treated much like a civil lawsuit. The party bringing the action is known as the plaintiff, and the party against whom the complaint is brought is referred to as the defendant. The plaintiff files a formal complaint with the court and has that complaint served on the defendant. The bankruptcy court maintains the case under its own separate docket number known as an **adversary number**. This unique adversary number will be listed just below the docket number for the main bankruptcy case in any pleading concerning the adversary proceeding. The adversary proceeding requires a significant amount of preparation by the attorney and paralegal prior to the hearing. Discovery, including interrogatories and depositions of both the debtor and other expert and fact witnesses, must be dealt with prior to the hearing.

Paralegals must be aware of the time limitations under which the trustee or creditors may have to bring an adversary proceeding. 11 U.S.C. § 547, 548, and 549 govern the following limitations for the following voidable transfer actions. For preference actions, an action may be brought for transfers the debtor made within 90 days before filing the petition and within one year before filing the petition for transfers made to insiders. An action to void a fraudulent conveyance may be brought for conveyances that occurred within two years before the debtor filed the petition, and postpetition actions may be brought so long as the transfer occurred after the debtor filed the petition.

Paralegal's Role With Voidable Transfers and Voidance Actions

The paralegal is on the front lines in a law firm, and he or she is usually the first to know just about anything that might affect a client and the attorneys in the firm. This is why it is of the utmost importance for the paralegal to know his or her respective role in handling a bankruptcy case. The paralegal must also have a working knowledge of the law and be able to issue-spot while performing the usual tasks such as the initial intake and assisting the client with the petition, schedules, and other forms necessary for filing the case.

In most law firms, the paralegal will be spending the most time with the client during the initial phases of preparing for bankruptcy filing. This is true prior to and following the consultation the client may have with the attorney regarding how or under which chapter of the Bankruptcy Code his or her case should proceed. While the paralegal is assisting the client with the petition, schedules, and research on the required credit counseling, the debtor may bombard him or her with numerous questions. A debtor might ask, "I heard from my friend Susie that I could lose my house and my snowmobile during the bankruptcy. She recommended that I just transfer my house to her for a dollar and sell her my snowmobile for 50 dollars. She will hold on to my snowmobile until the bankruptcy case is over, and she will let me live in the house while the bankruptcy case is pending. That's okay, right?"

After reading this chapter, we hope that you are aware that these two transfers are clearly inadvisable. You should understand that those transfers may very well be voided at best. At worst, the client could lose the right to

adversary number

A separate docket number the bankruptcy court assigns to an adversary proceeding. This number is listed below the docket number for the main bankruptcy case.

exempt any value in her home and risk dismissal of her entire case. The paralegal may also notice, in the schedules and statement of financial affairs, potential voidable transfer issues.

The paralegal should not give any advice to the debtor about how to proceed because this would constitute the unauthorized practice of law. However, the paralegal should advise the client that he or she should not make any decisions on any transfer of property until speaking with the attorney. The paralegal should immediately inform his or her supervising attorney of any information the client shares that might have to do with a fraudulent transfer.

If the debtor is named as a defendant in a voidable transfer or, as it is sometimes referred to, an adversarial proceeding, the paralegal's role is also vital. When an adversarial proceeding is filed against the debtor, by either a creditor or the trustee, the paralegal will be at the center of all the action and will likely be involved in:

- Investigating the factual and legal allegations against the debtor.
- Drafting various pleadings, including communicating with and drafting subpoenas of factual and expert witnesses.
- Managing the adversarial proceeding docket.
- Reviewing documents to be presented at trial.
- Assisting with both reviewing and responding to discovery requests.
- Drafting and effecting service of discovery requests.
- Assisting the attorney in preparing the debtor for depositions.
- Attending and taking careful notes at depositions.
- Assisting attorneys at trial with evidence and presentation software.

Recall Ms. Schooner from the beginning of the chapter. She conveyed her home to her sister for very little value and likely left herself with very little in the way of assets for the trustee to pay her creditors. Although Ms. Schooner probably did not convey her house to her sister with the overt intention of defrauding her creditors, as you now know, the circumstances surrounding this transfer may be sufficient for the trustee to prove constructive fraud. If this is the case, the trustee will likely be successful in reversing the transfer Ms. Schooner made to her sister. The $1,500 loan Ms. Schooner repaid to her father six months prior to filing bankruptcy may also be reversed.

CHAPTER **SUMMARY**

The bankruptcy code helps maintain equity between the debtor and the creditors. It is designed to treat creditors in the same category, such as general unsecured creditors, fairly. After the debtor files for bankruptcy, the code's power to preserve all the parties' rights goes into effect. A voidable preference occurs when a debtor, within 90 days of filing for bankruptcy, makes a payment or transfers property to one of his or her creditors in repayment of a debt. With regard to a voidable preference, the debtor's intentions do not matter. The trustee can even reverse an involuntary transfer, such as a repossession, garnishment, or lien, if it occurred within 90 days of the bankruptcy filing.

The trustee may void a transfer to a creditor up to one year pre-petition if the creditor qualifies as an insider. An insider is a person or entity that has a close relationship to the debtor. The longer reach-back period for insiders correlates to the amount of control the insider likely had over the debtor. This is in contrast to a typical creditor, such as a credit card company, that is dealing with the debtor from a distance. A creditor may successfully defend itself against a trustee seeking to void a particular transfer if it can prove that, among others,

- The transfer involved a contemporaneous exchange whereby the debtor received sufficient new value from the creditor.
- It was made during the ordinary course of business between the debtor and the creditor.

- It resulted in an enabling loan in which a creditor records a security instrument for property it provided to the debtor.
- It resulted in subsequent new value to the debtor in exchange for a payment the debtor made.
- It resulted in a statutory lien such as a mechanic's lien or a tax lien.
- The transfer was for the payment of alimony or child support.

A fraudulent transfer is made when the debtor does so with the actual or constructive intent to defraud his or her creditors. The debtor's intention with respect to the transfer is to prevent some or all of his or her creditors from receiving what they would have gotten if the transfer had not occurred.

Fraudulent transfers can be categorized into actual fraud and constructive fraud. Actual fraud requires proof that the debtor had the actual intent to defraud creditors as a result of the transfer. Constructive fraud requires proof that the debtor received either nothing or less than reasonable market value for the transferred asset. A creditor or the trustee may bring an adversarial proceeding against the debtor to reverse a transfer.

An adversary proceeding in a bankruptcy case is treated much like a civil lawsuit. The party bringing the action is known as the plaintiff, and the party against whom the complaint is brought is referred to as the defendant. The plaintiff files a formal complaint with the court and has that complaint served on the defendant. The bankruptcy court maintains the case under its own separate docket number known as an adversary number. Any pleading concerning the adversary proceeding will list this unique adversary number just below the docket number for the main bankruptcy case. The paralegal's role in both recognizing and bringing potential problems with fraudulent transfers to the attorney's attention is vital. The paralegal also plays a vital role in assisting the attorney at adversarial proceedings.

CONCEPT REVIEW AND REINFORCEMENT

KEY TERMS

actual fraud	contemporaneous exchange	involuntary transfer
adversary number	enabling loan	statutory lien
adversary proceeding	fraudulent conveyance	voidable preferences or voidable
constructive fraud	insider	transfer

REVIEWING KEY CONCEPTS

1. Define and discuss the different types of voidable transfers a debtor may make. Why are these transfers voidable?
2. Explain the difference between actual fraud and constructive fraud.
3. What is an insider? Why are transfers the debtor makes to insiders treated differently from other types of transfers?
4. Describe fully what an adversarial proceeding is and what it involves. Who usually brings this type of action?
5. Describe the paralegal's role in adversarial proceedings and in recognizing possible fraudulent transfers.
6. What statutory limitations are imposed on preferences, fraudulent transfers, and postpetition transfers, respectively?

BUILDING YOUR PARALEGAL SKILLS

CASE FOR BRIEFING

In Re Meyer, 244 F.3d 352, CASE NO. 98-1534 C.A.4 (Va.), 2001

BUILDING A PROFESSIONAL PORTFOLIO

PORTFOLIO **EXERCISE**

You work for the law offices of Robert Davis, LLC, and your firm represents the debtor John Smith. John Smith is an individual debtor with primarily consumer debts. You have been working closely with the debtor by helping him fill out his petition and schedules. The debtor informed you that after speaking with his brother-in-law yesterday at a weekend gathering, he has decided to transfer his primary residence to his sister, Cleopatra Smith, for one dollar. He is very frightened that he will lose his home to the bankruptcy court and cannot bear the thought. His plan is to continue living at the residence, but it will be in his sister's name because he feels this will shield the home from his creditors.

After reading the foregoing chapter, you have learned that you should warn the debtor to refrain from making any transfers until he speaks with the attorney. Attorney Davis has asked you to draft a letter to the client on Attorney Davis's behalf, explaining all the potential consequences the debtor may face if he transfers his house to his sister for one dollar.

chapter 11

DISMISSAL, CONVERSION, AND CLOSING A BANKRUPTCY

LEARNING OBJECTIVES

After studying this chapter, you should be able to:

1. Recognize the effects of a dismissal in a bankruptcy case.

2. Explain the difference between a voluntary dismissal and an involuntary dismissal.

3. Identify the reasons for converting a bankruptcy case from one chapter to another.

4. Define a closed bankruptcy.

5. Understand the circumstances that can result in reopening a bankruptcy case.

Huy Nguyen, through his attorney, recently filed for Chapter 7 bankruptcy. Financially strained by credit card debt, car payments, living expenses, and the debt on his student loans, he just could not meet his obligations, especially on his low wage from his family's landscaping business. Huy was very pleased to hear that his income level was low enough to qualify for a Chapter 7 liquidation. A couple of months into his bankruptcy case, Huy received a promotion at work, which increased his annual income. He is wondering how his new income will affect his bankruptcy case. He really wants his debts to be wiped clean through Chapter 7 and be able to start over again. Should Huy tell his attorney about his increased income? How might his new income affect his Chapter 7 case? Will the bankruptcy court force Huy into a Chapter 13 case? If Huy is not honest with his attorney regarding his new earnings, could he risk his case being dismissed altogether? Read on and find out.

Introduction

The average person might be under the impression that a bankruptcy case terminates when the bankruptcy court discharges a debtor's obligations. However, there may be some twists and turns along the way. Some cases are dismissed, which is the equivalent of having the case thrown out of court. Others are converted when the bankruptcy judge waves a magic gavel and transforms the filing status of a case from one chapter to another. All cases, whether dismissed, converted, or discharged, eventually end and are closed in the eyes of the bankruptcy court. Even then, circumstances can exist that necessitate reopening the bankruptcy case so the court can take a second look.

Introduction to Bankruptcy Dismissals

A bankruptcy **dismissal** occurs when the bankruptcy court ceases administration of the case and no longer has jurisdiction over the matter, including any adversary proceedings that other parties have filed. In simple terms, a dismissal means that the debtor's case has been thrown out of court. The debtor's obligations are not discharged, the Automatic Stay terminates, and creditors are now free to pursue any legal collection efforts. A debtor, creditor, trustee, or other party in interest may seek a dismissal. Grounds for dismissal for each bankruptcy chapter are found in the following Bankruptcy Code sections:

- Chapter 7 - 11 U.S.C. § 707
- Chapter 11 - 11 U.S.C. § 1112
- Chapter 13 - 11 U.S.C. § 1307

dismissal
The bankruptcy court has closed the case, and the debtor does not obtain the benefit of a fresh start. The debtor's obligations are still due, and the court will take no further action on the case.

When a dismissal has been granted, any money or property that the trustee recovered for the benefit of the bankruptcy estate, as well as any funds collected for distribution to creditors that had not been disbursed at the time of the dismissal, are returned to the debtor.

Maintaining a good docketing system that is regularly updated is one of the best ways a paralegal can help bankruptcy clients avoid dismissals. Proper calendar maintenance makes it easier for law offices to monitor multiple cases and send reminders to clients regarding the fulfillment of their obligations during the course of the bankruptcy case.

CONSEQUENCES OF A BANKRUPTCY DISMISSAL

After the bankruptcy case is dismissed, the court no longer has any jurisdiction over the debtor, and the trustee is relieved of his or her duties. The dismissal, however, is not without its consequences for the debtor.

- The debtor loses the immediate protection of the Automatic Stay. Creditors are now free to pursue any legal actions against the debtor such as collections, foreclosures, and repossessions.
- The required payments under Chapter 13 repayment plan cease.
- The debtor now owes the original obligation to creditors. In a Chapter 13 case, the amount due to creditors is reduced according to any payments made while the Chapter 13 plan was in effect.
- The bankruptcy filing remains on the debtor's credit report and will affect the debtor's credit score. The Fair Credit Reporting Act states that a bankruptcy remains on the debtor's credit report for ten years.
- Automatic Stay protection may be limited if the debtor files subsequent bankruptcies and is considered a serial filer.

VOLUNTARY DISMISSAL

Bankruptcy dismissals are either voluntary or involuntary. In a **voluntary dismissal**, the debtor decides not to pursue the bankruptcy case and consents to its dismissal. The debtor may want to dismiss the case voluntarily when he or she finds new employment and now can pay creditors, reaches a settlement with creditors, or finds that the court has determined that some or all of the obligations are not dischargeable. A Chapter 13 debtor may easily seek a voluntary dismissal by

voluntary dismissal
When the debtor decides not to pursue the bankruptcy case and consents to its dismissal.

simply filing a form with the court, but the bankruptcy court judge must grant a dismissal of a Chapter 7 bankruptcy.

Debtors who have filed for bankruptcy under Chapter 7 and Chapter 11, or under a chapter converted from a Chapter 7 or Chapter 11, may seek a voluntary dismissal of their case but must show *cause* for the dismissal. This requirement is meant to discourage debtors from abusing the bankruptcy system. For example, some debtors faced with foreclosure might file bankruptcy to stop the foreclosure proceedings with the Automatic Stay. Debtors would then ask the court for a dismissal, which would require the creditor to restart the foreclosure proceedings. This would prolong the creditors' efforts to foreclose on the property and extend the time the debtor could remain in the home. Other examples of *cause* in a voluntary bankruptcy case include situations when the debtor:

- Determines that the bankruptcy petition was filed in error.
- Determines that the principal debt he or she sought to discharge is not dischargeable.
- Obtains employment that enables him or her to pay obligations.
- Cannot make the scheduled payments under a Chapter 13 repayment plan.

INVOLUNTARY DISMISSAL

involuntary dismissal
A dismissal the bankruptcy court judge initiates, acting on its own, or by motion of the U.S. trustee.

sua sponte
An action a court takes on its own motion.

An **involuntary dismissal** is initiated by the bankruptcy court judge acting **sua sponte** (on its own) or by the U.S. trustee. Creditors may also pursue an involuntary dismissal so that they will be free to pursue their legal remedies against the debtor without the constraints of the Automatic Stay.

An **involuntary dismissal** is typically initiated when the debtor has failed to comply with the requirements of the Bankruptcy Code or Federal Rules of Bankruptcy Procedure. In some circumstances, the bankruptcy court judge may give the debtor advance notice of the dismissal, allowing the debtor to cure the defect. This is not always the case, so compliance is paramount. The U.S. trustee may also file a motion to dismiss the debtor's case to give the debtor notice and an opportunity to object. Examples of actions that would result in an involuntary dismissal include cases when the debtor has failed to:

- Attend the 341 hearing
- File a Chapter 11 plan in a timely fashion
- File monthly financial statements (Chapter 11 cases)
- File tax returns over the previous four years
- File the proper documents
- Make payments under a repayment plan (Chapter 13 cases)
- Meet deadlines
- Participate in the required credit counseling and debt management courses
- Pay court fees or charges

DISMISSAL OF CHAPTER 7 CASES

Under 11 U.S.C. § 707(a), a Chapter 7 liquidation case may be dismissed for cause after notice is sent to all interested parties and a hearing takes place. Causes for dismissing a Chapter 7 include the following.

- Failure to file schedules pursuant to 11 U.S.C. § 521
- Failure to file tax returns
- Failure to meet the Means Test (for cases filed on or after October 17, 2005)

- Failure to pay court fees or charges
- Unreasonable delay that results in prejudice to creditors
- Failure to account for assets
- Fraud or misrepresentation
- Failure to read the bankruptcy petition and other documents to prevent the inclusion of false statements

The bankruptcy court or U.S. trustee may motion to dismiss the debtor's case if it is determined that granting relief would be considered a substantial abuse of the bankruptcy process. The bankruptcy court may deem a substantial abuse of process when:

- The debtor has engaged in serial filings on or after October 17, 2005.
- The debtor's obligation consists primarily of consumer debts.
- The debtor has filed the petition in bad faith.

Debtors are obligated to file their bankruptcy cases in good faith. The bankruptcy court can find cause to dismiss the debtor's case if it discovers a lack of good faith. A debtor acts in **bad faith** when he or she conceals or misrepresents assets, income, or expenses; intends to avoid paying a large debt to a creditor; or spends lavishly without regard for how to pay the bills.

> **bad faith**
> When a debtor conceals or misrepresents assets, income, or expenses; intends to avoid paying a large debt to a creditor; or spends lavishly without regard for how to pay the bills.

In contemplation of filing for bankruptcy, the debtor in the following case chose to treat himself and spend his bonus on luxury items rather than paying his creditors. Although the debtor filed for Chapter 7 relief, the bankruptcy court dismissed the case because the debtor's behavior constituted bad faith within the meaning of 11 U.S.C. § 707(b).

If a debtor's case is dismissed on the grounds of bad faith, fraud, bankruptcy crimes, willful disobedience of court orders, filing multiple cases in bad faith to delay creditors, or abusing the bankruptcy system, it may **dismiss with prejudice**. A dismissal with prejudice has serious consequences for the debtor. According to 11 U.S.C. § 109(g), a debtor is prohibited from filing another bankruptcy petition for 180 days from the date the court enters the dismissal order or the debtor voluntarily dismisses the case after the creditor files a motion to lift the Automatic Stay. This provision of the Bankruptcy Code prevents debtors from taking advantage of repetitive filings to institute the Automatic Stay when, for example, a secured creditor seeks to repossess a car or foreclose on the home.

> **dismissed with prejudice**
> The bankruptcy court dismisses a debtor's case and limits or prohibits the debtor from filing for bankruptcy at a later time due to the debtor's bad faith or abuse of the bankruptcy process.

It is also within the discretion of the bankruptcy court judge to extend the period during which the debtor may not file another bankruptcy case if the actions of the debtor were egregious. Under these circumstances, the debtor is also barred from obtaining a discharge on dischargeable debts included in a later bankruptcy petition. Bankruptcy cases that are dismissed on procedural grounds as listed previously are often **dismissed without prejudice**, thus allowing the debtor to file for bankruptcy again immediately and discharge the same debts included in the first petition.

> **dismissed without prejudice**
> The bankruptcy court dismisses the debtor's case, allowing the debtor to file for bankruptcy again immediately and discharge the same debts included in the first petition.

DISMISSAL OF CHAPTER 13 CASES

The debtor may request a voluntary dismissal of a Chapter 13. The process is quite simple, only requiring the debtor to file a form with the bankruptcy court. The bankruptcy court will grant the request unless the case was converted from another chapter, for example, from a Chapter 7 to a Chapter 13. The trustee may also request an involuntary dismissal if the debtor has failed to comply with

CASE **11.1** *In Re Kevin Francis James, Debtor*, 345 B.R. 664
(N.D. Iowa Jun. 30, 2006)

Memorandum Decision: U.S. Trustee's Motion to Dismiss Case

...James is employed *as* terminal manager for Jebro, Inc....James received a longevity bonus in the gross amount of $20,000.00 on or about September 30, 2005. By December 7, 2005, he received also a year-end bonus of $2,500.00....

...James's wife, Therese, did not file a bankruptcy petition. She has heart problems, and suffered a heart attack two and a half years ago....

James's bankruptcy schedules show that he has two secured debts. He owes Sun Trust Mortgage approximately $71,763.00 on a mortgage debt against his home. He values the home at $76,000.00. He owes Siouxland Federal Credit Union approximately $20,777.00 on a car loan. The loan is secured by a 2003 Chevrolet Z71 Silverado pickup truck valued by James at $16,500.00. He has reaffirmed both debts. His schedule of creditors holding unsecured nonpriority claims shows eight creditors, six of which are credit card lenders. One creditor was a furniture vendor, another was a cell phone service provider. The aggregate unsecured debt listed by James was $24,165.22. It appears that nearly all the unsecured debt was incurred prior to James receiving his longevity bonus.

...James has a savings account but not a checking account. He deposited the net proceeds of his longevity bonus in his savings account. He withdrew $7,500.00 in cash. He spent the money in a variety of ways.

...James did not use any part of the longevity bonus or the year-end bonus to pay existing debts. He said he made up his mind he couldn't pay his debts, and he decided to "treat" himself, to "reward" himself, in spending the bonus.

He purchased a new dog kennel for his Labrador retriever. It cost approximately $600.00. He bought a black powder muzzle loading rifle for $235.00, a bowling ball and bag for $200.00, hunting boots for $180.00, a shock collar for his dog for $150.00, a snowblower for approximately $535.00, a wheelbarrow for $60.00, a shop vac for $60.00, and new washing machine and clothes dryer for approximately $600.00. Also he purchased Christmas gifts for the nine adults and six children in his family. James also took a trip to Chicago with friends to watch the Chicago Bears football team play the San Francisco 49ers. He said the trip cost him about $800.00. He also paid his attorney's charges for bankruptcy representation. The attorney disclosed receiving compensation in the amount of $1,174.00. James said the remaining bonus money was spent on everyday living expenses.

The evidence shows significant medical bills for 2006. The couple has health insurance through his employer. James pays $394.83 per month for the coverage, which is deducted from his pay. James is responsible for some of the post-petition medical costs under his insurance plan.

James received a federal income tax refund for 2005. He received it in February 2006. He does not recall the amount of the refund. He spent it on "living expenses." James is an individual with primarily consumer debts.

...I consider an abuse to be a misuse of the bankruptcy provisions, to use them wrongly or improperly. I consider that bad faith has taken place when a debtor files a bankruptcy petition with motives that lack honesty of purpose or fair dealing. James acted in such a way....

...James's payment of a significant part of the bonuses to creditors might have made a subsequently filed chapter 13 plan feasible. Instead he spent the money on himself. This ensured that the chapter 7 means test would not require dismissal.

In summary, I find and conclude that spending significant cash assets on unnecessary luxury items with an intent to file bankruptcy and discharge existing indebtedness is bad faith within the meaning of 11 U.S.C. § 707(b).

bankruptcy court rules or has failed to make payments under the repayment plan. Likewise, the bankruptcy court may, sua sponte (on its own motion), dismiss the case when the debtor fails to complete a repayment plan.

Both the bankruptcy court and the U.S. trustee may also move to dismiss the case when the debtor has acted in bad faith, as discussed in the previous section. Creditors may also request a dismissal. If granted, the Automatic Stay terminates, allowing creditors to commence collections actions against the debtor. Chapter 13 debtors are required under BAPCPA to file with the court all tax returns for the previous four years one day before the 341 hearing (creditors' meeting). If not filed, the court can dismiss the Chapter 13 case or convert it to a Chapter 7.

DISMISSAL OF CHAPTER 11 CASES

Chapter 11 bankruptcies may be dismissed or converted to a Chapter 7 with the approval of the bankruptcy court. Dismissal does not always mean that the debtor failed to reorganize under the plan. The debtor and creditors may have reached an agreement that does not require the approval or further involvement of the bankruptcy court, and a dismissal is in order. In other cases, the debtor is unable to create a reorganization plan that satisfies either the court or its creditors. Here, the court will either dismiss or convert the case to a Chapter 7 liquidation.

Bankruptcy Conversions

INTRODUCTION

A **conversion** takes place when the debtor's original bankruptcy filing status is changed, either voluntarily or involuntarily, from one chapter to another. When a bankruptcy case is converted, it is considered a continuation of the original, not the beginning of a new case. There may, however, be some adjustments, depending on the provisions and requirements under the converted chapter. In addition, the debtor must meet the eligibility requirements of the converted chapter for the conversion to take effect. Conversion may also trigger changes in deadlines that must be monitored so the client files the requisite documents in a timely fashion. Conversions for Chapter 7, Chapter 11, and Chapter 13 cases are found in the following sections of the Bankruptcy Code.

> **conversion**
> A legal process that changes the debtor's original bankruptcy filing status, either voluntarily or involuntarily, from one chapter to another.

- Chapter 7 - 11 U.S.C. § 706
- Chapter 11 - 11 U.S.C. § 1112(a)
- Chapter 13 - 11 U.S.C. § 1307(a) and (g)

The most typical conversions involve converting from a Chapter 7 to a Chapter 13 or from a Chapter 13 to a Chapter 7. A debtor, creditor, trustee, or any other party in interest may move for a conversion. Creditors and other parties in interest are sent a **notice of conversion**, informing them of a potential change of status of the case and allowing them to raise objections.

The debtor or any one of the creditors may initiate a conversion, usually because it has been determined that another chapter is more suitable under the specific circumstances of the debtor's case. For example, a debtor who has filed for Chapter 13 with all good intentions to engage in a repayment plan may seek to convert to a Chapter 7 if there is no steady income due to recent unemployment or an unexpected

> **notice of conversion**
> A court notice sent to creditors and other parties in interest, informing them of a potential change of status of the case and allowing them to raise objections.

medical illness. On the contrary, a Chapter 7 debtor who acquires a new job with substantially more income may have to establish a repayment plan under Chapter 13.

It is important to note that in addition to dealing with dismissals and conversions when the attorney filed the original bankruptcy petition, the practice may also obtain a new client that initially filed his or her bankruptcy petition on a pro se basis. Clients in this position may have chosen a chapter that they are not eligible for or may be inappropriate for their situation. In these cases, the attorney may have to fend off a dismissal or move for a conversion to a more suitable chapter.

VOLUNTARY CONVERSIONS

voluntary conversion
The debtor seeks to change his or her bankruptcy filing status from one chapter to another.

As with dismissals, conversions may be either voluntary or involuntary. A **voluntary conversion** occurs when the debtor seeks to change his or her bankruptcy filing status from one chapter to another. The debtor has the right to convert from Chapter 7 to Chapter 11, Chapter 12, or Chapter 13 as long as he or she meets the eligibility requirements of that chapter. A debtor whose income cannot support a repayment plan may be unable to convert from a Chapter 7 to 13. Conversely, a debtor may be prohibited from converting from a Chapter 13 to a Chapter 7 if, for instance, a calculation of the Means Test determines that the debtor is not eligible for Chapter 7. There may be an exception if the debtor can convince the bankruptcy court that there is good cause to convert.

INVOLUNTARY CONVERSION

involuntary conversion
A bankruptcy conversion that is not initiated by the debtor but, rather, by the trustee, creditor, other party in interest or the bankruptcy court.

An **involuntary conversion** is a conversion that is not initiated by the debtor but, rather, by the trustee, creditor, other party in interest, or the bankruptcy court. Creditors, trustees, and other parties seeking an involuntary conversion must provide notice and a hearing so those objecting to a conversion have an opportunity to be heard. Here, the movant must convince the court that there is good cause for converting the case from its current filing status.

Facts that would justify an involuntary conversion would occur when a Chapter 7 debtor is ineligible for liquidation relief because of a finding of fraud and abuse by the debtor. Another example would be when a Chapter 7 debtor becomes gainfully employed, and it is determined that he or she has enough disposable income sufficient to support the repayment of creditors under Chapter 13.

CHAPTER 7 TO 13 CONVERSIONS

A conversion from Chapter 7 to Chapter 13 takes a bankruptcy case from liquidation to a repayment plan. Debtors who wish to convert from Chapter 7 to Chapter 13 must meet the eligibility requirements of a Chapter 13 case. It may be the best course of action for debtors who face a dismissal under Chapter 7. By converting to Chapter 13, they could arrange to pay their creditors under the supervision of the bankruptcy court rather than risk lawsuits, foreclosures, repossessions, and other collection efforts that would take place when the Automatic Stay is lifted. Debtors who acquire regular income, for example, often convert their Chapter 7 cases to Chapter 13. If a calculation of the Means Test determines that the debtor has sufficient disposable income to repay his or her creditors, the debtor may convert to a Chapter 13 to avoid the dismissal of the Chapter 7 case.

Although 11 U.S.C. § 706(a) gives a Chapter 7 debtor an absolute right to convert to Chapter 13, the bankruptcy court has the power to prevent abuse of the bankruptcy process. Converting to a Chapter 13 has its advantages because it would allow the debtor to keep more of his or her assets. The bankruptcy court, however, may deny the conversion if doing so would be an abuse under the provisions of the Bankruptcy Code or because of bad faith. Bad faith, for example, exists when the trustee determines that the debtor has failed to disclose pre-petition assets.

In *Marrama v. Citizens Bank of Massachusetts et al.,* 549 U.S. 365 (2007), the United States Supreme Court held that a Chapter 7 debtor who acted in bad faith by making misleading or inaccurate statements in connection with his assets and concealing assets on his bankruptcy schedules forfeited his right to convert to Chapter 13. In this case, the bankruptcy court denied the debtor's motion to convert from a Chapter 7 to a Chapter 13 bankruptcy because he acted in bad faith when he concealed assets and engaged in fraudulent transfers.

CHAPTER 13 TO CHAPTER 7 CONVERSIONS

A conversion from a Chapter 13 to a Chapter 7 involves a change from a repayment plan to liquidation. A debtor may wish to file for Chapter 13 protection, for example, if the goal is to keep assets such as the home or vehicle. This is done under the assumption that he or she will still have a job that allows him or her to meet the requirements of a repayment plan for the next three to five years. Unfortunately, life has surprises. A well-intentioned debtor may be unable to fulfill the terms of the Chapter 13 repayment plan because of unexpected changes such as job loss, decreased income, unexpected support of two households because of a divorce, medical illness or physical injury, or the death of a spouse. The debtor may also find that the Chapter 13 repayment plan, which can last from three to five years, is impractical and unsustainable when the reality of making payments and keeping up with daily living expenses sets in. The debtor may also reach a point when it is no longer practical to hold on to property that he or she originally sought to protect in a Chapter 13. Under these circumstances, a debtor may seek a voluntary conversion from a Chapter 13 to a Chapter 7.

The bankruptcy court may order a **forced conversion** when the debtor fails to create a Chapter 13 plan, successfully make payments under the Chapter 13 plan, or engage in some unreasonable delay that will cause harm to the creditors.

forced conversion
A bankruptcy court orders the debtor into liquidation for failure to create a Chapter 13 plan, failure to make payments successfully under the Chapter 13 plan, or engagement in some unreasonable delay that will cause harm to the creditors.

CHAPTER 13 TO CHAPTER 11 CONVERSIONS

A conversion from Chapter 13 to Chapter 11 involves a transition from a repayment plan to reorganization. Sometimes an entrepreneur or a professional in practice originally filed for Chapter 13 to structure a repayment plan with creditors. When this type of debtor finds it increasingly difficult to make payments under the plan, converting to Chapter 11 may be more practical.

For example, assume that a client, an accountant in private practice, files for bankruptcy under Chapter 13. The client works out a repayment plan of $4,000 a month for a period of 60 months. Unfortunately, the client is finding it harder to make these payments in addition to meeting her basic daily needs. The attorney may advise the client to convert to a Chapter 11 to allow the client to reorganize her financial obligations, obtain relief from others, and obtain debtor in possession (DIP) financing. After the debtor converts to Chapter 11, however, the creditors must confirm the proposed plan.

CHAPTER 11 TO CHAPTER 7 CONVERSIONS

A conversion from Chapter 11 to Chapter 7 involves changing from reorganization to liquidation. A Chapter 11 debtor may convert to Chapter 7 liquidation if Chapter 11 was filed as a voluntary petition and the debtor is a DIP. This conversion makes sense if assets are diminishing. Creditors, for example, may have motioned the court to lift the Automatic Stay, resulting in a seizure of property. A situation may arise as it did in the Hostess bankruptcy case when the company claimed that it would be unable to reorganize unless it obtained concessions from the union in the form of cuts to wages and pension benefits. Substantial postpetition taxes and attorneys' fees may also serve to decrease the possibility of reorganization.

Involuntary bankruptcies, either initially filed by creditors to force a debtor into bankruptcy or as a conversion, may be converted from a Chapter 11 to a Chapter 7 for cause. An example of cause to support an involuntary conversion from Chapter 11 to Chapter 7 is the unlikelihood that the debtor will be able to make payments under the reorganization plan and rehabilitate its business affairs.

Exhibit 11.1 is an example of the form used for a debtor's motion to convert.

Bankruptcy Closing and Reopening

CLOSING A BANKRUPTCY CASE

Bankruptcy clients might think, incorrectly, that a discharge is synonymous with a closed case. A discharge is the legal forgiveness of a debt, and is not necessarily equivalent to closing the case. In bankruptcy cases when a discharge is entered, the discharge *precedes* the closing of the case. Whether a bankruptcy case is discharged or dismissed, all cases will eventually be closed. A closed bankruptcy indicates that there is no longer any activity in the debtor's case. Under 11 U.S.C. § 350(a), the court shall close the case after the estate is fully administered and the court has discharged the trustee. It is when the bankruptcy court has officially determined that the case is over and no longer requires the court's involvement.

The bankruptcy case is closed when the trustee has completed administration and there is no longer any activity in the case. The closing of a bankruptcy case also does not necessarily mean that the debtor's case was discharged. As discussed in the previous chapter, a discharge specifically relieves the debtor of certain debts. A bankruptcy case may be closed without being discharged, for example, this may occur when the debtor has failed to participate in a court-approved debt management course.

Adversary proceedings against the debtor may also be pending regardless of whether the case has been closed. An adversary proceeding is a lawsuit related to the bankruptcy but filed as a separate case in the bankruptcy court. Creditors may file an adversary proceeding when they object to a discharge or wish to have a debt declared nondischargeable because of fraud by the debtor.

A Chapter 7 bankruptcy is closed after it has been either dismissed or discharged. Chapter 7 cases are closed when the trustee has liquidated the debtor's nonexempt assets and distributed the proceeds to creditors. Although the debtor's debts may be discharged, the Chapter 7 case may be prolonged if the sale of assets requires more time.

EXHIBIT 11.1 Debtor's Motion to Convert Case

Attorney or Party Name, Address, Telephone & FAX Numbers, and California State Bar Number	FOR COURT USE ONLY

Attorney for

UNITED STATES BANKRUPTCY COURT
CENTRAL DISTRICT OF CALIFORNIA

In re:

CHAPTER _____

CASE NUMBER

Debtor.

(No Hearing Required)

DEBTOR'S MOTION TO CONVERT CASE
UNDER 11 U.S.C. §§ 706(a), 1112(a) OR (d), 1208(a) OR 1307(d)

TO THE HONORABLE UNITED STATES BANKRUPTCY JUDGE:

1. Debtor hereby moves this Court for an Order converting the above Chapter _____ case to a case under Chapter _____ on the grounds set forth below:

2. **Filing Information:**

    a. ☐ A Voluntary Petition under Chapter ☐ 7 ☐ 11 ☐ 12 ☐ 13 was filed on:

    b. ☐ An Involuntary Petition under Chapter ☐ 7 ☐ 11 was filed on:
       ☐ An Order of Relief under Chapter ☐ 7 ☐ 11 was entered on:

    c. ☐ An Order of Conversion to Chapter ☐ 7 ☐ 11 ☐ 12 ☐ 13 was entered on:

    d. ☐ Other (specify):

3. **Procedural Status:**

    a. Name of Trustee Appointed (if any):

    b. Name of Attorney of Record for Trustee (if any):

(Continued on next page)

Rev. 5/98   This form is optional. It has been approved for use by the United States Bankruptcy Court for the Central District of California.   **F 1017-1.1**

EXHIBIT 11.1 Continued

Debtor's Motion to Convert Case - *Page 2* **F 1017-1.1**

In re	CHAPTER _____
Debtor.	CASE NUMBER

4. Debtor alleges that this case has not been previously converted and that Debtor is eligible for relief under the chapter for which conversion is requested.

WHEREFORE, Debtor prays that this Court issue an Order (the form of which is submitted herewith and has been served) converting this case from one under Chapter _____ to a case under Chapter _____.

Dated:

Respectfully submitted,

_____
Firm Name

By: _____

Name: _____
Attorney for Debtor/Trustee

PROOF OF SERVICE BY MAIL

STATE OF CALIFORNIA
COUNTY OF _____

I am employed in the above County, State of California. I am over the age of 18 and not a party to the within action. My business address is as follows:

On _____, I served the foregoing document described as: DEBTOR'S MOTION TO CONVERT CASE UNDER 11 U.S.C. §§ 706(a), 1112(a) or (d), 1208(a) or 1307(d) on the Chapter _____ Trustee (if any) and the United States Trustee at their last known addresses by placing a true and correct copy thereof in a sealed envelope with postage thereon fully prepaid in the United States Mail at _____, California, addressed as follows:

❏ Addresses continued on attached page

I declare under penalty of perjury under the laws of the United States of America that the foregoing is true and correct.

Dated:

_____
Type Name

_____
Signature

Rev. 5/98 This form is optional. It has been approved for use by the United States Bankruptcy Court for the Central District of California.   **F 1017-1.1**

REOPENING A CLOSED BANKRUPTCY CASE

A closed bankruptcy case may be reopened, at the court's discretion, by debtors, the trustee, or any party in interest. A **reopened bankruptcy** is a case that was closed but now reactivated and opened for further proceedings. Under 11 U.S.C. § 350(b), a bankruptcy case may be reopened to administer assets, accord relief to the debtor, or for other cause. The last prong of this Bankruptcy Code section allows the court some flexibility to define what *cause* would justify reopening a case.

reopened bankruptcy
A bankruptcy case that was once closed that is now reactivated and opened for further proceedings.

A debtor may want to reopen a case if it is alleged that one of the creditors engaged in some form of misconduct. An example of creditor misconduct would include trying to collect on a debt that has been lawfully discharged, which is prohibited by the Bankruptcy Code. A debtor in this position would have to reopen the bankruptcy case to pursue damages against the creditor. Debtors may also seek to reopen a case if they failed to list a creditor who is now seeking repayment. It is up to the bankruptcy court judge to determine whether the failure to list the creditor was an inadvertent mistake or deliberate. Creditors may wish to reopen a bankruptcy case if the debtor failed to disclose pre-petition assets. Reopening the case would allow creditors to make claims against this property.

The reopening of a bankruptcy case is within the discretion of the bankruptcy court. In the following case, the court denied the debtor's motion to reopen her case to pursue sanctions and damages against the holder of her student loans for an alleged violation of the discharge injunction.

CASE **11.2** *In Re Kellie Ward Smyth, Debtor,* 470 B.R. 459
(B.A.P. 6th Cir. 2012)

…Kellie Ward Smyth (the "Debtor") appeals from the bankruptcy court's order finding the Debtor's student loans had not been discharged in her no asset Chapter 7 case and denying the Debtor's motion to reopen her case to pursue an alleged violation of the discharge injunction by the holders of her student loans…

…The issue raised in this appeal is whether the bankruptcy court abused its discretion in denying the Debtor's motion to reopen her bankruptcy case …

…The Debtor filed a voluntary petition for relief under Chapter 7 of the Bankruptcy Code on July 17, 2003. No student loan debts were listed in her voluntary petition for relief. A notice of Chapter 7 Bankruptcy filing was sent to the creditors listed by the Debtor on her schedules. The notice directed creditors not to file a proof of claim unless and until they receive further notification.

On October 16, 2003, the Debtor filed an amended Schedule F which lists Edamerica as a creditor holding a student loan in the amount of $76,654.86. On October 23, 2003, the bankruptcy court issued a general Chapter 7 discharge to the Debtor. No adversary proceedings were commenced during the pendency of the Debtor's Chapter 7 case, and it is undisputed that no determination of undue hardship was requested of or made by the bankruptcy court. On April 29, 2004, the Chapter 7 Trustee filed a no asset report, and thereafter, the bankruptcy court entered a final decree and closed the case on May 21, 2004.

On February 28, 2011, the Debtor filed a motion to reopen her Chapter 7 case, not to seek a discharge of her student loans, but to pursue sanctions and damages against the holder of her student loans for an alleged violation of the discharge injunction. Edamerica, Inc. and various other parties, including the guarantor of the Debtor's student loans, opposed the motion to reopen. The bankruptcy court

(Continued)

(Continued)

held a hearing on the motion to reopen. At the conclusion of the hearing, the bankruptcy court denied the motion to reopen and entered an order in accordance with that ruling on April 29, 2011. The Debtor timely filed this appeal.

...Section 350(b) provides that a bankruptcy court, in its discretion, may reopen a bankruptcy case to provide relief to the debtor or for other cause.... Here, the only reason the Debtor seeks to reopen her case is to obtain relief from what she alleges is a violation of the discharge injunction. The appellees argue that the relief sought by the Debtor is unavailable or futile.

The Debtor relies on *United Student Aid Funds v. Espinosa,* 559 U.S. 260, 130 S.Ct. 1367, 176 L.Ed.2d 158 (2010), for the proposition that her student loan was discharged by the entry of the general discharge order in her no asset Chapter 7 case. As noted by the bankruptcy court in its order denying the Debtor's motion to reopen, *Espinosa* is not applicable to a Chapter 7 case and does not provide the Debtor with a basis for the relief sought in her motion to reopen.... Student loans are not discharged in bankruptcy absent a determination of undue hardship in an adversary proceeding....

...The bankruptcy court did not abuse its discretion in denying the Debtor's motion to reopen. The decision of the bankruptcy court is AFFIRMED....

After reading this chapter, you have learned that a debtor who conceals or misrepresents assets, income, or expenses can be found to have acted in bad faith. If the debtor is found to have acted in bad faith, his or her bankruptcy case is bound to be dismissed. Many debtors don't realize that concealing income, even an increase in income several weeks or months after the bankruptcy filing, can be interpreted by the bankruptcy court as bad faith. Remember our friend Huy Nuygen from the beginning of this chapter? He suddenly experienced an increase in income after his Chapter 7 case was well under way. As you are now aware, any change in financial circumstance must be disclosed to the bankruptcy attorney and, in turn, to the court. Huy's new income may still be low enough for his Chapter 7 case to continue. However, this is not his decision to make. If Huy's income is high enough to leave him with enough disposable cash each month to support a Chapter 13 repayment plan, this is the route he may have to take.

CHAPTER **SUMMARY**

A bankruptcy dismissal occurs when the bankruptcy court ceases administration of the case and no longer has jurisdiction over the matter, including any adversary proceedings that other parties have filed. In simple terms, a dismissal means that the debtor's case has been thrown out of court. Bankruptcy dismissals are either voluntary or involuntary. In a voluntary dismissal, the debtor decides not to pursue the bankruptcy case and consents to its dismissal. An involuntary dismissal is initiated by the bankruptcy court judge acting sua sponte (on its own) or by the U.S. trustee. Creditors may also pursue an involuntary dismissal so that they will be free to pursue their legal remedies against the debtor without the constraints of the Automatic Stay.

A conversion takes place when the debtor's original bankruptcy filing status is changed from one chapter to another. When a bankruptcy case is converted, it is considered a continuation of the original, not the beginning of a new case, but there may be some adjustments, depending on the provisions and requirements under the converted chapter.

Whether a bankruptcy case is discharged or dismissed, all cases will eventually be closed. A closed bankruptcy indicates that there is no longer any activity in the debtor's case. Under 11 U.S.C. § 350(a), the court shall close the case after the estate is fully administered and the court has discharged the trustee. A closed bankruptcy case may be reopened. A reopened bankruptcy is a case that was once closed but is now reactivated and opened for further proceedings. Under 11 U.S.C. § 350(b), a bankruptcy case may be reopened to administer assets, accord relief to the debtor, or for other cause.

CONCEPT REVIEW AND REINFORCEMENT

KEY **TERMS**

bad faith
conversion
dismissal
dismissed with
  prejudice

dismissed without prejudice
forced conversion
involuntary conversion
involuntary dismissal
notice of conversion

reopened bankruptcy
sua sponte
voluntary conversion
voluntary dismissal

REVIEWING **KEY CONCEPTS**

1. What happens when a bankruptcy case is dismissed with or without prejudice?
2. What effect does a dismissal have on a debtor? What about the creditors?
3. Describe the difference between a voluntary dismissal and an involuntary dismissal.
4. What is a conversion?
5. Describe the difference between a voluntary conversion and an involuntary conversion.
6. Explain why a debtor would want to convert a Chapter 7 case to a Chapter 13.

7. Explain why a debtor would want to convert a Chapter 13 case to a Chapter 7.
8. Why would a business that filed for a Chapter 11 reorganization wish to convert to a Chapter 7 liquidation?
9. What is a forced conversion?
10. What does it mean when a bankruptcy case is closed? What grounds must be satisfied for reopening a bankruptcy case?

BUILDING YOUR PARALEGAL SKILLS

CASE FOR **REVIEW**

Marrama v. Citizens Bank of Massachusetts et al., 549 U.S. 365 (2007)

BUILDING A PROFESSIONAL PORTFOLIO

PORTFOLIO **EXERCISE**

You work for the law firm of Cleveland, Delaney & Garrett. Latasha Green, a bankruptcy client, calls looking for Attorney Rose Delaney, who is in court. She appears agitated and relates the following facts to you. Ms. Green filed for Chapter 13 because it was determined that she had sufficient income from her job to repay her creditors. She has heard through the grapevine, however, that layoffs at her place of employment are inevitable. Ms. Green is also five months pregnant and is concerned that if she is laid off, she will have a hard time finding a job. She is afraid that if this happens, she will be unable to make the payments under a Chapter 13 plan. Ms. Green wants to know what to do. Draft a letter to Ms. Green on Attorney Delaney's behalf, explaining her options under the Bankruptcy Code.

chapter 12

THE BANKRUPTCY DISCHARGE

LEARNING OBJECTIVES

After studying this chapter, you should be able to:

1. Recognize the power the Bankruptcy Code has to discharge certain debts.

2. Summarize the types of debt that are nondischargeable.

3. Describe the difference between denial of discharge and nondischargeable debt.

4. Explain the right and the process by which a creditor can bring an action against a debtor to declare certain debts nondischargeable.

5. Identify the actions a debtor may take that could result in a denial of discharge.

Johnny Debt, like many Americans, is fortunate enough to have a high-paying job as a real estate investment agent at a very prestigious firm in New York City. Jane Debt, Johnny's second wife, has a high-paying job as an associate in a very large accounting firm. Johnny and Jane both enjoyed the high life. Their dual income brought their annual salary into the high $200,000s. Several years ago, the Debts bought an old home in Westchester County for $500,000, and they updated each square foot of the home with everything from granite countertops to Brazilian cherry floors. They owe several contractors significant sums. Johnny also owes more than $3,200 in back child support to his ex-wife, Jill Smith.

To keep up with this lifestyle, the Debts have taken out several home equity lines of credit on their home over the past five to six years. Recently, Johnny lost his job at the real estate investment firm after he caused a very bad accident in which several people were hurt. Johnny was arrested for DUI in connection with the accident. Several personal injury claims are pending against Johnny from this accident. Further, both of the Debts have significant student loan debt from the private liberal arts colleges they attended. The bills keep piling up, but Johnny is not worried; he figures he can just file bankruptcy and have all of his debts discharged. Is he correct? Will all his debts be discharged? Read on and find out.

INTRODUCTION

The prevailing public belief seems to be that bankruptcy is the answer to all of one's debt problems. We hope that you have gathered from previous chapters in this book that it is not quite that easy. It is often said that the Bankruptcy Code has the power to absolve the debtor of *most* of his or her debts. The simple truth is that the object of any personal bankruptcy case is ultimately to unburden the debtor of most, if not all of his or her unsecured debt.

This chapter discusses the benefits and limitations of **discharge**, which is literally the legal cancellation of a debt for the debtor. After a debt is discharged, the creditor claiming such debt cannot pursue the debtor for the debt any longer. To do so would be illegal, and the

discharge
A document a bankruptcy judge issues that releases the debtor from liability and prohibits the creditor from pursuing any legal action to collect those debts.

creditor may be subject to sanctions if it takes such action. The types of debt that are **nondischargeable** due to public policy concerns will also be discussed. Further, the actions a debtor may take, such as concealing assets, making fraudulent transfers, and not scheduling debts, and the effect these actions can have on the **dischargeability** of certain debts, will also be reviewed.

Discharge of Debt

The effect the Bankruptcy Code has on the debtor's dischargeable debt is powerful. Under 11 U.S.C. § 524(a)(1)(2), the discharge of debt through bankruptcy acts as a statutory injunction against any collection efforts the creditor asserts. In other words, not only is it unlawful for the creditor to pursue the debtor after the petition has been filed, it is equally, if not more, unlawful for the creditor to pursue the debtor post-discharge. There is however, an exception to this rule. If the debtor enters into a reaffirmation agreement with the creditor, the creditor retains all its legal and equitable rights to collect the debt and may pursue the debtor.

If any creditor attempts to collect a discharged debt from the debtor by any means, including harassing phone calls, letters, and commencing legal action, that creditor may be subject to court-imposed sanctions. To report such action to the Bankruptcy Court, the debtor would need to file a motion in the court that handled the bankruptcy case. The court will hear the motion and, if it determines that the creditor was in willful contempt of the court's ruling on discharge, the creditor may be ordered to pay sanctions. Sanctions against a creditor can include compensatory damages, including attorney fees and lost wages to the debtor for his or her time away from work to attend court hearings and to meet with his or her attorney.

In the sections that follow, we discuss certain debts that are always nondischargeable in bankruptcy. We also discuss the debts that may be susceptible to a denial of discharge by the court because of some action by the debtor or because the creditor filed for an **adversary proceeding** with the court.

Nondischargeable Debt

According to 11 U.S.C. § 523, certain debts cannot be discharged through bankruptcy. For one reason or another, Congress deemed the discharge of certain debts to be against public policy. "Against public policy" means that Congress felt that absolving individual or business debtors of certain debts would not be in the interest of promoting the public good. These types of debts are viewed not merely as debts but as obligations. To allow a debtor to avoid such debts would likely cause a person of reasonable sensibilities to stand up and exclaim, "That's outrageous!" As mentioned in a previous chapter, and as you will see, this makes sense. As you read on, you will learn that some of these debts are always nondischargeable without any creditor action. You will also see that some of the debts are nondischargeable only when the creditor files for an adversary proceeding in the Bankruptcy Court to determine the dischargeability of a debt based on the debtor's actions. The most prevalent nondischargeable debts are:

1. Spousal and child support.
2. Government-sponsored student loans.
3. Governmentally imposed debts such as certain taxes or traffic tickets and orders to pay restitution to victims of a crime.

nondischargeable
Certain debts that cannot be eliminated in bankruptcy due to public policy concerns.

dischargeability
Determining whether a debt may be eliminated in bankruptcy.

adversary proceeding
A separate lawsuit filed within a bankruptcy case, which must be resolved by the judge before the case may proceed to discharge.

4. Debts incurred by fraudulent means.
5. Homeowners' association fees.
6. Debt for personal injury caused to another because of the debtor's operation of a motor vehicle while intoxicated.
7. Debts incurred by a debtor who, while acting as a fiduciary, obtained funds from a creditor by way of fraud or defalcation of duty.
8. Debts incurred due to the debtor's malicious and willful injury of another, e.g., assault and battery of the creditor who now has medical bills and pain and suffering as a result.

Nondischargeable Debts Not Requiring Creditor Action

ALIMONY AND CHILD SUPPORT

Generally, spousal and child support are court-ordered obligations that a debtor may not avoid through bankruptcy. If a debtor, (also known as an obligor in domestic support cases) who is ordered to pay child support, misses several payments, this arrearage cannot be discharged through bankruptcy. The debtor, however, may have an opportunity to dispute the amount owed to the **custodial parent** on his or her bankruptcy petition. The custodial parent has custody of the minor children. The creditor—custodial parent—must file a Proof of Claim within 60 days of the meeting of the creditors. The bankruptcy court cannot deal with the debtor's ongoing obligation to pay domestic support. The debtor must turn to the family court in his or her state to determine, adjust, or modify child support or other domestic support obligations. **Alimony**, or financial support paid to an ex-spouse, is treated in a similar way. Issues with what qualifies as alimony or property division sometimes arise, and the bankruptcy court can make those types of determinations. For example, a court may order one ex-spouse to pay at least half of the car payments on the other ex-spouse's car. If a dispute over the dischargeability of this debt arises, the bankruptcy court would likely deem this a support obligation rather than an issue of property division and, as such, nondischargeable.

STUDENT LOANS

Student loans may be included on a Chapter 13 plan to make payments more manageable for a debtor. However, student loans are generally not dischargeable. This has been the case since 1976 for government-sponsored loans, and in 1984, private student loans became exempt from discharge. The Bankruptcy Code allows for the partial or complete discharge of student loans in only very rare cases if the debtor can show extreme undue hardship in his or her ability to repay a student loan when it becomes due. In determining whether a debtor cannot repay a student loan, several but not all bankruptcy courts have applied a three-pronged test to determine undue hardship. These courts have considered whether "the debtor cannot maintain, based on current income and expenses, a 'minimal' standard of living for herself and her dependents if forced to repay the loans;...that additional circumstances exist indicating that this state of affairs is likely to persist for a significant portion of the repayment period of the student loans; and...that the

custodial parent
The parent with residential custody of minor children.

alimony
Court-ordered financial support paid to an ex-spouse.

debtor has made good faith efforts to repay the loans." See *Brunner vs. New York State Higher Education Services Corp*, 831 F. 2d 395, 396 (1987).

TAXES

Most taxes levied against the debtor by the federal, state, or local government are generally not dischargeable. This includes sales tax, estate tax, payroll tax, trust fund tax, and tax on personal property. Income tax may be dischargeable in Chapter 7, Chapter 13, and Chapter 11 cases if the date on which the tax was due (usually April 15 of the year following the tax year) is more than three years prior to the debtor filing for bankruptcy.

Further, to be eligible for a discharge of income tax, the debtor must have correctly and accurately filed a tax return for the year or years that the taxes were due. If the debtor incurred income taxes charges due to fraud or willful tax evasion, the taxes cannot be discharged. For example, Harriet Nance failed to include the rental income she receives from the second floor she rents in her two-family home. The IRS and state revenue services send her a tax deficiency notice. If Nance files for bankruptcy, she will be unable to discharge these tax debts.

Dischargeable tax debts are considered unsecured debts in Chapter 11 and Chapter 13 cases. The taxing authority will be treated similarly to the debtor's general unsecured creditors under the repayment or reorganization plan.

Although the bankruptcy court may discharge some tax debt, it cannot discharge a lawfully filed tax lien. A **tax lien** is a claim the government files against a taxpayer's property for unpaid back taxes. The outstanding tax lien encumbers the title on the property and must be paid before the property may be sold. Federal and state tax liens are not dischargeable in bankruptcy. Tax liens are different from tax levies. According to the Internal Revenue website, "a [tax] levy is a legal seizure of your property to satisfy a tax debt. . . . A lien is a claim used as security for the tax debt, while a levy actually takes the property to satisfy the tax debt."

If nondischargeable federal and state taxes are not paid, the government tax authorities may seize and sell the taxpayer's property to satisfy these obligations. For example, the government may seize and sell the taxpayer's home, automobile, or boat. The government could also levy property that belongs to the taxpayer but is in the possession of another. For example, this would include the taxpayer's wages, which are in the employer's possession, bank accounts, commissions, dividends, rental income, accounts receivables, or cash values on life insurance.

Although tax debts generally cannot be discharged, debtors may consider negotiating with the IRS or other taxing authority to reach a compromise to settle their tax debt for less than the full amount owed or enter into an installment agreement to pay the debt over time. This strategy helps the debtor minimize the tax penalties that can accumulate during the bankruptcy process and beyond.

FINES IMPOSED BY GOVERNMENT

If the debtor is fined for violating a law, this type of debt is nondischargeable. Again, in accordance with public policy, the bankruptcy courts do not want to encourage or reward those who have broken the law with a discharge of this type of debt. Another example of a nondischargeable fine imposed by the government would be restitution to a victim of the debtor's crime.

HOMEOWNERS' ASSOCIATION DUES

If the debtor is filing for bankruptcy and owns a condominium unit, cooperative, planned unit development unit, or other property subject to **homeowners' association fees (HOA),** these fees may not be completely discharged. **HOA** fees the debtor incurs after he or she has filed the bankruptcy petition are nondischargeable. These fees remain the debtor's responsibility up to the time the property is no longer in the debtor's name whether by way of a sale or foreclosure. The fees the association may incur, such as attorney fees, to collect association dues postpetition are often nondischargeable. This type of nondischargeable debt came about because of the Bankruptcy Abuse Prevention and Consumer Protection Act of 2005 (BAPCPA) in 2005.

Many bankruptcy courts have held that a debtor may be liable for HOA fees *after* filing for bankruptcy, even though the property is no longer in the debtor's name. For example, the debtor's condominium may have been foreclosed upon and title transferred to a sheriff or marshal after the sale. In this case, the debtor may not have a possessory interest in the property but, in many states, may have a **right of redemption** in the property. If the debtor loses property in foreclosure, he or she can reclaim the property within a specified time if he or she can somehow pay the balance or structure a payment plan with the mortgage company. The HOA may file a post-discharge in rem action, which is against the actual property and not *in personam*, that is, not against the debtor. Many courts have held the debtor liable for the HOA fees during the term of the debtor's residency, even though the property is no longer in the debtor's name.

DEBT INCURRED FROM DUI

According to 11 U.S.C. § 523(a)(9), a debtor may not discharge a debt for death or personal injury he or she caused by operation of a motor vehicle, vessel, or aircraft if such operation was unlawful because the debtor was intoxicated from using alcohol, a drug, or another substance. It does not matter whether the debtor filed for Chapter 7 or Chapter 13. The creditor has the burden of proving that the debtor was intoxicated at the time of the accident. However, the protection afforded to this type of creditor is so strong that the creditor only needs to prove that the debtor was intoxicated while operating the vehicle at the time the injuries occurred. The creditor does not need to prove that the intoxication was the actual cause of the injury nor does there need to be a criminal conviction for DUI as a result. There have been cases in which the creditor was able to show, by using witness testimony and a preponderance of the evidence, that more likely than not the debtor was intoxicated at the time of the accident. Bankruptcy courts have held that "[l]egal intoxication…does not have to be specifically adjudicated by a state court for the purposes of determining nondischargeability under [11 U.S.C.] § 523(a)(9)." See *In re Phalen*, 145 B.R. 551 (N.D. Ohio Jul. 23, 1992).

The Bankruptcy Code does not want to reward a debtor who injured or damaged the property of another due to his or her drunk driving. The innocent third party, who has a claim for personal injury or property damage against a person who was intoxicated at the time he or she caused the injury, should not be barred from eventually recovering money from the debtor in a situation like this.

Debts Nondischargeable if Successfully Challenged

DEBT INCURRED BY FRAUD

A debtor may not discharge debt incurred by fraudulent means. This includes loans, credit card debt, mortgages, and lines of credit obtained under false pretenses. A creditor, according to 11 U.S.C. § 523(a)(2)(A), must prove that the debtor made a misrepresentation of his or her financial condition that was a **material fact**. A material fact is one on which one or both parties rely when making a decision to enter into a contract with the other. The debtor must have made the misrepresentation, knowing it to be false, with the intent to deceive the creditor. Therefore, lying on credit card applications, loan applications, and applications for lines of credit all include deception that existed at the time the debt was incurred. For example, a debtor who knows he or she will never be able to repay a debt at the time the debt is incurred will likely be unable to discharge that debt. Merely being uncertain whether a debtor can repay a debt probably will not render a debt nondischargeable.

material fact
Facts on which one or both parties rely when making a decision to enter into a contract with the other.

DEFALCATION BY FIDUCIARY

According to 11 U. S. C. § 523(a)(4), debts that are incurred by a **fiduciary** through fraud, embezzlement, or defalcation are not dischargeable. A fiduciary is someone who holds a position of trust and generally manages the money of another person or persons. A classic example would be an executor or administrator of a deceased person's estate. There is little doubt that knowingly committing **embezzlement**, or misappropriating the funds of another person, creates a nondischargeable debt. However, defalcation, a loosely defined term, by a fiduciary, will result in nondischargeable debt. The courts have defined defalcation as a mere dereliction of duty or neglect of duty by a fiduciary. In other words, a fiduciary's action could be considered a defalcation if he or she unintentionally used funds for a reason that was not appropriate. For example, a fiduciary transfers $50,000 to herself, without probate court approval, as compensation from a large estate she is handling. She honestly believes she is entitled to the money for all her hard work. The probate court will likely replace that fiduciary with another fiduciary, and the estate she handled will file a claim for the $50,000 if the fiduciary files for bankruptcy. This debt will not be dischargeable due to the fiduciary's defalcation.

fiduciary
One who holds a position of trust and generally manages the money of another person or persons and has similar powers to those of a Chapter 11 trustee.

embezzlement
Misappropriating the funds of another person.

"A debt is nondischargeable as the result of defalcation when a preponderance of the evidence establishes: (1) a pre-existing fiduciary relationship, (2) a breach of that relationship, and (3) resulting loss." *In re Patel,* 565 F.3d 963, 968 (6th Cir. 2009) (citing *In re Bucci,* 493 F.3d 635, 642 (6th Cir.2007)) In *Patel,* the court held that the debtor's conduct was objectively reckless when he "paid his own operating expenses including payroll, utilities, taxes and wages to himself," before paying subcontractors. Although the debtor had no actual intent to defraud, he was guilty of defalcation because of his inadequate accounting skills and sloppy business operations.

The following case, *Bullock v. Bankchampaign, N.A.,* travels from Bankruptcy Court, Federal District Court, Circuit Court of Appeals, and finally, to the Supreme Court of the United States. This case illustrates that not all debts may be discharged, or released from obligation, in bankruptcy, especially those incurred

defalcation
A culpable state of mind requirement involving knowledge of, or gross recklessness in respect to, the improper nature of the fiduciary behavior.

by fraud or **defalcation**, a term in desperate need of a clear definition to resolve a century and a half of confusion. Ultimately, the Court determined that defalcation involves "a culpable state of mind requirement involving knowledge of, or gross recklessness in respect to, the improper nature of the fiduciary behavior."

CASE 12.1 *Bullock v. BankChampaign, N.A.,* 133 S. Ct. 1754 (2013)

…Section 523(a)(4) of the Federal Bankruptcy Code provides that an individual cannot obtain a bankruptcy discharge from a debt "for fraud or defalcation while acting in a fiduciary capacity, embezzlement, or larceny." 11 U. S. C. § 523(a)(4). We here consider the scope of the term "defalcation." We hold that it includes a culpable state of mind requirement akin to that which accompanies application of the other terms in the same statutory phrase. We describe that state of mind as one involving knowledge of, or gross recklessness in respect to, the improper nature of the relevant fiduciary behavior.

In 1978, the father of petitioner Randy Bullock established a trust for the benefit of his five children. He made petitioner the (nonprofessional) trustee; and he transferred to the trust a single asset, an insurance policy on his life.… The trust instrument permitted the trustee to borrow funds from the insurer against the policy's value (which, in practice, was available at an insurance-company-determined 6% interest rate).…

In 1981, petitioner, at his father's request, borrowed money from the trust, paying the funds to his mother who used them to repay a debt to the father's business. In 1984, petitioner again borrowed funds from the trust, this time using the funds to pay for certificates of deposit, which he and his mother used to buy a mill. In 1990, petitioner once again borrowed funds, this time using the money to buy real property for himself and his mother.… Petitioner saw that all of the borrowed funds were repaid to the trust along with 6% interest.…

In 1999, petitioner's brothers sued petitioner in Illinois state court. The state court held that petitioner had committed a breach of fiduciary duty. It explained that petitioner "does not appear to have had a malicious motive in borrowing funds from the trust" but nonetheless "was clearly involved in self-dealing."…It ordered petitioner to pay the trust "the benefits he received from his breaches" (along with costs and attorney's fees).… The court imposed constructive trusts on petitioner's interests in the mill and the original trust, in order to secure petitioner's payment of its judgment, with respondent BankChampaign serving as trustee for all of the trust.… After petitioner tried unsuccessfully to liquidate his interests in the mill and other constructive trust assets to obtain funds to make the court-ordered payment, petitioner filed for bankruptcy in federal court.…

BankChampaign opposed petitioner's efforts to obtain a bankruptcy discharge of his state-court-imposed debts to the trust. And the Bankruptcy Court granted summary judgment in the bank's favor. It held that the debts fell within § 523(a)(4)'s exception "as a debt for defalcation while acting in a fiduciary capacity."…Hence, they were not dischargeable.

The Federal District Court reviewed the Bankruptcy Court's determination. It said that it was "convinced" that BankChampaign was "abusing its position of trust by failing to liquidate the assets," but it nonetheless affirmed the Bankruptcy Court's decision.…

In turn, the Court of Appeals affirmed the District Court. It wrote that "defalcation requires a known breach of a fiduciary duty, such that the conduct can be characterized as objectively reckless." ... And it found that petitioner's conduct satisfied this standard....

Petitioner sought certiorari. In effect he has asked us to decide whether the bankruptcy term "defalcation" applies "in the absence of any specific finding of ill intent or evidence of an ultimate loss of trust principal." ... The lower courts have long disagreed about whether "defalcation" includes a scienter requirement and, if so, what kind of scienter it requires. Compare *In re Sherman*, 658 F. 3d 1009, 1017 (CA9 2011) ("defalcation" includes "even innocent acts of failure to fully account for money received in trust" (internal quotation marks and brackets omitted)), with *In re Uwimana*, 274 F. 3d 806, 811 (CA4 2001) (defalcation occurs when "negligence or even an innocent mistake...results in misappropriation"), with 670 F. 3d, at 1166 ("defalcation requires...conduct [that] can be characterized as objectively reckless"), and with *In re Baylis*, 313 F. 3d 9, 20 (CA1 2002) ("defalcation requires something close to a showing of extreme recklessness"). In light of that disagreement, we granted the petition.

Congress first included the term "defalcation" as an exception to discharge in a federal bankruptcy statute in 1867.... And legal authorities have disagreed about its meaning almost ever since....

...We base our approach and our answer upon one of this Court's precedents. In 1878, this Court interpreted the related statutory term "fraud" in the portion of the Bankruptcy Code laying out exceptions to discharge. Justice Harlan wrote for the Court:

"[D]ebts created by 'fraud' are associated directly with debts created by 'embezzlement.' Such association justifies, if it does not imperatively require, the conclusion that the 'fraud' referred to in that section means positive fraud, or fraud in fact, involving moral turpitude or intentional wrong, as does embezzlement; and not implied fraud, or fraud in law, which may exist without the imputation of bad faith or immorality." *Neal v. Clark*, 95 U. S. 704, 709 (1878).

We believe that the statutory term "defalcation" should be treated similarly.

Thus, where the conduct at issue does not involve bad faith, moral turpitude, or other immoral conduct, the term requires an intentional wrong. We include as intentional not only conduct that the fiduciary knows is improper but also reckless conduct of the kind that the criminal law often treats as the equivalent. Thus, we include reckless conduct of the kind set forth in the Model Penal Code. Where actual knowledge of wrongdoing is lacking, we consider conduct as equivalent if the fiduciary "consciously disregards" (or is willfully blind to) "a substantial and unjustifiable risk" that his conduct will turn out to violate a fiduciary duty.... That risk "must be of such a nature and degree that, considering the nature and purpose of the actor's conduct and the circumstances known to him, its disregard involves *a gross deviation* from the standard of conduct that a law-abiding person would observe in the actor's situation."

...Several considerations lead us to interpret the statutory term "defalcation" in this way. First, as Justice Harlan pointed out in *Neal*, statutory context strongly favors this interpretation. Applying the canon of interpretation *noscitur a sociis*, the Court there looked to fraud's linguistic neighbor, "embezzlement." It found that both terms refer to different forms of generally similar conduct. It wrote that both are "*'ejusdem generis,'*" of the same kind, and that both are "'referable to the same subject-matter.'" ... Moreover, embezzlement requires a showing of wrongful intent...(noting that embezzlement "involv[es] moral turpitude or intentional wrong")....Hence, the Court concluded, "fraud" must require an equivalent showing. *Neal* has been the law for more than a century. And here, the additional neighbors ("larceny" and, as defined in *Neal*, "fraud") mean that the canon *noscitur a sociis* argues even more strongly for similarly interpreting the similar statutory term "defalcation."

(Continued)

(Continued)

Second, this interpretation does not make the word identical to its statutory neighbors.... As commonly used, "embezzlement" requires conversion, and "larceny" requires taking and carrying away another's property.... "Defalcation," as commonly used (hence as Congress might have understood it), can encompass a breach of fiduciary obligation that involves neither conversion, nor taking and carrying away another's property, nor falsity.... Nor are embezzlement, larceny, and fiduciary fraud simply special cases of defalcation as so defined. The statutory provision makes clear that the first two terms apply outside of the fiduciary context; and "defalcation," unlike "fraud," may be used to refer to *nonfraudulent* breaches of fiduciary duty....

Third, the interpretation is consistent with the longstanding principle that "exceptions to discharge 'should be confined to those plainly expressed.'"... It is also consistent with a set of statutory exceptions that Congress normally confines to circumstances where strong, special policy considerations, such as the presence of fault, argue for preserving the debt, thereby benefiting, for example, a typically more honest creditor. See, *e.g.*, 11 U. S. C. §§ 523(a)(2)(A), (a)(2)(B), (a)(6), (a)(9) (fault). See also, *e.g.*, §§ 523(a)(1), (a)(7), (a)(14), (a)(14A) (taxes); § 523(a)(8) (educational loans); § 523(a)(15) (spousal and child support). In the absence of fault, it is difficult to find strong policy reasons favoring a broader exception here, at least in respect to those whom a scienter requirement will most likely help, namely *nonprofessional* trustees, perhaps administering small family trusts potentially immersed in intrafamily arguments that are difficult to evaluate in terms of comparative fault.

Fourth, as far as the briefs before us reveal, at least some Circuits have interpreted the statute similarly for many years without administrative, or other practical, difficulties....

Finally, it is important to have a uniform interpretation of federal law, the choices are limited, and neither the parties nor the Government has presented us with strong considerations favoring a different interpretation. In addition to those we have already discussed, the Government has pointed to the fact that in 1970 Congress rewrote the statute, eliminating the word "misappropriation" and placing the term "defalcation" (previously in a different exemption provision) alongside its present three neighbors.... The Government believes that these changes support reading "defalcation" without a scienter requirement. But one might argue, with equal plausibility, that the changes reflect a decision to make certain that courts would read in similar ways "defalcation," "fraud," "embezzlement," and "larceny." In fact, we believe the 1970 changes are inconclusive.

In this case the Court of Appeals applied a standard of "objective[e] reckless[ness]" to facts presented at summary judgment.... We consequently remand the case to permit the court to determine whether further proceedings are needed and, if so, to apply the heightened standard that we have set forth. For these reasons we vacate the judgment of the Court of Appeals and remand the case for further proceedings consistent with this opinion.

It is so ordered.

DEBTS INCURRED BY DEBTOR'S MALICIOUS AND/OR WILLFUL MISCONDUCT

According to 11 U.S.C. § 523(a)(6), any debt that comes about because of the "willful and malicious injury by the debtor to another entity or to the property of another entity" is nondischargeable. For an action to be considered willful, the debtor must knowingly and intentionally act in a certain way that he or she knows will likely cause harm to another person. For example, a debtor who commits a battery or assault on another person should know that his or her actions would result in harm to the other party for which the debtor could be monetarily liable. The bankruptcy court cannot discharge this type of debt.

Problems occur when questions about the debtor's intent are raised. The bankruptcy courts look at how the state courts have handled issues surrounding the intent of the person who inflicted the harm when deciding whether a claim the creditor makes is nondischargeable. Other issues concerning the definition of "malicious" may occur. There is no doubt that assaulting and battering another individual is quite malicious, but maliciousness is not required in order to have a willful act. The courts have held that the "willful injury requirement of § 523(a)(6) is met when it is shown either that the debtor had a subjective motive to inflict the injury *or* that the debtor believed that injury was substantially certain to occur as a result of his conduct." See *In re Jercich*, 238 F.3d 1202, 1208 (2001).

There is a fine line between willful and malicious when considering the intention of the debtor. When considering a malicious injury, think about the debtor who strongly dislikes his or her neighbor and purposely destroys his or her neighbor's car out of spite. A **malicious injury** has been defined as involving "a wrongful act,...done intentionally,...which necessarily causes injury, and...is done without just cause or excuse." See *In re Jercich*, 238 F.3d 1202, 1209 (2001).

malicious injury
A wrongful, intentional act that causes injury to another or his or her property.

Denial of Discharge

In addition to the debts previously described, which are dischargeable if successfully challenged, there are situations when a debt that normally would have been discharged may become nondischargeable. For example, most folks think of credit card debt as always dischargeable. However, if the debtor obtained credit fraudulently, and the creditor can prove it, debt in connection with the credit card may be ruled nondischargeable. In a **denial of discharge**, some action the debtor takes, whether innocent or fraudulent, may cause a particular debt or all debts to become nondischargeable prior to the conclusion of the bankruptcy case. The trustee may also, within one year of discharge or the closing of the case, request a **revocation of discharge**. A revocation of discharge cannot take effect against a debtor unless the debtor has an opportunity to be heard by the court.

denial of discharge
Declaring nondischargeable a debt that normally would have been discharged.

revocation of discharge
The bankruptcy court's removal of a debtor's discharge.

According to 11 U.S.C. § 727, in the following instances, a debt may become nondischargeable if:

1. The debtor purposely conceals, destroys, or hinders any information pertaining to his or her assets.
2. The debtor purposely, with the intent to defraud or hinder the handling of a bankruptcy case, conceals, destroys, or transfers any property in the bankruptcy estate within one year of filing for bankruptcy or after the petition has been filed.
3. The debtor lies or fails to cooperate with the trustee.
4. The debtor fails to explain adequately any loss of assets to the court.
5. The debtor refuses to cooperate with and comply with any orders from the bankruptcy court.

Nondischargeability Adversarial Actions by Creditors and Debtors

The trustee, debtor, or creditor may initiate an adversarial proceeding. An adversary proceeding in a bankruptcy case is a civil proceeding and, therefore, the Federal Rules of Civil Procedure and Federal Rules of Evidence apply. The party bringing the action is known as the plaintiff, and the party against whom the complaint is brought is referred to as the defendant. The plaintiff files a formal complaint with the court, and the complaint is served on the defendant. The bankruptcy court maintains the case under its own separate docket number known as an adversary number. This unique adversary number will be listed just below the docket number for the main bankruptcy case on any pleading concerning the adversary proceeding.

The trustee may file an adversary proceeding against the debtor to ask the court to deny discharge or dismiss the case if the debtor has been uncooperative or dishonest with the trustee. However, most often, a creditor will initiate an action to determine nondischargeability of a particular debt. The types of debt for which a creditor will initiate such an action involve debt incurred by the alleged fraud, willful and/or malicious conduct, defalcation, or asset division by way of a divorce. Other actions to determine dischargeability are sometimes brought by the debtor. For example, let's say a debtor owes back taxes that were due in excess of three years from the date the debtor filed for bankruptcy. The debtor, if he or she would like the court to consider this normally nondischargeable debt dischargeable, would be the person to bring such an action to the court. In addition, a debtor who wishes to assert extreme hardship in connection with his or her student loans would be the appropriate plaintiff in an action to determine dischargeability of this debt.

According to 11 U.S.C. § 523(c), a debtor or creditor may bring an adversarial action in bankruptcy court to determine the dischargeability of a certain debt. A creditor is required to bring this action within 60 days of the date of the first meeting of the creditors. A debtor may bring such an action at any time during the bankruptcy case.

Remember our friends, the Debts, from the beginning of the chapter? Unfortunately for them, they have probably learned by now that not all their debts will be discharged. Unless the Debts can prove significant hardship, their student loan debts will not be discharged. Johnny Debt's indebtedness to the folks who were injured from his DUI will not be discharged. Certain debts cannot be discharged through bankruptcy. Congress deemed the discharge of certain debts to be against public policy. Johnny's $3,200 in back child support to his ex-wife, Jill Smith, is not going anywhere until he pays it. Imagine the result if the Bankruptcy Code allowed a debtor to wipe clean every one of his or her debts. The results could be devastating for many, and it is clear that certain types of behavior such as drunk driving or delinquency on child support payments, should not be rewarded with a discharge.

CHAPTER **SUMMARY**

The Bankruptcy Code has the power to absolve the debtor of most of his or her debts. The object of any personal bankruptcy case is ultimately to unburden the debtor of most, if not all, of his or her unsecured debt. Discharge of debt is a very powerful result of a successful bankruptcy case. It is literally the legal cancellation of a debt for the debtor. Under 11 U.S.C. § 524(a)(1)(2), the discharge of debt through bankruptcy acts as a statutory injunction against any collection efforts the creditor asserts. Any creditor that pursues the debtor for a discharged debt may be subject to sanctions that could include the debtor's attorney fees and general damages such as loss of income.

According to 11 U.S.C. § 523, certain debts cannot be discharged through bankruptcy. Congress deemed the discharge of these debts to be against public policy. Certain nondischargeable debts include debts owed for domestic support of a former spouse or children; debts imposed by the government; and debts the debtor incurred through fraud, defalcation, or drunk driving. Some debts, such as domestic support and certain taxes, are considered always nondischargeable, and no action is required of the creditor to deem such debts nondischargeable.

There are other debts, such as debts incurred by fraud, defalcation, or the debtor's alleged malicious and willful actions, that can only be deemed dischargeable by the court at an adversarial proceeding. The creditor in this situation would be the proper plaintiff in an adversarial proceeding and would bear the burden of proof. On the other hand, the court can only deem typically nondischargeable debts such as student loans or taxes dischargeable during an adversary proceeding. The debtor in these situations would be the proper plaintiff to bring this type of adversary proceeding.

An adversary proceeding in a bankruptcy case is treated much like a civil lawsuit. The trustee may bring an adversary proceeding to deny discharge of one or all the debtor's debts because of some action the debtor takes, whether innocent or fraudulent, prior to the conclusion of the bankruptcy case. If information regarding the debtor's dishonesty, lack of cooperation with the trustee, or failure to obey an order of the court comes to light after discharge has been granted, the discharge may be revoked. The trustee may request a revocation of discharge within one year of discharge or the closing of the case. A revocation of discharge cannot take effect against a debtor unless the debtor has an opportunity to be heard by the court at an adversarial proceeding.

CONCEPT REVIEW AND REINFORCEMENT

KEY TERMS

adversary proceeding
alimony
custodial parent
defalcation
denial of discharge

discharge
dischargeability
embezzlement
fiduciary
malicious injury

material fact
nondischargeable
revocation of
   discharge
right of redemption

REVIEWING KEY CONCEPTS

1. What type of actions the debtor takes would result in a possible denial of discharge?
2. What type of sanctions, if any, can be imposed on a creditor that pursues a debtor after a discharge of debt has taken effect?
3. Explain the difference between nondischargeable debt and denial of discharge. In what ways are these two concepts similar?

4. Provide three examples of a debt that would be classified as always nondischargeable.
5. Explain the concept of revocation of discharge. When could this happen and what possible actions by the debtor give rise to a revocation of discharge?

BUILDING YOUR PARALEGAL SKILLS

CASE FOR REVIEW

In re Jordan, 521 F.3d 430 (4th Cir. 2008)

BUILDING A PROFESSIONAL PORTFOLIO

PORTFOLIO **EXERCISE**

You work for the law offices of LeMay and Charette, LLC, and your firm represents the debtor Jane Stanley. Ms. Stanley is an individual debtor with primarily consumer debts. Jane has been reading many self-help books regarding bankruptcy, and she learned that not all her debts will be dischargeable. Jane has a personal injury claim pending against her because of an accident she caused a year ago. The case has not been brought to court yet, and Jane's criminal attorney was able to have the DUI charges against her dropped because it was her first offense and she agreed to pay a hefty fine.

Jane feels quite embarrassed about the whole situation. It would just devastate her if the trustee at the bankruptcy court found out about her drunk driving. She feels that because there is no public record of her intoxication and the resulting personal injury claim, she would rather settle with the person she injured quietly and not report this debt on her bankruptcy schedules. Based on what you have learned from reading this chapter and any outside research, draft a letter to the client on behalf of Attorney Charette, explaining all the possible ramifications that might result if Jane conceals this debt from the bankruptcy trustee.

chapter 13

BANKRUPTCY INTERSECTIONS

Shareen, a former fashion designer, has fallen significantly behind on her mortgage payments ever since she lost her six-figure job six months ago. Eight years ago, she bought the house of her dreams, a 1950s bungalow that she updated from the basement to the second floor. Shareen updated every room of the house with new mahogany pegged hardwood flooring and gave the kitchen a complete remodel with quartz countertops and tiled backsplashes—and, of course, top of the line stainless steel appliances were installed in the kitchen. After all, what would her friends think if she had all white appliances? She is finding it very expensive to keep up with this "impress-your-friends" way of life. Shareen took out several personal loans and ran the debt up on her credit cards significantly to help pay for living expenses and all the updates in the home.

Despite losing her job six months ago, she managed to build up quite a bit of equity in her home. She was fortunate enough to owe less than her home's value. However, this fact did little to keep her lender from filing a foreclosure action against her when she fell behind on her mortgage payments. While out in the garden one day, a neighbor whose friend was interested in buying her home approached Shareen. Shareen was excited at the idea of selling her home privately and not losing it to the bank. At this point, Shareen decided she needed to see a lawyer. She was looking for a firm that had attorneys and paralegals who could help her with the foreclosure matter, help her sell her home, and help her file for bankruptcy. Shareen, like many folks, needs a law firm that can help her with an array of legal problems. Read on and discover how bankruptcy law intersects with so many other areas of law and why a cross-trained paralegal is so essential to a law practice!

LEARNING OBJECTIVES

After studying this chapter, you should be able to:

1. Define the term *intersection* as it applies to the practice of law.

2. Identify the ten most common bankruptcy-related crimes.

3. Explain the purpose of a UCC filing.

4. Summarize the effect of family, foreclosure, personal injury, and real estate law on a bankruptcy case.

Introduction

Law cannot be practiced in a neatly compartmentalized vacuum. Inevitably, situations will arise when one area of law collides with another. Legal practitioners call this interplay an intersection. Although attorneys and paralegals alike are often encouraged to specialize, having a broad knowledge of various disciplines is critical. Even the most specialized boutique practice will encounter many intersections that need to be addressed either by the bankruptcy attorney or a specialist in the respective field. Although this chapter is not exhaustive in describing all bankruptcy intersections, it will help the paralegal recognize those four-way stops on the road to helping clients in bankruptcy matters.

intersection

When one area of legal practice is influenced by another area of the law.

A legal **intersection** occurs when one area of legal practice is influenced by another. Bankruptcy is a specialty that is not confined to just one field of practice. Attorneys and paralegals are well aware that although bankruptcy is considered a specialized field of practice, an understanding of how other areas of law affect a client's case is essential. It is essential, therefore, for legal professionals to recognize when these intersections occur and either become proficient in handling these matters in-office or seek the advice of or refer the matter to someone else.

Criminal Law

In the case of *United States v. Colasuonno*, 697 F.3d 164 (2d Cir. 2012), the Second Circuit Court of Appeals held that "bankruptcy laws are not a haven for criminal offenders, but are designed to give relief from financial over-extension." The legislative intent of our bankruptcy system is not to shield criminals from punishment but to provide those in financial distress with a fresh start.

Unfortunately, whenever money is involved, some wrongdoers turn to the bankruptcy court in an effort to wipe out the consequences of their misdeeds. In March 2013, the United States Department of Justice Executive Office for United States Trustees issued a report to Congress regarding the criminal referrals by the U.S. Trustee Program for the fiscal year of 2012. The United States Trustee Program made 2,120 bankruptcy and bankruptcy-related criminal referrals during that year and found that there was a 7.7% percent increase over the 1,968 criminal referrals made during 2011. According to this report, the ten most common allegations of bankruptcy and bankruptcy-related crimes are:

1. Tax fraud
2. False oath/statement
3. Concealment
4. Bankruptcy fraud scheme
5. ID theft and use of false/multiple SSNs
6. Mortgage/real estate fraud
7. Mail/wire fraud
8. Bank fraud
9. Concealment/destruction/withholding of documents
10. Perjury/false statement

Efforts of the United States Trustee Program to combat fraud and abuse in the bankruptcy system include detecting and referring fraud schemes, collaborating with law enforcement partners, and providing specialized training. The most valuable partner in the U.S. Trustee Office's attempts to protect the integrity of the bankruptcy system is the X Factor. Ex-business partners, ex-spouses, ex-employees, as well as creditors are considered a valuable resource in helping identify bad acts that would often go undetected. This proves the old saying heard in many law offices that there is "always someone who knows where the dead bodies are buried!"

BANKRUPTCY-RELATED CRIMES

Bankruptcy-related crimes are found in Title 18 of the United States Code. Paralegals working with bankruptcy clients should review the federal statutes for the bankruptcy crimes such as concealment of assets, false oaths and claims, and bribery. One of the functions of bankruptcy attorneys and paralegals is to impress on clients the importance of truthfulness and accuracy in their dealings with the bankruptcy court and the potential consequences if clients break the law. Clients do not want to trigger an audit, where the accuracy, veracity, and completeness of petitions, schedules, and other information they provide is scrutinized by the U.S. Trustee Office. Although honest mistakes may be overcome with corrections and explanations, criminal acts such as concealment of assets and fraud will be prosecuted. Federal statute 18 U.S.C.A § 152 makes such activities a federal offense carrying a sentence of up to five years in prison, a fine of up to $500,000, or both.

18 U.S.C. § 152 (2011) CONCEALMENT OF ASSETS, FALSE OATHS AND CLAIMS, BRIBERY

A person who:

1. Knowingly and fraudulently conceals from a custodian, trustee, marshal, or other officer of the court charged with the control or custody of property, or, in connection with a case under title 11, from creditors or the United States Trustee, any property belonging to the estate of a debtor;
2. Knowingly and fraudulently makes a false oath or account in or in relation to any case under title 11;
3. Knowingly and fraudulently makes a false declaration, certificate, verification, or statement under penalty of perjury as permitted under section 1746 of title 28, in or in relation to any case under title 11;
4. Knowingly and fraudulently presents any false claim for proof against the estate of a debtor, or uses any such claim in any case under title 11, in a personal capacity or as or through an agent, proxy, or attorney;
5. Knowingly and fraudulently receives any material amount of property from a debtor after the filing of a case under title 11, with intent to defeat the provisions of title 11;
6. Knowingly and fraudulently gives, offers, receives, or attempts to obtain any money or property, remuneration, compensation, reward, advantage, or promise thereof for acting or forbearing to act in any case under title 11;
7. In a personal capacity or as an agent or officer of any person or corporation, in contemplation of a case under title 11 by or against the person or any other person or corporation, or with intent to defeat the provisions of title 11, knowingly and fraudulently transfers or conceals any of his property or the property of such other person or corporation;
8. After the filing of a case under title 11 or in contemplation thereof, knowingly and fraudulently conceals, destroys, mutilates, falsifies, or makes a false

entry in any recorded information (including books, documents, records, and papers) relating to the property or financial affairs of a debtor; or

9. After the filing of a case under title 11, knowingly and fraudulently withholds from a custodian, trustee, marshal, or other officer of the court or a United States Trustee entitled to its possession, any recorded information (including books, documents, records, and papers) relating to the property or financial affairs of a debtor, shall be fined under this title, imprisoned not more than 5 years, or both.

18 U.S.C. § 157 (2011) BANKRUPTCY FRAUD

A person who, having devised or intending to devise a scheme or artifice to defraud and for the purpose of executing or concealing such a scheme or artifice or attempting to do so:

1. Files a petition under title 11, including a fraudulent involuntary petition under section 303 of such title;
2. Files a document in a proceeding under title 11; or
3. Makes a false or fraudulent representation, claim, or promise concerning or in relation to a proceeding under title 11, at any time before or after the filing of the petition, or in relation to a proceeding falsely asserted to be pending under such title, shall be fined under this title, imprisoned not more than 5 years, or both.

Another important federal statute is 18 U.S.C. § 3284, which states that the "concealment of assets of a debtor in a case under title 11 shall be deemed to be a continuing offense until the debtor shall have been finally discharged or a discharge denied, and the period of limitations shall not begin to run until such final discharge or denial of discharge." The federal statute of limitations establishing the time frame for which criminal charges of bankruptcy fraud may be filed against a debtor is five years from the date of discharge.

Clients facing allegations of federal crimes should be represented by an expert criminal defense attorney with experience in handling these types of cases. The consequences are too great for an attorney who attempts to dabble in criminal cases. Federal prosecutors faced with defendants accused of bankruptcy and bankruptcy-related crimes may decide to throw the book at them and add additional, nonbankruptcy-related charges such as fraud, perjury, bribery, embezzlement, money laundering, and destruction of records as well as seek forfeiture of the debtor's assets.

Fans of Bravo channel's reality show, *The Real Housewives of New Jersey* may be familiar with the trials and tribulations of Teresa Giudice and Giuseppe "Joe" Giudice. This case is a classic example of a situation that involves the intersection of bankruptcy, criminal, and immigration law. The Giudices filed a voluntary Chapter 7 petition in October 2009; their debts were never discharged. During the course of the bankruptcy proceedings, the U.S. trustee raised serious accusations of concealment of assets and fraud. When questioned, the couple took refuge under the Fifth Amendment of the U.S. Constitution and remained silent in an effort not to incriminate themselves. The Giudices withdrew their petitions in hopes of avoiding possible criminal prosecution.

Unfortunately for the Giudices, on July 29, 2013, the United States Department of Justice filed an indictment in the United States District Court of New Jersey that included 39 counts, including allegations of bankruptcy fraud, specifically concealment of assets, false oaths, and false declarations, not to mention a whole host of other federal crimes. In November 2013, the government added two new charges of bank fraud and loan application fraud to the indictment, alleging that Teresa Giudice lied about her income and employment situation on a mortgage loan application.

In March 2014, the Giudices pleaded guilty to mortgage fraud and several counts of bankruptcy fraud, conspiracy to commit mail fraud and wire fraud, and failure to pay taxes. The Giudices were sentenced in October 2014. Teresa Giudice was to serve 15 months in prison on conspiracy and bankruptcy charges. Joe Giudice was sentenced to 41 months on fraud.

Commercial Law

A **Uniform Commercial Code (UCC) filing** is often used by creditors to secure rights to collateral specified in secured financing agreements. The creditor files the agreement with the Secretary of State's office lender and thus puts the public on notice that the creditor has a legally recognized interest in the collateral until it is fully paid for; it also establishes the creditor's legal title in the assets if the debtor defaults.

USA Bank gives Park City Chocolate Company a loan to purchase a delivery truck in the state of Connecticut and, in the course of their transaction, the parties enter into a security agreement. A **secured financing agreement** is a contract between the creditor and the debtor by which the debtor agrees to give the creditor an interest in specific assets pledged as collateral. It must be in writing, signed by both the creditor and the debtor, describe the collateral, and contain specific language expressly stating the that debtor is granting a security interest to the creditor. The security agreement must also be supported by consideration. The creditor records the secured financing agreement with the office of the secretary of state in the jurisdiction where the business is located.

In this example, USA Bank files a UCC financing statement with the Connecticut Secretary of the State, naming Park City Chocolate Company as the debtor and the new delivery truck as collateral. This process is called **perfecting the security interest in the property**. Article 9 of the Uniform Commercial Code has created categories of collateral subject to perfection of security interests. The categories are agricultural liens, chattel paper (including electronic chattel paper), commercial tort claims, deposit accounts, documents, general intangibles, goods (including consumer goods, fixtures, equipment, inventory), instruments (including promissory notes), investment property, letter of credit rights, manufactured homes, and proceeds. Practically speaking, it means that Park City Chocolate Company cannot sell or dispose of the property without first paying off the debt owed to USA Bank. If Park City Chocolate Company files for bankruptcy, the lender is now considered a secured creditor and thus a secured claim. Recall that a secured claim is in a better position in a bankruptcy case than one that is unsecured.

UCC filings often appear in bankruptcy proceedings. Paralegals who work in law offices that represent creditors may prepare UCC filings. When representing debtors, it is often the job of the paralegal to review and summarize UCC, judgment, tax, and other lien searches for the attorney. Learning how to draft UCC filings and research the state's database is an important function of the paralegal. The paralegal should become familiar with the secretary of state's website in the jurisdiction where the paralegal is employed because each state has different forms, requirements, and search methods on its website.

Uniform Commercial Code (UCC) filing
Often used by creditors to secure rights to collateral specified in secured financing agreements. The creditor files the agreement with the Secretary of State's office lender and thus puts the public on notice that the creditor has a legally recognized interest in the collateral until it is fully paid for; it also establishes the creditor's legal title in the assets if the debtor defaults.

secured financing agreement
A contract between the creditor and the debtor by which the debtor agrees to give the creditor an interest in specific assets pledged as collateral.

perfecting the security interest in the property
The process by which the creditor records a secured financing agreement with the office of the secretary of state in the jurisdiction where the business is located.

Family Law

Spouses may file for bankruptcy while the marriage is intact or when the parties have decided to file for divorce. In either instance, some issues in the bankruptcy case might be complicated because of the marital relationship.

THE DECISION TO FILE JOINTLY OR SEPARATELY

The intersection between bankruptcy and family law occurs whenever a spouse or divorcing spouse files for bankruptcy. If a spouse has incurred debt in his or her name only, it is practical for that spouse alone to file for bankruptcy protection. When spouses have debt in which both are considered joint and severally liable, however, both should file for bankruptcy. Why? If one spouse receives a discharge on joint debts in a Chapter 7 case, creditors are free to pursue collection on the debt from the nonfiling spouse. In a Chapter 13 repayment case, however, the nonfiling spouse is protected from creditor claims as a co-debtor by the co-debtor stay under 11 U.S.C. § 1301 as long as the filing spouse makes regular payments under the plan.

In community property states, namely Arizona, California, Idaho, Louisiana, Nevada, New Mexico, Texas, Washington, and Wisconsin, both spouses own any debts or any property acquired during the marriage. The advantage of living in a community property state is that creditors cannot touch any property the nonfiling spouse acquires after the filing spouse's bankruptcy has been discharged according to 11 U.S.C. § 524. In addition, joint community debts are also discharged and beyond reach of the creditors. Creditors may, however, sue the nonfiling spouse to collect on a debt but are only allowed to pursue collection against the nonfiling spouse's separate property that was acquired either before the marriage or by gift or inheritance.

WHICH TO FILE FIRST: BANKRUPTCY OR DIVORCE?

The result of a study released in 2013 by researchers at Kansas State University revealed something that the legal profession has known for years. The number one reason for divorce is fights over money. Financial stress not only leads to divorce, but, in many cases, family law and bankruptcy law will intersect, whether before or after the couple is divorced. Spouses may be jointly liable for taxes, joint credit cards or loans, and other contracts of joint obligation or cosigning arrangement. When the marriage is going well, spouses mutually support one another financially and with best intentions, not often contemplating what may happen in the event of a breakdown of the marriage coupled with a bankruptcy.

Couples who have incurred substantial debt during the course of the marriage should, in most circumstances, file a joint bankruptcy petition before finalizing their divorce. Doing so in this order will help minimize the complications associated with the distribution of marital assets as well as marital debts. The divorce is simplified because the dischargeable debts have been eliminated, and more funds are now available for support obligations such as spousal and child support.

There are circumstances that make filing for bankruptcy *after* the divorce more advantageous. This would require an assessment of the Means Test by reviewing the couple's income for the six months prior to the bankruptcy filing and, in a separate calculation, the client's income under a similar test. If a client earns much less than the spouse, it might be advisable for them to wait until after the divorce is final so they could qualify for Chapter 7 instead of Chapter 13.

Another reason to file after the divorce is when the client's state does not allow doubling of exemptions. In this case, it may make more sense to file separately.

EFFECT OF THE AUTOMATIC STAY

What the Automatic Stay does not stop is the debtor's obligation to pay tax debts, child support, and alimony. These obligations remain intact and enforceable. If the divorce has been filed already, and then an Automatic Stay is issued, any property that is part of the bankruptcy estate is subject to the Automatic Stay. For example, Jillian and David are in the process of divorce. They have been unable to pay their mortgage, so the bank is seeking to foreclose on the marital home, which has no equity. The Automatic Stay, however, prohibits any action on the property without an order from the bankruptcy court. Under these circumstances, the bank could petition to have the stay lifted and proceed with the foreclosure proceedings because there is nothing to save on property that is financially under water. The Automatic Stay also does not affect evictions and criminal prosecutions. This is particularly important to know in matters involving the prosecution of domestic violence cases that may arise in family-related matters.

DISCHARGEABILITY ISSUES

Prior to the passage of the Bankruptcy Abuse Prevention and Consumer Protection Act of 2005 (BAPCPA), debtors used bankruptcy as a means of discharging, or avoiding, financial responsibilities such as court-ordered alimony, child support, and property distribution. BAPCPA remedied this practice by classifying alimony, maintenance, and child support payments as domestic support obligations (DSOs) and subject to first priority in bankruptcy proceedings. Other creditors cannot receive any payments owed to them until the domestic support obligations are fulfilled, and these obligations cannot be discharged in bankruptcy under either Chapter 7 or Chapter 13. The debtor is responsible for paying DSOs even after receiving a discharge in bankruptcy. The ability to discharge debts that are the result of a property settlement, however, depends on whether the debtor has filed for Chapter 7 or 13. In general, property settlement obligations are not dischargeable in a Chapter 7 bankruptcy but may be discharged in a Chapter 13 case.

ADVERSARY PROCEEDINGS

A situation may arise when a divorce client contacts the office to inform the attorney that he or she has received a notice from a bankruptcy court informing him or her that his or her former spouse has filed for bankruptcy. Although DSOs are not dischargeable, some property settlements are subject to discharge, and the debtor may be seeking to do away with these obligations. This notice should not be ignored and requires immediate action to preserve the client's rights. The client should file an **adversary proceeding complaint** in the bankruptcy case. This is a civil case filed with the bankruptcy court, and filing it will permit the client to argue to the judge that discharging nonsupport obligations will have an adverse effect on the client. Although property division and nonsupport orders for the benefit of a spouse are not dischargeable in Chapter 7, they are in Chapter 13.

adversary proceeding complaint
The initiating document in an adversary proceeding. The plaintiff files a formal complaint with the court and has that complaint served on the defendant.

The client may wish to add a clause to the property settlement portion of the separation agreement that acknowledges that property division and the support obligations of alimony and child support are connected and that any property settlement arrangement for the transfers of assets and payment of debts are to be considered domestic support obligations under the Bankruptcy Code. Basically, the clause establishes that if either of the parties files for bankruptcy, the purpose behind it is to seek relief from creditors, not to avoid obligations to the spouse. Furthermore, the parties would agree in writing that no obligations owed to the family pursuant to the agreement are dischargeable in the event of either spouse filing for post-divorce bankruptcy. This will give the client fodder to dispute attempts by the former spouse to discharge property or debt settlement arrangements in a Chapter 13 bankruptcy.

Foreclosure Law

foreclosure
A legal proceeding a lender, usually a bank or mortgage trust company, files against a debtor who defaults on a mortgage loan on a parcel of real property. The lender seeks to force the sale of real property secured by a mortgage to recover the money and interest due and the legal costs of the foreclosure when the borrower fails to make payments.

Job loss, medical bills for major illnesses or injuries, crushing student loans for one or both spouses, lack of health insurance, along with turning to credit cards to pay for everyday necessities may result in making monthly mortgage payments out of reach. It is not uncommon for a family in this position to find itself facing the intersection of foreclosure and bankruptcy law. A **foreclosure** is a legal proceeding by which the lender seeks to force the sale of real property secured by a mortgage to recover the money and interest due and the legal costs of the foreclosure when the borrower fails to make payments. When a homeowner files for bankruptcy either under Chapter 7 or Chapter 13, the Automatic Stay goes into effect and stops all foreclosure proceedings. The foreclosure sale will be delayed unless the foreclosure notice has already been filed or the creditor files a motion with the bankruptcy court to lift the Automatic Stay.

In a Chapter 7 case, the effect of filing for bankruptcy delays the foreclosure proceedings and buys the debtor a little more time to regroup. In a Chapter 13, a repayment plan when the debtor has sufficient income and a considerable amount of equity in the home may enable the debtor to save the home from foreclosure. Filing under Chapter 13 also allows for lien stripping, which is the ability to remove or strip junior mortgages or liens from the home and discharge them as unsecured debts when the home has a value lower than the amount of the senior mortgage. The result of lien stripping is that the junior mortgage or lien becomes an unsecured nonpriority debt that may be discharged in bankruptcy.

Personal Injury Law

Although Bankruptcy Code 11 U.S.C. § 522(d) (10)(C) exempts a debtor's "right to receive a disability, illness, or unemployment benefit" in a worker's compensation claim, personal injury cases, on the other hand, present varying issues when they intersect with bankruptcy law. During the course of the initial interview, a well-drafted bankruptcy worksheet or questionnaire will include questions regarding personal injury and worker's compensation claims. Although workers compensation claims are exempt, the claim should be listed on the bankruptcy petition as exempt property. Personal injury cases however, require special treatment.

DEBTOR AS TORTFEASOR

A concern among many personal injury plaintiffs is whether a tortfeasor may seek to avoid liability by filing for bankruptcy. A tortfeasor may not discharge a financial obligation incurred as a result of an intentional tort such as assault, battery, false imprisonment, libel, and slander or drunk driving. Other torts are dischargeable. Tort claims are considered unsecured debts and generally receive less protection than secured creditors in the order of priorities.

Asbestos litigation cases have led to protections in the Bankruptcy Code for victims suffering from mesothelioma or other asbestos-related illnesses. Asbestos defendants who want to remain in business by filing for reorganization are required under 11 U.S.C. § 524(G) to refrain from tort litigation and, instead, to set up asbestos trusts to pay victims' current and future claims. The bankruptcy court must approve the amount of funds set aside in the asbestos trust before approving the reorganization.

DEBTOR AS INJURED PARTY

A bankruptcy debtor who is also an injured party in a personal injury case must inform his or her bankruptcy attorney of the existence of a claim. The failure to disclose a pending personal injury claim is considered a crime. When the bankruptcy petition is filed, the trustee assumes control over the personal injury matter and has the authority to settle or litigate the case. Unfortunately, the debtor has no authority to accept or reject a settlement, participate in its negotiation, or decide whether to go to trial. Any funds obtained become part of the bankruptcy estate and are available to pay creditors. Federal and state exemptions are available for personal injury proceeds; however, they are limited in the amount the debtor may shield. As of April 1, 2013, the exemption for payments on account of personal bodily injury is $22,975.

Only those medical expenses incurred at the time the bankruptcy action was commenced are eligible for discharge. Medical expenses incurred during the pendency of the bankruptcy are not considered dischargeable medical debts, but they are considered an administration expense, and the trustee determines the payments made to medical service providers. For the debtor, this means that the remaining debt owed to medical service providers is the responsibility of the debtor.

Failure to disclose pending claims to the bankruptcy court may result in dismissal or revocation of the debtor's bankruptcy case, thereby exposing the debtor to criminal prosecution. Furthermore, debtors who fail to disclose a pending personal injury case to the bankruptcy court also run the risk of having their personal injury case dismissed. Defense attorneys who represent insurance companies make it a practice to instruct their paralegals to check the public bankruptcy court records for pending cases. Under the doctrine of judicial estoppel, the debtor, as personal injury plaintiff, is barred from proceeding in the tort case when he or she fails to disclose the action as an asset in a bankruptcy petition, as illustrated in the following case.

CASE **13.1** *Berge v. Kuno Mader and DMG America, Inc.,* 354 Ill.Dec. 374, 957 N.E.2d 968 (1st Dist. 2011)

In April 2006, plaintiff, Shirley Berge, filed for bankruptcy under chapter 13. (11 U.S.C. § 101, *et seq* (2007)). The following month, she was involved in an auto accident with a car owned by defendant DMG America, Inc., and driven by DMG's employee, defendant Kuno Mader. Plaintiff filed her negligence complaint concerning this accident in state court in November 2007 which is now the subject of this appeal. In May 2009, plaintiff converted her chapter 13

(Continued)

(Continued)

bankruptcy petition to a chapter 7 petition. (11 U.S.C. § 101, *et seq* (2007)). In October 2009, she received a "no assets" discharge of her debts in bankruptcy court and her chapter 7 petition was closed as fully resolved. It is undisputed that plaintiff never disclosed her state court claim against the defendants to the bankruptcy court while her chapter 13 and 7 petitions were pending, although plaintiff had numerous opportunities to do so. Defendants independently learned of plaintiff's bankruptcy case and filed a motion, captioned as one for summary judgment, which requested the state trial court to apply the doctrine of judicial estoppel and dismiss the case for plaintiff's failure to disclose the negligence claim in her list of statutorily required disclosures in bankruptcy court. After initial briefing of defendants' motion, plaintiff also returned to bankruptcy court to reopen her discharged case to disclose the instant case.

Plaintiff raises for the first time on appeal that the state court does not have jurisdiction to decide whether this personal injury case can proceed because of the plaintiff's non-compliance with the statute that requires her to list any lawsuit as an asset in her bankruptcy case, as required by statute. The argument presented is that only the bankruptcy court can decide issues stemming from the bankruptcy filing. This argument is without merit. It is the state court, in the first instance, that decides whether it has or does not have jurisdiction in any particular case. Defendants' position is that plaintiff is barred from raising this jurisdictional issue because the plaintiff failed to raise it in the trial court. However, it is axiomatic that jurisdictional issues can be raised at any time, even *sua sponte…*

This case presents this court with a simple question: Should plaintiff's failure to disclose a cause of action as an asset in her bankruptcy case prevent her from proceeding with that cause of action in state court under the doctrine of judicial estoppel?

The Illinois courts have determined that judicial estoppel has five separate elements, as follows:

> (1) the two positions must be taken by the same party; (2) the positions must be taken in judicial proceedings; (3) the positions must be given under oath; (4) the party must have successfully maintained the first position, and received some benefit thereby; and (5) the two positions must be totally inconsistent.

All five elements are present in this case. First, plaintiff presented two conflicting positions. Her position in bankruptcy court was that she had no pending lawsuits. Her pursuit of this state court action was to the contrary. Secondly, plaintiff made these conflicting positions in separate judicial proceedings. Plaintiff never disclosed her lawsuit in bankruptcy court, but she then turned around and actively pursued her pending personal injury case against defendants in state court. Third, plaintiff's complaint in this case and her many representations in her bankruptcy case were filings made under oath. Fourth, plaintiff benefitted by having her debts discharged in bankruptcy without giving her creditors any knowledge of her potential to recover a money judgment. In other words, plaintiff's failure to disclose left her with the ability to permanently avoid her debts after recovering a money judgment. Lastly, the final element is present and could not be clearer. Plaintiff never disclosed she had a lawsuit to the bankruptcy court while actively maintaining a lawsuit in Illinois state court.

For the foregoing reasons, we affirm the trial court's decision dismissing this lawsuit on judicial estoppel grounds. We find that the trial court did not abuse its discretion when it ruled that plaintiff was judicially estopped from pursuing her negligence case.

Probate Law

In the probate process, the decedent's personal representative has the responsibility of gathering the decedent's assets, paying his or her debts, and then distributing that which is left over either to the heirs at law or beneficiaries under the will. Although the personal representative may file lawsuits and other legal actions on behalf of the decedent's estate, he or she cannot file for bankruptcy in hopes of discharging the decedent's debts. If the decedent died without enough funds to pay any existing debts, the estate is, at this point, insolvent.

Probate law and bankruptcy intersect when the debtor is either an heir at law or beneficiary of the deceased's estate. The debtor must disclose a potential inheritance to the bankruptcy attorney, whether that potential exists at the time of the initial interview or occurs during the pendency of the bankruptcy case. Exemptions allow for the debtor to keep some of his or her inheritance; however, if the amount of the inheritance is greater than the exemption and the debtor has already filed for bankruptcy, the funds are now considered part of the bankruptcy estate. If the debtor has not yet filed, is it advisable for him or her to wait before filing for bankruptcy? The inheritance, if substantial enough, may help the debtor avoid having to file for bankruptcy and possibly take advantage of one of the bankruptcy alternatives.

A client who receives an inheritance within 180 days after filing a Chapter 7 case has a duty to disclose the inheritance, and the funds become part of the bankruptcy estate. Exemptions allow the client to keep a certain amount; however, any excess funds may be distributed to creditors. Chapter 13 clients must disclose the inheritance, and the nonexempt amount is factored into the debtor's repayment plan. If the inheritance is received after 180 days after the filing of the petition has lapsed, the Chapter 7 debtor may keep the inheritance. Inheritances obtained by a Chapter 13 debtor, however, may result in the reevaluation of the repayment plan and an amendment in favor of creditors.

Trusts also present problems when they intersect with bankruptcy cases. Some clients are under the mistaken impression that they can protect their assets by simply transferring them to their children or other family members. Funds or property transferred into trusts for the purposes of avoiding the creditors' reach may be deemed fraudulent transfers by the court. Debtors are also required to disclose all assets on the bankruptcy schedules, and that includes trusts. The trustee will also inquire whether the debtor is the beneficiary of a trust, which could mean that the debtor is receiving or entitled to receive funds. It is important to research state trust law, the type of trust created, the debtor's interest, and the specific terms of a trust when trusts and bankruptcies intersect.

Real Estate Law

After the debtor files for bankruptcy, any real property the debtor owns is now part of the bankruptcy estate and under the control of the trustee. A debtor does not have the authority to sell or refinance any real property without the approval of the bankruptcy court. The debtor must provide notice to any interested parties, and a hearing must take place under 11 U.S.C. § 363. Problems often arise when real estate law and bankruptcy intersect because the debtor usually obtains a discharge of debts before the trustee has had the opportunity to evaluate the property. A debtor may not understand that the bankruptcy case has not terminated until it has been closed. In this interim period, the debtor may mistakenly transfer the property through a sale because market conditions and rates have improved or an interested buyer has emerged. If a transfer or refinancing does take place, the trustee has the authority to undo the sale. This creates problems for the debtor and the new buyer. Therefore, it is vital for the debtor to wait until the bankruptcy case is officially closed or seek the court's permission before going forward with the sale. The closing of the case will signal to the debtor that any asset that was not administered during the course of the bankruptcy proceedings is now deemed abandoned and the debtor is free to sell the property.

Do you remember Shareen from the beginning of the chapter? She represents most clients who come to the attorney's office with several legal issues that all intersect. When working in a law firm, you will find that many clients, like Shareen, have intersecting legal issues that they are hoping your firm will resolve. It sounds like Shareen needs the legal assistance of a real estate lawyer, foreclosure lawyer, and a bankruptcy lawyer all at the same time. If Shareen's home is in foreclosure, she will need a foreclosure attorney to help negotiate with the bank to allow her to sell her home privately. She will also need a real estate lawyer to represent her at the closing on her home. Unfortunately, due to her significant credit card debt and personal loans, it looks like she might need the assistance of a bankruptcy lawyer as well. A paralegal able to assist an attorney with all these areas of law will be worth his or her weight in gold to an attorney faced with a client in need of multiple legal services.

CHAPTER **SUMMARY**

A legal intersection occurs when one area of legal practice is influenced by another. Bankruptcy is one of those specialties not confined to just one field of practice. Bankruptcy-related crimes are addressed in Title 18 of the United States Code. Paralegals working with bankruptcy clients should review the federal statutes for bankruptcy crimes such as concealment of assets, false oaths and claims, and bribery. UCC filings often appear in bankruptcy proceedings. Paralegals who work in law offices that represent creditors may prepare UCC filings. When representing debtors, it is often the job of the paralegal to review and summarize UCC, judgment, tax, and other lien searches for the attorney. Spouses may file for bankruptcy while the marriage is intact or when the parties have decided to file for divorce. In either instance, some issues in the bankruptcy case may be complicated because of the marital relationship. It is not uncommon for a family

in this position to find itself facing the intersection of foreclosure and bankruptcy law. Personal injury cases require special treatment.

Tort claims are considered unsecured debts and generally receive less protection than secured creditors in the order of priorities. Probate law and bankruptcy intersect when the debtor is either an heir at law or beneficiary of the deceased's estate. The debtor must disclose a potential inheritance to the bankruptcy attorney whether that potential exists at the time of the initial interview or occurs during the pendency of the bankruptcy case. After the debtor files for bankruptcy, any real property the debtor owns is now part of the bankruptcy estate and under the control of the trustee. A debtor does not have the authority to sell or refinance any real property without the approval of the bankruptcy court.

CONCEPT REVIEW AND REINFORCEMENT

KEY **TERMS**

adversary proceeding complaint
foreclosure
intersection

perfecting the security interest in the property
secured financing agreement

Uniform Commercial Code (UCC)
filing

REVIEWING **KEY CONCEPTS**

1. What does the term *intersection* mean and how does it apply to legal professionals?
2. What are the five most common allegations of bankruptcy and bankruptcy-related crimes?
3. Identify the U.S. Trustee's Office most valuable partner in detecting bankruptcy crime offenders.
4. What is a UCC filing? Describe its relevance in a bankruptcy case.
5. Define the term *secured financing agreement*. What does the phrase "perfecting the security interest in property" mean?
6. What is the effect of the Automatic Stay on child support and alimony payments?
7. What is the effect of the Automatic Stay in a Chapter 7 case?
8. During the initial interview, a new bankruptcy client, Penny Pincher, confides in you that she was injured in a car accident and has a pending lawsuit against the other driver. She asks you not to tell your supervising attorney about the case. What do you do?
9. Mark Rapalo, a new bankruptcy client, informs you that his mother has just been admitted to hospice and, unfortunately, has about a week to live. Mark's mother was diagnosed with pancreatic cancer six months ago and immediately executed a will leaving her entire estate, valued at $1 million dollars, to her only son. His friend from the gym, an auto mechanic, told him that he should file for bankruptcy and discharge his debts so that when his mother's probate estate settles, he can enjoy his inheritance free and clear of any debt. Mark thinks this is a great idea. Do you? Did Mark's friend give him good advice?
10. Suresh Singh, one of the firm's bankruptcy clients, recently received a discharge in his bankruptcy case. Suresh owns a small parcel of land that was listed on his bankruptcy petition. His neighbor has approached him and offered a good price for the property. Suresh calls and wants to know whether his bankruptcy attorney can also represent him in the sale of the property. What advice do you think your supervising attorney will give Suresh?

BUILDING YOUR PARALEGAL SKILLS

CASE FOR **REVIEW**

State Bank of Arthur v. Miller (*In re Miller*), 2012 WL 3589426 (C.D. Ill. Aug. 17, 2012)

BUILDING A PROFESSIONAL PORTFOLIO

PORTFOLIO **EXERCISES**

You are a newly hired paralegal for the law firm of Acevedo, Bedollo, & Carreras. The three attorneys met in law school and decided to open their own firm upon passing the bar. One of the areas of legal practice for the firm will be bankruptcy law, representing both creditors and debtors. Attorney Lillian Acevedo has asked you to research your jurisdiction's secretary of state website and prepare an interoffice memo for the office staff about how to conduct a lien search in your state's UCC filing system. She would also like you to search the Internet and include in this memo some basic information about the importance of using a debtor's exact name on a UCC financing statement to perfect a security interest. Specifically, she wants you to include a section that discusses what happens if the debtor's name is wrong on a financing statement or on a search request.

chapter 14

BANKRUPTCY LAW ETHICS AND THE ROLE OF THE PARALEGAL

LEARNING OBJECTIVES

After studying this chapter, you should be able to:

1. Recognize the basic ethical issues that affect a bankruptcy practice.

2. Explain the role of the bankruptcy paralegal.

3. Identify the qualifications and requirements for a position as a bankruptcy paralegal.

4. Define the role of the bankruptcy petition preparer.

5. Analyze the ethical considerations for paralegals in a bankruptcy practice.

Casey graduated at the top of his paralegal studies class in college last year and landed a job at a prestigious bankruptcy law firm in his town. Casey felt very prepared to tackle the challenges of this area of law after acing a very detailed course in bankruptcy law. He also felt very knowledgeable about the subject area because he had filed for a Chapter 7 bankruptcy himself several years ago.

Casey started his job, and all seemed to be going quite well for the first year or so. With his comfort level with the clients continuing to rise, Casey began to take more liberties with clients on his job. After all, he had completed numerous intake interviews with new bankruptcy clients and sat in on many clients' consultations with his supervising attorney. After helping some clients with their bankruptcy forms and schedules, Casey found himself giving advice to some clients. Casey's advice included discussions with clients regarding which chapter of the Bankruptcy Code he felt might be best for them. In addition, Casey began explaining to the clients the various ways they can use Chapter 13 to keep some of their property and how they could cramdown specific secured loans. Is Casey treading on thin ice here? What ethical rule is Casey violating? What could he be accused of if his behavior continues? Read on to discover some categories of ethical behavior that could help Casey.

Introduction

Bankruptcy law is considered an advanced course in most paralegal programs and is typically offered later in the curriculum. Although this chapter is entitled "Bankruptcy Law Ethics and the Role of the Paralegal," it is offered with the knowledge that the student reading this text has already taken general courses in the paralegal profession and ethics and has a basic understanding of the topic. This chapter begins with a discussion of the four C's, the most common ethical issues that arise in bankruptcy practice: conflict of interest, competency, confidentiality, and compensation. The chapter also defines the role of the bankruptcy paralegal and the bankruptcy petition preparer. More important, this chapter equips paralegal students with the knowledge required to avoid engaging in the unauthorized practice of law when working in the field of bankruptcy.

Bankruptcy Law Ethics

INTRODUCTION

Although all of rules of professional conduct may apply to a bankruptcy case, depending on its specific circumstances, the four most common ethical issues involved in practice are conflicts of interest, competency, confidentiality, and compensation. It is important for the bankruptcy paralegal to become acquainted with these issues to assist the attorney in complying with these rules and alert the attorney when problems arise.

CONFLICTS OF INTEREST

State ethical codes prohibit an attorney from representing a new client whose interests are materially adverse to those of a former client if the new matter and the former matter are substantially related to each other. This is known as a **conflict of interest**. For example, a bankruptcy attorney who represents a debtor as well as one of the debtor's creditors has a conflict of interest. In the Detroit bankruptcy for example, a conflict of interest issue arose involving the law firm of Miller, Canfield, Paddock and Stone. The firm represents the city of Detroit, the debtor in this case, as well as one of its creditors, the Public Lighting Authority. The potential conflict of interest came to light during a hearing regarding the use of utility taxes to finance $210 million in repairs for the more than 40,000 broken street lights in the city. U.S. Bankruptcy Judge Steven Rhodes indicated that he may disqualify the firm from representing the Public Lighting Authority unless the legal briefs he ordered the parties to file regarding the issue could convince him otherwise.

It is not uncommon for attorneys who practice bankruptcy law to work on the creditors' side in other cases, so this type of conflict is not unlikely. Before agreeing to represent a bankruptcy client, the attorney, with the assistance of a paralegal, must conduct a **conflicts check** to determine whether a potential problem exists in representing the new client. A conflicts check requires a review of the client database to determine whether the firm has formerly or is currently representing a client whose interest may conflict with a potential new client. It is better to know this information before taking on the representation of a new client and running the risk that a court may disqualify the firm.

During the initial interview, the client should be encouraged to disclose not only all creditors but any others that may have an interest in the debtor's bankruptcy. Potential problems can arise if the attorney currently represents opposing parties or has represented the opposing party in the past and is now armed with confidential information that can be used in favor of a new client to the detriment of a former client. Another situation may occur if a former client now becomes an adversary against a new client. Although codes of professional conduct for individual states have sections addressing conflicts of interest, so does the U.S. Bankruptcy Court. This means that the bankruptcy attorney must pay attention

conflict of interest
Relationships or circumstances that compromise the duty of loyalty that attorneys and paralegals owe to their clients.

conflicts check
A formal review of the law firm's client database to determine whether the firm has formerly or is currently representing a client whose interest may conflict with a potential new client.

to both. Generally, the states' codes prohibit an attorney from representing a new client whose interests are materially adverse to those of a former client if the new matter and the former matter are substantially related to each other. Ethical codes allow clients to sign a waiver, allowing the attorney with conflicting interest to assume representation. In such a case, if the client does not sign such a waiver, the attorney is disqualified and must withdraw from the case. The Bankruptcy Code, however, has stricter standards and contains no provision for waivers.

Bankruptcy law places additional rules regarding conflicts of interest on attorneys practicing in the field. The bankruptcy court judge must determine whether there is a conflict of interest by applying sections of the Bankruptcy Code as well as the Federal Rules of Bankruptcy Procedure. Bankruptcy Code 11 U.S.C. § 327 addresses the issue of employment of professional persons, which includes lawyers, by a trustee or debtor in possession in Chapter 11 reorganizations. Under this section, a professional person cannot "… represent or hold any interest adverse to the debtor or to the estate …" and must be a disinterested party. Bankruptcy Code 11 U.S.C. § 101(14) defines a disinterested person as follows.

(14) The term "disinterested person" means a person that:
(A) Is not a creditor, an equity security holder, or an insider;
(B) Is not and was not, within 2 years before the date of the filing of the petition, a director, officer, or employee of the debtor; and
(C) Does not have an interest materially adverse to the interest of the estate or of any class of creditors or equity security holders, by reason of any direct or indirect relationship to, connection with, or interest in, the debtor, or for any other reason.

A **disinterested party** in a bankruptcy case is someone who does not have any interest materially adverse to a creditor because of his or her association with the debtor.

When applying for approval for employment, professional persons must disclose, according to Fed. R. Bankr. P. 2014, "to the best of the applicant's knowledge, all of the person's connections with the debtor, creditors, any other party-in-interest, their respective attorneys and accountants, the United States Trustee, or any person employed in the office of the United States Trustee."

COMPETENCY

competency
An ethical rule that requires attorneys and paralegals to possess the knowledge, skill, preparation, and thoroughness to represent bankruptcy clients adequately.

The ethical rule of **competency** requires attorneys and paralegals to possess the knowledge, skill, preparation, and thoroughness to represent bankruptcy clients adequately. Bankruptcy law is a specialty in the legal profession, requiring an understanding of the Bankruptcy Code and how it applies to clients' cases. Lawyers who represent consumers in Chapter 7 and Chapter 13 cases tend to have more problems with the issue of competency than those who work on the more complex Chapter 11 reorganizations. Reorganizations require a higher level of legal skill given the complexities of both the Bankruptcy Code and an understanding of finances.

Unfortunately, some unwary attorneys tread into bankruptcy under the perception that it just involves filling out a few forms. Such an attorney could easily be exposed to malpractice when adopting this attitude. Some attorneys dabble, out of interest or necessity, in areas of the law in which they have no training or knowledge.

Paralegals who work for bankruptcy attorneys should have a basic understanding of the bankruptcy procedure, terminology, client interviews, and preparation of relevant documents. It is also a good idea for both attorneys and paralegals to attend regular continuing education programs. Reading updates on bankruptcy law and relevant cases is also advisable and particularly easy with use of the Internet. Another way to remain competent is to attend meetings and events sponsored by the bankruptcy law section of the state bar association or paralegal association. Some states permit paralegals to join state bar associations as nonvoting members.

CONFIDENTIALITY

The decision to walk into a bankruptcy attorney's office does not come easily, and it is one step that clients deliberate over and over again in their minds. A huge concern among clients is the shame and embarrassment around this issue and the concern that friends, families, acquaintances, employers, coworkers, and customers will find out. These individuals will most likely not find out about the bankruptcy unless they are in the position of creditors. State codes of professional responsibility require attorneys and their paralegals to protect clients' **confidentiality**. Information regarding the client's case shall not be divulged to a third party unless the client consents or the attorney is required to do so under the law. Clients should be assured that both the attorneys and nonattorneys in the office will safeguard their confidentiality, and others will not know unless clients choose to disclose. Bankruptcy clients are not required by law to disclose their filings publicly, and there is no equivalent to a police blotter as in a criminal case or publication as in probate matters.

The confidential communications between the bankruptcy attorney and the client are protected by **attorney–client privilege**. This rule prevents the attorney from disclosing privileged information unless the client waives the privilege, clearing the way for the attorney to discuss the contents of the communications with a third party. A situation could arise in which a trustee, for example, questions a bankruptcy client during a 341 hearing, and the client may wish to use the attorney–client privilege to refuse to answer a question that was part of a legal discussion with the attorney.

Clients must know, however, that bankruptcy filings are a matter of public record. The general rule under 11 U.S.C. § 107(a) is that documents filed in bankruptcy matters are open to examination by the public except for information such as social security and financial account numbers, for example, which are protected from disclosure. Clients should be assured that (other than such confidential account numbers) this information is discoverable by someone who is actively looking for it. Such an individual must actually go to the U.S. district court and pull the file or access those records electronically. The best form of protection is for clients not to discuss the issue with outsiders or those they do not trust. There are, however, exceptions to the public access requirement, and clients who qualify for these exceptions may ask permission of the court to seal such information from the public eye.

confidentiality
An ethical rule that prohibits attorneys from disclosing information regarding the client's case to a third party unless the client consents or the attorney is required to do so under the law.

attorney–client privilege
An ethical rule that prohibits an attorney from disclosing privileged information unless waived by the client, clearing the way for the attorney to discuss the contents of the communications with a third party.

11 U.S.C. § 107 (2011): Public Access to Papers

(A) Except as provided in subsections (B) and (C) and subject to section 112, a paper filed in a case under this title and the dockets of a bankruptcy court are public records and open to examination by an entity at reasonable times without charge;

(B) On request of a party in interest, the bankruptcy court shall, and on the bankruptcy court's own motion, the bankruptcy court may;

(1) Protect an entity with respect to a trade secret or confidential research, development, or commercial information; or

(2) Protect a person with respect to scandalous or defamatory matter contained in a paper filed in a case under this title.

(C) (1) The bankruptcy court, for cause, may protect an individual, with respect to the following types of information to the extent the court finds that disclosure of such information would create undue risk of identity theft or other unlawful injury to the individual or the individual's property:

(a) Any means of identification (as defined in section 1028(d) of title 18) contained in a paper filed, or to be filed, in a case under this title.

(b) Other information contained in a paper described in subparagraph (a).

(2) Upon ex parte application demonstrating cause, the court shall provide access to information protected pursuant to paragraph (1) to an entity acting pursuant to the police or regulatory power of a domestic governmental unit.

(3) The United States trustee, bankruptcy administrator, trustee, and any auditor serving under section 586(f) of title 28—

(a) shall have full access to all information contained in any paper filed or submitted in a case under this title; and

(b) shall not disclose information specifically protected by the court under this title.

Ultimately, it is important to encourage clients to disclose anything and everything that could affect their bankruptcy case. It is better for the attorney to know all at the beginning of the case so that he or she may properly represent the client. That is why thorough intakes and client interviews are crucial in establishing a relationship of trust and confidence and eliciting responses to carefully crafted questions.

COMPENSATION

compensation
Payment for legal services. The rules of ethics require attorney compensation or fees to be reasonable, and the attorney must provide an explanation to the client regarding the scope of representation and the basis of the fee.

When it comes to fees, ethical codes require an attorney's **compensation** or fee to be reasonable, and the attorney must provide an explanation to the client regarding the scope of representation and the basis of the fee. According to 11 U.S.C. § 329, "any attorney representing a debtor in a case under this title, or in connection with such a case, whether or not such attorney applies for compensation under this title, shall file with the court a statement of the compensation paid or agreed to be paid, if such payment or agreement was made after one year before the date of the filing of the petition, for services rendered or to be rendered in contemplation of or in connection with the case by such attorney, and the source of such compensation." Bankruptcy attorneys must provide the court with an itemized accounting, including the time spent on the case, fees charged, and the complexity involved. Paralegals assisting bankruptcy attorneys must carefully document time spent on the case as well as details regarding the work performed by the office so proper disclosure may be provided to the court. The bankruptcy court may review the reasonableness of the fee for all debtors' attorneys regardless of whether they applied for compensation in the bankruptcy case.

If the compensation exceeds the reasonable value of any of these services, the bankruptcy court has the authority to cancel the agreement or order the return of the excessive payment.

Bankruptcy Code 11 U.S.C. § 330 (a) (3) states that in determining the amount of reasonable compensation to be awarded, the court shall consider the nature, the extent, and the value of such services, taking into account all relevant factors, including:

(A) Time spent on such services;

(B) Rates charged for such services;

(C) Whether the services were necessary to the administration of, or beneficial at the time at which the service was rendered toward the completion of, a case under this title;

(D) Whether the services were performed within a reasonable amount of time commensurate with the complexity, importance, and nature of the problem, issue, or task addressed;

(E) With respect to a professional person, whether the person is board certified or otherwise has demonstrated skill and experience in the bankruptcy field; and

(F) Whether the compensation is reasonable based on the customary compensation charged by comparably skilled practitioners in cases other than cases under this title.

In addition, Fed. R. Bankr. P. 2016(b) requires attorneys to disclose any compensation that "the attorney has shared or agreed to share with any other entity." The bankruptcy court has the authority to order professional persons to **disgorge** or give up excessive fees. The court may also disallow fees entirely if counsel fails to comply with applicable disclosure rules or has provided the client with incompetent representation.

The Role of the Bankruptcy Paralegal

INTRODUCTION

A **bankruptcy paralegal** is a nonattorney who works under the supervision of a bankruptcy lawyer. Bankruptcy paralegals must be highly organized individuals who are knowledgeable in bankruptcy law and able to handle the demands of a fast-paced, document-intensive practice. Although many paralegals work as employees in law offices, others choose to work independently as bankruptcy petition preparers.

bankruptcy paralegal
A nonattorney who works under the supervision of a bankruptcy lawyer.

THE BANKRUPTCY PARALEGAL

Many bankruptcy attorneys prefer to hire paralegals with some form of legal training, either a degree or certificate in paralegal studies. This ensures that the paralegal has learned the basic principles in areas of substantive and procedural law and legal ethics. Most paralegal education programs include a basic course in bankruptcy. Although these basic courses do not make one an expert in the field, a basic understanding of the bankruptcy laws and court proceedings is essential. Expertise is attained over years of practice and regular attendance and participation in continuing legal education seminars.

One of the main responsibilities of the bankruptcy paralegal is initial and follow-up meetings with clients. The paralegal should possess good people skills and the ability to communicate effectively. Paralegals may be responsible for scheduling the initial intake as well as any additional meetings during the course of representation. Assisting clients with data collection is another function paralegals may be of great help with to a busy bankruptcy lawyer. Before a petition is even drafted, the law office must obtain the most accurate and verifiable information for assessing clients' financial position, providing them with legal advice from the attorney, and preparing the appropriate legal documents. Clients need help and direction in gathering the proper forms to facilitate filing their bankruptcy. This process may take weeks or months because all clients are different. Therefore, the paralegal must develop a good working relationship with clients to guide them through the process. This might include phone calls and other forms of reminders.

Another major responsibility of the bankruptcy paralegal is the preparation of forms and documents, all under the supervision of an attorney. Bankruptcy forms are either prepared online or through the use of bankruptcy software the law office purchases. The different types of software are discussed in a later chapter.

After clients have retained the services of an attorney either to file for bankruptcy or pursue an alternative, the office must deal with the creditors. The bankruptcy paralegal is often responsible for notifying creditors that the debtor has retained counsel and is either filing for bankruptcy or retaining the office for another purpose such as debt negotiation. Here the paralegal generates correspondence on behalf of the attorney, documents all dealings with creditors in client files, and follows through with instructions from the attorney.

Although the bankruptcy court schedules the mandatory 341 creditors meeting, the paralegal may also be responsible for scheduling other hearings through the bankruptcy court clerk's office. This may also require rescheduling other hearings or meetings that the attorney has to accommodate to attend the 341 creditors meeting. Bankruptcy paralegals may also be called on to assist the attorney with research to answer questions regarding the Bankruptcy Code, Federal Rules of Bankruptcy Procedure, relevant case law, and information obtained through public domain sources. The paralegal should also become familiar with the website the United States Bankruptcy Court maintains for the particular federal district in which the attorney practices for valuable information that is used daily.

QUALIFICATIONS AND JOB REQUIREMENTS

The qualifications for an entry-level job as a bankruptcy paralegal may include:

- Possession of a paralegal degree or certificate
- Knowledge of basic bankruptcy law and procedure
- Knowledge of Chapter 7, Chapter 11, and Chapter 13
- Understanding of legal ethics and the unauthorized practice of law
- Proficiency in Microsoft Word, Outlook, and Excel
- Proficiency in accurate typing and good spelling and grammar
- Familiarity with PACER and bankruptcy form preparation software
- Ability to prioritize and meet deadlines
- Ability to communicate effectively, both orally and in writing
- Good people skills
- A professional attitude and appearance

The bankruptcy paralegal may be required to perform some of the following functions in addition to, sometimes, working for more than one attorney in the practice.

- Accessing bankruptcy forms
- Taking detailed notes and keeping accurate records
- Calendaring and tracking hearings and deadlines
- Corresponding with clients and third parties
- Reviewing credit reports and financial documents
- Managing cases and files
- Meeting deadlines
- Maintaining competency through seminars, workshops, and affiliations to stay current with the latest developments
- Drafting correspondence, certificates of service, discovery requests, petitions, schedules, pleadings, and motions
- Interviewing and following up with bankruptcy clients
- Preparing and filing proof of claims
- Understanding creditors' rights
- Researching pending collections actions or lawsuits against the debtor
- Understanding credit reports
- Researching land records and other public information

THE BANKRUPTCY PETITION PREPARER

Bankruptcy Code 11 U.S.C. § 110(a)(1) defines a **bankruptcy petition preparer** as "a person, other than an attorney for the debtor or an employee of such attorney under the direct supervision of such attorney, who prepares for compensation a document for filing." Bankruptcy petition preparers are independent paralegals and do not work as employees under the direct supervision of attorneys.

Paralegals who work under the direct supervision of an attorney therefore are not considered bankruptcy petition preparers under the definition of the Bankruptcy Code. This does not, however, stop a paralegal from engaging in this enterprise outside of the law office, which will subject them to Bankruptcy Code regulations.

Debtors who are cash strapped and short of funds may seek the assistance of bankruptcy petition preparers to type the petition and schedules. Debtors then file the initiating documents and represent themselves before the bankruptcy court. Bankruptcy petition preparers, however, cannot give legal advice. They can only enter information as it is provided to them on the bankruptcy forms and can charge only a reasonable fee.

Local bankruptcy court rules limit what the bankruptcy petition preparer can charge, with nominal fees ranging from $100 to $150. The Bankruptcy Abuse Prevention and Consumer Protection Act of 2005 places strict requirements on preparers as well as penalties for those who fail to comply with the statute. The concerns of the U.S. bankruptcy courts regarding bankruptcy petition preparers are expressed in the following article.

Increased Use of Bankruptcy Petition Preparers Raises Concerns

U.S. bankruptcy courts increasingly are concerned with abuses committed by some non-lawyers in the business of helping prepare bankruptcy filing documents for a fee.

bankruptcy petition preparer
A person, other than an attorney for the debtor or an employee of such attorney under the direct supervision of such attorney, who prepares for compensation a document for filing.

A growing number of people who seek bankruptcy protection navigate that challenging process without a lawyer's help, as so-called "pro se" filers. But federal bankruptcy law also allows them to pay non-lawyers to prepare petitions for them.

The law defines a "bankruptcy petition preparer" (BPP) as "a person other than an attorney for the debtor or an employee of such attorney…who prepares for compensation a document for filing."

Many preparers operate within the strict limits the law imposes on them, but some do not.

> "We have seen an increase in abuse," said U.S. Bankruptcy Judge Maureen Tighe in the Central District of California. "The increase in 'foreclosure rescue' and 'loan modification' services seems to be the source in the past three years. The homeowners are desperate and take advice from the most questionable sources. There is a wide range of BPPs, from those who are well-meaning but still are giving legal advice, to out-and-out fraud perpetrators—and the down-and-out consumer debtor doesn't know the difference most of the time."

In Tighe's district, several petition preparers have been fined for, among other infractions, the unauthorized practice of law and collecting higher petition-preparation fees than the $200 allowed by the bankruptcy court. (Petition-preparation fee limits vary in the 91 bankruptcy courts.)

In its fiscal year 2011 report, the U.S. Trustee Program said bankruptcy trustees nationwide had filed 504 actions against BPPs, with a success rate of 98.8 percent. More than $1.9 million in fines were imposed and some $419,000 in fees recovered during that year, the report said.

The U.S. Trustee Program, part of the Department of Justice, features a warning on its website (Justice.gov) for those who might seek help filing for bankruptcy protection.

> "Non-attorney bankruptcy petition preparers may type bankruptcy documents with information supplied by the debtor. They may not provide legal services, such as helping you choose whether to file under Chapter 7 or Chapter 13 or identifying your property that is exempt from the reach of creditors," it states. "Bankruptcy petition preparers may advertise their services under 'document preparation services' and similar categories of services, but not under 'legal services.' If a bankruptcy petition preparer offers to provide legal services to you or fails to disclose that he or she is not an attorney and may not provide legal services, please report this to a U.S. Trustee Program field office."

> Efforts to thwart fraud by BPPs are hampered in some districts by cultural differences. "Our challenge is exacerbated by the large Latino population who confuses notaries with 'notarios' because 'notarios' actually can carry out simple legal functions in Central America," Tighe said. "Some of our BPPs just advertise as 'notarios' and reel them in."

Source: United States Courts website, dated June 18, 2012

Bankruptcy petition preparers are required to notify clients, in writing, that they are not attorneys and that because of their lack of attorney status, they cannot render legal advice or engage in the practice of law.

Paralegal Ethics and Bankruptcy Practice

Paralegals who work as either employees in a bankruptcy law firm or bankruptcy petition preparers must refrain from engaging in the unauthorized practice of law. The individual states have statutes regulating who may practice law and which activities, when engaged in by a nonattorney, are considered the unauthorized practice of law. Paralegals who engage in the unauthorized practice of law may be committing a crime under the laws of their state and exposing themselves and their law firms to lawsuits. The following section explores the supervisory role of the attorney as well some of the most common activities that define the unauthorized practice of law as it relates to paralegals working in a bankruptcy law practice.

THE SUPERVISORY ROLE OF THE BANKRUPTCY ATTORNEY

Bankruptcy attorneys are responsible for the conduct of their paralegal employees according to Guideline One of the *ABA Model Guidelines for the Utilization of Paralegal Services*. This means that attorneys are not only responsible for the quality of work their paralegal assistants produce, they must also make sure that their conduct is consistent with the rules of professional conduct for the jurisdiction in which the attorneys practice. Attorneys are allowed to delegate certain tasks to their paralegal assistants, but they cannot delegate the practice of law. Activities that are considered practicing law include giving legal advice, representing clients in court, drafting legal documents, and conducting depositions.

Although legal malpractice insurance typically covers nonattorney assistants, paralegals must be well versed in the rules of professional conduct for both attorneys and paralegals to avoid exposing attorneys to lawsuits for their acts. Disgruntled clients will pursue malpractice lawsuits against attorneys because they obviously have deeper pockets than their paralegal assistants. Paralegals, however, are not immune to lawsuits, especially when they act outside of their scope of employment.

Some bankruptcy paralegals are so efficient and competent that an attorney may have the utmost trust and confidence in their abilities to handle a bankruptcy case from its inception to its end. Although paralegals play a vital role in bankruptcy law practices, the attorney must keep in mind that it is he or she who must maintain a direct relationship with clients.

ESTABLISHING THE ATTORNEY–CLIENT RELATIONSHIP AND SETTING LEGAL FEES

Will you represent me? How much is filing for bankruptcy going to cost? These two questions must be answered by attorneys. Although paralegals may conduct initial interviews with bankruptcy clients, the question of whether the attorney will take on the client's representation is decided only by attorneys.

LEGAL ADVICE AND OPINIONS

Bankruptcy paralegals cannot give legal advice. Legal advice requires the application of legal principles to the bankruptcy clients' specific circumstances, which may include recommendations on courses of action or predictions regarding the outcome of certain actions. Even if paralegals are absolutely sure of the answer to a client's question, it is up to the attorneys to provide legal advice. It is perfectly fine to tell clients that the paralegal is not licensed to practice law and cannot answer the question, but the paralegal will communicate the matter to the attorney for his or her assessment of the situation. The paralegal may, in these instances, take notes regarding the clients' inquiries and relay these concerns to the attorney for resolution. Listening, recording facts, and following through with the supervising attorney are the roles of the paralegal when legal advice is elicited.

Various decisions must be made in the course of representing bankruptcy clients that require some degree of legal interpretation and advice. Although a bankruptcy paralegal may assist the attorney in performing numerous functions, the interpretation of bankruptcy law as it applies to clients is the job of the attorney. In a bankruptcy practice, for example, the following issues require interpretations of the law that must be rendered by licensed attorneys and should not be addressed by the paralegal assistants. This includes advice on:

- Clients' rights under bankruptcy law
- Alternatives to bankruptcy
- Which bankruptcy alternatives to pursue
- Determining the most appropriate chapter under which to file
- How to deal with creditors
- The applicability of real and personal property exemptions
- The legal ramification of any concealed debts
- How bankruptcy law intersects with other areas of the law
- Tax consequences of filing for bankruptcy
- The dischargeability of debts
- Whether certain debts should be repaid or reaffirmed
- Which assets the debtor will be able to keep

REPRESENTING CLIENTS IN BANKRUPTCY COURT

Bankruptcy paralegals cannot appear in court to represent clients. They may, however, accompany the attorney and the client to court to provide assistance to the attorney. Paralegals cannot represent clients at 341 hearings because it is considered the unauthorized practice of law.

Pennsylvania Bar Association Unauthorized Practice of Law Committee

Opinion 96-108

SUBJECT: Does the appearance of an attorney's non-lawyer representative at a Bankruptcy 341 Meeting, at which meeting the non-attorney is asking questions that are focused on certain legal matters in the Bankruptcy Code as opposed to merely general information gathering, constitute the unauthorized practice of law, as does the "representation" of petitioning bankrupts by non-attorneys?

It is the **OPINION** of the Pennsylvania Bar Association Unauthorized Practice of Law Committee that non-attorneys participating in Bankruptcy 341 Meetings and whose questioning goes beyond mere information gathering to questions focused on legal matters in the Bankruptcy Code are engaged in the unauthorized practice of law as set forth in 42 Pa. C.S.A. § 2524.

DRAFTING LEGAL DOCUMENTS AND SIGNATURES

The preparation of legal documents involves legal expertise. The bankruptcy court forms are deceiving to the untrained person in that the very act of selecting a box or including a miscalculated figure may have long-term ramifications for the unwary. Legal document preparation carries with it consequences as well as the necessity to communicate the potential issues to clients and provide them with legal advice. Although bankruptcy petition preparers are, in a clerical capacity, allowed under the Bankruptcy Code to assist with filling out the bankruptcy forms, they often run afoul of engaging in the unauthorized practice of law when they encounter a situation in which a legal judgment must be made. A paralegal working under the supervision of an attorney may draft legal documents for clients. The attorney is responsible for the paralegal's work product and must ultimately answer if mistakes are made.

All forms and documents filed with the bankruptcy court in conjunction with clients' cases are to be signed by the attorney. Bankruptcy court forms and documents are filed electronically with the appropriate United States District Court, and only attorneys are allowed as Filing Users. Practically speaking, an attorney is permitted to use an authorized agent, such as his or her paralegal, to use the attorney's password for electronic filing purposes. The attorney, however, is responsible for the contents of the filings and should review any drafts before they are officially filed. Failure to supervise and review a paralegal's work product may result in the client filing a legal malpractice action against the attorney.

REFRAINING FROM EX-PARTE COMMUNICATIONS

Paralegals communicate with not only clients, but a variety of third parties on a daily basis. One of the functions of the bankruptcy paralegal is to deal with scheduling conflicts as well as other matters for the attorney, which might include contact with the bankruptcy court. Communicating with the bankruptcy court clerks is perfectly fine and acceptable. It is important to note, though, that Fed. R. Bankr. P. 9003 prohibits ex-parte contact by "any examiner, any party in interest, and any attorney, accountant, or employee of a party in interest" with bankruptcy judges regarding "matters affecting a particular case or proceeding." Ex parte is a Latin phrase that means "on one side only; by or for one party." Practically speaking, it means that any of the parties involved in the bankruptcy case may not engage in any form of communications or discussions with the bankruptcy judge unless all the parties involved in the matter are present. Fed. R. Bankr. P. 9003 also states that "United States Trustee and assistants to and employees or agents of the United States Trustee shall refrain from ex parte meetings and communications with the court concerning matters affecting a particular case or proceeding." The U.S. trustee however, may discuss with the court general problems of administration and improvement of bankruptcy administration, including the operation of the U. S. Trustee system.

The ethics chapter in any legal textbook is perhaps one of the most important chapters an aspiring paralegal can read. As you saw with Casey at the beginning of this chapter, after working in the field for a couple of years and having completed numerous bankruptcy client intakes, a paralegal's knowledge begins to seem on par with his or her attorney supervisor. Casey fell into the trap of giving legal advice to clients who were contemplating bankruptcy. It is fine for a paralegal to answer procedural questions and to inform a client of his or her obligation to attend credit counseling prior to filing and prior to receiving a discharge of debt. However, it is quite another story for a paralegal to listen to an individual's financial situation and offer advice about which bankruptcy chapter would be best for that client. Only an attorney should give legal advice to the client. As the example at the beginning of the chapter illustrated, by providing legal advice to his firm's clients, Casey was dangerously close to being grieved for the unauthorized practice of law.

CHAPTER **SUMMARY**

Although all rules of professional conduct may apply to a bankruptcy case, depending on its specific circumstances, the four most common ethical issues involved in practice are conflicts of interest, competency, confidentiality, and compensation. State ethical codes prohibit an attorney from representing a new client whose interests are materially adverse to those of a former client if the new matter and the former matter are substantially related to each other. This is known as a conflict of interest. The ethical rule of competency requires attorneys and paralegals to possess the knowledge, skill, preparation, and thoroughness to represent bankruptcy clients adequately. State codes of professional responsibility require attorneys to protect clients' confidentiality unless required to disclose under the law. This means that information regarding the client's case shall not be divulged to a third party unless the client consents or the attorney is required

to do so under the law. When it comes to fees, ethical codes require an attorney's fee to be reasonable, and the attorney must provide an explanation to the client regarding the scope of representation and the basis of the fee.

The role of the bankruptcy paralegal, under the supervision of an attorney, is to assist the attorney with various tasks that do not involve engaging in the unauthorized practice of law. Restricted activities include giving legal advice, accepting clients, setting legal fees, representing clients in court or at 341 hearings, and drafting legal documents. Some paralegals work as employees of bankruptcy attorneys and others are independent paralegals who function as bankruptcy petition preparers. Both cannot engage in the unauthorized practice of law, which includes rendering legal advice, both in communicating with clients and preparing bankruptcy-related forms.

CONCEPT REVIEW AND REINFORCEMENT

KEY **TERMS**

attorney–client privilege
bankruptcy paralegal
bankruptcy petition preparer

compensation
competency
confidentiality

conflict of interest
conflicts check

REVIEWING **KEY CONCEPTS**

1. List the four most common ethical issues encountered in a typical bankruptcy practice.
2. Give an example of a conflict of interest in a bankruptcy case.
3. What is a conflicts check and why is it important to conduct one before taking on the representation of a bankruptcy client?
4. Define the ethical rule of competency and the steps a bankruptcy paralegal may take in fulfilling this ethical obligation.
5. What are the confidentiality concerns for bankruptcy clients?
6. List five factors the bankruptcy court shall consider in determining the reasonableness of an attorney's fee.

7. How are bankruptcy petition preparers different from bankruptcy paralegals who are employed by bankruptcy attorneys?
8. What are some of the concerns of the U.S. Bankruptcy Court regarding bankruptcy petition preparers?
9. A close friend has decided to file for bankruptcy on her own because she does not trust lawyers. She calls you and wants to know which bankruptcy chapter would be most appropriate given her circumstances. What do you say to her? Explain your answer.
10. Your supervising attorney is going on vacation and asks you to attend a 341 hearing. What do you say to him? Explain your answer.

BUILDING YOUR PARALEGAL SKILLS

CASE FOR **REVIEW**

In re Mark Albert Boettcher, Jr., Debtor, No. 01-10004 (Bankr. N.D. Cal. Apr. 2, 2001)

BUILDING A PROFESSIONAL PORTFOLIO

PORTFOLIO **EXERCISES**

You are the head paralegal employed with the Pelletier Law Group. Otto Pelletier, your supervising attorney, has expressed his desire to encourage both associate attorneys and nonattorneys working in the office to participate in more continuing legal education. He has had a meeting with the partners, and the firm will reimburse employees for the cost of continuing legal education that is either located within the state or on online. Specifically, it will cover the cost of the course and materials. Employees are responsible for travel expenses and meals. In addition, it will also pay the employee for the day if the seminar requires their physical attendance on a work day, but it will not pay for any out-of-state seminars.

Attorney Pelletier has asked you to prepare an inter-office memo informing employees of the new policy and include a list of seminars, workshops, and courses available in your area or online. Assume the Pelletier Law Group is located in your city. Research the Internet, including local and state bar associations, paralegal associations, and online continuing legal education courses related to the field of bankruptcy. Remember that cost is important, and Attorney Pelletier would appreciate you taking that into consideration when evaluating potential programs.

chapter 15

THE BANKRUPTCY CLIENT: INITIAL INTAKE AND RELATED MATTERS

LEARNING OBJECTIVES

After studying this chapter, you should be able to:

1. Explain the psychology of bankruptcy.

2. Identify the alternatives to bankruptcy.

3. Explain what takes place at the initial client interview.

4. Recognize the importance of disclosure in a bankruptcy case.

5. Explain the impact of social networking on a debtor's case.

6. Summarize the basic clauses in disclosure and retainer agreements.

Virginia Giordano is a wealthy businesswoman and real estate investor in the midst of a nasty divorce. She is notorious in the business community for being a hard-nosed negotiator with an obsession for getting what she wants. Virginia's husband, Angelo, filed for divorce last year after he caught her in the throes of adultery with her commercial property appraiser. He is asking for full custody of the minor children, child support, alimony, and a percentage of the couple's assets. Their attempts at reaching a settlement have gone from bad to worse, with Virginia refusing to budge an inch. After the last disastrous four-way conference with their attorneys, Virginia emailed Angelo and told him that it would be a cold day in hell before she gives him a nickel and that she would rather have their dog Maxine raise their kids than give him custody. She also told him in writing that she intended to file for bankruptcy to ensure that he would get nothing.

Virginia eventually filed for bankruptcy and concealed assets that she had transferred into other people's names. She specifically hired her tennis doubles partner's son, Phillip Baines, Jr., who just passed the bar, to file the bankruptcy petition. He and his paralegal were so intimidated by her that she took control of the initial interview. When the attorney tried to broach the issue of disclosure with her, Virginia screamed and exclaimed, "How dare you tell me what to put in this petition! I was handling complicated business deals before you were even born!" The attorney backed off, and the paralegal reached for an antacid. Phillip did not want to upset Virginia, desperately wanting to please her and gain access to her social and business circle. Phillip's paralegal was instructed to prepare the petition but questioned the veracity of the figures. The paralegal was immediately ordered to file everything as is and without further inquiry. Meanwhile, Angelo received notice of her bankruptcy filing and the Automatic Stay. Angelo immediately asked his attorney to look into her assets or supposed lack thereof. An investigation revealed what Angelo suspected. Read on to find out the legal consequences of this client interview!

Introduction

The role of the legal team is to process the client's bankruptcy efficiently and effectively through a daunting legal maze that is laden with traps for the unwary. This chapter begins with a short discussion of the psychology of bankruptcy and how paralegals can assure clients that the fresh start afforded by a bankruptcy discharge is protected in our Constitution. The chapter will then discuss the initial interview process with emphasis on the importance of disclosure. Clients should be able to provide evidence proving the information supplied on the bankruptcy petition and the accompanying schedules. Clients who conceal and fail to disclose assets and income to the bankruptcy court run the risk of not only having their cases dismissed but also facing criminal fraud charges. The traps inherent in the use of social networking will also be highlighted along with sections on important matters related to the establishment of the attorney–client relationship in the bankruptcy practice.

The Psychology of Bankruptcy

A valued social norm in our culture is to pay debts and meet obligations to others. Our identities are often shaped by our occupations and in the things we have accumulated. Bankruptcy clients may experience shame, embarrassment, and fear when faced with the possibility of being unable to afford the basic necessities of life. It takes a lot of effort for clients to make the ultimate decision to file for bankruptcy. They may view themselves as failures and worry that their friends, family, employers, and acquaintances may find out about their financial troubles and think negatively of them.

The role of the bankruptcy attorney and paralegal is to process the client's case through the legal maze of rules, regulations, and legal forms. Providing mental health counseling is outside the scope of the legal team's practice. Clients who are experiencing emotional problems should be referred to those in the **financial therapy industry**. The financial therapy industry consists of professional mental health counselors specializing in assisting debtors dealing with the emotionality of being in financial distress and the accompanying problems they face.

financial therapy industry
Professional mental health counselors specializing in assisting debtors dealing with the emotionality of being in financial distress and the accompanying problems they face.

With that said, legal professionals cannot ignore the emotional toll bankruptcy takes on clients. It is important to remind them that our bankruptcy laws are rooted in the history of our Constitution and were created to give debtors a fresh start. Commend clients for taking control of their lives. If the bankruptcy is the result of the client's poor money management habits, encourage the client to seek remedies for that behavior by taking advantage of counseling and budgeting. If the bankruptcy was caused by sources outside of the client's control such as illness or job loss, remind the client that the bankruptcy laws were written to protect people in this position and that no one is immune to such a catastrophe. It is also comforting for clients to know that they are not the only ones filing for bankruptcy and that declaring bankruptcy is legal and sometimes the only option.

Reassure clients that they are not obligated to tell anyone they do not trust about their bankruptcy and that the office will maintain their confidentiality. Although bankruptcy filings are public record, finding this information requires knowing where to look and what to look for. It is best to encourage clients to focus their attention on working toward a fresh start rather than dwelling on the negativity associated with bankruptcy. Gathering information, developing a budget, and getting professional counseling are all proactive steps clients can take toward a new beginning.

Debtors and Employment Discrimination

Many employers conduct a background check on prospective employees to determine their suitability. The Fair Credit Reporting Act allows prospective employers to obtain information from applicants' credit report when screening for employment purposes. Employers may consider an applicant's bad credit when making a hiring decision. Unfortunately, although no one needs a job more than an unemployed person, the reality is that a negative credit report could lead to employment discrimination, especially in fields in which the prospective employee may have to deal with money. In addition to the stigma of bankruptcy, the reality from an employer's perspective is that hiring a person with bad credit may pose a risk. Employers may have some legitimate concerns when they are seeking to fill jobs during which the employee has access to money and may be tempted to engage in some form of theft.

Bankruptcy Code 11 U.S.C. § 525 prohibits private and public (government) employers from terminating an active employee because they sought protection under the bankruptcy laws. Under 11 U.S.C. § 525, federal, state, and local governments cannot deny, revoke, suspend, or refuse a license, permit, charter, franchise, or similar grant solely because the client has a history of bankruptcy. This does not mean that a client cannot be denied employment on other grounds. Private employers, however, are not held to the same standard.

A private employer may not terminate the employment of an employee who has sought bankruptcy protection. The statute, however, does not protect prospective employees during the screening process for a new job when they are interviewing with private employers. The issue of whether it is considered discriminatory to deny a person employment based on a bankruptcy is being litigated across the United States. Although some courts have found that employers cannot discriminate based on a history of bankruptcy because it denies one a fresh start, other courts have ruled in favor of the employer. Ultimately, this issue will have to be decided by the United States Supreme Court unless the statute is amended to protect applicants.

The best action for a client to take when the employer will conduct a credit check is to address the issue of the bankruptcy early on in the job interview. This allows the client to be up-front with the employer and, given the recent recession, it would not be the first time an employer has had to deal with the issue.

Alternatives to Bankruptcy

Although filing for bankruptcy may mean a fresh start, there are inherent costs and consequences. Clients have to spend money to get the relief they seek from the bankruptcy court. This includes legal fees, court filing fees, and the cost of credit counseling. Clients must also expend a lot of time and effort gathering information for the attorney and paralegal, completing worksheets, meeting with the attorney and paralegal, and attending the 341 hearing. There are other disadvantages to filing that also have to be considered before the bankruptcy petition is filed. A bankruptcy will:

- Remain on the client's credit report for ten years. This will make it difficult for the client to obtain loans or mortgages.
- Result in the loss of any nonexempt property. Remember that the U.S. trustee will liquidate the debtor's nonexempt property to raise as much cash as possible to pay creditors.
- Possibly subject the debtor to housing and employment discrimination.

Although filing for bankruptcy may eventually result in a fresh start for clients in debt, it is not always the most practical solution. It is the responsibility of the attorney to review clients' financial circumstances and determine whether pursuing an alternative to bankruptcy makes more sense.

JUDGMENT PROOF

This alternative to bankruptcy is based on the old adage that you can't get blood out of a stone. A client who has little or no assets or income is **judgment proof**. This means that even if creditors sue the debtor and obtain a judgment, collecting the debt will be impossible because the debtor has no property to attach or wages to garnish.

judgment proof
The inability of a creditor to obtain a judgment on a debt because the debtor has no property to attach or wages to garnish.

NEGOTIATING A DEBT SETTLEMENT WITH CREDITORS

Instead of filing for bankruptcy, it is possible for some debtors to negotiate some form of compromise with creditors, the effect of which provides the debtor with some relief and assures the creditor of some payment. A **debt settlement** is a lump sum payment to the creditor, from 30% to 50% of the total debt, in satisfaction of the entire obligation. Instead of pursuing a bankruptcy case, the attorney may represent the debtor in the negotiation process rather than the debtor having to deal with aggressive collection agencies or creditors' attorneys. Some debtors seek the assistance of **debt management agencies** in negotiating a debt settlement. Debt management agencies are nonprofit entities that promise to negotiate a payment plan with creditors. A list of legitimate Consumer Credit Counseling Services is available on the United States Trustee's website.

debt settlement
A lump sum payment to the creditor, from 30% to 50% of the total debt, in satisfaction of the entire obligation.

debt management agencies
Nonprofit entities that promise to negotiate a payment plan with creditors.

In contrast, **debt consolidation** is a bankruptcy alternative that requires the debtor to obtain a large loan to pay off existing debts. The debtor is left with one loan payment, usually at a lower interest rate than those on the multiple debts originally owed. Loans extended as part of debt consolidation are secured, meaning that an asset must be pledged as collateral. A debtor who has numerous credit card debts, for example, may consolidate her debt by obtaining a large loan, secured by her home, which she will use to pay off her credit cards. If she defaults, however, she can lose her home.

debt consolidation
A bankruptcy alternative that requires the debtor to obtain a large loan to pay off existing debts.

CREATING A BUDGET

In addition to negotiating a payment plan with creditors, debtors may be encouraged to create a budget and reduce expenses. They may be able to eliminate unnecessary expenses and readjust their lifestyle to make ends meet. Budget assistance may be provided by courses on the Internet, adult education classes, credit counseling services, or a financial professional.

CLIENT'S DEBTS ARE NONDISCHARGEABLE

If the majority of the client's debts are considered nondischargeable, it might make more sense for the client to file under Chapter 13. Recall that nondischargeable debts may include child support and alimony payments, most student loans, court fines and penalties, tax debts, restitution to victims of crime or personal injury perpetrated or caused by the debtor.

Initial Client Interview

Although the structure of the initial meeting varies from practice to practice, a simple bankruptcy case requires three important meetings with the client and the attorney: the **initial client interview**, the signing of the bankruptcy petition and related documents, and the 341 hearing (meeting of creditors).

initial client interview
The bankruptcy client's first meeting with the attorney and his or her paralegal. It is when the attorney provides the client with legal advice; takes the initial steps to determine which bankruptcy chapter is appropriate, considering the client's circumstances; and establishes the attorney–client relationship.

The initial client interview is the bankruptcy client's first meeting with the attorney and his or her paralegal. It is when the attorney provides the client with legal advice; takes the initial steps to determine which bankruptcy chapter is appropriate, considering the client's circumstances; and establishes the attorney–client relationship. A paralegal is often present at the initial interview because it is the paralegal who has most contact with the client. The paralegal's main function during the initial interview is to take notes and assist the attorney in the information-gathering process.

Upon meeting a new client, it is important to make him or her feel welcomed. Paralegals should disclose their nonattorney status to the client and remember that he or she cannot give legal advice, accept or reject the case, or set the legal fee for the service, three functions that are considered engaging in the practice of law and the attorney should address. In addition to the initial meeting, paralegals often meet with clients throughout the course of the bankruptcy case to obtain documentation to justify figures on the petitions and schedules and to supervise document signing. The paralegal may also accompany the attorney and client to assist the attorney at the 341 hearing or any other proceedings.

Although legal professionals are not therapists, they do need to establish a rapport with the client so that he or she gains trust and confidence in the legal team. The client should be given space and encouragement to tell his or her story regarding the financial circumstances as well as the emotional issues around having made the decision to file for bankruptcy. Pulling out a questionnaire at the outset is insulting and not a recommended tactic in establishing a good relationship with a new client.

An unsettling reality of working with bankruptcy clients is that it is not uncommon for debtors to attempt to conceal assets from the process. Some clients do not intentionally conceal assets but may not consider certain matters such as back child support, tax refunds due, or a pending personal injury case relevant. It is the legal team's responsibility to ferret out this information with the use of detailed questionnaires and worksheets.

Clients must be directed to disclose any and all information so that accurate data may be included on petitions and schedules. Disclosure also requires clients to inform the law office immediately of any changes that occur after the petition has been filed and during the pendency of the bankruptcy case. The attorney must have a frank and candid discussion with the client of the implications of the failure to disclose truthful information and should warn the client not to incur any further debt unless the attorney is consulted. A bankruptcy client whose car breaks down during the course of the bankruptcy case may need to purchase a reasonably priced and reliable car to get to work, but a client should not go on a shopping spree or exhaust credit cards just because he or she is going bankrupt.

Clients should be encouraged to be truthful with all disclosures and warned that failure to do so could not only result in dismissal of the case but could also lead to criminal penalties. Remember that giving legal advice is applying the law to the client's specific circumstances. Telling a client that he or she has an obligation to tell the truth or face serious consequences is not an application of the law to a client's particular circumstances. It is general information that applies to all those filing for bankruptcy. Clients should also be encouraged to speak with the attorney if questions arise during the course of the bankruptcy because well-meaning friends and family may be dispensing poor legal advice.

The attorney will explain the bankruptcy process to the client, answer any legal questions the client may have and provide the client with legal advice. The attorney will also advise the client regarding the professional fees and costs associated with the bankruptcy filing. Very often, a financially strapped client will need some time after the initial meeting with the attorney to gather the funds to pay for the bankruptcy.

Bankruptcy Worksheet

At the initial meeting, the client will be instructed to gather detailed financial information, which, depending on the client's circumstances, will take considerable time to assemble. The client is given the task of completing a **bankruptcy worksheet** before the next meeting with the attorney. A bankruptcy worksheet is a detailed questionnaire that guides the client in identifying the information necessary for the attorney to assess the client's financial circumstances and determine the best course of action to take regarding the client's debt.

bankruptcy worksheet
A detailed questionnaire that guides the client in identifying the information necessary for the attorney to assess the client's financial circumstances and determine the best course of action to take regarding the client's debt.

It is often during the second meeting that the client will give the attorney a completed bankruptcy worksheet, credit counseling certificate, professional fee and costs, and any other documentation the attorney requests. The attorney then must analyze the bankruptcy worksheet, paying close attention to the client's assets, debts, income, expenses, and past financial transactions before any meaningful legal advice can be rendered. This information is used to calculate the Means Test, the result of which, in many cases, will dictate the appropriate bankruptcy chapter. The information in the bankruptcy worksheet provides the necessary data for the paralegal to prepare the bankruptcy petition and accompanying schedules. Additional appointments may have to be scheduled for information-gathering purposes during the course of bankruptcy document preparation.

The bankruptcy worksheet is typically a long document and can overwhelm some clients. They must be informed that filing for bankruptcy is a process highly regulated by federal law, and it is important to gather and verify the information that is requested in the worksheet. The use of worksheets also ensures that the attorney and paralegal will not miss certain information during the course of the client interview.

Documentation

Along with the bankruptcy worksheet, the client should also bring the following general documentation to the initial meeting with the attorney.

- A detailed list of all debts, including name and address of creditor, amount owed, minimum payment due, and interest rates
- A detailed list of monthly expenses such as rent or mortgage, utility, food, child care, clothing, schooling, medical, dental, car operation, insurance bills, back taxes, unreimbursed work expenses, storage, and student loan payments
- Any and all correspondence from creditors and bill collectors
- Appraisals or assessments of real property
- Arrearage statements on any real or personal property
- Court orders such as child or spousal support
- Credit report from Experian, Equifax, or TransUnion
- Divorce decrees
- Documentation regarding any previous bankruptcies filed
- Federal and state tax returns for the past three years
- Insurance policies
- Inventory of all real and personal property
- Judgments entered against or in favor of debtor
- Lawsuits papers served or received
- Mortgages, notes, leases
- Most recent statements for any accounts such as checking, savings, money market, retirement, investment, medical savings, college funds, education IRAs, pension plans, and insurance policies
- Original Social Security card
- Partnership or shareholder agreements in which debtor holds an interest
- Pay stubs for last six months of debtor's employment or any other documentation of income such as W-2 or 1099 forms, royalty statements, and financial statements; verification of spouse's income
- Recent checkbook register
- Repossession documentation
- Residential addresses for the past three years
- Trust agreements in which debtor is beneficiary
- Valid driver's license or state identification card
- Wage garnishments

Due Diligence and the Verification of Information

Bankruptcy law requires clients to submit complete, accurate, and truthful information. In practice, the office will obtain this information by having the client complete a bankruptcy worksheet and supplying the documentation to verify the data in the worksheet. Although the attorney and paralegal must stress to the client the importance of such a requirement and the consequences that may result for lack of compliance, the information the client provides must be verified by the law office. The process of verifying the client's financial information is called **due diligence**. A simple rule to remember is that the client should be able to provide evidence proving the information supplied on the bankruptcy petition

due diligence
The process of verifying the client's financial information.

and accompanying schedules. It is not enough just to take the client's word for the veracity of the information provided.

Bankruptcy Code 11 U.S.C. § 707(b), as amended by the Bankruptcy Abuse Prevention and Consumer Protection Act (BAPCPA), states that:

> The signature of an attorney on a petition, pleading, or written motion shall constitute a certification that the attorney has:
>
> (i) Performed a reasonable investigation into the circumstances that gave rise to the petition, pleading, or written motion; and
>
> (ii) Determined that the petition, pleading, or written motion
>
> (iii) (I) is well grounded in fact; and (II) is warranted by existing law or a good faith argument for the extension, modification, or reversal of existing law and does not constitute an abuse under paragraph (1).
>
> (iv) The signature of an attorney on the petition shall constitute a certification that the attorney has no knowledge after an inquiry that the information in the schedules filed with such petition is incorrect.

In the case of *In re Withrow, Debtor*, 391 B.R. 217 (Bankr. D. Mass. 2008), the United States Bankruptcy Court for the District of Massachusetts provides bankruptcy attorneys with a five-step analysis to determine whether the attorney has fulfilled his or her obligation to exercise due diligence. Paralegals should be well versed in these steps because a main function of the paralegal in a bankruptcy firm is information gathering.

The five steps in the *Withrow* case are:

(1) Did the attorney impress upon the debtor the critical importance of accuracy in the preparation of documents to be presented to the Court?

(2) Did the attorney seek from the debtor, and then review, whatever documents were within the debtor's possession, custody or control in order to verify the information provided by the debtor?

(3) Did the attorney employ such external verification tools as were available and not time or cost prohibitive (e.g., on-line real estate title compilations, on-line lien search, tax "scripts")?

(4) Was any of the information provided by the debtor and then set forth in the debtor's court filings internally inconsistent—that is, was there anything which should have obviously alerted the attorney that the information provided by the debtor could not be accurate?

(5) Did the attorney act promptly to correct any information presented to the Court which turned out, notwithstanding the attorney's best efforts, to be inaccurate?

These questions can be further simplified and reduced to one question, their common denominator: Did the attorney do his or her level best to get it right? More cannot, and should not, be asked of any attorney.

Social Networking and its Impact on Bankruptcy Cases

Social networking on popular sites such as Facebook, Twitter, Google+, LinkedIn, and Instagram has become the way in which people stay in touch and communicate through the posting of photographs, comments, and discussions. Although clients may perceive sharing on social media as an innocent endeavor, unchecked disclosure of even the simplest details of a client's life may have legal ramifications. Filing for bankruptcy requires clients to disclose certain information to the bankruptcy court and exerts a continuing duty to disclose during the pendency of the case. Failure to do so may result in allegations of bankruptcy fraud, and social media may be used to substantiate these accusations, resulting in a denial of discharge as well as criminal fraud charges.

Clients should be warned that what appears on social media could negatively affect their bankruptcy case. Trustees, creditors, and third parties may have access to information that could later backfire for the debtor. Setting high privacy settings will not help because creditors and trustees may subpoena social media sites for access to information, or third parties such as ex-spouses may have access through friends and family who simply print copies of the offending content. Remember that information is never truly deleted and, with a subpoena, is never private. Although many attorneys instruct their clients to cease all participation in social media, it does not take the place of complete honesty and disclosure with the bankruptcy court.

Displaying the following activities on social networking sites may pose serious problems for bankruptcy filers.

- **New possessions** Uploading photographs of the debtor with new material possessions such as a fur coat, jewelry, new flat-screen TV, or any newly acquired possession can raise questions about the client's spending. Remember that debtors who file for bankruptcy must disclose any property they acquire after the petition has been filed with the court.
- **New employment, a raise, job promotion, or starting a new business** Debtors must disclose all sources of income. Debtors who file for Chapter 13 are required to make payments to their creditors based on their disposable income. The bankruptcy court should be notified of the new job so the payment to creditors may be adjusted. Posting this on LinkedIn before making it known to the trustee may result in an accusation of fraud. The trustee may petition the bankruptcy court to increase monthly payment obligations.
- **Luxury spending** Although credit card debts are generally discharged in bankruptcy, an exception is credit card purchases for luxury items purchased within 90 days of the filing of a bankruptcy petition. Posting pictures of a new Harley Davidson or that pricey diving trip to the Cayman Islands may provide the U.S. trustee and creditors with evidence of a better financial condition than previously revealed to the court.

Concealing assets and perpetrating a fraud on the court may result in dismissal of the debtor's case, the result of which is that all his or her debts are left intact and owed to the creditors. There are also criminal penalties for making false statements on the bankruptcy petitions and schedules. For example, a client indicates on his statement of financial affairs that he sold an expensive Bowflex home gym and elliptical trainer fully equipped with features such as a CD player, a fan, and TV screen in the two years before filing for bankruptcy. Recently posted photographs on his Facebook account, however, show him working out on these machines along with boasts about how fit he's become as a result. A U.S. trustee who has reviewed the debtor's timeline may conclude that the debtor concealed the machine and may move to have the debtor's case dismissed. His bankruptcy filing, which he declared under penalty of perjury, included a schedule of all of his personal property that he knew to be false. Hiding assets from the bankruptcy court is considered a serious criminal offense. A seemingly innocent comment and uploaded photograph on a social media timeline will not only result in a dismissal of the debtor's case but also trigger a criminal case.

The Law Office as Debt Relief Agency

As discussed in Chapter 3, the BAPCPA amendments to the Bankruptcy Code include attorneys in the definition of a **debt relief agency**. A debt relief agency is "any person who provides any bankruptcy assistance to an assisted person in return for the payment of money or other valuable consideration, or who is a bankruptcy petition preparer." The law office is a debt relief agency because it assists debtors by providing information, advice, counsel, document preparation, or filing or attendance at a creditors' meeting or appearance in a case or proceeding or legal representation on behalf of another.

The United States Supreme Court, in the case of *Milavetz, Gallop & Milavetz, P.A. v. United States*, 130 S.Ct. 1324, 176 L.Ed 2d 79 (2010), held that the BAPCPA provisions placing attorneys in the category of a debt relief agency applies to debtors' attorneys working on behalf of the debtor. Bankruptcy attorneys may also represent creditors and other third parties in bankruptcy matters, but the debt relief agency requirements only apply when representing debtors.

debt relief agency
Any person who provides any bankruptcy assistance to an assisted person in return for the payment of money or other valuable consideration, or who is a bankruptcy petition preparer.

Disclosure Agreements

New bankruptcy clients should be given a copy of the mandatory disclosures found in 11 U.S.C. § 527. The **disclosure agreement** is a document that lists all the mandatory disclosures required in Section 527. It should be read to the client during the initial meeting, and then the client should be asked to sign the agreement, which will be filed for safekeeping.

Although the text of this code section is included in Chapter 3, a summary of the mandates in Section 527 includes:

disclosure agreement or disclosure statement
A document that lists all the mandatory disclosures required by 11 U.S.C. § 527, Section 527. It includes information such as the financial details of the debtor's business, enough to allow the creditors to determine how their interests will be affected.

- An advisement to the client that the attorney is a debt relief agency and as such counsels those who file for bankruptcy.
- The requirement that there must be a written contract between the attorney and the client, and the contract must specify what the attorney will do for the client and how much this service will cost.
- An advisement to the client that all information provided by the client must be complete, accurate, and truthful. The client must completely and accurately disclose all assets and all liabilities in the bankruptcy petition. The client must also be warned that failure to provide accurate, complete, and truthful information may result in dismissal of the case or other sanction, including a criminal sanction.
- The requirement that the client must participate in a credit counseling course and financial management course.

The disclosure agreement should also include a **notice of non-representation**. This is a clause in the disclosures that informs the client that the attorney–client relationship is not established until the client signs a retainer agreement and pays the attorney's fee.

notice of non-representation
A disclosure statement that informs the client that the attorney–client relationship is not established until the client signs a retainer agreement and pays the attorney's fee.

The client must also be given a copy of Bankruptcy Form B201A in accordance with § 342(b) of the Bankruptcy Code. This is a preprinted notice that briefly describes the services available from credit counseling services and the purposes, benefits, and costs of the four types of bankruptcy proceedings; it informs the client about bankruptcy crimes and that the U.S. Attorney General may examine all information the client supplies. The client then signs Bankruptcy Form B201B, which is a certification that states that the client received and read the notice. A copy should be made for the client, and the originals are filed with the bankruptcy petition.

Retainer Agreement

retainer agreement
An agreement between an attorney or law firm and a client to provide the client with legal services.

A **retainer agreement** is an agreement between an attorney or law firm and a client to provide the client with legal services. Retainer agreements are required by law and memorialize the role of each party in writing. They should be written in plain language and easy to read so clients understand what they are signing. At the very least, a bankruptcy retainer should contain

- A clause stating that the attorney is rendering bankruptcy services for the client. It should specify, for example, that the attorney will represent the client in a Chapter 7 or Chapter 13 case. Clients may have myriad legal issues, and the attorney needs to clarify in the retainer agreement the specific services offered. Clients often have the misperception that just because they have hired an attorney, he or she will represent them in any other matters for which they need legal representation.

For example, suppose the attorney contracts with a client to provide bankruptcy services to file for Chapter 7 on behalf of the client. During the course of the case, the client conceals assets and commits other fraudulent acts and is now facing criminal prosecution. The client may turn to the bankruptcy attorney for representation, but the bankruptcy attorney only agreed to represent the client in the bankruptcy matter.

- A clause stating how much the attorney's services will cost and how the client will be billed for bankruptcy court filing fees, faxes, telephone calls, copying charges, and other expenses related to the bankruptcy case.
- A clause indicating what services the basic fee does not cover and the cost of additional services that may arise during the course of the bankruptcy.

Fee Arrangements in Bankruptcy Cases

Bankruptcy attorneys often provide prospective clients with a free consultation. If the attorney will charge for the initial consultation, then the client should be told the fee and the length of time it covers. For example, some attorneys provide prospective clients with a free half hour consultation and will then charge a fee for any additional time spent.

fixed or flat fee
A one-time fee an attorney charges for filing the bankruptcy case and assisting the client through the bankruptcy administration process.

The most common type of fee arrangement in bankruptcy cases is the fixed or flat fee arrangement. A **fixed** or **flat fee** means that the attorney charges one fee for filing the bankruptcy case and assisting the client through the bankruptcy administration process. A Chapter 7 no-asset case, for example, could cost from $1,000 to $2,500. The costs can vary, depending on the jurisdiction, the specific circumstances of the case, the difficulties presented in the case, and other factors.

Debtors are often cash strapped, and paying a fixed fee to a bankruptcy attorney might be difficult. For clients in this predicament, attorneys might accept a payment plan. A **payment plan** is a fee arrangement that allows the client to pay the attorney in installments. Some attorneys will commence representation of the client with the first payment, whereas others wait until the client has paid the entire fixed fee for the attorney's services. An attorney who accepts a payment plan always runs the risk of becoming another one of the debtor's creditors. In some federal districts, if the client is filing under a Chapter 13 repayment, the attorney's fee in an installment plan is included in the repayment plan, and the attorney must be listed as a creditor. If a situation arises during the course of the client's case that requires the attorney to render additional services to the client in conjunction with the bankruptcy, the attorney must file a supplemental fee application. This informs the bankruptcy court that the client requires further assistance from the attorney.

payment plan
A fee arrangement that allows the client to pay the attorney in installments.

Another fee arrangement in bankruptcy cases is to charge an **hourly fee**. Here the client is billed for every billable hour the attorney or paralegal spends working on the case. Ethical codes allow an attorney to bill separately for paralegal services, which, in the long run, saves clients' money because the hourly rate for a paralegal is lower than the attorney's rate. Although debtor fees are often fixed, attorneys representing creditors or trustees bill clients by the hour.

hourly fee
An arrangement for the payment of legal fees by which a client is billed for every billable hour the attorney or paralegal spends working on the case.

Regardless of whether the fee is fixed, payment plan, or hourly, the U.S. trustee as well as the bankruptcy court may examine the fee for reasonableness, as discussed in the previous chapter.

ATTORNEY'S FEE DISCLOSURE REQUIREMENTS

Bankruptcy Code 11 U.S.C. § 329(a) and Fed. R. Bankr. P. 2016(b) requires attorneys representing debtors to disclose the "compensation paid or agreed to be paid, if such payment or agreement was made after one year before the date of the filing of the petition," within 15 days after the case is filed. A statement of attorney's fees is filed with the bankruptcy court and served on the U.S. trustee. Sometimes a friend or family member, as a kind gesture, gives the debtor the money to hire an attorney so that he or she may be relieved of his or her financial pressures. If a third party pays all or any portion of the attorney's fees, this information should be included in the statement. It is important to note that regardless of who pays the client's attorney fee, ethical codes require legal professionals to remain loyal to the client and not to the individual who signed the check.

For example, a client may come to the initial consultation with her mother, who will pay for her adult daughter's bankruptcy. A conflict of interest may arise if the attorney and office staff are not careful. The client is the adult daughter, not her mother, and care should be taken to protect the daughter's confidentiality. The client should be interviewed privately, and then the mother could join the session when the matter of payment arises. The mother should also be told that regardless of who pays, the direct relationship is with the client, and the details of the client's case remain confidential. If the client wishes to share these details with her mother, that is her decision. If mother calls the office, however, looking for information on the daughter's case, a paralegal should refrain from discussing the matter with anyone other than the client. A supplemental statement must be filed within 15 days of receipt of any payment that was not previously disclosed. This occurs when the attorney charges the client any additional fees in the course of the bankruptcy case. Bankruptcy lawyers who fail to comply with the attorney fee disclosure requirements may be ordered by the court to disgorge the entire fee.

Checking Pending Litigation

Pending litigation or potential claims must be disclosed when filing for bankruptcy. A failure to disclose any pending litigation or potential claims in which the debtor is currently involved or could be involved in, as plaintiff, defendant, or third party, may result in dismissal of the bankruptcy case and expose the client to charges of bankruptcy fraud. In addition, a client who does not disclose a personal injury claim or any other type of claim may find that he or she cannot legally pursue the claim under the doctrine of collateral estoppel. For example, a client who was injured in a minor car accident several months before filing for bankruptcy must disclose the potential lawsuit against the driver of the other car. If the client fails to disclose this information on his bankruptcy petition, he will be estopped from filing a lawsuit in the personal injury case. Then bankruptcy court and U.S. trustee must be notified of any potential claims that arise after the bankruptcy petitions and schedules have been filed. Clients must be instructed to contact their bankruptcy attorney immediately so that the appropriate amendments may be filed.

Although questions regarding pending and potential lawsuits are listed in bankruptcy worksheets and questionnaires, an important function of the paralegal is to check the state and federal court websites for any pending litigation in which the debtor is involved. The state's judicial branch website may be easily accessed to review the civil, small claims, and family law dockets. Paralegals may also check for pending federal cases through Public Access to Court Electronic Records (PACER), an electronic public access service that allows users to obtain case and docket information from federal appellate, district, and bankruptcy courts.

Credit Counseling and Financial Management Course

The client must be advised that a certificate of completion from a credit counseling course is required before the bankruptcy petition can be filed. In addition, he or she must obtain a certificate of completion from a financial management course after the client has filed for bankruptcy but before the case may be discharged. This form is called the Debtor's Certification of Completion of Instructional Course Concerning Financial Management.

There are only a few exceptions to this requirement.

- The debtor lives in an area where no such course is available. This excuse is rarely acceptable because these courses are available by telephone or online at little cost to the debtor. If the client does not have computer skills, he or she can bring them into the office with their credit card and set them up on an office computer.
- The debtor is mentally incompetent to the point of inability to comprehend the course contents. Debtors who are physically disabled may conveniently take the course online or by telephone.
- The debtor is on active duty in a military zone.

The agency providing these courses must be approved by the U.S. trustee, and a list is available on the U.S. trustee's website. A bankruptcy administrator administers a similar list for clients living in the District of Alabama and the District of North Carolina.

The paralegal should prepare a list of approved courses for the client's convenience. If the law firm represents non-English–speaking clients, approved agencies offer these courses in Spanish and other languages. The paralegal should include the appropriate services on the list for such foreign-language clients.

Effect of Bankruptcy on Credit Ratings and How to Repair Damaged Credit

The first question that comes to the mind of many individuals who are contemplating filing for bankruptcy is how bankruptcy will affect their **credit scores**. A credit score is a number that summarizes the information in an individual's credit report. Credit scores range from 300 to 850. The rule is that the higher the credit score, the more creditworthy the debtor. Negative information such as bankruptcy, debt collections, judgments, foreclosures, and liens on a credit report will lower the credit score. Businesses use the credit score as a basis for extending credit, and many employers have instituted the practice of checking a prospective employee's credit score.

The prevailing belief seems to be that a bankruptcy filing can only do irreparable damage to an individual's credit score with no hope for recovery. Although there is definitely some truth to the belief that a bankruptcy filing will have a negative impact on one's credit score, it is also true that it depends on how low one's credit score was before the bankruptcy filing. It seems that the lower the credit score one has, the less of a negative impact a bankruptcy filing has on his or her credit score. The opposite is true for the individual who has a relatively good score before filing for bankruptcy; this individual experiences the greatest impact to his or her credit score. Putting all of this aside, anyone contemplating bankruptcy is likely to have a less than good credit score, so a fresh start through bankruptcy is more like hitting the reset button on his or her financial health.

CREDIT REPORTS

Most of us have a good idea of what a **credit report** is, but not all of us are aware of just how much information is reflected in this report and for how long. A credit report is a detailed snapshot of an individual's financial history. It is a report that prospective employers request when considering an applicant for employment, and lenders use it to determine whether they will lend money to an individual and, if so, at which interest rate. A future property owner considering an individual's rent application might also request a credit report.

credit report
A detailed snapshot of an individual's financial history.

A credit report is generally divided into four sections. The first section of the credit report contains personal information such as the individual's full name and any alias the person might have used, his or her address and previous addresses, date of birth, and current and past employment information. The next set of data contains credit information. All of the debtor's current and closed credit card accounts and mortgages and home equity lines of credit appear in this section. The third section contains a listing of all pertinent public records such as the individual's bankruptcy filings, civil judgments, tax liens, and wage garnishments. Finally, an individual's credit report will show who has requested a copy of the report for various reasons, and these requests show up as inquiries.

Many clients are concerned with how long a bankruptcy filing will stay on his or her credit report. Many law firms recommend that their bankruptcy clients, as part of taking inventory of all the creditors that need to be scheduled, order a free copy of his or her credit report from one of the three major credit bureaus, Equifax, Experian, or TransUnion. It is important to remember that a credit report is only a start with respect to taking an inventory of creditors. Not all the debtor's creditors will be listed on the report, so a thorough interview with the client is essential to determine whether creditors other than those listed in the credit report need to be identified. In addition, it is important to review the credit report thoroughly with the client to make sure the credit report is accurate and identify any errors that need to be corrected on the part of the client.

REPAIRING A DAMAGED CREDIT SCORE

Generally, a Chapter 7 case that proceeds normally and ends up in a discharge of debt for the debtor will appear on the debtor's credit report for ten years. A Chapter 13 case usually remains on a debtor's credit report for seven years; however, this time frame can vary from state to state. In California, for example, judgments are enforced up to 10 years and can be renewed for an additional 10-year period. Many debtors fear this fact and perhaps even worry unduly about it. Often, debtors may be persuaded to seek the assistance of a **credit repair organization (CRO)**. These businesses promise to repair a client's credit report for a fee. Many credit counselors and financial advisors advise against this because seeking this type of help may only serve to cost the debtor a great deal of money. There were numerous issues with types of organizations, so much so that Congress was prompted to enact the **Credit Repair Organizations Act (CROA)** 15 U.S.C. § 1679(a)(1996), which reads:

credit repair organization (CRO)
Businesses that promise to repair a client's credit report for a fee.

Credit Repair Organizations Act (CROA)
A federal law passed in 1996 designed to protect the public from unfair or deceptive advertising and business practices by credit repair organizations.

(a) Findings

The Congress makes the following findings:

(1) Consumers have a vital interest in establishing and maintaining their credit worthiness and credit standing in order to obtain and use credit. As a result, consumers who have experienced credit problems may seek assistance from credit repair organizations which offer to improve the credit standing of such consumers.

(2) Certain advertising and business practices of some companies engaged in the business of credit repair services have worked a financial hardship upon consumers, particularly those of limited economic means and who are inexperienced in credit matters.

(b) Purposes

The purposes of this subchapter are:

(1) To ensure that prospective buyers of the services of credit repair organizations are provided with the information necessary to make an informed decision regarding the purchase of such services; and

(2) To protect the public from unfair or deceptive advertising and business practices by credit repair organizations.

Rather than seek the advice of a CRO, many credit counselors advise that the road to repairing your credit score is better paved with simple actions taken after a bankruptcy case rather than seeking "professional help" to repair his or her credit score. It seems better for the debtor not to dwell on what is contained in his or her credit report and to take steps to improve his or her credit score. Credit counselors recommend some of the following actions to repair a broken credit score.

1. Order a copy of the credit report and check it for inaccuracies.
2. Open a modest checking and savings account with a reputable credit union or bank.
3. Make a strict budget that only includes necessities.
4. Attempt to pay all bills on time.
5. Open a high-interest or a secured credit card with a reputable bank.

The last item on this list, a **secured credit card,** is an option that could have the most significant impact on improving one's credit score. A financial institution may be persuaded to offer a credit card to an individual with poor credit if that person provides it with a monetary deposit, which serves as a security, similar to how a property owner collects a security deposit prior to leasing property to the lessee. With this type of credit card, the amount the cardholder puts down as a deposit usually matches the credit limit the bank extends. The cardholder is allowed to use the secured credit card up to the limit like any other card. If the cardholder makes monthly payments toward the balance on time, this adds significantly to rebuilding his or her credit score. Over time, if the cardholder continues to make timely monthly payments, a higher credit limit can be requested. This will require an additional security deposit from the cardholder. When the cardholder wishes to pay off and close the account, the card issuer is supposed to return the security deposit to the cardholder, much like a property owner–tenant situation. On some occasions, a bank may offer the cardholder an unsecured credit card, provided it had a significant history of timely payments toward the balance on the secured card. Credit counselors warn that this type of card should only be sought from a reputable, FDIC-insured bank.

> **secured credit card**
> A credit card issued to an individual with poor credit; the cardholder provides the credit card company with a monetary deposit, which serves as a security similar to how a property owner collects a security deposit prior to leasing property to the lessee.

Obtaining precise information from the prospective client is paramount. Clients who conceal information and control the intake and information divulged on the petition often experience negative outcomes such as dismissal and even criminal prosecution in some cases. Remember Virginia Giordano from the beginning of the chapter? Her goals seemed to be focused more on how she could deny her husband as many assets as she could from her divorce case. Virginia was dealing with a bankruptcy attorney who was still celebrating his bar passage just months before. As a result, Virginia controlled the intake meeting, and her attorney essentially allowed her to misrepresent information on her petition. He also allowed her to conceal certain financial transactions that could have been construed as fraudulent conveyances. For this and many other reasons, most practitioners prefer this meeting to be face to face with the prospective client. Many attorneys feel that it is not good to determine important issues on a prospective client's bankruptcy filing based on a simple questionnaire. Don't misinterpret—questionnaires are great. However, they should not be the sole method for an initial intake. In the case with Virginia Giordano, the paralegal was correct to question the veracity of the information he or she was given when filing Ms. Giordano's petition. The attorney was flat-out wrong for insisting that the paralegal file the petition as is. Lesson learned: Trust your instincts. If it looks like a rat, it probably is a rat.

CHAPTER **SUMMARY**

Bankruptcy clients can experience shame, embarrassment, and fear when faced with the possibility of being unable to afford the necessities of life. Clients who are experiencing emotional problems should be referred to those in the financial therapy industry. Although filing for bankruptcy may eventually result in a fresh start for clients in debt, it is not always the most practical solution. It is the responsibility of the attorney to review clients' financial circumstances and determine whether pursuing an alternative to bankruptcy makes more sense.

The initial client interview is the bankruptcy client's first meeting with the attorney and his or her paralegal. The paralegal's main function during the initial interview is to take notes and assist the attorney in the information-gathering process. Clients should be encouraged to be truthful with all disclosures and informed that failure to do so could not only result in their case being dismissed, but could also lead to criminal penalties. Additional appointments may have to be scheduled for information-gathering purposes during the course of bankruptcy document preparation. Although the attorney and paralegal must stress to the client the importance of such a requirement and the consequences that can result for lack of compliance, the law office must still verify the information the client provides.

The process of verifying the client's financial information is called due diligence. A simple rule to remember is that the client should be able to provide evidence proving the information supplied on the bankruptcy petition and accompanying schedules. Clients should be warned that what appears on social media might affect their bankruptcy case negatively. Trustees, creditors, and third parties may have access to information that could later backfire for the debtor. The most common type of fee arrangement in bankruptcy cases is the fixed or flat fee arrangement. Others include an hourly fee or payment plan. Clients must also disclose any potential claims to the attorney. In addition, an important function of the paralegal is to check the state and federal court websites for any pending litigation the debtor might be involved in.

The first question that comes to the mind of many individuals who are contemplating filing for bankruptcy is how bankruptcy will affect their credit scores. A credit score is a number that summarizes the information in an individual's credit report. A credit report is a detailed snapshot of an individual's financial history. Generally, a Chapter 7 case that proceeds normally and ends up in a discharge of debt for the debtor will appear on the debtor's credit report for ten years. A Chapter 13 case usually remains on a debtor's credit report for seven years; however, this time period can vary from state to state.

CONCEPT REVIEW AND REINFORCEMENT

KEY **TERMS**

Bankruptcy worksheet
credit repair organization (CRO)
Credit Repair Organizations Act (CROA)
credit report
debt consolidation
debt management agencies

debt relief agency
debt settlement
disclosure agreement or disclosure statement
due diligence
financial therapy industry
fixed (or flat) fee

hourly fee
initial client interview
judgment proof
notice of non-representation
payment plan
retainer agreement
secured credit card

REVIEWING **KEY CONCEPTS**

1. Briefly describe the alternatives to bankruptcy.
2. May a private employer discriminate against an applicant on the basis of a bankruptcy discharge listed on the applicant's credit report?
3. What is a bankruptcy worksheet and what is its purpose?
4. Why is it important for the legal team to gather documentation carefully when representing a debtor in a bankruptcy case?
5. Define due diligence.
6. What is the five-step analysis used to determine whether an attorney has fulfilled his or her obligation to exercise due diligence?
7. What impact can social networking have on a bankruptcy case?
8. Describe the basic clauses that should be included in a disclosure agreement.
9. Describe the basic clauses that should be included in a retainer agreement.
10. Name the resources a paralegal may use in checking pending litigation in a bankruptcy case.

BUILDING YOUR PARALEGAL SKILLS

CASE FOR **REVIEW**

U.S. v. Cluck, 87 F.3d 138 (1996)

BUILDING A PROFESSIONAL PORTFOLIO

PORTFOLIO **EXERCISES**

You are a bankruptcy paralegal at the law office of Maxine Frank. Attorney Frank is not happy with the current bankruptcy worksheet the office is using during the initial client interview. She asks you to review the numerous bankruptcy worksheets available on the Internet and combine the best of what you find to draft a new worksheet for the office.

LEARNING OBJECTIVES

After studying this chapter, you should be able to:

1. Identify the electronic resources available to bankruptcy paralegals.

2. Explain the differences between federal and local bankruptcy forms.

3. Describe the bankruptcy court privacy rules and how to avoid breaches of confidentiality.

4. Explain how PACER and CM/ECF are used in bankruptcy practice.

5. Summarize the use of bankruptcy software and the considerations when choosing a vendor.

6. Recognize the human factor component when using bankruptcy software.

Bankruptcy attorney Nancy Kholman's practice has grown since opening her doors in 2012. She is busier than ever and now with a newborn son, Fitzroy, Nancy has decided to hire a paralegal to help her around the office. Nancy drafted the following ad and forwarded it to Debbie Pastore, head of Career Services at the local paralegal school, hoping to find a recent graduate to fill the position. Attorney Kholman is particularly interested in hiring someone who has some basic knowledge of electronic filing and bankruptcy petition preparation software. These skills are extremely important in the modern-day, technology-based bankruptcy law practice.

The Law Office of Nancy Kholman is seeking an entry-level bankruptcy paralegal. Applicants should have functional proficiency and skills in the following areas:

- Paralegal certificate preferable
- Basic understanding of the fundamentals of Chapters 7, 11, and 13
- Basic knowledge of electronic filing (CM/ECF registration), PACER, and Best Case software
- Ability to prioritize and multitask
- Detail oriented
- Strong communication skills
- Excellent computer skills
- Ability to handle large volume of work
- Ability to meet deadlines

Hours are 9 AM–5 PM

Please submit résumé, cover letter, and salary requirements (hourly rate).

Debbie calls Nancy and tells her she has the perfect candidate! The student's name is Orlando Cabrera, and he is in his final term at the school. Orlando has had some office experience and worked in a bank for several years. Nancy tells Debbie that the last time she tried to hire an entry-level paralegal, she received a lot of résumés from candidates showing no exposure to electronic filing, PACER, or any form of bankruptcy software. Although she is willing to work with an employee who is right out of paralegal school, she wants someone who at least has some basic knowledge of PACER and the latest bankruptcy filing software. Debbie assures her that curriculum changes were made to the bankruptcy course last year to ensure that the bankruptcy law course at the school includes basic instruction in these practical skills. Read on to find out what electronic resources provide paralegals with the tools to succeed.

Introduction

Lawyers and paralegals may recall the days when they physically had to go to the district court to pick up bankruptcy forms from the clerk's office. They brought these forms back to the office, prepared them on a typewriter, and delivered them in their completed form to the clerk's office. Deadlines were especially hectic, requiring a race to the courthouse before the doors locked at the close of business. Research was conducted in books available in the office or with a trip to the local law library. Technology, however, has dramatically changed the way in which bankruptcy-related services are rendered. Legal documents are now prepared and filed online, eliminating the need for typewriters, last-minute searches for a parking space, and the mad dash to the clerk's office. Legal research is available at the touch of a button, and forms are filled out and filed online. This chapter examines how bankruptcy documents are electronically prepared and delivered, addresses the use of bankruptcy software in a bankruptcy law practice, and introduces the reader to some of the online resources bankruptcy paralegals use in answering day-to-day questions and keeping abreast of the changes in bankruptcy law. Also discussed in this chapter are the rules created to protect client privacy in an increasingly online world.

The Internet has provided legal professionals and self-represented parties with access to legal documents and the ability to file cases electronically. Legal documents were traditionally mailed, fax filed, or hand delivered to the courthouse, opposing parties, and other individuals or agencies associated with bankruptcy matters. Law firms looking for space often want offices conveniently situated near the courthouse because parking (or lack thereof) and parking tickets are always an issue in congested courthouse districts. With e-filing, however, case-related documents and pleadings can easily be filed from any computer with Internet access, eliminating those last-minute mad dashes to the clerk's office.

Bankruptcy Court Forms: Federal and Local Forms

FEDERAL FORMS

Official forms must be used to file and process a bankruptcy case. These forms must be used in all district courts throughout the country and are specified in the Federal Rules of Bankruptcy Procedure. Most forms include instructions unless the instructions are undergoing revisions and are temporarily unavailable. When filing for bankruptcy, the bankruptcy courts require use of the Official Bankruptcy

Forms and Procedural Forms. National (federal) and local bankruptcy court forms are available online for public use. Procedural forms are also available online and may be used during the course of a bankruptcy proceeding. The bankruptcy forms section of the U.S. Courts website is divided into three categories:

- Part I - Official Forms, Instructions, and Committee Notes
- Part II - Procedural Forms and Instructions
- Links to Related Material

Part I – Official Forms, Instructions, and Committee Notes

The necessary forms for filing bankruptcy under Chapter 7, Chapter 11, Chapter 12, or Chapter 13 are found in Part I. The paralegal must carefully choose the appropriate form to file for the client's specific needs. The forms on this website are **fillable**, which means that they may be completed online and saved for later use or to work on later. A form entry for a *List of Creditors Holding 20 Largest Unsecured Claims* looks like this:

fillable
Electronic forms that may be completed online and saved for later use or to work on later.

> **B4   List of Creditors Holding 20 Largest Unsecured Claims (12/07)**
>   **Instructions | Committee Notes**

Notice that each entry includes a link to the form, instructions for completing the document, and the effective date of the form. It includes a link to **Committee Notes**. These notes are created by the Judicial Conference Advisory Committee on Rules of Bankruptcy Procedure, or **Advisory Committee**, which consists of federal judges and bankruptcy attorneys and makes recommendations about bankruptcy rules, forms, and procedures. The Committee Notes provide details of the changes in bankruptcy forms and the reasons for the revisions. The Advisory Committee is only involved in policy and has no involvement in the daily operations and management of the courts. The Committee Notes for Official Form B4 are included here and illustrate how changes were made to protect the anonymity of minor children who, for example, may be the subject of an adversary proceeding to address child support the debtor owes.

Committee Notes
Notes the Judicial Conference Advisory Committee on Rules of Bankruptcy Procedure creates to provide details of the changes in bankruptcy forms and the reasons for the revisions.

Advisory Committee
A committee consisting of federal judges and bankruptcy attorneys that makes recommendations about bankruptcy rules, forms, and procedures.

B4 (Official Form 4) LIST OF CREDITORS HOLDING 20 LARGEST UNSECURED CLAIMS

Official Form 4 - Cumulative Committee Note

2005–2007 COMMITTEE NOTE

The form is amended to direct that the name of any minor child not be disclosed. The amendment implements § 112 of the Code, which was added by the Bankruptcy Abuse Prevention and Consumer Protection Act of 2005, Pub. L. No. 109-8, 119 Stat. 23 (April 20, 2005). In addition, the form is amended to add to the reference to Rule 1007(m) a direction to include for noticing purposes the name, address, and legal relationship to the child of "a person described" in that rule. Rule 1007(m) requires the person named to be someone on whom process would be served in an adversary proceeding against the child.

2005 COMMITTEE NOTE

The form is amended to direct that the name of any minor child not be disclosed. The amendment implements § 112 of the Code, which was added by the Bankruptcy Abuse Prevention and Consumer Protection Act of 2005, Pub. L. No. 109-8, 119 Stat. 23 (April 20, 2005).

Part II – Procedural Forms and Instructions

Part II includes procedural forms and instructions and other forms that are filed during the course of the bankruptcy proceeding, for example:

- Additional forms the debtor needs, such as Official Form B202 Statement of Military Service when a debtor is requesting a suspension of the bankruptcy proceedings because he or she is on active duty.
- Forms creditors use, such as Official Form B104 Adversary Proceeding Cover Sheet filed by a former spouse seeking child support.
- Forms the bankruptcy court uses for its convenience, such as Official Form 15S Order Finally Approving Disclosure Statement and Confirming Plan in a Chapter 11 reorganization.

Links to Related Materials

This section includes general information on the bankruptcy law and process. It includes three links: *Bankruptcy Basics, Court Links–Court Locator*, and *Pending Changes in Bankruptcy Forms*.

LOCAL FORMS

Paralegals working in a bankruptcy law practice should be aware that the U.S. Bankruptcy Court for the specific district where the client's case will be filed may require filing additional forms to comply with **local bankruptcy rules**. The individual district courts may draft their own rules specifically for the administration and case management of bankruptcy matters through that particular court system. **Local bankruptcy forms** are created by the individual district courts and may vary from one federal district to another. Paralegals should also take note of whether local forms are either mandatory or recommended. Some federal district courts only require filing of the Official Forms found on the U.S. Courts website. An example of a local, mandatory form is found on the U.S. Bankruptcy Court, District of New Jersey website, entitled *Amendment to Schedules D, E, F, G, H or List of Creditors*. Although each district may draft its own local Bankruptcy Rules and Forms, it must be consistent with Acts of Congress, the Federal Rules of Bankruptcy Procedure, and the Federal Rules of Civil Procedure.

local bankruptcy rules
Bankruptcy rules drafted by individual district courts, specifically for the administration and case management of bankruptcy matters in that particular court system.

local bankruptcy forms
Bankruptcy forms created by the individual district courts that may vary from one federal district to another.

Electronic Filing with Public Access Court Electronic Records (PACER)

PACER is an acronym for **Public Access to Court Electronic Records**, an Internet-based public access system that allows registered users to obtain basic case information, docket information, opinions, and documents filed in federal appellate, district, and bankruptcy courts. The PACER system is considered a public record, so any entity with a registered PACER account, such as banks or credit card companies, may have access to the information. Although PACER provides the public with access to information filed on the system, personally identifiable information such as the first five digits of a Social Security number, financial account numbers, the name of a minor, a person's date of birth, and home addresses in a criminal case are specifically kept out of the public eye. Access to PACER requires the user to create an account and password. The website charges a fee of ten cents per page to view or print pages, payable by credit card.

PACER (Public Acces to Court Electronic Records)
An acronym for **Public Access to Court Electronic Records,** an Internet-based public access system that allows registered users to obtain basic case information, docket information, opinions, and documents filed in federal appellate, district, and bankruptcy courts.

CM/ECF (Case Management/Electronic Case Files)
Acronym for **Case Management/Electronic Case Files**, a system that enables attorneys and paralegals to file and download documents related to bankruptcy cases when the firm represents the debtor, creditor, or other interested party.

CM/ECF, the acronym for the **Case Management/Electronic Case Files** system, enables attorneys and paralegals to file and download documents related to bankruptcy cases when the firm represents the debtor, creditor, or other interested party. Although PACER and CM/ECF may appear as separate databases, registered users have access to the same information, regardless of which portal is used. Bankruptcy cases, however, are actually filed and managed through CM/ECF. Each bankruptcy court has control over the system in its district, so paralegals and attorneys filing cases for clients must log on to the CM/ECF database for that particular court. There is no fee, however, for electronically filing documents with the bankruptcy court by using CM/ECF. Viewing and printing documents in existing cases will generate a per-page charge, though.

Case Management/Electronic Case Files (CM/ECF)

e-filing
The electronic filing of legal pleadings and documents now implemented in many courts across the country.

Learning how to file documents electronically is a must for paralegals employed in a bankruptcy law firm. **E-filing** is the electronic filing of legal pleadings and documents now implemented in many courts across the country. The benefits of e-filing for law firms include decreased costs of printing, postage, and file storage. Quick access to documents is also an advantage. Pleadings, documents, and information may be reviewed at any time, and e-filing eliminates the time it takes for an attorney or assistant to go to the courthouse physically to review files. It also facilitates better control of case management because all the necessary documents can be accessed through the judicial branch's website.

The convenience of filing documents after the courthouse closes and the ability to deliver the same electronically to opposing counsel and other interested parties is also a convenience. E-filing also benefits the clerk's office and court staff. An effective e-filing system eliminates the manual input of data regarding each case because it can automatically populate data from the state's judiciary website into the state's case management system. Court clerks do not have to spend time entering and scanning documents because they are immediately filed through the e-filing process. It also cuts down on visits to the clerk's counter and relieves the clerks of having to retrieve files, transport them, and pull them for the court hearings. Clerks do not have to prepare the file physically for court because judges can review the file directly from the bench without waiting for the clerk's office to bring the file to the actual courtroom. The courts can also eliminate or significantly reduce the need to maintain and store paper files.

Most of the U.S. bankruptcy, federal district, and appellate courts use the CM/ECF system or are implementing it now, and most bankruptcy documents today are filed through the CM/ECF system. Bankruptcy courts that have implemented CM/ECF create their own procedural rules, so it is important to become familiar with the local rules. Although CM/ECF is the vehicle for filing electronically in federal courts, access to court records is available through PACER.

TRAINING FOR CM/ECF AND PACER

Training for CM/ECF and PACER is available at no cost through the PACER website. Paralegals who wish to work in a bankruptcy practice or any other federally based practice should make it a point to take advantage of the free training. Learning the system is a must because most bankruptcy cases are filed electronically. The website organizes the material in training modules that include instruction about tasks such as opening a new bankruptcy case. Mastering the use of CM/ECF and PACER requires practice. Familiarity with these resources is not only vital as part of a paralegal bankruptcy course curriculum, but should also be reviewed before an interview with a bankruptcy law firm. Bankruptcy attorneys will most likely ask prospective employees whether they are familiar with these resources and have the requisite skills to work in a bankruptcy practice that uses them.

Knowledge of CM/ECF and PACER should also be included on a paralegal résumé because it is most often a requirement for employment in a bankruptcy practice. Paralegals should be familiar with how a bankruptcy case is filed electronically, how to access and scan documents, and save documents as a Portable Document Format (PDF). Paralegals will find that when it comes to electronic filing or accessing documents, practice makes perfect. The free training is available at any time and may need to be revisited until use of these systems becomes routine. Several other approaches to educating legal professionals in CM/ECF and PACER include seminars bar association or paralegal groups offer and training sessions the courts offer.

PROTECTING PRIVACY IN THE BANKRUPTCY SYSTEM

Unlimited public access can have devastating effects on those seeking a fresh start under the bankruptcy system because it makes available private information that can be used to perpetrate identity theft and credit fraud. Rules exist, however, to help balance the public's right to know and the individual's right to privacy. Paralegals employed in bankruptcy law firms are integral partners in protecting privacy in a system that makes individuals' personal information available for public view. This section addresses three important privacy laws, namely, bankruptcy court privacy rules, the Fair Credit Reporting Act, and the Gramm-Leach-Bliley Act.

BANKRUPTCY COURT PRIVACY RULES

Federal law requires **personally identifiable information**, or any information that can be used to identify a specific individual, to be protected from public view, whether the information is filed electronically or in paper form. This type of confidential, sensitive information must be omitted if unnecessary or redacted or sealed if the law requires. The bankruptcy court system must balance the public's right to access to public documents and protection of personal privacy. Most courts have or are in the process of scanning paper filings so both are available for electronic access. Although both versions are accessible to the public, personal data identifiers contained in those documents are not. If this information is not protected, it will become accessible to the public over the Internet. The login page for CM/ECF or PACER displays the following notice:

> IMPORTANT NOTICE OF REDACTION RESPONSIBILITY: All filers must redact: Social Security or taxpayer-identification numbers; dates of birth; names of minor children; financial account numbers; and, in criminal cases, home addresses, in compliance with Fed. R. Civ. P. 5.2 or Fed. R. Crim. P. 49.1. This requirement applies to all documents, including attachments.

Many e-filed documents are publicly available at the touch of a button. Furthermore, confidentiality police are not sitting in the clerk's office ready to review filings for

personally identifiable information
Any information that can be used to identify a specific individual; it must be protected from public view, whether the information is filed electronically or in paper form.

confidential information and alert the attorney's office of potential problems. To protect personal privacy and combat identity theft, the bankruptcy court has enacted Fed.R.Bankr.P. 9037, which closely parallels Fed.R. Civ. P. 5.2, titled *Privacy Protection for Filings Made with the Court.* Although Fed.R.Bankr.P. 9037 requires removal of personal data contained in bankruptcy documents, the court clerk does not perform this function. It is the responsibility of the attorney and his or her staff to ensure that confidentiality is maintained in the e-filing process, and the attorney will most likely entrust the bankruptcy paralegal with this redacting.

redacting
Striking out confidential words, phrases, or numbers by blacking out the information with a marker or using computer software that performs this process through electronic means.

Redacting is defined as striking out confidential words, phrases, or numbers by blacking out the information with a marker or using computer software that performs this process through electronic means. Documents that are uploaded, such as pay stubs, should be reviewed and redacted with a thick, black marker before scanning. Attorneys and paralegals working on their behalf and under their supervision are required to redact personally identifiable information from any electronic or paper filings. Failure to do so could expose the attorney to a malpractice suit, administrative grievances, or invasion of privacy lawsuits. Although paralegals often review documents for redacting purposes, the attorney is ultimately responsible for supervising nonattorney assistants and for any breaches of confidentiality. Attorneys logging on to the CM/ECF system, and paralegals who log on on their behalf, are required to click a box indicating that they are aware of the redaction requirements, further emphasizing the importance and responsibilities under the law. Given the importance of Fed.R.Bankr.P. 9037, both bankruptcy paralegals and attorneys should have a strong working knowledge of this rule and its requirements.

Fed.R.Bankr.P. 9037 Privacy Protection For Filings Made With The Court

(a) Redacted Filings. Unless the court orders otherwise, in an electronic or paper filing made with the court that contains an individual's social-security number, taxpayer-identification number, or birth date, the name of an individual, other than the debtor, known to be and identified as a minor, or a financial-account number, a party or nonparty making the filing may include only:

   (1) the last four digits of the social-security number and taxpayer-identification number;
   (2) the year of the individual's birth;
   (3) the minor's initials; and
   (4) the last four digits of the financial-account number.

(b) Exemptions From the Redaction Requirement. The redaction requirement does not apply to the following:

   (1) a financial-account number that identifies the property allegedly subject to forfeiture in a forfeiture proceeding;
   (2) the record of an administrative or agency proceeding unless filed with a proof of claim;
   (3) the official record of a state-court proceeding;
   (4) the record of a court or tribunal, if that record was not subject to the redaction requirement when originally filed;
   (5) a filing covered by subdivision (c) of this rule; and
   (6) a filing that is subject to § 110 of the Code.

(c) Filings Made Under Seal. The court may order that a filing be made under seal without redaction. The court may later unseal the filing or order the entity that made the filing to file a redacted version for the public record.

(d) Protective Orders. For cause, the court may by order in a case under the Code:

    (1) require redaction of additional information; or

    (2) limit or prohibit a nonparty's remote electronic access to a document filed with the court.

(e) Option for Additional Unredacted Filing Under Seal. An entity making a redacted filing may also file an unredacted copy under seal. The court must retain the unredacted copy as part of the record.

(f) Option for Filing a Reference List. A filing that contains redacted information may be filed together with a reference list that identifies each item of redacted information and specifies an appropriate identifier that uniquely corresponds to each item listed. The list must be filed under seal and may be amended as of right. Any reference in the case to a listed identifier will be construed to refer to the corresponding item of information.

(g) Waiver of Protection of Identifiers. An entity waives the protection of subdivision (a) as to the entity's own information by filing it without redaction and not under seal.

AVOIDING E-FILING PITFALLS

There are many pitfalls that if not anticipated can lead to disastrous repercussions if a legal professional is not forewarned. It is imperative for attorneys, paralegals, and anyone else in the office working on e-filing to be aware of what can actually go wrong before beginning the process. As the old saying goes, "Forewarned is forearmed."

Check, Double Check, Check Again

The paralegal should carefully review all information entered in the CM/ECF system to ensure its accuracy. In addition, documents uploaded to the system must be carefully identified to make sure that the right document is selected. Although these precautions seem obvious, it is often easier said than done in a busy bankruptcy law practice. Other common mistakes include:

- Entering incorrect party or event codes.
- Failure to identify exhibits.
- Failure to include a certificate of service.
- Failure to include attachments.
- Failure to redact confidential information.
- Failure to segregate documents.
- Failure to update changes in email addresses.
- Failure to update firm credit card information. (Filing may be rejected for lack of payment of fees.)
- Failure to include proper signatures.
- Uploading files that are too large. (Filing may be rejected and deadline may be missed.)

Pay Attention to Deadlines

Traditionally, filing paper document at the last minute required a race to the courthouse before the doors closed. Now that more courts have adopted e-filing, it is imperative for the manner in which the particular court determines the close of business day to be clearly understood. How does the court define the close of business day? Knowing the exact time, as well as date deadlines, is important not only for e-filing documents but also for e-service to other parties involved in the case. Post reminders of deadlines in the office so they are always visible. The paralegal should also be aware of the different time zones throughout the United States when determining filing deadlines. For example, a paralegal who is accustomed to filing in California, which is controlled by Pacific Standard Time, may miss a deadline when filing in Illinois, which follows Central Time.

File the Right Documents

Make sure that the proper document or pleading is being filed by making it a habit to double and triple check before clicking the Send or File icon.

Check before Deleting Email Messages

All incoming email messages should be checked for electronic notifications of pleading and documents filed in pending cases. If the law firm changes the email address the office uses to receive notifications from the CM/ECF system, it is important to log on to the CM/ECF account and update the email address section. Also, make sure that junk email and spam filters are not set to block court notices and check this folder regularly to make sure relevant emails are not left unattended. Set these filters to allow court domains, clients, agencies, or any other entity when communication is necessary. Changes may need to be made with the Internet service provider (ISP) as well as the law office email settings.

Email Notification Management

Some firms designate a separate email account exclusively for email notifications so that several members of the legal team may have access to court notices if the employee who is currently working on the case is on vacation, out on sick leave, or unavailable. Some firms have court notices delivered not only to the paralegal but also to the supervising attorney and another staff member to ensure continuity of case management.

Checking the Court Docket

Checking the court docket on a daily basis is a good way to ensure that all electronically filed documents and pleadings have been properly uploaded and that cases are properly monitored for any changes that can occur.

Protecting Privacy in a Public Records Environment

With the increase in electronic filing on the federal level, the trend to use technology for convenience and cost savings is also creating serious privacy concerns. Legal professionals should become proficient in FRBP 9037 and carefully review and redact documents to ensure client privacy.

Learn the Local Court Rules

Each bankruptcy court may adopt its own local rules in establishing the specific requirements for electronic filing. Therefore, it is essential to find the local rules for the federal bankruptcy court where the client's case will be filed. Bankruptcy attorneys may be filing in different courts, so the local rules should not be taken for granted; they may differ from jurisdiction to jurisdiction.

Last-Minute Filings

The old adage, "Whatever can go wrong will go wrong," is true when filing bankruptcy documents at the last minute. It is good to have a cushion of time to deal with technological problems that may arise during the electronic filing process. Furthermore, rushing through a filing can result in mistakes that could have been avoided if more attention was paid to the file.

Although paralegals are often delegated the task of electronically filing bankruptcy petitions and related documents, the attorney is not relieved of the supervisory responsibility. As illustrated in the following case, care should be taken by both attorneys and paralegals alike to ensure competent representation of clients, regardless of who is to blame for the mistake.

CASE **16.1** *Satterlee v. Allen Press, Inc.*, 455 F. Supp. 2d 1236 (D. Kan. 2006)

...[T]he Court sees no excuse for counsel's inadvertence in filing plaintiff's summary judgment response without supporting documents or his failure to recognize that these documents had not been attached at the time the response was filed. Plaintiff's counsel has had extensive experience filing and litigating cases in this district. While plaintiff's counsel now contends that the documents were not filed because their large size exceeded the maximum amount allowed by the electronic filing system and that this was the fault of his legal assistant, plaintiff's counsel bears responsibility for this oversight as well.

The electronic filing system notified plaintiff's counsel and his legal assistant of the electronic filings in this case at three different email addresses. According to the receipt for plaintiff's response, filed on May 11, 2006, electronic notification was sent to plaintiff's counsel, Mr. David O. Alegria, at the following email addresses: davidalegria@mcwala.com, DOAlegria@ aol.com, and jackierogers@mcwala.com. This notice described the filing as: "MEMORANDUM in Opposition by Plaintiff Karla Satterlee re [33] MOTION for Summary Judgment." Plaintiff's counsel was notified in this email that the response had been filed, and there is no indication that supporting documents accompanied this response. To illustrate this process, when plaintiff filed the reply to this motion in which a supporting document was properly attached, he received electronic notice described as "REPLY to Response to Motion by Plaintiff Karla Satterlee re: [46] MOTION for Reconsideration re [45] Judgment (Attachments: # (1) Exhibit A)," indicating that this motion was filed with an attachment. Plaintiffs counsel's failure to file supporting documents and failure to recognize that none had been filed, when he received these notices specifically indicating no attachments, is not excusable neglect.

Further, plaintiff's counsel apparently did not realize that these documents were not attached until the Court pointed this out in the July 31 Order. Between the

(Continued)

(Continued)

filing of the response on May 11, 2006 and the issuance of the July 31 Order, plaintiff's counsel could have checked the docket sheet in this case. Had he done so in this two month period, plaintiff's counsel would have realized that he had provided no supporting documents with his response. Additionally, counsel should have been alerted to the failure to file the documents upon receipt of defendant's reply. On the first page of defendant's reply, defendant asserts that plaintiff's response failed to comply with D. Kan. R. 56.1 in several respects. When plaintiff purported to controvert facts in the response and defendant replied that the facts were unsupported or contradicted by the record, that should have prompted defendant to check the record, particularly when neither the electronic notice and the docket sheet indicated that any attachments had been filed. Thus, the Court finds plaintiffs counsel's neglect in this case was inexcusable, and refuses to grant plaintiff relief under Rule 60....

The law office will have to create an e-filing account with CM/ECF. It is important to create the account before a case actually has to be filed so technological glitches can be resolved without the pressure of an impending deadline. After the account is created, the office will receive a user ID and password, which will permit the filing of new cases or representation of clients in matters that have already been filed. The reality is that paralegals and other legal staff members, with their supervising attorney's consent, use the attorney's login information to file and monitor client cases. Although this might be a common practice, the attorney is responsible for the filing, the content, and any of the consequences arising out of authorizing a member of the office staff to e-file on his or her behalf.

According to the *Case Management Electronic Case Files (CM/ECF) Attorney's User Guide*, paralegals do not qualify as Filing Users under this system. However, the reality is that paralegals often file bankruptcy petitions and related documents. The *Administrative Procedures for Electronic Filing in Civil and Criminal Cases,* available on individual district courts' websites, allows the attorney's authorized staff members to use the attorney's CM/ECF login ID and password. The attorney, however, is prohibited from knowingly allowing an unauthorized party to have access to the system. For example, although the attorney might allow his or her paralegal to access the system to file a bankruptcy petition, the attorney cannot give his or her best friend the information to find data about an old love interest.

OTHER FEDERAL PRIVACY STATUTES

The Fair Credit Reporting Act and the Gramm-Leach-Bliley Act are two privacy statutes that, in addition to federal bankruptcy law, also address issues regarding the use and collection of information regarding a debtor in the bankruptcy process.

Fair Credit Reporting Act

Fair Credit Reporting Act
A federal law that prohibits reporting inaccurate or incomplete information on the client's credit report.

After the court has discharged a client's bankruptcy, the **Fair Credit Reporting Act** prohibits reporting inaccurate or incomplete information on the client's credit report. According to federal law, although a consumer reporting agency may include delinquencies on debts discharged in bankruptcy in consumer reports, it is required to note the status of the debt accurately. If the client owed $3,457 to XYZ Credit Card Company, and this debt was discharged in bankruptcy, the client's credit report must indicate that the debt was discharged. A credit report that simply includes the unpaid balance is inaccurate and prohibited by law. The legal remedies for violating the Act depend on whether the breach was intentional or negligent and may include actual damages, punitive damages, attorneys' fees, and costs. In the following case, the United States District Court Central District of California agrees with the plaintiffs when it indicates that when retrieving information from PACER, TransUnion could dramatically enhance the accuracy of information on its credit reports for consumers with discharged debts.

CASE 16.2 *White v. Trans Union, LLC.*, 462 F. Supp. 2d 1079 (C.D. Cal. 2006)

...Plaintiffs brought this class action lawsuit on behalf of themselves, and others similarly situated, to restrain TransUnion from employing credit reporting practices that they allege falsely declare their discharged debts to be "due and owing" and thereby inappropriately taint Plaintiffs' credit reports. Specifically, Plaintiffs allege that TransUnion employs procedures regarding its reporting of such debts that produce twice as many erroneous reports than it does accurate ones, and that TransUnion does so willfully and in conscious disregard of Plaintiffs' statutory right to protection from the transmission of inaccurate information.... To vindicate these rights, Plaintiffs now seek statutory and punitive damages, injunctive relief, and attorneys' fees and costs....

...The First and Second Causes of Action allege negligent and willful failure to employ reasonable procedures to ensure maximum accuracy of Credit Reports in violation of the Fair Credit Reporting Act ("FCRA"), 15 U.S.C. §§ 1681e(b) and the California Consumer Credit Reporting Agency Act ("CCRAA"), Cal. Civ. Code section 1785.14(b). TransUnion current relies solely on consumers' creditors to voluntarily update the status of accounts belonging to consumers that receive Chapter 7 discharge orders. Plaintiffs complain that TransUnion knows, or should know, that the information these creditors furnish regarding the status of pre-bankruptcy debts is highly unreliable and that procedures for reporting such debts therefore fail to assure "maximum possible accuracy."...

...TransUnion moves to dismiss Plaintiffs' First and Second Causes of Action on the grounds that a credit reporting agency cannot be held liable for inaccurate reporting if the procedures used to prepare that reporting were reasonable.... The crux of this argument is that the texts of the FCRA and the CCRAA do not expressly require that credit reporting agencies must describe the legal implications of a bankruptcy discharge order on a Credit Report. TransUnion further maintains that because the legal effect of such bankruptcy discharge orders is not readily apparent to entities, such as credit reporting agencies, that are not actual parties to the bankruptcy proceeding, it must be reasonable for them to rely exclusively upon the public record and information voluntarily provided to update the status of discharged accounts.

...The FCRA and the CCRAA both obligate credit reporting agencies to "follow reasonable procedures to assure maximum possible accuracy of the information concerning the individual about whom the report relates." 15 U.S.C. § 1681e(b); Cal. Civ.Code section 1785.14(b). Each of these statutes impose additional obligations on credit reporting agencies relating to consumers who have filed petitions for bankruptcy that require such agencies to report the particular chapter of Title 11

(Continued)

(Continued)

under which the petition was filed and that limit the amount of time they may report bankruptcy information to a maximum of ten years. 15 U.S.C. §§ 1681c; Cal. Civ. Code section 1785.13(c). But nothing in these statutory provisions suggests that there is an exception to an agency's standard obligation to employ reasonable procedures to ensure maximum possible accuracy for bankruptcy-related information. *See also* 16 C.F.R. 600 app. § 607(3)(A)(6); *id.* § 607(3)(F)(2) ("[A] consumer reporting agency may include delinquencies on debts discharged in bankruptcy in consumer reports, but must accurately note the status of the debt (e.g., discharged, voluntarily repaid).") ...("A consumer reporting agency must employ reasonable procedures to keep its file current on past due accounts [e.g., by requiring its creditors to notify the credit bureau when a previously past due account has been paid or discharged in bankruptcy....").

There is no basis here upon which the Court could find that TransUnion's procedures are reasonable to ensure maximum possible accuracy as a matter of law. The SACC references a survey of 960 Credit Reports issued by TransUnion showing that in sixty-four per cent of the cases involving no-asset Chapter 7 bankruptcy proceedings, TransUnion erroneously listed one or more of the consumer's discharged debts as due and owing.... The average number of falsely listed debts in this sample was between three and four per report, and some reports contained as many as ten or more such errors.... This allegation by itself is capable of demonstrating the type of repetitive and systematic errors in TransUnion's procedures that could render those procedures unreasonable.... Not once in its sixteen page motion or its twenty-one page reply brief does TransUnion confront this error rate or attempt to explain how a set of procedures that it contends to be reasonable could cause for nearly two thirds of the Credit Reports it issues involving debts discharged through Chapter 7 bankruptcy proceedings to contain the same type of error.

The Plaintiffs' allegations go further still, however, and outline specific alternative procedures that TransUnion could follow to dramatically enhance the accuracy of the Credit Reports it issues for consumers with discharged debts. Specifically, they explain that TransUnion already obtains every discharge order issued in Chapter 7 proceedings through the electronic PACER court reporting service and that information as to whether a debt has been reaffirmed or successfully challenged is easily retrievable through this PACER service. By commanding its computers to utilize this resource in an effort to determine which debts have been discharged and which remain, Plaintiffs allege that TransUnion "could achieve close to 100 percent accuracy in the reporting of the status of pre-bankruptcy debts." ...TransUnion never even mentions the PACER system in its filings on this Motion.

The fact that TransUnion has elected to ignore Plaintiffs' allegations supporting its claim of unreasonableness does not change the fact that these allegations nevertheless exist and make out a cognizable legal theory. Accordingly, Plaintiffs' First and Second Causes of Action cannot be dismissed on this theory.

Gramm-Leach-Bliley Act of 1999 (Financial Services Modernization Act of 1999)
A federal law that requires financial institutions to limit the disclosure of consumers' personal financial information, to advise consumers of the institution's privacy policies, and to allow consumers to opt out of sharing their personal financial information.

GRAMM-LEACH-BLILEY ACT OF 1999

The **Gramm-Leach-Bliley Act of 1999,** also known as the **Financial Services Modernization Act of 1999**, 15 U.S.C. §§ 6801-6809, requires financial institutions to limit the disclosure of consumers' personal financial information, to advise consumers of the institution's privacy policies, and to allow consumers to opt out of sharing their personal financial information. Consumers see this law in action every time they receive a privacy notice or privacy policy insert in their bank or credit card statements. The financial institution may disclose such information to its business affiliates, and this provision in the statute is not affected if the consumer selects the opt-out provision. Although consumers may opt out of disclosures to third parties, limited financial information included in the bankruptcy petition and related documents is public record and, unfortunately, bypasses the opt-out provisions of the Gramm-Leach-Bliley Act.

Bankruptcy Software

INTRODUCTION

Bankruptcy software has increasingly become an essential tool for bankruptcy law practitioners and their paralegals. It assists with preparation of the bankruptcy petition, schedules, statement of financial affairs and creditor matrix, calculation of the Means Test, and case management. Bankruptcy software streamlines the document preparation process and saves precious time in a busy practice. Although the official bankruptcy forms and instructions are available and filed online, bankruptcy software has become especially important since the enactment of the Bankruptcy Abuse Prevention and Consumer Protection Act of 2005 (BAPCPA) and the requirement of the Means Test calculation to determine whether the client qualifies for Chapter 7 liquidation or a Chapter 13 repayment plan.

When interviewing with a bankruptcy attorney, the prospective paralegal employee should determine what type of bankruptcy software the office uses. Many vendors sell these products to law firms, so usage can vary from practice to practice. Every bankruptcy software program is different, so becoming familiar with the system the bankruptcy law firm uses is an important skill. If a paralegal is hired by a bankruptcy law firm that uses unfamiliar bankruptcy software, the paralegal should take the initiative to access the vendor's website or directly contact the vendor to determine what type of resources are available for learning the system. Most bankruptcy software providers offer online manuals, demos, and tutorials to assist legal professionals in learning how to use the software. A **tutorial** is an online resource that provides the user with step-by-step instruction in how to use the bankruptcy software and is an invaluable resource when learning new software.

tutorial
An online resource that provides the user with step-by-step instruction in how to use the bankruptcy software and is an invaluable resource when learning new software.

Although some paralegals are employed in established law offices that have systems and software in place, some paralegals are employed by new attorneys or attorneys choosing to add the representation of clients in bankruptcy proceedings. These paralegals may be asked to assist the attorney in evaluating bankruptcy software, especially because the paralegals will be assisting the attorney.

CHOOSING BANKRUPTCY SOFTWARE

Careful consideration should be taken when choosing bankruptcy software for a busy law office. Purchasing software that is user friendly avoids the frustration of spending unbillable hours of valuable law firm time in solving technical glitches. In addition to the preparation of petitions and related initial documents, the software should also include a Means Test calculator and postpetition forms, PDF generators, free tech support, and regular maintenance.

If the paralegal is involved in the decision process, he or she should determine whether the U.S. Bankruptcy Court for the district or districts in which the attorney practices have tested the software with its CM/ECF system. Bankruptcy software should be functionally compatible with the CM/ECF system used in the district, enabling the attorney or paralegal to upload case data from the software to CM/ECF. Bankruptcy petition software vendors have created software that allows for automatic case upload from their application into CM/ECF. Although the bankruptcy courts do not endorse or recommend any specific software vendor, they will provide a list on their websites of the bankruptcy petition programs that have been tested with that district's electronic filing system.

The following is a list of some bankruptcy petition software that can be used in conjunction with CM/ECF. Please note that this list is not exhaustive, and care should be taken to verify software compatibility:

- Bankruptcy Plus
- Bankruptcy PRO
- Best Case® Bankruptcy
- EZ Filing
- Fresh$tart$even
- Lexis/Nexis Collier TopForm
- New Hope Bankruptcy2014
- West-Specialty Software/ Chap 7…13

A bankruptcy law practice should purchase software that is specifically created for attorneys. There are many bankruptcy software vendors, some of which cater to consumers who are representing themselves or bankruptcy petition preparers. Bankruptcy software for attorneys, as opposed to software for consumers, is a specialized product and a considerable investment for a bankruptcy law firm. Cost and yearly maintenance fees are important considerations for firms in the market for bankruptcy software. Although the software geared to attorneys may be more expensive, the attorney is paying for not only the expertise involved in the creation of the software but also for maintenance and updating features.

For example, software that includes a Means Test calculator must include the latest numerical values from the Bureau of the Census, Department of Justice, and Internal Revenue Service. Bankruptcy software that is not updated will produce inaccurate figures on behalf of the client. Bankruptcy law practitioners should choose software that includes regular updates, which will obviously cost the attorney additional subscription fees for the service, but this is a cost that cannot and should not be avoided, because the rules of professional conduct for attorneys require continuing competence in the field of practice. Law is ever changing, and failure to keep abreast of relevant changes may not only expose the attorney to malpractice suits and grievance proceedings but, more important, can damage a client's financial future.

It is also essential to determine how many people in the office will be using the software and how many times the attorney may install the software on different devices and for various staff members. Bankruptcy software is protected by copyright law. The owner of the copyright, however, has the right to license the software to those willing to pay the licensing fee. A **license** is the right to use another's

license
The right to use another's creative work under certain terms and conditions.

creative work under the terms and conditions of the license. There are two types of licenses to consider when dealing with bankruptcy software. A **single-user license** allows one person to use the software. A **multi-user license** allows more than one person to use the software. Understanding the licensing agreement will clarify the terms of how the software may be used. A multi-user license is a must in a busy bankruptcy office where several attorneys and paralegals may need access to the system to do their work.

single-user license
A license that allows one person to use the software.

multi-user license
A license that allows more than one person to use software.

THE HUMAN FACTOR

Preparing bankruptcy petitions and related documents with the assistance of software is not simply a clerical function. The software does not do the actual work for either the attorney or the paralegal. The adage, "Garbage in, garbage out," rings true whenever unreliable and unverified information is used in the preparation of any computer-assisted system. Legal professionals must interview clients thoroughly, review financial records, and sift out verifiable data in the preparation of documents. It is not enough just to fill in the blanks and check off the boxes. Although bankruptcy software can make filing petitions and other documents online easier, the input of data requires the skill of an attorney or paralegal trained in the foundations of bankruptcy law and procedure.

Knowledge of substantive bankruptcy law and procedure, and how it applies to the client's specific circumstances, requires a trained eye. Bankruptcy paralegals will find themselves stopping during the course of preparing documents, whether done so manually or with software, to ask the attorney what should be done in a particular situation. Filing for bankruptcy and the many decisions that must be made on the road to discharge may require the strategy that only an experienced attorney can provide. Regardless of which bankruptcy software vendor is used, the experienced legal professional should be able to review the document and determine whether the software functioned properly and accurately.

INTERNET RESOURCES

The legal profession now does most of its work with the aid of technological resources. Bankruptcy resources are accessed online. Bankruptcy research is conducted online. Bankruptcy petition, schedules, and pleadings are filed online. Bankruptcy cases are managed online. In light of the online nature of bankruptcy practice, bankruptcy paralegals are highly recommended to become familiar with the tools and resources available through the Internet. The following list is not exhaustive. A simple Google or Bing search will yield numerous resources for the bankruptcy professional.

GOVERNMENT WEBSITES

Administrative Office of the U.S. Courts

The Administrative Office of the U.S. Courts website provides information about bankruptcy statistics. This is a particularly good resource when the paralegal is enlisted to assist the attorney or firm in the preparation of content for a continuing legal education seminar in bankruptcy, writing an article for the local newspaper or law firm website, or is preparing a presentation for the local paralegal association.

IRS Bankruptcy Tax Guide

The IRS Bankruptcy Tax Guide website includes IRS Publication 908, which explains the federal tax aspects of bankruptcy. This is a very important resource for paralegals to research the implications of Internal Revenue rules as they apply to bankruptcy law.

United States Department of Justice, United States Trustee Program

United States Department of Justice, United States Trustee Program is the official government website for the U.S. Trustee Program that includes valuable information about the federal bankruptcy system. It includes information about credit counseling and debtor education, consumer resources, fee guidelines, Means Testing, bankruptcy reform, and information about the trustee program.

U.S. Courts

U.S. Courts is the official website of the United States federal courts. It is an absolutely essential resource for bankruptcy professionals. The website's Bankruptcy Basics section includes the following topics and resources:

- Process
- The Discharge in Bankruptcy
- Chapter 7. Liquidation Under the Bankruptcy Code
- Chapter 9. Municipality Bankruptcy
- Chapter 11. Reorganization Under the Bankruptcy Code
- Chapter 12. Family Farmer Bankruptcy or Family Fisherman Bankruptcy
- Chapter 13. Individual Debt Adjustment
- Chapter 15. Ancillary and Other Cross-Border Cases
- SCRA. Service Members' Civil Relief Act
- SIPA. Securities Investor Protection Act
- Glossary - Terms You Need to Know
- Bankruptcy Forms

The website also includes links to bankruptcy courts in each federal district and tutorials for CM/ECF and PACER.

BANKRUPTCY LAW NEWS AND INFORMATION

American Bankruptcy Institute

The American Bankruptcy Institute's website provides useful information for bankruptcy professionals by reporting on bankruptcy news, bankruptcy code and regulations, online resources, and information about conferences and workshops.

Bankruptcy Law Topics –ABA Journal

The *ABA Journal*'s Bankruptcy Law Topics provides links to articles related to bankruptcy law. Readers may also elect to subscribe by RSS feed to receive updates.

Bernstein's Dictionary of Bankruptcy Terminology

Bernstein's Dictionary of Bankruptcy Terminology provides definitions and explanations of commonly used bankruptcy terms.

Kelley Blue Book

Kelley Blue Book is an excellent resource for researching the value of both new and used vehicles.

Legal Information Institute Cornell Law School

Cornell Law School's Legal Information Institute is a valuable resource that includes federal statutes and regulations, state statutes, and court opinions related to bankruptcy law as well as a general overview on bankruptcy law.

NADA

NADA is another website that may be used to obtain the value of new and used vehicles.

Nolo's Bankruptcy Information

Nolo is a company that publishes legal resources that are actually written in plain language, making the law accessible and understandable. Nolo's Bankruptcy Information website provides a wellspring of articles about bankruptcy law on topics such as the different bankruptcy chapters, exemptions, small business bankruptcy, and bankruptcy procedure, for example.

Zillow

Zillow is a website that allows users to search for property values. It can be useful in accessing property values to determine homestead exemptions in bankruptcy cases. Although Zillow may be used to access these figures, the trustee or bankruptcy court may require the debtor to obtain an appraisal of the property if a more accurate value is desired. The paralegal should also obtain a copy of the most recent tax assessment of the property.

BANKRUPTCY BLOGS

A **blog** is a webpage or website created by an individual or an organization that frequently expresses its opinions about various topics. Many blogs address the specific area of bankruptcy law. Bankruptcy Law–ABA Journal is a useful website that provides a list of bankruptcy-related blogs along with links for easy access. The following are examples of several bankruptcy blogs that may be of interest to paralegal professionals.

blog
A webpage or website created by an individual or organizations who frequently express their views and opinions on various topics.

Bankruptcy Law Network

Bankruptcy Law Network provides bankruptcy information to the general public.

Credit Slips

Credit Slips includes blog articles on credit and bankruptcy, written by attorneys and law professors.

Wall Street Journal's *Bankruptcy Beat*

Bankruptcy Beat reports on the latest trends in bankruptcy law as well as corporate bankruptcies.

Recall Attorney Kohlman from the beginning of the chapter? She is the bankruptcy attorney who had a busy practice. Attorney Kohlman, like virtually all other bankruptcy attorneys, is not just looking for a paralegal who is detail oriented and possesses strong communication skills. She is interested in recruiting a well-trained, new paralegal graduate from the local career school. In particular, she is looking for a graduate who is trained in the latest bankruptcy file management software and is familiar with the federal court's online filing and indexing system. Her employment ad specified that she needed a paralegal who was familiar with e-filing and online resources. After reading this chapter, you have learned that e-filing is the electronic filing of legal pleadings and documents and has been implemented in many courts across the country. Learning how to file documents electronically is a must for paralegals employed in a bankruptcy law firm. In addition, paralegals should be comfortable looking up the values on vehicles and real property and should know how to navigate online assessor databases, real property records, and both state and federal court dockets. A paralegal graduate who has had exposure to such things as PACER, online state court dockets, bankruptcy file management software, vehicle and real property valuation websites, and property assessors' databases, has a definite leg up on the competition. Just think how glad Orlando Cabrera will be that he took the time to learn as much as he could about the electronic resources for bankruptcy practice.

CHAPTER SUMMARY

Technology has dramatically changed the way in which bankruptcy related services are rendered. National (federal) and local bankruptcy court forms are available online and available for public use. Paralegals working in a bankruptcy law practice should be aware that the U.S. Bankruptcy Court for the specific district where the client's case will be filed may require the filing of additional forms to comply with local bankruptcy rules. The individual district courts may draft their own rules specifically for the administration and case management of bankruptcy matters through that particular court system. Local bankruptcy forms are created by the individual district courts and may vary from one federal district to another.

PACER is an acronym for Public Access to Court Electronic Records, an Internet-based public access system that allows registered users to obtain basic case information, docket information, and opinions and documents filed in federal appellate, district, and bankruptcy courts. The Case Management/Electronic Case Filing (CM/ECF) system is an electronic case management system most of the bankruptcy courts use, as do federal district and appellate courts. Most bankruptcy documents today are filed through the CM/ECF system. Federal law requires personally identifiable information, or any information that can be used to identify a specific individual, to

be protected from public view, whether the information is filed electronically or in paper form. This type of confidential, sensitive information must be omitted if unnecessary or redacted or sealed if the law requires. There are many pitfalls to using this system that, if not anticipated, can lead to disastrous repercussions if a legal professional is not forewarned. It is imperative for attorneys, paralegals, and anyone else in the office working on e-filing to be aware of what can actually go wrong before beginning the process.

Bankruptcy software has increasingly become an essential tool for bankruptcy law practitioners and their paralegals. It can assist with preparation of the bankruptcy petition, schedules, statement of financial affairs and creditor matrix, calculation of the Means Test, and case management, but it does not do the actual work for either the attorney or the paralegal. The adage, "Garbage in, garbage out," rings true whenever unreliable and unverified information is used in the preparation of any computer-assisted system. Legal professionals must interview clients thoroughly, review financial records, and sift out verifiable data in the preparation of documents. In light of the online nature of bankruptcy practice, bankruptcy paralegals are highly recommended to become familiar with the tools and resources available through the Internet.

CONCEPT REVIEW AND REINFORCEMENT

KEY **TERMS**

Advisory Committee
blog
CM/ECF (Case Management/
Electronic Case Files)
Committee Notes
e-filing
Fair Credit Reporting Act

fillable
Gramm-Leach Bliley Act of 1999
(Financial Services Modernization
Act of 1999)
license
local bankruptcy forms
local bankruptcy rules

multi-user license
PACER (Public Access to Court
Electronic Records)
personally identifiable information
redacting
single-user license
tutorial

REVIEWING **KEY CONCEPTS**

1. List and briefly explain the three categories of bankruptcy forms available on the U.S. Court's website.
2. What is the function of local bankruptcy rules and forms in bankruptcy practice?
3. What is PACER and how is it used in bankruptcy practice?
4. What is CM/ECF and how is it used in bankruptcy practice?
5. Explain the significance of the notice of redaction responsibility on the login page for PACER and CM/ECF.
6. What is the main goal of Fed.R. Bankr. P. 9037?
7. Paralegals do not qualify as Filing Users in the CM/ECF system. How, then, may paralegals legally file

bankruptcy petitions on behalf of their attorney supervisors?
8. You have just been hired as a paralegal for a bankruptcy law firm that uses Best Case bankruptcy software. You are unfamiliar with how to use this software, and your new job starts in two weeks. What do you do?
9. Your supervising attorney would like to purchase inexpensive bankruptcy software. One of the reasons the cost is so low is that he doesn't intend to purchase a subscription that updates the software. Is this a good idea?
10. Find an interesting blog written by a bankruptcy attorney. Explain why this would be a useful resource in bankruptcy practice.

BUILDING YOUR PARALEGAL SKILLS

CASE FOR **REVIEW**

Amina Anwar et al. v. D. Lee Johnson et al., No. 11-16612 (9th Cir. 2013)

PRACTICAL EXERCISES

PACER AND **CM/ECF TRAINING ASSIGNMENT**

Free training for PACER and CM/ECF is available on the Internet. Please note that training is in the form of tutorials and that actual access to PACER and CM/ECF requires you to set up an account. In building your paralegal skills, do the following exercises.

PACER   Conduct an Internet search on either Google or Bing and find the PACER Video Training Site on the PACER website. Learn how to use PACER by viewing the tutorials available on this page. The tutorials may be viewed by simply clicking the links.

CM/ECF   Conduct an Internet search on either Google or Bing and locate the PACER website. Click the E-File tab. This takes you to the CM/ECF system page. Click Training on the E-File menu located on the left side of this page. Learn how to use CM/ECF by clicking the available links to access the learning modules:

Streaming Video

"CM/ECF: The Attorney's Perspective" streaming video

Bankruptcy Courts

Version 3.+ Electronic Learning Modules
Version 4.+ Electronic Learning Modules
Version 5.+ Electronic Learning Modules

Best Case Tutorial Assignment

Learn the basics of Best Case® Bankruptcy Software, at *http://bestcase.com*/edu/students, where you can attend a free on-line demonstration and learn how to:

- Prepare a voluntary petition and other bankruptcy schedules and forms
- Open a new client file
- Use the Best Case Means Test Calculator

For additional practice, a free educational version of Best Case is available for download. The training exercises contained on the website provide an opportunity to prepare a sample voluntary petition and corresponding schedules, Statement of Financial Affairs, and there is also an exercise on electronic filing.

BUILDING A PROFESSIONAL PORTFOLIO

PORTFOLIO EXERCISES

You work as a paralegal for the bankruptcy law firm of Marietta & Naisby. Maxine Bell is a client whose bankruptcy was discharged last year. She recently obtained a copy of her credit report from VERIFY, a credit reporting agency, and found that a $6,390 debt that was discharged is currently listed on her credit report as due. She is furious! She thought that filing for bankruptcy would give her a fresh start, but this is not the case. She wants to know whether this is legal and what, if anything, can be done about it.

Using an Internet search engine such as Google or Bing, research the remedies for violating the Fair Credit Reporting Act. Draft a letter to Ms. Bell on behalf of Attorney Joan Naisby explaining her legal rights under the Act and the available remedies. Include alternative courses of action that Ms. Bell may take to rectify this problem without the expense of a lawsuit against VERIFY.

chapter 17

PETITIONS, SCHEDULES, AND OTHER FORMS

After graduating near the top of his class at the local career college, Solomon Feinstein secured a job as a paralegal at a very prestigious law firm. Solomon was surprised that one of his first tasks on the job was to help the firm formulate a new intake questionnaire because the one they were using was more than 10 years old. He is certainly glad that he took Bankruptcy Law as an elective in his paralegal program at school. In his Bankruptcy class, he learned the importance of being as thorough and accurate as possible with respect to the information the debtor must represent to the bankruptcy court. Solomon was already familiar with the petition, forms, and schedules and understood the consequences a bankruptcy debtor could face if the information in those forms was inaccurate. Read on to discover what Solomon learned that has helped make him successful at his new job as a paralegal.

LEARNING OBJECTIVES

After studying this chapter, you should be able to:

1. Understand how to prepare and file the necessary forms and schedules accurately in a typical bankruptcy case.

2. Summarize the petition and the various forms and their respective purposes in a bankruptcy filing.

3. Describe the paralegal's role and his or her limitations when assisting a bankruptcy client with the forms and schedules.

4. Explain how to assist clients accurately with preparing the Means Test calculation.

5. Identify the potential issues a paralegal must be able to spot while assisting the client with the petition, schedules, and Statement of Financial Affairs.

Introduction

In previous chapters, we introduced you to the various tasks you will perform in your role as paralegal. After you complete the intake and assist the client with locating an approved credit counseling agency online or in person, your work begins to intensify. The paralegal's responsibilities, especially at the beginning of a bankruptcy case, are intense. In most law firms, it will be your responsibility to complete the client intake as well as prepare the petition, schedules, and other necessary forms. In the following pages, we review all the necessary forms your firm's clients will need to file a successful liquidation or reorganization case. You will learn how to categorize and properly document the client's assets as well as his or her debts. We introduce you to a fictitious couple, Otto and Christina Schuler, who have run into a little trouble financially in the past few years. After meeting the

Schulers, you will discover that they have had just about every problem most couples could have with consumer debt. Consumer debt has been defined as debt incurred through the purchase of nonappreciable assets such as clothing, food, and the latest personal, must-have gadgets that are not related to business. You will have an opportunity to practice preparing each of the schedules and forms you might encounter with similar real-life clients in your future position as a bankruptcy paralegal. You will prepare and calculate the Means Test form to verify whether the Schulers are eligible for a liquidation filing or must file a reorganization case.

Preparing The Voluntary Petition

voluntary petition

A court form, similar to an application, that the debtor must complete in order to be eligible for bankruptcy relief.

Think of the **voluntary petition** as an application the debtor must fill out to be eligible for bankruptcy relief. As you will see, the petition contains many sections and box-checking areas that may or may not apply to your client. After successfully completing an intake with the client, you should be able to prepare and select the appropriate sections of the petition.

Name Section Indicate the debtor and joint debtor's full, proper, and legal names on the petition. No nicknames or commonly known as names are acceptable on the petition. Any names or aliases the debtor used within the past eight years must be captured on the form as well.

Nature of Debt Indicate the nature of your client's debts. For most individual clients, this will be non-business–related consumer debt.

Filing Fee You must indicate whether your client is paying the full fee, has applied for a fee waiver (rare in bankruptcy cases), or will pay the fees in installments. If your client's intention is to pay the filing fee in installments, you must prepare a Form 3A, Application and Order to Pay Filing Fee in Installments. If your client chooses to pay in installments, he or she will be allowed four installments. The entire amount of the filing fee must be paid off within 120 days after filing the petition.

Statistical Information In this section, the debtor indicates whether there will be assets to distribute to the creditors. This section is particularly important in a liquidation case. It gives a creditor an indication of whether it should file a proof of claim with the court. When considering how to answer this question on the petition, the debtor must consider the property he or she owns and how much of it, if any, will be exempt or nonexempt.

Prior Bankruptcy Cases within Last Eight Years The debtor must disclose all bankruptcy cases he or she (and spouse if applicable) has previously filed in the past eight years. Accurate disclosure in this section is important because restrictions apply on how often and how long a debtor must wait to file another bankruptcy case.

Exhibit A This section is for individuals or businesses filing for Chapter 11 bankruptcy.

Exhibit B This section applies when the debtor is represented by an attorney. The bankruptcy attorney must attest that he or she explained all the client's options under Chapters 7, 11, 12, or 13. In addition, the attorney must attest that the debtor has been advised in accordance with the requirements under 11 U.S.C. 342(b).

(b) Before the commencement of a case under this title by an individual whose debts are primarily consumer debts, the clerk shall give to such individual written notice containing:

(1) A brief description of:

(A) Chapters 7, 11, 12, and 13 and the general purpose, benefits, and costs of proceeding under each of those chapters; and

(B) The types of services available from credit counseling agencies; and

(2) Statements specifying that:

(A) A person who knowingly and fraudulently conceals assets or makes a false oath or statement under penalty of perjury in connection with a case under this title shall be subject to fine, imprisonment, or both; and

(B) All information supplied by a debtor in connection with a case under this title is subject to examination by the Attorney General.

Exhibit C This section asks the debtor to disclose whether he or she owns any property that might cause harm to the public health and safety.

Exhibit D This section references Official Form 1, Exhibit D, which is available on the Bankruptcy Court's website. This form discloses whether the debtor has completed the **mandatory credit counseling** within 180 days prior to filing. Mandatory credit counseling is required prior to filing the petition and once again prior to receiving a discharge of debt. This type of counseling focuses on training the debtor how to handle his or her own finances. If the debtor has not received credit counseling and feels that he or she is exempt due to factors such as military status or incapacity, the debtor may indicate so on the form.

> **mandatory credit counseling**
> Required counseling that focuses on training the debtor how to handle his or her own finances.

Information Regarding the Debtor – Venue In this section, the debtor indicates whether he or she meets the domicile requirements for the district he or she plans to file in. In most cases, the debtor must have resided or had a principal asset or place of business in the district for at least 180 days immediately preceding the date of filing.

Certification of Debtor Who Resides as a Tenant of Residential Property This section applies to debtors who reside as tenants in a rental property and are in default on rent. This section helps the court discover whether the Automatic Stay applies to the eviction proceedings. If the debtor's proprietor has already obtained a judgment for possession of the property prior to the debtor's bankruptcy filing, the Automatic Stay likely will not apply. If the debtor is behind on his or her rent, but there was no judgment for possession of the property before the debtor files, the Automatic Stay will halt the eviction process at least temporarily.

Signature Section – Attorney and Client Must Sign This section of the petition indicates where the debtor must sign, attesting that all information contained in the petition is true and correct. The attorney or the petition preparer must also sign on this page. (See Appendix A: Official Form 1 Voluntary Petition.)

Involuntary Petition

According to 11 U.S.C. § 303(a), "[a]n involuntary case may be commenced only under chapter 7 or 11 of this title, and only against a person, except a farmer, family farmer, or a corporation that is not a moneyed, business, or commercial corporation, that may be a debtor under the chapter under which such case is commenced."

involuntary petition
A petition that is brought against the debtor by several creditors.

An **involuntary petition** is similar to a voluntary petition. The involuntary petition, however, is brought against the debtor by several of the creditors. Individuals as well as companies may be the object of an involuntary bankruptcy, but involuntary cases against an individual are uncommon. Most of the targets of an involuntary case are debtors with substantial means. If a group of creditors feels that the debtor is giving an unfair preference to other unsecured creditors, they may collaborate and file an involuntary petition. To file against the debtor, the debtor must have 12 or more unsecured creditors, and at least three unsecured creditors must be filing the petition together. The three creditors who file against the debtor must be owed, between them, at least $14,425.00. An involuntary case may also be filed by one creditor alone whose claim meets or exceeds $14,425.00.

After the petition is filed, the debtor has 20 days to respond. If the debtor responds within the required time frame, the court will set the case down for a hearing to determine the merits of going forward. If the debtor does not respond within the required time frame, he or she will be forced to go forward with the bankruptcy case. Only Chapter 7 and 11 cases may be brought involuntarily against a debtor.

Cover Sheet for Schedules

The Cover Sheet for Schedules, also known as Form 6 or B6, must precede the debtor's completed schedules when they are filed with the court. (See Appendix B: Official Form 6 Cover Sheet for Schedules.)

SCHEDULE A – REAL PROPERTY

real property
Land owned by the debtor or any property that has a direct relationship to the land such as a house or other type of permanent structure.

In this schedule, the debtor must list all of the **real property** he or she owns. Real property refers to any land and the structures or buildings attached to the land that the debtor may own. When completing this form, the debtor must provide a description of the property. The property's full address suffices. The debtor must also indicate the ownership interest he or she has (i.e., joint tenancy, community property, or tenant in common) and the current value of the property as well as the amount of the secured claim. The amount of the secured claim is the loan balance left on property that is due and owing to the secured creditor. The paralegal can assist the debtor in locating the value of real property through the Zillow website. The Kelley Bluebook website is an example of a website to use to determine the current value of automobiles. (See Appendix C: Official Form 6A Schedule A: Real Property.)

SCHEDULE B – PERSONAL PROPERTY

tangible property
Personal property that can be seen or felt, such as cars or furniture.

intangible property
Items that have value but cannot be felt or touched, such as stock in a company.

On Schedule B (Official Form 6B), the debtor must list all **tangible property** and **intangible property**. Tangible items can be seen or felt, such as cars or furniture. Intangible items have value but cannot be felt or touched, such as stock in a company.

In the extreme left column of Schedule B, categories of personal property are numbered 1 through 35. The debtor must be very thorough in this section. Listing everything the debtor owns, including the kitchen sink, is advisable here. The debtor cannot over-disclose in this section! The categories on the left of this form act as a guide to the paralegal when assisting the debtor with this schedule. Certain sections are very specific, such as the "Boats, Motors, and Accessories" section and others that are not as specific, such as the "Household Furnishing" section. The debtor must indicate the type of interest he or she has in the property (i.e., community property, jointly held, or husband or wife's property). This is indicated by placing a C, J, H, or W in the appropriate area. The replacement value or current value of the item must also be indicated. If a category does not apply, the debtor must indicate it by placing an X in the appropriate area. (See Appendix D: Official Form 6B Schedule B: Personal Property.)

SCHEDULE C – PROPERTY CLAIMED AS EXEMPT

Schedule C (Official Form 6C) requires the debtor to disclose all **exempt property** that he or she is claiming. Exempt property is property the debtor owns that he or she wishes to be beyond the reach of the trustee to seize and sell for cash to pay the creditors. The debtor, after speaking with the supervising attorney, will know whether the federal exemptions or the applicable state's exemptions apply. Most states require the debtor to use that state's exemptions. Some states, such as Connecticut, allow the debtor to choose between the federal or the state exemptions but not both. If a debtor chooses the federal exemptions, the box next to 11 U.S.C. § 522(b)(2) should be selected. If the debtor is choosing the state exemptions, the box next to 11 U.S.C. § 522(b)(3) should be selected. Remember that the state the debtor resides in currently might not be the state whose exemptions would apply if the debtor is choosing state over federal exemptions. If a debtor resided in his or her current state of residency for at least two years prior to filing, that state's exemptions would apply. Thus, if the debtor did not reside in his or her current state of residency for the full two-year period, the laws of the state where the debtor resided for the majority of the six-month period prior to the two years will apply. (See Appendix E: Official Form 6C Schedule C: Property Claimed as Exempt.)

exempt property
Property that is exempt from seizure by creditors.

SCHEDULE D – CREDITORS HOLDING SECURED CLAIMS

As previous chapters have reviewed, a secured debt is one in which the debtor has pledged collateral. For example, when a debtor buys a home with money a bank has loaned him or her, the house is the collateral that will help satisfy the debt if the debtor defaults on the loan. Schedule D (Official Form 6D) requires the debtor to list all of his or her secured creditors and indicate the name and account number associated with each creditor. If there is a co-debtor, the debtor must indicate this with an X in the appropriate column. In addition, the debtor must indicate his or her interest in the property and whether it is in the husband's or wife's name only or jointly held. The debtor must also indicate whether the debt is contingent, unliquidated, or disputed. A **contingent debt** depends on an event happening. If the debtor cosigned on a loan, but that loan hasn't gone into default yet, the claim is contingent. If **unliquidated debt** is claimed, the amount of the debt has not been determined. If **disputed debt** is claimed, the debtor and creditor disagree about the amount of the debt. Disputed debt can also refer to the debtor's feeling that he or she is not indebted to the creditor at all.

contingent debt
A debt that depends on an event happening such as a loan that the debtor co-signed that has not defaulted.

unliquidated debt
A debt of which the amount has yet to be determined.

disputed debt
Debt where the debtor and creditor disagree regarding the amount.

On Schedule D, the debtor must provide a description of the property with its current value, which is subject to the secured debt. For example, the debtor may indicate a 2008 Scion TC with a current value of $8,674 in fair condition. Continuing with this example, say the debtor still owes $10,000 on the loan. The $10,000 would be indicated in the box under the "Amount of Claim Without Deducting Value of Collateral" heading. The unsecured portion would be $1,326. The unsecured portion of the debt will be treated in the same manner as the debtor's other unsecured, nonpriority debts. (See Appendix F: Official Form 6D Schedule D: Creditors Holding Secured Claims.)

SCHEDULE E – CREDITORS HOLDING UNSECURED PRIORITY CLAIMS

Unsecured priority claims or debt is not secured by collateral. Further, this type of debt is given priority over other types of unsecured debt. For example, a debtor's child support debt would be given priority over his or her credit card debt. Schedule E (Official Form 6E) contains a listing of all the debtor's priority unsecured claims. The first page of the form contains a listing of all the possible types of priority claims. The debtor must select the box next to each type of priority debt he or she has. Each type of priority debt should be scheduled using a new continuation sheet. For instance, if the debtor owes both back alimony and back child support, these two debts would be combined on one continuation sheet, whereas the debtor's back taxes would be filed on an additional continuation sheet of the Schedule E form. At the end of page 2 of Schedule E, the debtor must indicate how many continuation sheets are attached. (See Appendix G: Official Form 6E Schedule E: Creditors Holding Unsecured Priority Claims.)

SCHEDULE F – CREDITORS HOLDING UNSECURED NON-PRIORITY CLAIMS

Schedule F (Official Form 6F) is the busiest schedule in most bankruptcy filings. A typical debtor's debt consists mostly of unsecured, nonpriority debt. This is where the debtor schedules debt such as medical bills, credit card debt, personal loans, student loans, debts owed to utility companies, and secured loan deficiencies. This type of debt is considered after the debtor's priority debts have been paid. (See Appendix H: Official Form 6F Schedule F: Creditors Holding Unsecured Non-Priority Claims.)

SCHEDULE G – EXECUTORY CONTRACTS AND UNEXPIRED LEASES

On Schedule G (Official Form 6G) the debtor must list all of his or her unexpired leases and executory contracts. An example of an unexpired lease can be a lease agreement for an apartment for which the term has not ended or a lease of equipment for a term that has not expired yet. **Executory contracts** are contracts that have not been fully performed. An example would be if the debtor contracted with a painting company to paint the exterior of his house. If the debtor has paid the painting company and it has not performed its end of the bargain yet, it would

executory contract
A contract under which insufficient or incomplete performance has occurred on either side of the contract.

qualify as an executory contract. This information is important for the trustee to know about because the trustee has the power to accept or reject these special types of contracts. (See Appendix I: Official Form 6G Schedule G: Executory Contracts and Unexpired Leases.)

SCHEDULE H – CO-DEBTORS

Schedule H (Official Form 6H) requires the debtor to make a list of all his or her co-debtors. A **co-debtor** is a person who has cosigned on a loan with the debtor and must receive notification that the debtor has filed bankruptcy. (See Appendix J: Official Form 6H Schedule H: Codebtors.)

co-debtor
A person who has co-signed on a loan with the debtor who must receive notification that the debtor has filed for bankruptcy.

SCHEDULE I – CURRENT INCOME OF INDIVIDUAL DEBTOR

Schedule I (Official Form 6I) requires the debtor to document all of his or her income as well as that of any joint or non-joint–filing spouse. Remember that it is the debtor and joint debtor's monthly income that must be listed. All forms of income must be captured on this form, both traditional, employer income and nontraditional income such as alimony, rent, royalties, and unemployment income. (See Appendix K: Offical Form B 61 Schedule I: Your Income.)

SCHEDULE J – CURRENT EXPENDITURES OF INDIVIDUAL DEBTOR

Schedule J (Official Form 6J) captures all of the debtor and joint debtor's monthly expenses. This form is very important because the information contained on it along with Schedule I will dictate which chapter the debtor files under. The debtor must list all his or her dependents without including their names. When calculating expenses, remember that the debtor cannot list any items such as payroll deductions that were indicated on Schedule I. It is also important for the debtor to be as accurate as possible with this form or risk dismissal of the case. (See Appendix L: Official Form B 6J Schedule J: Your Expenses.)

DECLARATION CONCERNING DEBTOR'S SCHEDULES

After completing the schedules, the debtor, whether an individual filing his or her own bankruptcy or a president of a company filing for bankruptcy, must swear that the information contained in the foregoing schedules is true and accurate. The debtor does this by completing the Declaration Concerning Debtor's Schedules, Official Form 6 – Declaration. The total number of pages included with the schedules must be indicated. This helps the clerk know how many pages to expect and may prompt the clerk to alert the debtor or the debtor's attorney if pages are missing.

In the case of an individual debtor filing jointly, both spouses must sign the form. If the debtor is found to have made an intentional misrepresentation of the information in the forms, serious consequences could result. For example, the case could be dismissed, or the debtor could face prison time or a steep fine. (See Appendix M: Official Form 6 Declaration Concerning Debtors.)

STATEMENT OF FINANCIAL AFFAIRS

The Statement of Financial Affairs (Official Form 7) consists of a series of questions the debtor must answer thoroughly and truthfully about his or her recent financial affairs. The information the debtor must provide includes recent property transfers, payments to creditors, and gifts. Other financial affairs include a recent **wage garnishment**, closed bank accounts, repossessions, foreclosures, and lawsuits. A wage garnishment is the deduction, from his or her wages, of an amount the debtor owes, usually because of a court order. The debtor is also required to document losses from gambling and fire.

The debtor's accurate documentation of the previously mentioned financial information is crucial for the bankruptcy trustee to get a complete picture of the debtor's financial situation. In the consultation with the debtor, the bankruptcy attorney will caution the debtor about the importance of capturing this information honestly and completely. If not, the debtor could face the dismissal of the entire bankruptcy case and might endure the consequences of perjury.

When helping the client with this form, the paralegal should remind the debtor of his or her duty to be honest in answering the questions. The paralegal is often the first person to see this completed form and should read it carefully and bring any suspicious financial transactions to the attention of the supervising attorney immediately. The attorney can determine whether any voidable transfers or preferences can be expected that would necessitate meeting with the client again.

All debtors must answer questions 1–18 on the Statement of Financial Affairs, and questions 19–25 must be answered by commercial or business debtors. All debtors must sign an affirmation, under penalty of perjury, that the answers to the questions on the Statement of Financial Affairs are true and correct. (See Appendix N: Official Form 7 Statement of Financial Affairs.)

DISCLOSURE OF ATTORNEY COMPENSATION FORM

Fed. R. Bankr. P. 2016(b) and 329(a) require the attorney representing a debtor in a bankruptcy case to disclose to the court the fees that he or she is charging the debtor. The source of that compensation must also be disclosed. Fed. R. Bankr. P. 329(b) and 2017 give the bankruptcy court the power to review the attorney's fee to ensure that it adheres to the district court's guidelines for what is reasonable. If an attorney fee is deemed unreasonable, the court may order the attorney to refund a portion or the entire fee to the debtor. The court may also order the attorney to return a fee to the client if the court has found the attorney to be incompetent in handling the bankruptcy case.

The paralegal, when preparing this form, must first determine the amount of the fee his or her supervising attorney is charging. Next, the paralegal must determine whether the client will be paying the fee or someone else will be paying the fee on the client's behalf. The identity of the person paying the fee on the client's behalf is required. Further, the paralegal must determine whether the fee will be paid in full, up front, or paid in two installments. The attorney must attest that he or she will not be sharing the fees collected with anyone other than attorneys or associates of the firm. The type of legal work done in exchange for the fee must be disclosed as well. For example, sometimes, in addition to filing the petition and schedules, the attorney may assist the client with preparing reaffirmation of debt agreements, negotiating values on collateral, and so on. (See Appendix O: Disclosure of Compensation of Attorney for Debtor.)

wage garnishment
A wage deduction of a certain amount of money that the debtor owes usually pursuant to a court order.

Chapter 7 Individual Debtor's Statement of Intention

A debtor must file the Individual Debtor's Statement of Intention (Official Form 8) if he or she owns secured property or has an unexpired lease on some type of property. The Chapter 7 debtor must file this form within 30 days after filing the petition. The debtor may file the form with the petition and the schedules but does not have to. As long as this form is prepared accurately and filed in time for the meeting of the creditors, the debtor has complied with this requirement.

Section A of the form asks the debtor to indicate his or her intentions with regard to all items of secured property in his or her possession. The trustee will then know whether the debtor intends to keep or surrender the property. If the former is the case, the debtor must indicate whether he intends to redeem the property, reaffirm the debt, or describe any other plans he has for the property. Let's say the debtor decides to redeem the property. With **redemption**, the debtor pays either the value or the loan balance on a piece of exempt property, in a lump sum to the creditor, whichever figure is less. The debtor may also reaffirm a secured debt and keep the collateral. In **reaffirmation of debt**, the debtor reinstates the debt on a secured loan. In doing so, the debtor will remain liable for the debt even after the debtor receives a discharge of debt. If the debtor has other plans for the debt, he or she would choose "other" on the form.

Section B of the form requires the debtor to indicate whether any lease of property (i.e., a car, RV, or work equipment) will be assumed or terminated. If the Chapter 7 trustee rejects the lease, the debtor is free to assume it or terminate it. (See Appendix P: Official Form 8 Chapter 7 Individual Debtor's Statement of Intention.)

redemption
A situation where the debtor pays either the value or the loan balance on a piece of exempt property, whichever figure is less.

reaffirmation of debt
A situation where the debtor reinstates the debt on a secured loan.

Statement of Current Monthly Income and Means Test Calculation (Chapter 7)

All individual debtors must complete the Statement of Current Monthly Income and Means Test Calculation (Official Form 22A). By properly preparing this form, the debtor can find out whether he or she qualifies for a Chapter 7 liquidation case or must file for Chapter 13. As discussed in previous chapters, if the debtor's income is at or below the median income for a family of her size in her state, it is presumed that the debtor may file for Chapter 7. However, if the debtor's household income is above the median, he or she must take the **Means Test**. This allows the debtor to deduct certain government-allowed expenses, such as health care and other living expenses, to see whether the debtor will have enough money left over at the end of the month to make payments on a repayment plan.

Some debtors immediately qualify for Chapter 7 and do not have to complete the Means Test calculations. They find this information in Part I of Official Form 22A, which includes disabled veterans, debtors who have primarily business debts, and certain members of the armed forces such as members of the reserve component of the National Guard or people on active duty or involved with homeland defense security.

Part II of the form requires the debtor to provide information about all sources and types of income in the past six months. If the debtor is married, filing jointly, or married, filing individually, with his or her spouse living in the same

Means Test
A formula designed to determine whether debtors have income and the ability to restructure their debt and pay off their creditors.

median household income
The income level that falls exactly in the middle of the range of incomes for a particular family size in the debtor's state.

household, the spouse's and petitioner's income from the six months preceding the date of the filing is totaled. The average income from the past six months is what the court uses to determine an average annual income for the debtor. For instance, if the debtor files the petition on January 5, the debtor's monthly income from the previous July to December would be used to calculate the average income. The average monthly income taken from the past six months is then multiplied by 12. The resulting figure is the debtor's average household income. The debtor's annual household income is then compared to the **median household income** in the debtor's state, which represents the income level that falls exactly in the middle of the range of incomes for a particular family size. The paralegal can find a listing of all the states' median household incomes on the U.S. Trustee website.

If the debtor's income is at or below the median income for the debtor's state, the debtor may select the check box that states, "The presumption does not arise," on page 1 of the form and then complete section VIII of the form. If the debtor's income is above the median income in the debtor's state, the debtor must complete the remaining questions on the Means Test. The remaining questions in parts IV and V determine whether the debtor will have enough disposable monthly income, after deducting certain allowed expenses, to make payments on a Chapter 13 repayment plan. The allowed expenses can be found on the U.S. Trustee website. (See Appendix Q: Official Form B 22A1 Chapter 7 Statement of Your Current Monthly Income; and Official Form B 22A2 Chapter 7 Means Test Calculation.)

Statement of Current Monthly Income and Calculation of Commitment Period and Disposable Income (Chapter 13)

The Statement of Current Monthly Income and Calculation of Commitment Period and Disposable Income (Official Form 22C), must be filled out by all Chapter 13 filers. This form is quite similar to the Statement of Current Monthly Income and Means Test Calculation (Chapter 7) that we discussed. However, this test uses the debtor's household income and certain allowed expenses to determine the length of the Chapter 13 plan (3 or 5 years) and how much the debtor must pay the creditors through the plan. (See Appendix R: Official Form B 22C1 Chapter 13 Statement of Your Current Monthly Income and Calculation of Commitment Period; and Official Form B 22C2 Chapter 13 Calculation of Your Disposable Income.)

Debtor's Certification of Completion of Instructional Course Concerning Financial Management

After filing the petition and before receiving a discharge of debt, the debtor must file the Debtor's Certification of Completion of Instructional Course Concerning Financial Management (Official Form 23). All Chapter 7 and Chapter 13 debtors must complete this form; there are a very few, narrow exceptions to the requirement to file this form. Some of the exceptions include the debtor being disabled so severely that the course would be a hardship, the debtor being on active duty, or the absence of available courses in the debtor's area. The last one is as rare as a blue moon with the advent of online, approved credit counseling.

If the debtor is filing jointly with his or her spouse, both spouses must file his or her own Form 23. Even if the debtor qualifies for an exception from the debt counseling requirement, he or she must still file this form with the court indicating so.

EXPEDITED/EMERGENCY FILING: PETITION AND MASTER LIST OF CREDITORS

Some situations might lead a debtor to file an **emergency filing** when a debtor needs the protection of the Automatic Stay but cannot wait longer than a day or two for all the forms and schedules to be filed. The emergency filing is a last-resort type of filing and is done when the debtor is facing immediate foreclosure, trial for a debt collection case, or an imminent eviction. An emergency filing requires the debtor to file the petition and a master list of known creditors along with their addresses. In some courts, the debtor must also file a Statement of Social Security Number (Form B21) and a Certificate of Credit Counseling from an approved credit counseling agency. Emergency filings are sometimes referred to as barebones or skeleton filings.

emergency filing
A situation where the debtor needs the protection of the Automatic Stay but cannot wait longer than a day or two for all the forms and schedules to be filed.

Introduction to Otto and Christina Schuler

Otto and Christina Schuler have contacted our office and set up an appointment to meet with you for an initial client intake. The following fact pattern provides you with enough information to complete the Voluntary Petition, Schedules A–J, Statement of Financial Affairs, Means Test Calculation, and Disclosure of Attorney Fees. This will assist your attorney with filing the Schuler's case at the appropriate bankruptcy court in your state.

Mr. and Mrs. Schuler have been married for six years, and they reside at 4 Carriages Crossing Way, Anytown, YS (Your State) 07000. They have lived at this address since getting married, and they own the house as joint tenants. Mr. Schuler's SSN is XXX-XX-2222 and Mrs. Schuler's SSN is XXX-XX-4444. Both Mr. and Mrs. Schuler have been married before, and both have children from a prior marriage. The Schulers have three children, Otto Schuler, Jr., age 6; Grace Schuler, age 4; and Ralph Schuler, age 2. Mrs. Schuler's son, George Jones, age 15, is a child from her previous marriage to Brian Jones. George Jones primarily resides with the Schulers, and Christina receives $85 per week for child support from her ex-husband, Brian Jones. Mr. Schuler has one daughter, Lisa Schuler, age 16, who resides with her mother, Linda Schuler. (Linda kept her married name.) Otto pays $105 in child support per week to Linda Schuler to support Lisa, his eldest daughter. According to Mr. Schuler, he has an arrearage of $500 for child support to Linda Schuler, who lives at 45 Pay Me Way, Anytown, YS 07000. He disputes the amount that Linda Schuler claims he owes her ($600) in back child support.

Otto, Jr., and Grace both attend private school for kindergarten and preschool, respectively. It costs the Schulers a total of $3,200 per year for both kids.

Otto works at Sugar Factory (a rival of Hostess), which is famous for its Golden Toes, which are remarkably similar in appearance to the Hostess Twinkie, but moister and lower in calories. Otto earns $45,000 per year as a manager at the factory's Ocean Grove, YS, plant, and he is paid once a month. He currently has a balance of $32,000 in his 401(k), which is managed by Fidelity Investments, Inc. His pay is reduced by $275 per month for his contribution to his 401(k) plan. (Use an online search engine to find a payroll calculator to calculate Mr. Schuler's deductions and his net pay for YS. Usually, you base this information on the client's paystubs.)

Christina Schuler worked at a hair salon called Oh That Hair, located in Bradley, YS, which was very successful until a year and a half ago, when Superstorm Stacey came up the coast and completely destroyed the salon. When the salon was successful, Christina's income was $37,000 per year. The loss of Christina's income in the past year or so has dealt a severe blow to the family's financial health. The Schulers have found it hard to keep up with all of their bills, and they are contemplating filing for bankruptcy. They hope to file chapter 7 jointly to help them get back on their feet financially as soon as possible. Otto Schuler owns a lawn-mowing service, Otto's Lawn Service, LLC, and he still owes $300 in wages to a former worker named Charles Burgh. Mr. Burgh resides at 121 Smith Way, Anytown, YS, 07111. Otto dissolved the LLC approximately six months ago.

In an attempt to begin working independently, Mrs. Schuler leased some hairstyling equipment for $150 per month from Connie's Hair Equipment Supply, Inc., located at 5 Jones Drive, in Anytown, YS, 07000. The lease was for one year, but Mrs. Schuler stopped paying after six months because she simply could not keep up with the payments. Mrs. Schuler did not get one client out of this venture.

The Schulers have approximately $150 in cash on hand and $523 in their joint checking account with Anytown Savings Bank.

Approximately two years ago, Mr. Schuler bought a winning scratch-off lottery ticket and, after taxes, he took home $9,000. Instead of using that money to pay the family's bills, he bought a 2009 Crossfire snowmobile for $6,500. He spent the other $2,500 on a pearl ring for Mrs. Schuler, just because.

The Schulers have two cars. They jointly own a 2010 Scion TC that is financed through Toyota Financial, Inc. (loan# 8978768787), with a balance of $13,500. The TC is currently valued at $11,500. They also have a 2006 Toyota Camry that Mrs. Schuler owns solely. The Camry is financed through Toyota Financial, Inc. (loan#: 345768993), with a balance of $4,500 left on the loan. The vehicle is worth about $6,850. Mrs. Schuler's father, John Burke, who resides at 34 Lucian Avenue, in Anytown, YS 07000, cosigned the car loan with Mrs. Schuler. Both vehicles are dangerously close to repossession. When they can make the payments, the combined amount is approximately $512 per month.

In the past year, the Schulers have done very well to keep up with their mortgage payments and, thankfully, Mr. Schuler has a good insurance policy that covers him, Mrs. Schuler, and the children. They own their house jointly, and it is currently worth $125,000. They have an outstanding mortgage balance of $75,000 with Thrifty Mortgage Company. Their mortgage payment of $625 per month includes their escrowed real estate taxes. Their property insurance, which is not included with their mortgage payment, with Anycompany Mutual, costs them $39.42 per month. They got such a good deal on their house insurance because they have a security system with Don't Even Think About It Home Security Company, which costs them $37.95 per month.

Most of Mr. Schuler's income is spent on their mortgage, and the Schulers used credit to help pay for food and utility bills such as phone, gas, heating oil, and electricity. Mr. Schuler has a $500,000 term life insurance policy that costs him $75 per month. The Schulers pay $185 per month for electricity, and they use electricity to heat the house, so there is no separate fuel bill. Their water and sewer bill is paid quarterly and is usually about $52 per quarter. They pay $25 per year for their safe deposit box.

The Schulers pay about $1,200 per month for food which includes dining out and school lunches for the two children attending school. As a family, they spend approximately $300 per month on entertainment, which includes movie rentals, pay-per-view, and nights out at the movies. They pay $350 per month for clothing. (The kids are growing fast!) The Schulers are on the family plan with Acme Wireless, and their phone bill for unlimited text and talk with a 2-gigabyte data plan costs $95 per month. They pay $125 per month to Acme Cable Company. Their average monthly cost for dry cleaning is $38. Medical expenses for the family run approximately $50 dollars per month because Christina takes a prescription for her chronic acid reflux, and Otto suffers from chronic allergies. They estimate that their routine home maintenance, repair, and yard upkeep costs them approximately $75 per month. The Schulers don't have regular transportation expenses aside from Christina's annual flight down to Florida to visit her mom. This costs approximately $625 per year because she usually takes one of the kids with her.

The Schulers have three joint credit cards. One of their cards is with DiscoverCharge (account# 9999999) with a balance of $14,875. Their other credit card, MasterCharge (account# 8888000), has a balance of $12,543. Mrs. Schuler has a Kohl's charge card (account# 5555555) that she has used to pay for the family's clothing and other essentials; that card has a balance of $3,200.

The Schulers spend approximately $3,000 per year in pet care expenses for their cat Minou and their dog Eldo.

Otto and Christina put a new roof on the house last year, which cost $9,000. They charged half up front, and they still owe Smith's Roofing Service, LLC, of 34 Anystreet, Anytown, YS 07000, $4,500. Currently, a small-claims case is pending against the Schulers in state court in YS, styled *Smith's Roofing Service, LLC vs. Otto Schuler et al.*, Docket# CV15-2333456342.

Just about six months ago, Otto was on a winning streak at the Acme Casino in YS. He got carried away, though, and lost about $1,765 that night at the blackjack table.

The Schulers estimate that their family's wearing apparel has a replacement value of about $2,200. They also estimate that their essential household furnishings (including beds, tables, desks, sofa, and so on) are worth approximately $6,500.

Because your supervising attorney feels that the Schulers may qualify for a no asset Chapter 7 case, the Schulers will be paying $306 for their Chapter 7 fee, and they will be paying your attorney $2,500 in two installments for attorney fees associated with the bankruptcy filing. The Schulers read some self-help books prior to consulting your attorney, and they both completed the required credit counseling, which cost them $45 total. See Portfolio Exercise at the end of this chapter for instructions on how to help the Schulers prepare their bankruptcy forms.

Solomon Feinstein, our newly minted paralegal at the beginning of the chapter, gave you an idea of how important it is to have a deep understanding of the forms and schedules in a bankruptcy case. Aside from the initial intake, assisting the debtor with the forms and schedules is, perhaps, representative of how the bankruptcy paralegal spends most of his or her time. Under the close supervision of an attorney, the paralegal uses the information gathered from the debtor to not only complete the forms and schedules, but to help answer any procedural questions the debtor may have about the forms. By understanding the forms in depth, Solomon will be able to help not only his law firm's clients, but his attorney spot problems and inconsistencies in the forms and schedules before they become issues. One of the first tasks Solomon was asked to complete was to update his new employer's bankruptcy client intake form. Having a solid and up-to-date understanding of the forms and schedules will help Solomon create a thorough intake questionnaire for his supervising attorney, which will lead to more effective intake meetings with future bankruptcy clients.

CHAPTER **SUMMARY**

After completing the client intake, the paralegal's role in assisting the client begins to intensify. His or her responsibilities, especially at the beginning of a bankruptcy case, are intense. In most law firms, it will be the paralegal's responsibility to complete the client intake as well as prepare the petition, schedules, and other necessary forms discussed in this chapter. The paralegal's role in helping the client prepare all the required forms will help the attorney do what is necessary to facilitate the client's successful liquidation or reorganization case. After meeting the Schulers, you have discovered that they had a fairly representative cross section of financial problems that many couples can have with consumer debt. You now have an opportunity to practice preparing each of the schedules and forms for a Chapter 7 bankruptcy filing similar to real-life clients in your future position as a bankruptcy paralegal.

CONCEPT REVIEW AND REINFORCEMENT

KEY **TERMS**

co-debtor
contingent debt
disputed debt
emergency filing
exempt property
executory contracts

involuntary petition
intangible property
mandatory credit counseling
Means Test
median household income
reaffirmation of debt

real property
redemption
tangible property
unliquidated debt
voluntary petition
wage garnishment

REVIEWING **KEY CONCEPTS**

1. Define and discuss the difference between a voluntary and an involuntary petition. In which type of circumstances may an involuntary petition be brought?
2. Explain the difference between tangible and intangible personal property.
3. What is an insider? Why are transfers the debtor makes to insiders treated differently from other types of transfers?
4. On Schedule D, there is a column labeled Unsecured Portion If Any. What is that section referring to and how is that portion of the creditor's claim treated?

5. Why is it crucial for the debtor to respond to the questions on the Statement of Financial Affairs thoroughly and truthfully? Explain your answer and give examples.
6. Define an emergency filing. In which types of situations is an emergency filing warranted and what do most district courts require to be filed in these instances?

BUILDING YOUR PARALEGAL SKILLS

CASE FOR **REVIEW**

In re Ablavsky, No. 12-18167 (Bankr. D. Mass., Jan. 23, 2014)

BUILDING A PROFESSIONAL PORTFOLIO

PORTFOLIO **EXERCISE**

Using the fact pattern at the end of the chapter regarding Otto and Christina Schuler, prepare their bankruptcy joint petition, schedules A through J, the Statement of Financial Affairs, Disclosure of Attorney Compensation, and the Means Test calculation. Please feel free to insert any information that the fact pattern has not provided such as your attorney's name and address, a local court address in your state, and any other information you may need to prepare the forms. Use your imagination. You can use the sample version of Best Case™, that you downloaded while reading Chapter 16, to complete the forms for this exercise. Or, you may use the Official Forms available at uscourts.gov/forms/bankruptcy-forms.

chapter 18

MOTION PRACTICE AND ADVERSARY PROCEEDINGS IN BANKRUTPCY

LEARNING OBJECTIVES

After studying this chapter, you should be able to:

1. Describe the various motions filed in bankruptcy court.

2. Summarize the various situations that would prompt a party in a bankruptcy case to file a motion with the bankruptcy court.

3. Describe the different parties who may file a motion in a bankruptcy case and the various types of relief these parties might seek from the bankruptcy court.

4. Explain the formal process in connection with drafting, serving, and defending certain motions along with the paralegal's role in the process.

5. Identify the defenses a party may assert in an adversary proceeding to defeat the moving party's motion.

Stefania Kowalczyk recently filed her own Chapter 13 case to help get back on her feet financially. She has been struggling to pay bills for the past several years after she needed to take a reduction in pay at work or lose her job. Stefania chose the former and kept working despite the loss in income. After reading *You Can File Your Own Bankruptcy Case* by DIY Publishers, she successfully filed her own Chapter 13 plan. Stefania did not qualify for Chapter 7 because she had sufficient disposable income left over each month to make at least some payments to her creditors.

After her case was filed, she continued to read her self-help book, and she learned that she could ask the court for a cramdown of her car loan. Stefania checked an online appraisal service for her car and realized that her car's value had diminished significantly below the current balance on her loan with ACME Auto Finance. Stefania wrote a letter to the bankruptcy clerk and asked the court to cramdown the balance of her car loan to the current market value of her car.

The clerk called Stefania and told her that she would need to file a motion to put the matter in front of a judge for consideration. Stefania decided she was in over her head and called a lawyer for help. What type of motion does Stefania need to file with the court to take advantage of the option to cramdown her car loan? What other types of motions might Stefania or her lawyer have to file in the future? Read on and find out.

Introduction

In an existing bankruptcy case, one must file a motion with the court in order to seek the court's ruling on any issue that may arise. This is very similar to many other civil proceedings. By filing a motion, a party is literally moving the court to take notice of an issue or make a ruling on an issue. As such, the party filing the motion, whatever it is for, is referred to as the movant. Just like any other proceeding in civil court, formalities come along with this process and can involve a hearing on the issue or an adversary proceeding, which resembles a small trial. In a bankruptcy case, a motion may be filed by any of three parties. The trustee may file a motion to have the case dismissed due to some type of misrepresentation alleged against the debtor. On the other hand, the trustee may request the debtor's case to be converted to another chapter. In a Chapter 13 case, the debtor may file a motion for valuation on an item of collateral to cramdown a loan. In addition, a secured creditor may file a motion for relief from the Automatic Stay if there is very little equity in the collateral or evidence that the debtor will have difficulty continuing to make payments on the loan. This chapter reviews the most prevalent motions a paralegal may encounter in consumer bankruptcy cases. It also reviews the paralegal's role in assisting the attorney with filing and responding to these motions and presents examples of the more prevalent motions.

Most of the time, a reorganization or liquidation case proceeds through the bankruptcy process without incident. A typical bankruptcy case takes the debtor through the process with very little involvement from the bankruptcy court or the bankruptcy judge. The most formal proceeding for most debtors is usually the **meeting of the creditors**. Sometimes, the debtor never sets foot in the bankruptcy court again after this meeting.

Usually, a reorganization plan of repayment is approved after a couple of sessions with the trustee and the court. Most often, a liquidation case does not involve **nonexempt property**. If there is nonexempt property, the debtor is usually cooperative. There is usually no suspicion of anything untoward by the debtor regarding the value or ownership status of such property.

However, there are times when one of the parties in a bankruptcy case will raise an issue that only the judge can resolve. Examples include issues of hidden assets, the debtor's dishonesty, improperly transferred property, or permission to proceed with a foreclosure or repossession. As mentioned previously, a **motion** is the appropriate way to bring these and other types of issues to the attention of the bankruptcy court for resolution. *Motion* is a term that describes a verbal or written request for the court to take some type of action. Sometimes, a small lawsuit, called an **adversary proceeding**, might need to be brought before the court for certain issues such as voidable transfers. Whatever the reason for bringing an issue before the court, this chapter discusses the procedures involved and the paralegal's role in the process. The following pages discuss the most prevalent motions the paralegal will encounter while handling liquidation and reorganization cases.

Introduction to Motion Practice

RELIEF FROM AUTOMATIC STAY

Bankruptcy Code 11 U.S.C. § 362 governs what is called the **Automatic Stay**. The Automatic Stay acts as an injunction preventing the creditors from proceeding with any action against the debtor to recover a debt. As pointed out in previous chapters, this injunction, imposed by the Bankruptcy Code, is rock solid. Any creditor wishing to avoid the effect of this injunction must bring a motion, with good cause, before the bankruptcy court to receive the court's permission to proceed with collecting its debt. The Automatic Stay is very powerful; even when the debtor has agreed to surrender the collateral to the creditor, the creditor must still obtain approval from the bankruptcy court.

meeting of the creditors (341 hearing)
The first court appearance the debtor makes in a bankruptcy case. This meeting may also be referred to as the 341 meeting, named after the Bankruptcy Code section where it is found. The debtor must attend this meeting or face the possibility that the court will dismiss his or her case.

nonexempt property
Property that becomes part of the bankruptcy estate and may be sold by the bankruptcy trustee to raise funds to pay back creditors.

motion
A request filed by a party in a legal case when a court ruling is required on important issues or in contested matters requiring a resolution by the judge.

adversary proceeding
A separate lawsuit filed within a bankruptcy case, which must be resolved by the judge before the case may proceed to discharge. An adversary proceeding in a bankruptcy case is treated much like a civil lawsuit would be treated.

Automatic Stay
An injunction against the debtor's creditors and claimants that stops all court lawsuits and collection efforts against the debtor until the stay is lifted or removed by the bankruptcy court or the case ends.

This type of motion is often filed by a secured creditor seeking permission to continue with its foreclosure action or repossess the collateral. Upon showing the debtor's failure to make postpetition payments either by failing to make payments or providing for payments in a reorganization plan, the creditor may be allowed to proceed with collection. This collection often takes the form of allowing foreclosure to continue or repossession of the debtor's vehicle. Most motions of this nature are brought by secured creditors in connection with a car loan when the debtor is not making adequate postpetition payments. The creditor may bring this type of motion successfully if it can show that the collateral is inadequately protected. Examples of this would include a showing that there is little to no equity in the collateral or that the collateral is uninsured.

Most liquidation cases are deemed **no asset cases**. No-asset cases exist when a debtor has only exempt property and nothing the trustee may take to liquidate. In these cases, creditors receive nothing from the bankruptcy estate. These cases are relatively short-lived at three to five months in duration. As a result, you are not likely to see too many motions for relief from Automatic Stay in your travels. Most secured creditors will be content to wait out the three to five months it might take for a debtor to complete his or her liquidation case.

On rarer occasions, you might see unsecured creditors, such as recipients of spousal or child support and criminal restitution victims, file a motion for relief from stay. This happens most often in Chapter 7 cases because these creditors are often adequately provided for in a debtor's Chapter 13 reorganization plan. The argument this type of creditor might make in a Chapter 7 case would relate to the nondischargeable nature of the debt, which would allow it to survive the debtor's bankruptcy case.

The paralegal's role in recognizing this type of motion and helping the attorney adequately respond to it is paramount. The court might automatically grant a motion of this nature if it isn't opposed or objected to within two weeks. The debtor's silence might be considered evidence of his or her consent to lifting the Automatic Stay for a certain creditor. This is customary in bankruptcy practice, but remember that even if the debtor agrees to surrender an item of collateral to one of his or her creditors, the creditor still must file a motion for relief from stay. In this type of case, the debtor would remain silent and not offer a defense. The motion would then be granted, allowing the creditor to proceed with collection efforts. When the debtor intends to object to any relief from stay from a certain creditor, the debtor, most often through an attorney, would timely file an objection citing any number of defenses. Most often, defenses might declare that the collateral is adequately protected, that payments toward the debt are being made, or that the collateral is adequately insured.

When filing a Motion for Relief from Automatic Stay, the moving party must draft and include with the motion the following items:

- The motion for relief from Automatic Stay
- A notice of hearing and opportunity to object
- A memorandum, not to exceed 20 pages, supporting the motion
- A certificate of service

An example of several of these items follows to familiarize you with this type of motion. (See Appendix S: Notice of Hearing and Motion for Relief from Stay.)

no-asset case
A bankruptcy case in which most of the debtor's assets are exempt from the proceedings, leaving no nonexempt property for the trustee to sell.

Motion to Dismiss or Convert

A bankruptcy case may be dismissed by any of the parties involved. The debtor may request a **voluntary dismissal** in rare instances. After a bankruptcy case is filed, a debtor cannot simply decide to withdraw the case at his or her convenience. There must be a good reason, and not wanting to go through with it will not pass muster with the court. The court must be satisfied that no harm or prejudice will befall the creditors. Prejudice to a creditor can occur when one creditor is given preferential treatment over another unfairly. Suddenly coming into money is not a good reason for the debtor to request a dismissal of his or her case voluntarily. The court will simply view that as an opportunity to distribute assets to the creditors. The debtor must show that he or she has worked out an arrangement with the creditors or other plausible arrangement providing for the creditors' interests. The debtor must follow the proper protocol, which involves notifying all interested parties and, of course, filing the motion to dismiss. This can be done by using Form 20A of the Official Bankruptcy Forms. The trustee will likely raise objections, to which the debtor must be prepared to respond.

A creditor or the trustee may move to dismiss the debtor's bankruptcy case for one reason or another, as the following example will describe. In the case of a court dismissal, one of several possibilities might prompt a sudden court dismissal often described as **sua sponte**. Sua sponte refers to a decision the court makes on its own motion or objection from one of the parties. For instance, a debtor might miss a filing fee installment or fail to file the necessary documentation post-petition if he or she filed the case as an emergency. As previously mentioned, if a debtor is facing a civil trial for collections or an imminent foreclosure, he or she may file the petition along with a list of creditors to invoke the Automatic Stay. The Code has relaxed rules in this situation, allowing the debtor to file the schedules and other necessary forms within 15 days after filing the petition. If the debtor did not obtain an extension on this subsequent filing deadline, he or she may face a dismissal by the court.

The trustee's role in a dismissal depends largely on the type of case involved. A trustee in a reorganization case is often concerned, at least after the court approves the reorganization plan, only with the receipt of timely payments from the debtor. Under 11 U.S.C. § 109, a trustee may dismiss or convert a bankruptcy filing if the debtor does not qualify for a certain chapter. For example, if a pro se debtor does not pass the Means Test and files for Chapter 7 anyway, the case may be dismissed or converted after the trustee files a motion. Further, the trustee may file a motion to dismiss the case if the debtor is discovered to have made any misrepresentation to the court regarding assets, income, or illegal transfers.

Under 11 U.S.C. § 707(a)(1), a creditor may move to have a bankruptcy case dismissed if the debtor has caused an unreasonable delay in the case that resulted in prejudice to the creditor. Section 11 U.S.C. § 707(b)(1) allows a creditor to move to dismiss a case if it can prove that allowing a Chapter 7 case to go forward would result in abuse to the Bankruptcy Code. This is true even if the debtor has passed the Means Test. Passing the Means Test creates, by the Bankruptcy Code, a mere presumption that the debtor is not in abuse of the Code. If the creditor has evidence to the contrary regarding the debtor's income, assets, and the like, it may be able to dismiss the case successfully and continue with normal debt collection. (See Appendix T for an example of a typical Motion to Dismiss that a Chapter 13 trustee would bring.)

voluntary dismissal
When the debtor decides not to pursue the bankruptcy case and consents to its dismissal.

sua sponte
An action a court takes on its own motion.

Objection to Claim

Whenever a debtor files bankruptcy, the court forwards a notification to all the creditors listed on Schedules D, E, and F. After the creditors receive the notification, they must file an Official Form B10 Proof of Claim with the court. The creditor must indicate the amount of the claim as of the date of the filing of the bankruptcy case and, if applicable, provide sufficient evidence of the claim.

Any party who has an interest in the amount of money a creditor is claiming may file an objection to the creditor's proof of claim. These entities are known as **parties in interest**. Examples of parties in interest would be the trustee, other creditors, and, most importantly, the debtor. The reasons for filing an Objection to a Proof of Claim vary. Most often, the debtor disagrees with the amount the creditor is claiming. The trustee, or a debtor through his or her attorney, may file an objection because of a discrepancy or a dispute over how much of a particular claim is subject to priority. Another reason a trustee or debtor might file an objection may be due to a disagreement regarding the secured status of all or part of a claim.

Objections to a Proof of Claim are not very common in Chapter 7 cases that are deemed no-asset cases. This is true because there will be no distribution to creditors. However, in liquidation cases that involve nonexempt assets or reorganization cases, these types of objections are more common.

After a Proof of Claim is filed, the court considers its contents prima facie evidence of the creditor's claim. If the debtor, trustee, or another creditor files a timely objection, the burden of proof then shifts to the creditor to refute the objection. The hearing on an objection is scheduled for 30 days after the objection is filed. Sometimes, if necessary, the court will order discovery to be exchanged by the parties prior to the hearing. If the creditor does not respond to the objection or attend the hearing, the court will sustain the objection, and the creditor will be barred from receiving any funds distributed from the bankruptcy case.

As you will see in the following case, in most instances, the Federal Rules of Bankruptcy Procedure discourage an interested party from filing multiple objections in a single filing. Instead, the interested party should bring separate objections against different creditors and follow the proper filing and notice procedure for all objections.

parties in interest
Any party that has an interest in the amount of money a creditor is claiming may file an objection to the creditor's proof of claim.

> **Fed. R. Bankr. P. 3007**
>
> (a) **Objections to Claims.** An objection to the allowance of a claim shall be in writing and filed. A copy of the objection with notice of the hearing thereon shall be mailed or otherwise delivered to the claimant, the debtor or debtor in possession, and the trustee at least 30 days prior to the hearing.
>
> (b) **Demand for Relief Requiring an Adversary Proceeding.** A party in interest shall not include a demand for relief of a kind specified in Rule 7001 in an objection to the allowance of a claim, but may include the objection in an adversary proceeding.
>
> (c) **Limitation on Joinder of Claims Objections.** Unless otherwise ordered by the court or permitted by subdivision (d), objections to more than one claim shall not be joined in a single objection.
>
> (d) **Omnibus Objection.** Subject to subdivision (e), objections to more than one claim may be joined in an omnibus objection if all

the claims were filed by the same entity, or the objections are based solely on the grounds that the claims should be disallowed, in whole or in part, because:

(1) They duplicate other claims;

(2) They have been filed in the wrong case;

(3) They have been amended by subsequently filed proofs of claim;

(4) They were not timely filed;

(5) They have been satisfied or released during the case in accordance with the Code, applicable rules, or a court order;

(6) They were presented in a form that does not comply with applicable rules, and the objection states that the objector is unable to determine the validity of the claim because of the noncompliance;

(7) They are interests, rather than claims; or

(8) They assert priority in an amount that exceeds the maximum amount under § 507 of the Code.

(e) **Requirements for Omnibus Objection.** An omnibus objection shall:

(1) State in a conspicuous place that claimants receiving the objection should locate their names and claims in the objection;

(2) List claimants alphabetically, provide a cross-reference to claim numbers, and, if appropriate, list claimants by category of claims;

(3) State the grounds of the objection to each claim and provide a cross-reference to the pages in the omnibus objection pertinent to the stated grounds;

(4) State in the title the identity of the objector and the grounds for the objections;

(5) Be numbered consecutively with other omnibus objections filed by the same objector; and

(6) Contain objections to no more than 100 claims.

(f) **Finality of Objection.** The finality of any order regarding a claim objection included in an omnibus objection shall be determined as though the claim had been subject to an individual objection.

Motion to Value Collateral: Lien Avoidance

Bankruptcy Code 11 U.S.C. § 522(f) allows a debtor to avoid two lien types. Typically the debtor may avoid a judicial lien and a nonpossessory, nonpurchase money lien in bankruptcy. The debtor can only avoid a lien to the extent that the lien interferes with an exemption that the debtor listed on Schedule C. For instance, consider the debtor who has a home worth $200,000 that is encumbered by a mortgage in the amount of $100,000 and a judgment lien of $60,000. The homestead exemption in the debtor's state is $50,000. After considering the mortgage and the homestead exemption of $50,000, the judgment lien of $60,000 will be reduced by $10,000 to $50,000. If, on the other hand, the mortgage in this example was $150,000, the judgment lien would completely impair the exemption, and the judgment creditor would receive nothing.

In the case of a nonpossessory, nonpurchase money lien, if the debtor has pledged household items, jewelry, or clothing to secure a loan with a finance company, the debtor may avoid the lien or liens. This is tied more to the fact that sometimes these types of liens are attached to exempt property.

cramdown
Court-ordered modifications made to loans that are crammed down the creditors' throats.

As discussed in previous chapters, one of the benefits of filing a Chapter 13 bankruptcy is the debtor's ability to persuade the court to **cramdown** the balance of a secured claim to the fair market value of the collateral. Further, the debtor might be able to cramdown secured claims on nonresidence real property or strip off all or a portion of (a process known as lien stripping) a secondary secured lien on his or her primary residence to the extent that the collateral lacks sufficient value.

valuation motion (Motion to Value Collateral)
A motion filed to ask the court to determine the value of the collateral securing a particular loan or loans.

Sometimes the debtor and the secured creditor can reach an agreement regarding the fair market value of the collateral at the first 341 meeting of the creditors. Usually, debtors aren't fortunate enough to make such an agreement with a secured creditor, and the debtor or debtor's attorney files a **Motion to Value Collateral,** or a **valuation motion**. Such a motion asks the court to determine the value of the collateral securing a particular loan or loans. If the court determines that the value of the collateral is lower than the balance of a loan on, say, a vehicle, that loan balance will be reduced to the current value of the collateral. The same goes for a secondary loan on the debtor's primary residence or a senior loan on the debtor's nonprimary residence. If the value of the collateral, in the case of a mortgage, fails to secure the loan, the secondary loan may be stripped off and treated as an unsecured claim in the debtor's repayment plan. In the case of a nonprimary residence, a primary loan may be reduced to the fair market value of the home.

Many jurisdictions have form motions that the debtor may file with the court to give proper notification to the secured creditor in interest. The debtor must indicate what he or she feels the value of the collateral is and what that value is based on. Of course, the debtor must indicate which secured loan he or she wishes to revalue, and some forms allow the debtor to file this motion against multiple secured creditors. The process for filing such a motion usually requires the debtor to obtain a hearing date from the court and provide the creditor(s) with at least 21 days' notice of the hearing date. Most courts require the creditor to file any objection within two to seven days prior to the scheduled hearing. (See Appendix U for a Chapter 13 Plan Motion to Value Collateral; Notice of Deadline to Object.)

Motions for Abandonment

In a Chapter 7 case, all of the property the debtor owns and disclosed on the schedules becomes part of the bankruptcy estate. The trustee is charged with managing the estate and seeing that nonexempt property is sold. The money the trustee acquires from the sale of the nonexempt items is distributed hierarchically to the unsecured creditors.

Sometimes a trustee may deem certain property in the bankruptcy estate to be of little value and he or she may decide it is not worthwhile to sell. This may be true for several reasons:

- A particular piece of property may be so encumbered by liens or other encumbrances that it is completely devoid of value.

- An unencumbered article of property may not have enough value to make it worth selling after the costs associated with the sale and the trustee's commission are deducted.
- The portion of value in the item subject to exemption does not leave enough value in the item to warrant a sale.
- The item is fully exempt.
- The item is not popular for sale for one reason or another (i.e., a parcel of real property that is undesirable—no curb appeal).

If the trustee deems certain property to be worthy of abandonment, he or she must place all interested parties on notice of the proposed abandonment. Within 14 days of mailing the notice, any party in interest who wishes to object must do so. If an objection is raised according to the Federal Rules of Bankruptcy Procedure, the court sets the matter down for a hearing. If, at the hearing, the court either deems the property worthy of abandonment or overrules any objections, the property will no longer be part of the bankruptcy estate. The property, unless it is in the rightful possession of a creditor, will be returned to the debtor. Most objections raised prior to abandonment are raised by other creditors. If one or more creditors object to the abandonment of a certain item of property, they must prove that the property has value above any lien against the property and that this excess value is high enough to allow for a distribution to the creditors. Abandonment is not often an issue in a Chapter 13 case because the property of the estate is vested in the debtor when the reorganization plan is approved. According to the Federal Rules of Bankruptcy Procedure, the procedure for filing, serving, and carrying out a Motion to Abandon is as follows:

Fed. R. Bankr. P. 6007 Abandonment or Disposition Of Property

(a) **Notice of Proposed Abandonment or Disposition; Objections; Hearing.** Unless otherwise directed by the court, the trustee or debtor in possession shall give notice of a proposed abandonment or disposition of property to the United States trustee, all creditors, indenture trustees, and committees elected pursuant to § 705 or appointed pursuant to § 1102 of the Code. A party in interest may file and serve an objection within 14 days of the mailing of the notice, or within the time fixed by the court. If a timely objection is made, the court shall set a hearing on notice to the United States trustee and to other entities as the court may direct.

(b) **Motion by Party in Interest.** A party in interest may file and serve a motion requiring the trustee or debtor in possession to abandon property of the estate.

[(c) Hearing] (Abrogated Apr. 22, 1993, eff. Aug. 1, 1993)

Subdivision (c) requires a hearing when an objection under subdivision (a) is filed or a motion under subdivision (b) is made. Filing of an objection is sufficient to require a hearing; a separate or joined request for a hearing is unnecessary since the objection itself is tantamount to such a request.

Objections to Discharge of a Particular Debt

objection to discharge
When a creditor or the trustee formally opposes the bankruptcy court's grant of a discharge to the debtor.

Under 11 U.S.C. § 727(c)(1), a creditor or the trustee may file an **objection to discharge** of a particular debt or all the debts of a debtor in a bankruptcy case. The reasons a creditor or the trustee may object to a discharge vary. The reasons can include fraudulent transfers the debtor made, concealed assets, making a false oath, and purposely hindering the bankruptcy proceedings. The reasons can include just about any dishonest action by the debtor.

According to 11 U.S.C. § 727(c)(1)(2), "The trustee, a creditor, or the United States trustee may object to the granting of a discharge.... On request of a party in interest, the court may order the trustee to examine the acts and conduct of the debtor to determine whether a ground exists for denial of discharge."

revocation of discharge
The bankruptcy court's removal of a debtor's discharge.

Further, a creditor or the trustee can request a **revocation of discharge** that has already occurred. If it is discovered that the debtor engaged in any dishonest behavior in the case or for any of the reasons previously mentioned, a discharge can be successfully reversed. The ability to request a revocation of a discharge is subject to time limitations. The trustee and debtor have up to one year after a discharge is granted to successfully request that the court revoke the discharge.

Adversary Proceedings

The debtor, creditor, or the trustee may bring an adversary proceeding. Bankruptcy Code 11 U.S.C. §§ 547, 548, and 549 authorize the trustee to bring an adversary proceeding against a debtor for preference, fraudulent conveyance, and postpetition transfer actions, respectively. By filing an adversary proceeding against the debtor, the trustee may obtain the transferred property if the trustee can prove to the court that the transfer was made fraudulently. The burden of proof will fall on the trustee as the entity attempting to reverse a transfer or prevent the debtor from receiving his or her discharge.

Debtors are likely to bring an adversary proceeding against a creditor to determine whether a particular debt is dischargeable, to avoid a lien (known as lien stripping), or to stop a creditor from attempting to collect an already discharged debt.

Adversary proceedings that debtors file seeking to have a debt deemed dischargeable most often concern student loans, which are not typically dischargeable in bankruptcy; however, if a debtor can prove hardship, he or she may be able to have them deemed dischargeable. To show hardship, the debtor must prove a significant medical or mental issue prevents him or her from repaying student loans. Most often, expert testimony from doctors or psychotherapists is needed. In the case of a debtor bringing an adversary proceeding against a creditor who insists on collecting a debt that the court has already discharged, the bankruptcy court may invoke an injunction against the harassing creditor and order it to pay the debtor's attorney fees and other fees for lost wages and so on.

As discussed in previous chapters, Chapter 13 debtors who wish to avoid certain junior liens on property often end up in an adversary proceeding. At this type of adversary proceeding, the first issue is to determine the value of the collateral and whether the creditor's status is secured or unsecured. If, after hearing testimony and reviewing evidence the debtor and the creditor, a junior loan is deemed completely unsecured, that loan is stripped off and treated like the debtor's other unsecured debt.

Creditors may file an objection to discharge of a certain debt or all the debts the debtor incurred. The creditor might do this if it has evidence that the debtor acquired the debt in a fraudulent manner.

An adversary proceeding in a bankruptcy case is similar to a civil lawsuit. The plaintiff is the entity that files a formal complaint with the court. The complaint is then served on the defendant. The case is then assigned a number known as an **adversary number**. The adversary number appears just below the docket number for the main bankruptcy case on all pleadings in the adversary proceeding. A significant amount of preparation by the attorney and paralegal is required prior to the hearing. Discovery issues and exchanges must be dealt with prior to the hearing.

As stated in previous chapters, paralegals must be aware of the time limitations the trustee or creditors may have to bring an adversary proceeding. Bankruptcy Code 11 U.S.C. §§ 547, 548, and 549 govern the following limitations for the following voidable transfer actions. For preference actions, an action may be brought for transfers the debtor made within 90 days before filing the petition and within one year before filing the petition for transfers made to insiders. An action to void a fraudulent conveyance may be brought for conveyances that occurred within two years before the debtor filed the petition, and postpetition actions may be brought so long as the transfer occurred after the debtor filed the petition.

adversary number
A separate docket number the bankruptcy court assigns to an adversary proceeding. This number is listed below the docket number for the main bankruptcy case.

Jury Trials in Bankruptcy

The federal circuit courts are split regarding the bankruptcy judge's ability to preside over a jury trial. The seventh amendment of the U.S. Constitution states that individuals are entitled to a trial by jury in "suits at common law." That phrase has long been interpreted to refer to **legal rights** of individuals (monetary) and not **equitable rights**. Legal rights are concerned with the recovery of property or money in a lawsuit because of something the plaintiff is owed or has lost. Equitable rights are concerned with enforcing rules or statutes and often involve a court ordering someone to do or refrain from doing something.

Under Bankruptcy Code 28 U.S.C. § 157(e), "[i]f the right to a jury trial applies in a proceeding that may be heard under this section by a bankruptcy judge, the bankruptcy judge may conduct the jury trial if specially designated to exercise such jurisdiction by the district court and with the express consent of all the parties."

In bankruptcy practice, one of the most prevalent causes for a jury trial in bankruptcy court involves fraudulent transfer by the debtor. The case involves a person to whom property was delivered in an allegedly fraudulent manner or by way of a preference. If the trustee files for an adversary proceeding to reverse the fraudulent or preferential transfer, the defendant may request the case to be heard by a jury rather than the bankruptcy judge alone. Reasons for this request vary but, most often, the defendant or his or her attorney may feel that the judge is biased against the debtor. In many jurisdictions, requesting a jury in a case like this requires obtaining the consent of all parties involved in the bankruptcy case. If this is not possible, the case may need to be heard in the appropriate U.S. district court.

Remember Stefania from the beginning of the chapter? What she didn't realize while handling her own bankruptcy case was that the only way to accomplish certain objectives in her case was by filing the proper motion. Stefania was handling her own Chapter 13 case. Although she seemed to be very astute with regard to the benefits she could receive from Chapter 13, she wasn't quite on the

legal rights
Individual rights regarding the recovery of property or money in a lawsuit because of something the plaintiff is owed or has lost.

equitable rights
Individual rights concerned with enforcing rules or statutes; often involve a court ordering someone to do or refrain from doing something.

mark with how to avail herself properly of these benefits. After reading this chapter, you are now aware that the proper method for using such benefits as cramdown and lien stripping, is by filing the proper motion with the court. Stefania decided that calling a bankruptcy lawyer was the right choice for her. This will certainly make the process easier for her. Stefania's lawyer, after verifying that it is appropriate to do so, will file what is called a valuation motion. This will put her car loan issue in front of the court to consider whether a cramdown is appropriate. If Stefania's income continues to drop, she or her attorney might be able to file a motion to convert her case to a Chapter 7.

CHAPTER **SUMMARY**

Most of the time, a reorganization or liquidation case proceeds through the bankruptcy process without incident. A typical bankruptcy case takes the debtor through the process with very little involvement from the bankruptcy court or the bankruptcy judge. Most often, a liquidation case does not involve nonexempt property. Sometimes one of the parties in a bankruptcy case will raise issues such as hidden assets or a fraudulent transfer, and the judge is the only appropriate person to resolve such an issue. A motion is the appropriate way to bring these and other types of issues to the attention of the bankruptcy court for resolution. Any creditor wishing to avoid the effect of the Automatic Stay may, by showing good cause, bring a motion before the court to receive permission to proceed with collecting its debt from the debtor.

A debtor may opt to dismiss his or her own case, or the court might suddenly dismiss a case if the debtor misses an installment on the filing fee or fails to cooperate with the court by filing the schedules and other forms on time. A creditor may move to have a bankruptcy case dismissed if the debtor has caused an unreasonable delay in the case that resulted in prejudice to the creditor. A creditor might move to dismiss a case if it can prove that allowing a Chapter 7 case to go forward would result in abuse of the Bankruptcy Code. The trustee may dismiss or convert a bankruptcy filing if the debtor does not qualify for a certain chapter. The trustee may also file a motion to dismiss the case if he or she discovers that the debtor has made any misrepresentation to the court regarding assets, income, or illegal transfers. Sometimes debtors do not keep up with their plan payments in reorganization. The trustee may then file a motion to dismiss or convert the case to a Chapter 7. Any party who has an interest in the amount of money a creditor is claiming may file an objection to the creditor's proof of claim. The debtor may disagree with the amount the creditor is claiming, or the trustee may file an objection because of a discrepancy or dispute over how much of a particular claim is subject to priority.

In a Chapter 13 case, a debtor may file a valuation motion to cram the loan balance on a secured claim down to the current market value of the collateral. Sometimes a trustee may deem certain property in the bankruptcy estate to be of little value, and he or she decides it is not worthwhile to sell. If this is the case, the trustee will file a motion for abandonment with the court. Any party in interest who wishes to object to the motion for abandonment may do so within the proper time frame, and the matter will be set down for a hearing. Any creditor or the trustee may file an objection to discharge regarding a particular debt or all the debts in a bankruptcy case. The reasons the trustee or creditor may file this type of motion can include fraudulent transfers the debtor made, concealed assets, making a false oath, or purposely hindering the bankruptcy proceedings.

CONCEPT REVIEW AND REINFORCEMENT

KEY **TERMS**

adversary number	meeting of the creditors (341 meeting)	revocation of
adversary proceeding	motion	discharge
Automatic Stay	no-asset case	sua sponte
cramdown	nonexempt property	valuation motion (Motion to Value
equitable rights	objection to discharge	Collateral)
legal rights	parties in interest	voluntary dismissal

REVIEWING **KEY CONCEPTS**

1. Identify the different interested parties that may exist in a bankruptcy case. Based on the reading, please give two examples of the type of motion each of the parties may file in a bankruptcy case.
2. Explain the reasons a Motion to Value Collateral may be filed.
3. Discuss the reasons a trustee may want to abandon a certain article of property in the bankruptcy estate.
4. Cite at least two reasons the trustee may move to dismiss a debtor's bankruptcy case.
5. May a debtor simply withdraw his or her bankruptcy proceeding? If not, what process must he or she follow and why?
6. Discuss the parties who may file a Motion for Relief from Automatic Stay and discuss their respective reasons for filing such a motion.

BUILDING YOUR PARALEGAL SKILLS

CASE FOR **REVIEW**

In re Simmons, 200 F.3d 738 (11th Cir. 2000)

BUILDING A PROFESSIONAL PORTFOLIO

PORTFOLIO **EXERCISES**

You work for the law offices of David Smith, LLC, and your firm represents the debtor Jane Clark. Ms. Clark is an individual debtor with primarily consumer debts, and your office currently represents her in a Chapter 7 case. You have been working closely with the debtor by helping her fill out her petition and schedules. Recently Ms. Clark informed you that she bought a lottery scratch-off ticket last week and won $50,000. The client advised you that she wants to "just drop the bankruptcy case" because she feels she has enough money now and can pay off her debts on her own. Attorney David Smith would like you to draft a letter on his behalf to the client, explaining whether she may do this. Make sure your letter explains fully why she can or cannot do this. Be certain to explain the procedure the client must follow and any motions she must file. Don't forget to include all the ramifications of her actions that she might expect from the court, the trustee, and her creditors.

B1 (Official Form 1) (04/13)

UNITED STATES BANKRUPTCY COURT _____ District of _____	VOLUNTARY PETITION
Name of Debtor (if individual, enter Last, First, Middle):	Name of Joint Debtor (Spouse) (Last, First, Middle):
All Other Names used by the Debtor in the last 8 years (include married, maiden, and trade names):	All Other Names used by the Joint Debtor in the last 8 years (include married, maiden, and trade names):
Last four digits of Soc. Sec. or Individual - Taxpayer I.D. (ITIN)/Complete EIN (if more than one, state all):	Last four digits of Soc. Sec. or Individual - Taxpayer I.D. (ITIN)/Complete EIN (if more than one, state all):
Street Address of Debtor (No. and Street, City, and State): ZIP CODE	Street Address of Joint Debtor (No. and Street, City, and State): ZIP CODE
County of Residence or of the Principal Place of Business:	County of Residence or of the Principal Place of Business:
Mailing Address of Debtor (if different from street address): ZIP CODE	Mailing Address of Joint Debtor (if different from street address): ZIP CODE
Location of Principal Assets of Business Debtor (if different from street address above): ZIP CODE	

Type of Debtor
(Form of Organization)
(Check **one** box.)

☐ Individual (includes Joint Debtors)
   See Exhibit D on page 2 of this form.
☐ Corporation (includes LLC and LLP)
☐ Partnership
☐ Other (If debtor is not one of the above entities, check this box and state type of entity below.)

Nature of Business
(Check **one** box.)

☐ Health Care Business
☐ Single Asset Real Estate as defined in 11 U.S.C. § 101(51B)
☐ Railroad
☐ Stockbroker
☐ Commodity Broker
☐ Clearing Bank
☐ Other

Chapter of Bankruptcy Code Under Which the Petition is Filed (Check **one** box.)

☐ Chapter 7
☐ Chapter 9
☐ Chapter 11
☐ Chapter 12
☐ Chapter 13

☐ Chapter 15 Petition for Recognition of a Foreign Main Proceeding
☐ Chapter 15 Petition for Recognition of a Foreign Nonmain Proceeding

Chapter 15 Debtors

Country of debtor's center of main interests:

Each country in which a foreign proceeding by, regarding, or against debtor is pending:

Tax-Exempt Entity
(Check box, if applicable.)

☐ Debtor is a tax-exempt organization under title 26 of the United States Code (the Internal Revenue Code).

Nature of Debts
(Check **one** box.)

☐ Debts are primarily consumer debts, defined in 11 U.S.C. § 101(8) as "incurred by an individual primarily for a personal, family, or household purpose."

☐ Debts are primarily business debts.

Filing Fee (Check one box.)

☐ Full Filing Fee attached.

☐ Filing Fee to be paid in installments (applicable to individuals only). Must attach signed application for the court's consideration certifying that the debtor is unable to pay fee except in installments. Rule 1006(b). See Official Form 3A.

☐ Filing Fee waiver requested (applicable to chapter 7 individuals only). Must attach signed application for the court's consideration. See Official Form 3B.

Chapter 11 Debtors

Check one box:
☐ Debtor is a small business debtor as defined in 11 U.S.C. § 101(51D).
☐ Debtor is not a small business debtor as defined in 11 U.S.C. § 101(51D).

Check if:
☐ Debtor's aggregate noncontingent liquidated debts (excluding debts owed to insiders or affiliates) are less than $2,490,925 (*amount subject to adjustment on 4/01/16 and every three years thereafter*).

- -
Check all applicable boxes:
☐ A plan is being filed with this petition.
☐ Acceptances of the plan were solicited prepetition from one or more classes of creditors, in accordance with 11 U.S.C. § 1126(b).

Statistical/Administrative Information

☐ Debtor estimates that funds will be available for distribution to unsecured creditors.
☐ Debtor estimates that, after any exempt property is excluded and administrative expenses paid, there will be no funds available for distribution to unsecured creditors.

THIS SPACE IS FOR COURT USE ONLY

Estimated Number of Creditors

☐	☐	☐	☐	☐	☐	☐	☐	☐	☐
1-49	50-99	100-199	200-999	1,000-5,000	5,001-10,000	10,001-25,000	25,001-50,000	50,001-100,000	Over 100,000

Estimated Assets

☐	☐	☐	☐	☐	☐	☐	☐	☐	☐
$0 to $50,000	$50,001 to $100,000	$100,001 to $500,000	$500,001 to $1 million	$1,000,001 to $10 million	$10,000,001 to $50 million	$50,000,001 to $100 million	$100,000,001 to $500 million	$500,000,001 to $1 billion	More than $1 billion

Estimated Liabilities

☐	☐	☐	☐	☐	☐	☐	☐	☐	☐
$0 to $50,000	$50,001 to $100,000	$100,001 to $500,000	$500,001 to $1 million	$1,000,001 to $10 million	$10,000,001 to $50 million	$50,000,001 to $100 million	$100,000,001 to $500 million	$500,000,001 to $1 billion	More than $1 billion

B1 (Official Form 1) (04/13)   Page 2

Voluntary Petition *(This page must be completed and filed in every case.)*	Name of Debtor(s):

All Prior Bankruptcy Cases Filed Within Last 8 Years (If more than two, attach additional sheet.)

Location Where Filed:	Case Number:	Date Filed:
Location Where Filed:	Case Number:	Date Filed:

Pending Bankruptcy Case Filed by any Spouse, Partner, or Affiliate of this Debtor (If more than one, attach additional sheet.)

Name of Debtor:	Case Number:	Date Filed:
District:	Relationship:	Judge:

Exhibit A

(To be completed if debtor is required to file periodic reports (e.g., forms 10K and 10Q) with the Securities and Exchange Commission pursuant to Section 13 or 15(d) of the Securities Exchange Act of 1934 and is requesting relief under chapter 11.)

☐ Exhibit A is attached and made a part of this petition.

Exhibit B

(To be completed if debtor is an individual whose debts are primarily consumer debts.)

I, the attorney for the petitioner named in the foregoing petition, declare that I have informed the petitioner that [he or she] may proceed under chapter 7, 11, 12, or 13 of title 11, United States Code, and have explained the relief available under each such chapter. I further certify that I have delivered to the debtor the notice required by 11 U.S.C. § 342(b).

X _____
Signature of Attorney for Debtor(s)   (Date)

Exhibit C

Does the debtor own or have possession of any property that poses or is alleged to pose a threat of imminent and identifiable harm to public health or safety?

☐ Yes, and Exhibit C is attached and made a part of this petition.

☐ No.

Exhibit D

(To be completed by every individual debtor. If a joint petition is filed, each spouse must complete and attach a separate Exhibit D.)

☐ Exhibit D, completed and signed by the debtor, is attached and made a part of this petition.

If this is a joint petition:

☐ Exhibit D, also completed and signed by the joint debtor, is attached and made a part of this petition.

Information Regarding the Debtor - Venue
(Check any applicable box.)

☐ Debtor has been domiciled or has had a residence, principal place of business, or principal assets in this District for 180 days immediately preceding the date of this petition or for a longer part of such 180 days than in any other District.

☐ There is a bankruptcy case concerning debtor's affiliate, general partner, or partnership pending in this District.

☐ Debtor is a debtor in a foreign proceeding and has its principal place of business or principal assets in the United States in this District, or has no principal place of business or assets in the United States but is a defendant in an action or proceeding [in a federal or state court] in this District, or the interests of the parties will be served in regard to the relief sought in this District.

Certification by a Debtor Who Resides as a Tenant of Residential Property
(Check all applicable boxes.)

☐ Landlord has a judgment against the debtor for possession of debtor's residence. (If box checked, complete the following.)

_____
(Name of landlord that obtained judgment)

_____
(Address of landlord)

☐ Debtor claims that under applicable nonbankruptcy law, there are circumstances under which the debtor would be permitted to cure the entire monetary default that gave rise to the judgment for possession, after the judgment for possession was entered, and

☐ Debtor has included with this petition the deposit with the court of any rent that would become due during the 30-day period after the filing of the petition.

☐ Debtor certifies that he/she has served the Landlord with this certification. (11 U.S.C. § 362(l)).

Voluntary Petition	Name of Debtor(s):
(This page must be completed and filed in every case.)	

Signatures

Signature(s) of Debtor(s) (Individual/Joint)	**Signature of a Foreign Representative**

Signature(s) of Debtor(s) (Individual/Joint)

I declare under penalty of perjury that the information provided in this petition is true and correct.

[If petitioner is an individual whose debts are primarily consumer debts and has chosen to file under chapter 7] I am aware that I may proceed under chapter 7, 11, 12 or 13 of title 11, United States Code, understand the relief available under each such chapter, and choose to proceed under chapter 7.
[If no attorney represents me and no bankruptcy petition preparer signs the petition] I have obtained and read the notice required by 11 U.S.C. § 342(b).

I request relief in accordance with the chapter of title 11, United States Code, specified in this petition.

X _____
    Signature of Debtor

X _____
    Signature of Joint Debtor

    Telephone Number (if not represented by attorney)

    Date

Signature of a Foreign Representative

I declare under penalty of perjury that the information provided in this petition is true and correct, that I am the foreign representative of a debtor in a foreign proceeding, and that I am authorized to file this petition.

(Check only **one** box.)

☐ I request relief in accordance with chapter 15 of title 11, United States Code. Certified copies of the documents required by 11 U.S.C. § 1515 are attached.

☐ Pursuant to 11 U.S.C. § 1511, I request relief in accordance with the chapter of title 11 specified in this petition. A certified copy of the order granting recognition of the foreign main proceeding is attached.

X _____
    (Signature of Foreign Representative)

_____
    (Printed Name of Foreign Representative)

_____
    Date

Signature of Attorney*

X _____
    Signature of Attorney for Debtor(s)

    Printed Name of Attorney for Debtor(s)

    Firm Name

    Address

    Telephone Number

    Date

*In a case in which § 707(b)(4)(D) applies, this signature also constitutes a certification that the attorney has no knowledge after an inquiry that the information in the schedules is incorrect.

Signature of Non-Attorney Bankruptcy Petition Preparer

I declare under penalty of perjury that: (1) I am a bankruptcy petition preparer as defined in 11 U.S.C. § 110; (2) I prepared this document for compensation and have provided the debtor with a copy of this document and the notices and information required under 11 U.S.C. §§ 110(b), 110(h), and 342(b); and, (3) if rules or guidelines have been promulgated pursuant to 11 U.S.C. § 110(h) setting a maximum fee for services chargeable by bankruptcy petition preparers, I have given the debtor notice of the maximum amount before preparing any document for filing for a debtor or accepting any fee from the debtor, as required in that section. Official Form 19 is attached.

_____
Printed Name and title, if any, of Bankruptcy Petition Preparer

_____
Social-Security number (If the bankruptcy petition preparer is not an individual, state the Social-Security number of the officer, principal, responsible person or partner of the bankruptcy petition preparer.) (Required by 11 U.S.C. § 110.)

Signature of Debtor (Corporation/Partnership)

I declare under penalty of perjury that the information provided in this petition is true and correct, and that I have been authorized to file this petition on behalf of the debtor.

The debtor requests the relief in accordance with the chapter of title 11, United States Code, specified in this petition.

X _____
    Signature of Authorized Individual

    Printed Name of Authorized Individual

    Title of Authorized Individual

    Date

Address

X _____
Signature

_____
Date

Signature of bankruptcy petition preparer or officer, principal, responsible person, or partner whose Social-Security number is provided above.

Names and Social-Security numbers of all other individuals who prepared or assisted in preparing this document unless the   bankruptcy petition preparer is not an individual.

If more than one person prepared this document, attach additional sheets conforming to the appropriate official form for each person.

A bankruptcy petition preparer's failure to comply with the provisions of title 11 and the Federal Rules of Bankruptcy Procedure may result in fines or imprisonment or both. 11 U.S.C. § 110; 18 U.S.C. § 156.

B6 Cover (Form 6 Cover) (12/07)

FORM 6. SCHEDULES

Summary of Schedules
Statistical Summary of Certain Liabilities and Related Data (28 U.S.C. § 159)

Schedule A - Real Property
Schedule B - Personal Property
Schedule C - Property Claimed as Exempt
Schedule D - Creditors Holding Secured Claims
Schedule E - Creditors Holding Unsecured Priority Claims
Schedule F - Creditors Holding Unsecured Nonpriority Claims
Schedule G - Executory Contracts and Unexpired Leases
Schedule H - Codebtors
Schedule I - Current Income of Individual Debtor(s)
Schedule J - Current Expenditures of Individual Debtors(s)

Unsworn Declaration Under Penalty of Perjury

GENERAL INSTRUCTIONS: The first page of the debtor's schedules and the first page of any
amendments thereto must contain a caption as in Form 16B. Subsequent pages should be
identified with the debtor's name and case number. If the schedules are filed with the petition,
the case number should be left blank.

Schedules D, E, and F have been designed for the listing of each claim only once. Even when a
claim is secured only in part or entitled to priority only in part, it still should be listed only once.
A claim which is secured in whole or in part should be listed on Schedule D only, and a claim
which is entitled to priority in whole or in part should be listed on Schedule E only. Do not list
the same claim twice. If a creditor has more than one claim, such as claims arising from separate
transactions, each claim should be scheduled separately.

Review the specific instructions for each schedule before completing the schedule.

B6A (Official Form 6A) (12/07)

In re _____ ,   Case No. _____
                    Debtor   **(If known)**

SCHEDULE A - REAL PROPERTY

Except as directed below, list all real property in which the debtor has any legal, equitable, or future interest, including all property owned as a co-tenant, community property, or in which the debtor has a life estate. Include any property in which the debtor holds rights and powers exercisable for the debtor's own benefit. If the debtor is married, state whether the husband, wife, both, or the marital community own the property by placing an "H," "W," "J," or "C" in the column labeled "Husband, Wife, Joint, or Community." If the debtor holds no interest in real property, write "None" under "Description and Location of Property."

Do not include interests in executory contracts and unexpired leases on this schedule. List them in Schedule G - Executory Contracts and Unexpired Leases.

If an entity claims to have a lien or hold a secured interest in any property, state the amount of the secured claim. See Schedule D. If no entity claims to hold a secured interest in the property, write "None" in the column labeled "Amount of Secured Claim."

If the debtor is an individual or if a joint petition is filed, state the amount of any exemption claimed in the property only in Schedule C - Property Claimed as Exempt.

DESCRIPTION AND LOCATION OF PROPERTY	NATURE OF DEBTOR'S INTEREST IN PROPERTY	HUSBAND, WIFE, JOINT OR COMMUNITY	CURRENT VALUE OF DEBTOR'S INTEREST IN PROPERTY, WITHOUT DEDUCTING ANY SECURED CLAIM OR EXEMPTION	AMOUNT OF SECURED CLAIM
		Total ➡		

(Report also on Summary of Schedules.)

B 6B (Official Form 6B) (12/07)

In re _____,   Case No. _____
         Debtor   **(If known)**

SCHEDULE B - PERSONAL PROPERTY

Except as directed below, list all personal property of the debtor of whatever kind. If the debtor has no property in one or more of the categories, place an "x" in the appropriate position in the column labeled "None." If additional space is needed in any category, attach a separate sheet properly identified with the case name, case number, and the number of the category. If the debtor is married, state whether the husband, wife, both, or the marital community own the property by placing an "H," "W," "J," or "C" in the column labeled "Husband, Wife, Joint, or Community." If the debtor is an individual or a joint petition is filed, state the amount of any exemptions claimed only in Schedule C - Property Claimed as Exempt.

Do not list interests in executory contracts and unexpired leases on this schedule. List them in Schedule G - Executory Contracts and Unexpired Leases.

If the property is being held for the debtor by someone else, state that person's name and address under "Description and Location of Property." If the property is being held for a minor child, simply state the child's initials and the name and address of the child's parent or guardian, such as "A.B., a minor child, by John Doe, guardian." Do not disclose the child's name. See, 11 U.S.C. § 112 and Fed. R. Bankr. P. 1007(m).

TYPE OF PROPERTY	N O N E	DESCRIPTION AND LOCATION OF PROPERTY	HUSBAND, WIFE, JOINT, OR COMMUNITY	CURRENT VALUE OF DEBTOR'S INTEREST IN PROPERTY, WITH- OUT DEDUCTING ANY SECURED CLAIM OR EXEMPTION
1. Cash on hand.				
2. Checking, savings or other financial accounts, certificates of deposit or shares in banks, savings and loan, thrift, building and loan, and homestead associations, or credit unions, brokerage houses, or cooperatives.				
3. Security deposits with public utilities, telephone companies, landlords, and others.				
4. Household goods and furnishings, including audio, video, and computer equipment.				
5. Books; pictures and other art objects; antiques; stamp, coin, record, tape, compact disc, and other collections or collectibles.				
6. Wearing apparel.				
7. Furs and jewelry.				
8. Firearms and sports, photographic, and other hobby equipment.				
9. Interests in insurance policies. Name insurance company of each policy and itemize surrender or refund value of each.				
10. Annuities. Itemize and name each issuer.				
11. Interests in an education IRA as defined in 26 U.S.C. § 530(b)(1) or under a qualified State tuition plan as defined in 26 U.S.C. § 529(b)(1). Give particulars. (File separately the record(s) of any such interest(s). 11 U.S.C. § 521(c).)				

B 6B (Official Form 6B) (12/07) -- Cont.

In re _____,   Case No. _____
   Debtor   **(If known)**

SCHEDULE B - PERSONAL PROPERTY
(Continuation Sheet)

TYPE OF PROPERTY	N O N E	DESCRIPTION AND LOCATION OF PROPERTY	HUSBAND, WIFE, JOINT, OR COMMUNITY	CURRENT VALUE OF DEBTOR'S INTEREST IN PROPERTY, WITH-OUT DEDUCTING ANY SECURED CLAIM OR EXEMPTION
12. Interests in IRA, ERISA, Keogh, or other pension or profit sharing plans. Give particulars.				
13. Stock and interests in incorporated and unincorporated businesses. Itemize.				
14. Interests in partnerships or joint ventures. Itemize.				
15. Government and corporate bonds and other negotiable and non-negotiable instruments.				
16. Accounts receivable.				
17. Alimony, maintenance, support, and property settlements to which the debtor is or may be entitled. Give particulars.				
18. Other liquidated debts owed to debtor including tax refunds. Give particulars.				
19. Equitable or future interests, life estates, and rights or powers exercisable for the benefit of the debtor other than those listed in Schedule A – Real Property.				
20. Contingent and noncontingent interests in estate of a decedent, death benefit plan, life insurance policy, or trust.				
21. Other contingent and unliquidated claims of every nature, including tax refunds, counterclaims of the debtor, and rights to setoff claims. Give estimated value of each.				

B 6B (Official Form 6B) (12/07) -- Cont.

In re _____,   Case No. _____
    Debtor   **(If known)**

SCHEDULE B - PERSONAL PROPERTY
(Continuation Sheet)

TYPE OF PROPERTY	N O N E	DESCRIPTION AND LOCATION OF PROPERTY	HUSBAND, WIFE, JOINT, OR COMMUNITY	CURRENT VALUE OF DEBTOR'S INTEREST IN PROPERTY, WITH-OUT DEDUCTING ANY SECURED CLAIM OR EXEMPTION
22. Patents, copyrights, and other intellectual property. Give particulars.				
23. Licenses, franchises, and other general intangibles. Give particulars.				
24. Customer lists or other compilations containing personally identifiable information (as defined in 11 U.S.C. § 101(41A)) provided to the debtor by individuals in connection with obtaining a product or service from the debtor primarily for personal, family, or household purposes.				
25. Automobiles, trucks, trailers, and other vehicles and accessories.				
26. Boats, motors, and accessories.				
27. Aircraft and accessories.				
28. Office equipment, furnishings, and supplies.				
29. Machinery, fixtures, equipment, and supplies used in business.				
30. Inventory.				
31. Animals.				
32. Crops - growing or harvested. Give particulars.				
33. Farming equipment and implements.				
34. Farm supplies, chemicals, and feed.				
35. Other personal property of any kind not already listed. Itemize.				

_____continuation sheets attached   Total ➡ | $

(Include amounts from any continuation sheets attached.
Report total also on Summary of Schedules.)

B6C (Official Form 6C) (04/13))

In re_____,   Case No. _____
         Debtor   *(If known)*

SCHEDULE C - PROPERTY CLAIMED AS EXEMPT

Debtor claims the exemptions to which debtor is entitled under: ☐   Check if debtor claims a homestead exemption that exceeds
(Check one box) $155,675.*
☐   11 U.S.C. § 522(b)(2)
☐   11 U.S.C. § 522(b)(3)

DESCRIPTION OF PROPERTY	SPECIFY LAW PROVIDING EACH EXEMPTION	VALUE OF CLAIMED EXEMPTION	CURRENT VALUE OF PROPERTY WITHOUT DEDUCTING EXEMPTION

* *Amount subject to adjustment on 4/01/16, and every three years thereafter with respect to cases commenced on or after the date of adjustment.* *

B 6D (Official Form 6D) (12/07)

Schedule D: Creditors Holding Secured Claims

In re _____,   Case No. _____
       Debtor   **(If known)**

SCHEDULE D - CREDITORS HOLDING SECURED CLAIMS

State the name, mailing address, including zip code, and last four digits of any account number of all entities holding claims secured by property of the debtor as of the date of filing of the petition. The complete account number of any account the debtor has with the creditor is useful to the trustee and the creditor and may be provided if the debtor chooses to do so. List creditors holding all types of secured interests such as judgment liens, garnishments, statutory liens, mortgages, deeds of trust, and other security interests.

List creditors in alphabetical order to the extent practicable. If a minor child is the creditor, state the child's initials and the name and address of the child's parent or guardian, such as "A.B., a minor child, by John Doe, guardian." Do not disclose the child's name. See, 11 U.S.C. §112 and Fed. R. Bankr. P. 1007(m). If all secured creditors will not fit on this page, use the continuation sheet provided.

If any entity other than a spouse in a joint case may be jointly liable on a claim, place an "X" in the column labeled "Codebtor," include the entity on the appropriate schedule of creditors, and complete Schedule H – Codebtors. If a joint petition is filed, state whether the husband, wife, both of them, or the marital community may be liable on each claim by placing an "H," "W," "J," or "C" in the column labeled "Husband, Wife, Joint, or Community."

If the claim is contingent, place an "X" in the column labeled "Contingent." If the claim is unliquidated, place an "X" in the column labeled "Unliquidated." If the claim is disputed, place an "X" in the column labeled "Disputed." (You may need to place an "X" in more than one of these three columns.)

Total the columns labeled "Amount of Claim Without Deducting Value of Collateral" and "Unsecured Portion, if Any" in the boxes labeled "Total(s)" on the last sheet of the completed schedule. Report the total from the column labeled "Amount of Claim Without Deducting Value of Collateral" also on the Summary of Schedules and, if the debtor is an individual with primarily consumer debts, report the total from the column labeled "Unsecured Portion, if Any" on the Statistical Summary of Certain Liabilities and Related Data.

☐   Check this box if debtor has no creditors holding secured claims to report on this Schedule D.

CREDITOR'S NAME AND MAILING ADDRESS INCLUDING ZIP CODE AND AN ACCOUNT NUMBER *(See Instructions Above.)*	CODEBTOR	HUSBAND, WIFE, JOINT, OR COMMUNITY	DATE CLAIM WAS INCURRED, NATURE OF LIEN, AND DESCRIPTION AND VALUE OF PROPERTY SUBJECT TO LIEN	CONTINGENT	UNLIQUIDATED	DISPUTED	AMOUNT OF CLAIM WITHOUT DEDUCTING VALUE OF COLLATERAL	UNSECURED PORTION, IF ANY
ACCOUNT NO.								
			VALUE $					
ACCOUNT NO.								
			VALUE $					
ACCOUNT NO.								
			VALUE $					
_____ continuation sheets attached			Subtotal ▶ (Total of this page)				$	$
			Total ▶ (Use only on last page)				$	$
							(Report also on Summary of Schedules.)	(If applicable, report also on Statistical Summary of Certain Liabilities and Related Data.)

B 6D (Official Form 6D) (12/07) – Cont.   2

In re _____,   Case No. _____
                     Debtor   **(if known)**

SCHEDULE D - CREDITORS HOLDING SECURED CLAIMS
(Continuation Sheet)

CREDITOR'S NAME AND MAILING ADDRESS INCLUDING ZIP CODE AND AN ACCOUNT NUMBER *(See Instructions Above.)*	CODEBTOR	HUSBAND, WIFE, JOINT, OR COMMUNITY	DATE CLAIM WAS INCURRED, NATURE OF LIEN, AND DESCRIPTION AND VALUE OF PROPERTY SUBJECT TO LIEN	CONTINGENT	UNLIQUIDATED	DISPUTED	AMOUNT OF CLAIM WITHOUT DEDUCTING VALUE OF COLLATERAL	UNSECURED PORTION, IF ANY
ACCOUNT NO.								
			VALUE $					
ACCOUNT NO.								
			VALUE $					
ACCOUNT NO.								
			VALUE $					
ACCOUNT NO.								
			VALUE $					
ACCOUNT NO.								
			VALUE $					

Sheet no._____of_____continuation sheets attached to Schedule of Creditors Holding Secured Claims

Subtotal (s) ▶
(Total(s) of this page) $ $

Total(s) ▶
(Use only on last page) $ $

(Report also on Summary of Schedules.)   (If applicable, report also on Statistical Summary of Certain Liabilities and Related Data.)

B6E (Official Form 6E) (04/13)

In re _____,   Case No. _____
   Debtor   *(if known)*

SCHEDULE E - CREDITORS HOLDING UNSECURED PRIORITY CLAIMS

A complete list of claims entitled to priority, listed separately by type of priority, is to be set forth on the sheets provided. Only holders of unsecured claims entitled to priority should be listed in this schedule. In the boxes provided on the attached sheets, state the name, mailing address, including zip code, and last four digits of the account number, if any, of all entities holding priority claims against the debtor or the property of the debtor, as of the date of the filing of the petition. Use a separate continuation sheet for each type of priority and label each with the type of priority.

The complete account number of any account the debtor has with the creditor is useful to the trustee and the creditor and may be provided if the debtor chooses to do so. If a minor child is a creditor, state the child's initials and the name and address of the child's parent or guardian, such as "A.B., a minor child, by John Doe, guardian." Do not disclose the child's name. See, 11 U.S.C. § 112 and Fed. R. Bankr. P. 1007(m).

If any entity other than a spouse in a joint case may be jointly liable on a claim, place an "X" in the column labeled "Codebtor," include the entity on the appropriate schedule of creditors, and complete Schedule H-Codebtors. If a joint petition is filed, state whether the husband, wife, both of them, or the marital community may be liable on each claim by placing an "H," "W," "J," or "C" in the column labeled "Husband, Wife, Joint, or Community." If the claim is contingent, place an "X" in the column labeled "Contingent." If the claim is unliquidated, place an "X" in the column labeled "Unliquidated." If the claim is disputed, place an "X" in the column labeled "Disputed." (You may need to place an "X" in more than one of these three columns.)

Report the total of claims listed on each sheet in the box labeled "Subtotals" on each sheet. Report the total of all claims listed on this Schedule E in the box labeled "Total" on the last sheet of the completed schedule. Report this total also on the Summary of Schedules.

Report the total of amounts entitled to priority listed on each sheet in the box labeled "Subtotals" on each sheet. Report the total of all amounts entitled to priority listed on this Schedule E in the box labeled "Totals" on the last sheet of the completed schedule. Individual debtors with primarily consumer debts report this total also on the Statistical Summary of Certain Liabilities and Related Data.

Report the total of amounts <u>not</u> entitled to priority listed on each sheet in the box labeled "Subtotals" on each sheet. Report the total of all amounts not entitled to priority listed on this Schedule E in the box labeled "Totals" on the last sheet of the completed schedule. Individual debtors with primarily consumer debts report this total also on the Statistical Summary of Certain Liabilities and Related Data.

☐ Check this box if debtor has no creditors holding unsecured priority claims to report on this Schedule E.

TYPES OF PRIORITY CLAIMS (Check the appropriate box (es) below if claims in that category are listed on the attached sheets.)

☐ **Domestic Support Obligations**

Claims for domestic support that are owed to or recoverable by a spouse, former spouse, or child of the debtor, or the parent, legal guardian, or responsible relative of such a child, or a governmental unit to whom such a domestic support claim has been assigned to the extent provided in 11 U.S.C. § 507(a)(1).

☐ **Extensions of credit in an involuntary case**

Claims arising in the ordinary course of the debtor's business or financial affairs after the commencement of the case but before the earlier of the appointment of a trustee or the order for relief. 11 U.S.C. § 507(a)(3).

☐ **Wages, salaries, and commissions**

Wages, salaries, and commissions, including vacation, severance, and sick leave pay owing to employees and commissions owing to qualifying independent sales representatives up to $12,475* per person earned within 180 days immediately preceding the filing of the original petition, or the cessation of business, whichever occurred first, to the extent provided in 11 U.S.C. § 507(a)(4).

☐ **Contributions to employee benefit plans**

Money owed to employee benefit plans for services rendered within 180 days immediately preceding the filing of the original petition, or the cessation of business, whichever occurred first, to the extent provided in 11 U.S.C. § 507(a)(5).

Amount subject to adjustment on 4/01/16, and every three years thereafter with respect to cases commenced on or after the date of adjustment.

B6E (Official Form 6E) (04/13) – Cont.

In re _____ ,   Case No. _____
                    Debtor   *(if known)*

☐ **Certain farmers and fishermen**

Claims of certain farmers and fishermen, up to $6,150* per farmer or fisherman, against the debtor, as provided in 11 U.S.C. § 507(a)(6).

☐ **Deposits by individuals**

Claims of individuals up to $2,775* for deposits for the purchase, lease, or rental of property or services for personal, family, or household use, that were not delivered or provided. 11 U.S.C. § 507(a)(7).

☐ **Taxes and Certain Other Debts Owed to Governmental Units**

Taxes, customs duties, and penalties owing to federal, state, and local governmental units as set forth in 11 U.S.C. § 507(a)(8).

☐ **Commitments to Maintain the Capital of an Insured Depository Institution**

Claims based on commitments to the FDIC, RTC, Director of the Office of Thrift Supervision, Comptroller of the Currency, or Board of Governors of the Federal Reserve System, or their predecessors or successors, to maintain the capital of an insured depository institution. 11 U.S.C. § 507 (a)(9).

☐ **Claims for Death or Personal Injury While Debtor Was Intoxicated**

Claims for death or personal injury resulting from the operation of a motor vehicle or vessel while the debtor was intoxicated from using alcohol, a drug, or another substance. 11 U.S.C. § 507(a)(10).

* Amounts are subject to adjustment on 4/01/16, and every three years thereafter with respect to cases commenced on or after the date of adjustment.*

_____ continuation sheets attached

B6E (Official Form 6E) (04/13) – Cont.

In re _____ ,   Case No. _____
              Debtor   *(if known)*

SCHEDULE E - CREDITORS HOLDING UNSECURED PRIORITY CLAIMS
(Continuation Sheet)

Type of Priority for Claims Listed on This Sheet

CREDITOR'S NAME, MAILING ADDRESS INCLUDING ZIP CODE, AND ACCOUNT NUMBER *(See instructions above.)*	CODEBTOR	HUSBAND, WIFE, JOINT, OR COMMUNITY	DATE CLAIM WAS INCURRED AND CONSIDERATION FOR CLAIM	CONTINGENT	UNLIQUIDATED	DISPUTED	AMOUNT OF CLAIM	AMOUNT ENTITLED TO PRIORITY	AMOUNT NOT ENTITLED TO PRIORITY, IF ANY
Account No.									
Account No.									
Account No.									
Account No.									

Sheet no. ___ of ___ continuation sheets attached to Schedule of Creditors Holding Priority Claims

Subtotals ▸
(Totals of this page) $ $

Total ▸
(Use only on last page of the completed Schedule E. Report also on the Summary of Schedules.) $

Totals ▸
(Use only on last page of the completed Schedule E. If applicable, report also on the Statistical Summary of Certain Liabilities and Related Data.) $ $

B 6F (Official Form 6F) (12/07)

In re _____ ,   Case No. _____
             Debtor   **(if known)**

SCHEDULE F - CREDITORS HOLDING UNSECURED NONPRIORITY CLAIMS

State the name, mailing address, including zip code, and last four digits of any account number, of all entities holding unsecured claims without priority against the debtor or the property of the debtor, as of the date of filing of the petition. The complete account number of any account the debtor has with the creditor is useful to the trustee and the creditor and may be provided if the debtor chooses to do so. If a minor child is a creditor, state the child's initials and the name and address of the child's parent or guardian, such as "A.B., a minor child, by John Doe, guardian." Do not disclose the child's name. See, 11 U.S.C. § 112 and Fed. R. Bankr. P. 1007(m). Do not include claims listed in Schedules D and E. If all creditors will not fit on this page, use the continuation sheet provided.

If any entity other than a spouse in a joint case may be jointly liable on a claim, place an "X" in the column labeled "Codebtor," include the entity on the appropriate schedule of creditors, and complete Schedule H - Codebtors. If a joint petition is filed, state whether the husband, wife, both of them, or the marital community may be liable on each claim by placing an "H," "W," "J," or "C" in the column labeled "Husband, Wife, Joint, or Community."

If the claim is contingent, place an "X" in the column labeled "Contingent." If the claim is unliquidated, place an "X" in the column labeled "Unliquidated." If the claim is disputed, place an "X" in the column labeled "Disputed." (You may need to place an "X" in more than one of these three columns.)

Report the total of all claims listed on this schedule in the box labeled "Total" on the last sheet of the completed schedule. Report this total also on the Summary of Schedules and, if the debtor is an individual with primarily consumer debts, report this total also on the Statistical Summary of Certain Liabilities and Related Data..

☐   Check this box if debtor has no creditors holding unsecured claims to report on this Schedule F.

CREDITOR'S NAME, MAILING ADDRESS INCLUDING ZIP CODE, AND ACCOUNT NUMBER *(See instructions above.)*	CODEBTOR	HUSBAND, WIFE, JOINT, OR COMMUNITY	DATE CLAIM WAS INCURRED AND CONSIDERATION FOR CLAIM. IF CLAIM IS SUBJECT TO SETOFF, SO STATE.	CONTINGENT	UNLIQUIDATED	DISPUTED	AMOUNT OF CLAIM
ACCOUNT NO.							
ACCOUNT NO.							
ACCOUNT NO.							
ACCOUNT NO.							
				Subtotal ➤			$

_____continuation sheets attached

Total ➤ $

(Use only on last page of the completed Schedule F.)
(Report also on Summary of Schedules and, if applicable, on the Statistical Summary of Certain Liabilities and Related Data.)

B 6F (Official Form 6F) (12/07) - Cont.

In re _____,   Case No. _____
                    Debtor   **(if known)**

SCHEDULE F - CREDITORS HOLDING UNSECURED NONPRIORITY CLAIMS
(Continuation Sheet)

CREDITOR'S NAME, MAILING ADDRESS INCLUDING ZIP CODE, AND ACCOUNT NUMBER (See instructions above.)	CODEBTOR	HUSBAND, WIFE, JOINT, OR COMMUNITY	DATE CLAIM WAS INCURRED AND CONSIDERATION FOR CLAIM. IF CLAIM IS SUBJECT TO SETOFF, SO STATE.	CONTINGENT	UNLIQUIDATED	DISPUTED	AMOUNT OF CLAIM
ACCOUNT NO.							
ACCOUNT NO.							
ACCOUNT NO.							
ACCOUNT NO.							
ACCOUNT NO.							

Sheet no._____ of_____ continuation sheets attached
to Schedule of Creditors Holding Unsecured
Nonpriority Claims

Subtotal ➤ | $

Total ➤ | $
(Use only on last page of the completed Schedule F.)
(Report also on Summary of Schedules and, if applicable on the Statistical
Summary of Certain Liabilities and Related Data.)

B 6G (Official Form 6G) (12/07)

In re_____,   Case No._____ Debtor
                                            (if known)

SCHEDULE G - EXECUTORY CONTRACTS AND UNEXPIRED LEASES

Describe all executory contracts of any nature and all unexpired leases of real or personal property. Include any timeshare interests. State nature of debtor's interest in contract, i.e., "Purchaser," "Agent," etc. State whether debtor is the lessor or lessee of a lease. Provide the names and complete mailing addresses of all other parties to each lease or contract described. If a minor child is a party to one of the leases or contracts, state the child's initials and the name and address of the child's parent or guardian, such as "A.B., a minor child, by John Doe, guardian." Do not disclose the child's name. See, 11 U.S.C. § 112 and Fed. R. Bankr. P. 1007(m).

☐ Check this box if debtor has no executory contracts or unexpired leases.

NAME AND MAILING ADDRESS, INCLUDING ZIP CODE, OF OTHER PARTIES TO LEASE OR CONTRACT.	DESCRIPTION OF CONTRACT OR LEASE AND NATURE OF DEBTOR'S INTEREST. STATE WHETHER LEASE IS FOR NONRESIDENTIAL REAL PROPERTY. STATE CONTRACT NUMBER OF ANY GOVERNMENT CONTRACT.

appendix J Official Form 6H Schedule H: Codebtors

B 6H (Official Form 6H) (12/07)

In re_____,   Case No. _____ Debtor

SCHEDULE H - CODEBTORS

Provide the information requested concerning any person or entity, other than a spouse in a joint case, that is also liable on any debts listed by the debtor in the schedules of creditors. Include all guarantors and co-signers. If the debtor resides or resided in a community property state, commonwealth, or territory (including Alaska, Arizona, California, Idaho, Louisiana, Nevada, New Mexico, Puerto Rico, Texas, Washington, or Wisconsin) within the eight-year period immediately preceding the commencement of the case, identify the name of the debtor's spouse and of any former spouse who resides or resided with the debtor in the community property state, commonwealth, or territory. Include all names used by the nondebtor spouse during the eight years immediately preceding the commencement of this case. If a minor child is a codebtor or a creditor, state the child's initials and the name and address of the child's parent or guardian, such as "A.B., a minor child, by John Doe, guardian." Do not disclose the child's name. See, 11 U.S.C. § 112 and Fed. R. Bankr. P. 1007(m).

☐ Check this box if debtor has no codebtors.

NAME AND ADDRESS OF CODEBTOR	NAME AND ADDRESS OF CREDITOR

Fill in this information to identify your case:

Debtor 1 _____
First Name   Middle Name   Last Name

Debtor 2 _____
(Spouse, if filing) First Name   Middle Name   Last Name

United States Bankruptcy Court for the: _____ District of _____

Case number _____
(If known)

Check if this is:

☐ An amended filing

☐ A supplement showing post-petition
chapter 13 income as of the following date:
_____
MM / DD / YYYY

Official Form B 6I

Schedule I: Your Income

12/13

Be as complete and accurate as possible. If two married people are filing together (Debtor 1 and Debtor 2), both are equally responsible for supplying correct information. If you are married and not filing jointly, and your spouse is living with you, include information about your spouse. If you are separated and your spouse is not filing with you, do not include information about your spouse. If more space is needed, attach a separate sheet to this form. On the top of any additional pages, write your name and case number (if known). Answer every question.

Part 1:	Describe Employment

1. **Fill in your employment information.**

   If you have more than one job, attach a separate page with information about additional employers.

   Include part-time, seasonal, or self-employed work.

   Occupation may Include student or homemaker, if it applies.

	Debtor 1	Debtor 2 or non-filing spouse
Employment status	☐ Employed ☐ Not employed	☐ Employed ☐ Not employed
Occupation	_____	_____
Employer's name	_____	_____
Employer's address	_____ Number Street	_____ Number Street
	_____	_____
	_____ City State ZIP Code	_____ City State ZIP Code
How long employed there?	_____	_____

Part 2:	Give Details About Monthly Income

Estimate monthly income as of the date you file this form. If you have nothing to report for any line, write $0 in the space. Include your non-filing spouse unless you are separated.

If you or your non-filing spouse have more than one employer, combine the information for all employers for that person on the lines below. If you need more space, attach a separate sheet to this form.

	For Debtor 1	**For Debtor 2 or non-filing spouse**
2. **List monthly gross wages, salary, and commissions** (before all payroll deductions). If not paid monthly, calculate what the monthly wage would be.	2. $_____	$_____
3. **Estimate and list monthly overtime pay.**	3. + $_____	+ $_____
4. **Calculate gross income.** Add line 2 + line 3.	4. $_____	$_____

Debtor 1 _____   Case number (*if known*)_____
          First Name   Middle Name   Last Name

	For Debtor 1	For Debtor 2 or non-filing spouse
Copy line 4 here .... → 4.	$_____	$_____

5. **List all payroll deductions:**

		For Debtor 1	For Debtor 2 or non-filing spouse
5a. **Tax, Medicare, and Social Security deductions**	5a.	$_____	$_____
5b. **Mandatory contributions for retirement plans**	5b.	$_____	$_____
5c. **Voluntary contributions for retirement plans**	5c.	$_____	$_____
5d. **Required repayments of retirement fund loans**	5d.	$_____	$_____
5e. **Insurance**	5e.	$_____	$_____
5f. **Domestic support obligations**	5f.	$_____	$_____
5g. **Union dues**	5g.	$_____	$_____
5h. **Other deductions.** Specify: _____	5h.	+ $_____	+ $_____

6. **Add the payroll deductions.** Add lines 5a + 5b + 5c + 5d + 5e +5f + 5g +5h.   6. $_____ $_____

7. **Calculate total monthly take-home pay.** Subtract line 6 from line 4.   7. $_____ $_____

8. **List all other income regularly received:**

8a. **Net income from rental property and from operating a business, profession, or farm**

Attach a statement for each property and business showing gross receipts, ordinary and necessary business expenses, and the total monthly net income.   8a. $_____ $_____

8b. **Interest and dividends**   8b. $_____ $_____

8c. **Family support payments that you, a non-filing spouse, or a dependent regularly receive**

Include alimony, spousal support, child support, maintenance, divorce settlement, and property settlement.   8c. $_____ $_____

8d. **Unemployment compensation**   8d. $_____ $_____

8e. **Social Security**   8e. $_____ $_____

8f. **Other government assistance that you regularly receive**

Include cash assistance and the value (if known) of any non-cash assistance that you receive, such as food stamps (benefits under the Supplemental Nutrition Assistance Program) or housing subsidies.
Specify: _____   8f. $_____ $_____

8g. **Pension or retirement income**   8g. $_____ $_____

8h. **Other monthly income.** Specify: _____   8h.   + $_____   + $_____

9. **Add all other income.** Add lines 8a + 8b + 8c + 8d + 8e + 8f +8g + 8h.   9. $_____ $_____

10. **Calculate monthly income.** Add line 7 + line 9.
Add the entries in line 10 for Debtor 1 and Debtor 2 or non-filing spouse.   10. $_____ + $_____ = $_____

11. **State all other regular contributions to the expenses that you list in *Schedule J*.**

Include contributions from an unmarried partner, members of your household, your dependents, your roommates, and other friends or relatives.

Do not include any amounts already included in lines 2-10 or amounts that are not available to pay expenses listed in *Schedule J*.

Specify: _____   11.   + $_____

12. **Add the amount in the last column of line 10 to the amount in line 11.** The result is the combined monthly income.
Write that amount on the *Summary of Schedules* and *Statistical Summary of Certain Liabilities and Related Data*, if it applies   12. $_____

Combined monthly income

13. **Do you expect an increase or decrease within the year after you file this form?**

☐ No.

☐ Yes. Explain: _____

Fill in this information to identify your case:

Debtor 1 _____
First Name   Middle Name   Last Name

Debtor 2 _____
(Spouse, if filing) First Name   Middle Name   Last Name

United States Bankruptcy Court for the: _____ District of _____

Case number _____
(If known)

Check if this is:

☐ An amended filing

☐ A supplement showing post-petition chapter 13 expenses as of the following date:

_____
MM / DD / YYYY

☐ A separate filing for Debtor 2 because Debtor 2 maintains a separate household

Official Form B 6J

Schedule J: Your Expenses

12/13

Be as complete and accurate as possible. If two married people are filing together, both are equally responsible for supplying correct information. If more space is needed, attach another sheet to this form. On the top of any additional pages, write your name and case number (if known). Answer every question.

Part 1:   Describe Your Household

1. **Is this a joint case?**

   ☐ No. Go to line 2.
   ☐ Yes. **Does Debtor 2 live in a separate household?**

      ☐ No
      ☐ Yes. Debtor 2 must file a separate Schedule J.

2. **Do you have dependents?**

   Do not list Debtor 1 and Debtor 2.

   Do not state the dependents' names.

   ☐ No
   ☐ Yes. Fill out this information for each dependent..........................

Dependent's relationship to Debtor 1 or Debtor 2	Dependent's age	Does dependent live with you?
_____	_____	☐ No ☐ Yes
_____	_____	☐ No ☐ Yes
_____	_____	☐ No ☐ Yes
_____	_____	☐ No ☐ Yes
_____	_____	☐ No ☐ Yes

3. **Do your expenses include expenses of people other than yourself and your dependents?**

   ☐ No
   ☐ Yes

Part 2:   Estimate Your Ongoing Monthly Expenses

Estimate your expenses as of your bankruptcy filing date unless you are using this form as a supplement in a Chapter 13 case to report expenses as of a date after the bankruptcy is filed. If this is a supplemental *Schedule J*, check the box at the top of the form and fill in the applicable date.

Include expenses paid for with non-cash government assistance if you know the value of such assistance and have included it on *Schedule I: Your Income* (Official Form B 6I.)

Your expenses

4. **The rental or home ownership expenses for your residence.** Include first mortgage payments and any rent for the ground or lot.   4. $_____

   If not included in line 4:

   4a.   Real estate taxes   4a. $_____

   4b.   Property, homeowner's, or renter's insurance   4b. $_____

   4c.   Home maintenance, repair, and upkeep expenses   4c. $_____

   4d.   Homeowner's association or condominium dues   4d. $_____

Debtor 1 _____   Case number *(if known)* _____
     First Name   Middle Name   Last Name

		Your expenses

5. **Additional mortgage payments for your residence**, such as home equity loans   5. $_____

6. **Utilities:**

  6a. Electricity, heat, natural gas   6a. $_____

  6b. Water, sewer, garbage collection   6b. $_____

  6c. Telephone, cell phone, Internet, satellite, and cable services   6c. $_____

  6d. Other. Specify: _____   6d. $_____

7. **Food and housekeeping supplies**   7. $_____

8. **Childcare and children's education costs**   8. $_____

9. **Clothing, laundry, and dry cleaning**   9. $_____

10. **Personal care products and services**   10. $_____

11. **Medical and dental expenses**   11. $_____

12. **Transportation.** Include gas, maintenance, bus or train fare.
    Do not include car payments.   12 $_____

13. **Entertainment, clubs, recreation, newspapers, magazines, and books**   13. $_____

14. **Charitable contributions and religious donations**   14. $_____

15. **Insurance.**
    Do not include insurance deducted from your pay or included in lines 4 or 20.

  15a. Life insurance   15a $_____

  15b. Health insurance   15b $_____

  15c. Vehicle insurance   15c $_____

  15d. Other insurance. Specify:_____   15d $_____

16. **Taxes.** Do not include taxes deducted from your pay or included in lines 4 or 20.
    Specify: _____   16 $_____

17. **Installment or lease payments:**

  17a. Car payments for Vehicle 1   17a. $_____

  17b. Car payments for Vehicle 2   17b $_____

  17c. Other. Specify:_____   17c $_____

  17d. Other. Specify:_____   17d $_____

18. **Your payments of alimony, maintenance, and support that you did not report as deducted
    from your pay on line 5, *Schedule I, Your Income* (Official Form B 6I).**   18 $_____

19. **Other payments you make to support others who do not live with you.**
    Specify:_____   19 $_____

20. **Other real property expenses not included in lines 4 or 5 of this form or on *Schedule I: Your Income*.**

  20a. Mortgages on other property   20a. $_____

  20b. Real estate taxes   20b $_____

  20c. Property, homeowner's, or renter's insurance   20c $_____

  20d. Maintenance, repair, and upkeep expenses   20d $_____

  20e. Homeowner's association or condominium dues   20e $_____

Debtor 1 _____   Case number *(if known)*_____

First Name   Middle Name   Last Name

---

21. **Other**. Specify: _____   21.   +$_____

22. **Your monthly expenses.** Add lines 4 through 21.
    The result is your monthly expenses.   22. $_____

23. **Calculate your monthly net income.**

    23a.   Copy line 12 (*your combined monthly income*) from *Schedule I.*   23a. $_____

    23b.   Copy your monthly expenses from line 22 above.   23b.   – $_____

    23c.   Subtract your monthly expenses from your monthly income.
    The result is your *monthly net income.*   23c. $_____

24. **Do you expect an increase or decrease in your expenses within the year after you file this form?**

    For example, do you expect to finish paying for your car loan within the year or do you expect your
    mortgage payment to increase or decrease because of a modification to the terms of your mortgage?

    ☐ No.
    ☐ Yes.   Explain here:

B6 Declaration (Official Form 6 - Declaration) (12/07)

In re _____,   Case No. _____
           Debtor   if known)

DECLARATION CONCERNING DEBTOR'S SCHEDULES

DECLARATION UNDER PENALTY OF PERJURY BY INDIVIDUAL DEBTOR

    I declare under penalty of perjury that I have read the foregoing summary and schedules, consisting of _____ sheets, and that they are true and correct to the best of my knowledge, information, and belief.

Date _____   Signature: _____
                                                                    Debtor

Date _____   Signature: _____
                                                              (Joint Debtor, if any)

                                      [If joint case, both spouses must sign.]

DECLARATION AND SIGNATURE OF NON-ATTORNEY BANKRUPTCY PETITION PREPARER (See 11 U.S.C. § 110)

    I declare under penalty of perjury that: (1) I am a bankruptcy petition preparer as defined in 11 U.S.C. § 110; (2) I prepared this document for compensation and have provided the debtor with a copy of this document and the notices and information required under 11 U.S.C. §§ 110(b), 110(h) and 342(b); and, (3) if rules or guidelines have been promulgated pursuant to 11 U.S.C. § 110(h) setting a maximum fee for services chargeable by bankruptcy petition preparers, I have given the debtor notice of the maximum amount before preparing any document for filing for a debtor or accepting any fee from the debtor, as required by that section.

_____   _____
Printed or Typed Name and Title, if any,   Social Security No.
of Bankruptcy Petition Preparer   *(Required by 11 U.S.C. § 110.)*

If the bankruptcy petition preparer is not an individual, state the name, title (if any), address, and social security number of the officer, principal, responsible person, or partner who signs this document.

_____
_____
_____
Address

X_____   _____
Signature of Bankruptcy Petition Preparer   Date

Names and Social Security numbers of all other individuals who prepared or assisted in preparing this document, unless the bankruptcy petition preparer is not an individual:

If more than one person prepared this document, attach additional signed sheets conforming to the appropriate Official Form for each person.

A bankruptcy petition preparer's failure to comply with the provisions of title 11 and the Federal Rules of Bankruptcy Procedure may result in fines or imprisonment or both. 11 U.S.C. § 110; 18 U.S.C. § 156.

DECLARATION UNDER PENALTY OF PERJURY ON BEHALF OF A CORPORATION OR PARTNERSHIP

    I, the _____ [the president or other officer or an authorized agent of the corporation or a member or an authorized agent of the partnership] of the _____ [corporation or partnership] named as debtor in this case, declare under penalty of perjury that I have read the foregoing summary and schedules, consisting of _____ sheets (*Total shown on summary page plus 1*), and that they are true and correct to the best of my knowledge, information, and belief.

Date _____

                                     Signature: _____

                                         [Print or type name of individual signing on behalf of debtor.]

[An individual signing on behalf of a partnership or corporation must indicate position or relationship to debtor.]

Penalty for making a false statement or concealing property: Fine of up to $500,000 or imprisonment for up to 5 years or both. 18 U.S.C. §§ 152 and 3571.

B7 (Official Form 7) (04/13)

UNITED STATES BANKRUPTCY COURT

In re:_____,   Case No. _____
         Debtor   (if known)

STATEMENT OF FINANCIAL AFFAIRS

This statement is to be completed by every debtor. Spouses filing a joint petition may file a single statement on which the information for both spouses is combined. If the case is filed under chapter 12 or chapter 13, a married debtor must furnish information for both spouses whether or not a joint petition is filed, unless the spouses are separated and a joint petition is not filed. An individual debtor engaged in business as a sole proprietor, partner, family farmer, or self-employed professional, should provide the information requested on this statement concerning all such activities as well as the individual's personal affairs. To indicate payments, transfers and the like to minor children, state the child's initials and the name and address of the child's parent or guardian, such as "A.B., a minor child, by John Doe, guardian." Do not disclose the child's name. See, 11 U.S.C. § 112 and Fed. R. Bankr. P. 1007(m).

Questions 1 - 18 are to be completed by all debtors. Debtors that are or have been in business, as defined below, also must complete Questions 19 - 25. **If the answer to an applicable question is "None," mark the box labeled "None."** If additional space is needed for the answer to any question, use and attach a separate sheet properly identified with the case name, case number (if known), and the number of the question.

DEFINITIONS

"In business." A debtor is "in business" for the purpose of this form if the debtor is a corporation or partnership. An individual debtor is "in business" for the purpose of this form if the debtor is or has been, within six years immediately preceding the filing of this bankruptcy case, any of the following: an officer, director, managing executive, or owner of 5 percent or more of the voting or equity securities of a corporation; a partner, other than a limited partner, of a partnership; a sole proprietor or self-employed full-time or part-time. An individual debtor also may be "in business" for the purpose of this form if the debtor engages in a trade, business, or other activity, other than as an employee, to supplement income from the debtor's primary employment.

"Insider." The term "insider" includes but is not limited to: relatives of the debtor; general partners of the debtor and their relatives; corporations of which the debtor is an officer, director, or person in control; officers, directors, and any persons in control of a corporate debtor and their relatives; affiliates of the debtor and insiders of such affiliates; and any managing agent of the debtor. 11 U.S.C. § 101(2), (31).

---

1. **Income from employment or operation of business**

None
☐   State the gross amount of income the debtor has received from employment, trade, or profession, or from operation of the debtor's business, including part-time activities either as an employee or in independent trade or business, from the beginning of this calendar year to the date this case was commenced. State also the gross amounts received during the **two years** immediately preceding this calendar year. (A debtor that maintains, or has maintained, financial records on the basis of a fiscal rather than a calendar year may report fiscal year income. Identify the beginning and ending dates of the debtor's fiscal year.) If a joint petition is filed, state income for each spouse separately. (Married debtors filing under chapter 12 or chapter 13 must state income of both spouses whether or not a joint petition is filed, unless the spouses are separated and a joint petition is not filed.)

AMOUNT   SOURCE

2.   Income other than from employment or operation of business

None
☐

State the amount of income received by the debtor other than from employment, trade, profession, operation of the debtor's business during the **two years** immediately preceding the commencement of this case. Give particulars. If a joint petition is filed, state income for each spouse separately. (Married debtors filing under chapter 12 or chapter 13 must state income for each spouse whether or not a joint petition is filed, unless the spouses are separated and a joint petition is not filed.)

AMOUNT   SOURCE

---

3.   Payments to creditors

Complete a. or b., as appropriate, and c.

None
☐

a. *Individual or joint debtor(s) with primarily consumer debts:* List all payments on loans, installment purchases of goods or services, and other debts to any creditor made within **90 days** immediately preceding the commencement of this case unless the aggregate value of all property that constitutes or is affected by such transfer is less than $600. Indicate with an asterisk (*) any payments that were made to a creditor on account of a domestic support obligation or as part of an alternative repayment schedule under a plan by an approved nonprofit budgeting and credit counseling agency. (Married debtors filing under chapter 12 or chapter 13 must include payments by either or both spouses whether or not a joint petition is filed, unless the spouses are separated and a joint petition is not filed.)

NAME AND ADDRESS OF CREDITOR	DATES OF PAYMENTS	AMOUNT PAID	AMOUNT STILL OWING

None
☐

b. *Debtor whose debts are not primarily consumer debts: List each payment or other transfer to any creditor made within **90 days** immediately preceding the commencement of the case unless the aggregate value of all property that constitutes or is affected by such transfer is less than $6,225*. If the debtor is an individual, indicate with an asterisk (*) any payments that were made to a creditor on account of a domestic support obligation or as part of an alternative repayment schedule under a plan by an approved nonprofit budgeting and credit counseling agency. (Married debtors filing under chapter 12 or chapter 13 must include payments and other transfers by either or both spouses whether or not a joint petition is filed, unless the spouses are separated and a joint petition is not filed.)*

NAME AND ADDRESS OF CREDITOR	DATES OF PAYMENTS/ TRANSFERS	AMOUNT PAID OR VALUE OF TRANSFERS	AMOUNT STILL OWING

---

*Amount subject to adjustment on 4/01/16, and every three years thereafter with respect to cases commenced on or after the date of adjustment.

None ☐

c. *All debtors:* List all payments made within **one year** immediately preceding the commencement of this case to or for the benefit of creditors who are or were insiders. (Married debtors filing under chapter 12 or chapter 13 must include payments by either or both spouses whether or not a joint petition is filed, unless the spouses are separated and a joint petition is not filed.)

NAME AND ADDRESS OF CREDITOR AND RELATIONSHIP TO DEBTOR	DATE OF PAYMENT	AMOUNT PAID	AMOUNT STILL OWING

---

4. Suits and administrative proceedings, executions, garnishments and attachments

None ☐

a. List all suits and administrative proceedings to which the debtor is or was a party within **one year** immediately preceding the filing of this bankruptcy case. (Married debtors filing under chapter 12 or chapter 13 must include information concerning either or both spouses whether or not a joint petition is filed, unless the spouses are separated and a joint petition is not filed.)

CAPTION OF SUIT AND CASE NUMBER	NATURE OF PROCEEDING	COURT OR AGENCY AND LOCATION	STATUS OR DISPOSITION

None ☐

b. Describe all property that has been attached, garnished or seized under any legal or equitable process within **one year** immediately preceding the commencement of this case. (Married debtors filing under chapter 12 or chapter 13 must include information concerning property of either or both spouses whether or not a joint petition is filed, unless the spouses are separated and a joint petition is not filed.)

NAME AND ADDRESS OF PERSON FOR WHOSE BENEFIT PROPERTY WAS SEIZED	DATE OF SEIZURE	DESCRIPTION AND VALUE OF PROPERTY

---

5. Repossessions, foreclosures and returns

None ☐

List all property that has been repossessed by a creditor, sold at a foreclosure sale, transferred through a deed in lieu of foreclosure or returned to the seller, within **one year** immediately preceding the commencement of this case. (Married debtors filing under chapter 12 or chapter 13 must include information concerning property of either or both spouses whether or not a joint petition is filed, unless the spouses are separated and a joint petition is not filed.)

NAME AND ADDRESS OF CREDITOR OR SELLER	DATE OF REPOSSESSION, FORECLOSURE SALE, TRANSFER OR RETURN	DESCRIPTION AND VALUE OF PROPERTY

6.   Assignments and receiverships

None
☐

a. Describe any assignment of property for the benefit of creditors made within **120 days** immediately preceding the commencement of this case. (Married debtors filing under chapter 12 or chapter 13 must include any assignment by either or both spouses whether or not a joint petition is filed, unless the spouses are separated and a joint petition is not filed.)

NAME AND ADDRESS OF ASSIGNEE	DATE OF ASSIGNMENT	TERMS OF ASSIGNMENT OR SETTLEMENT

None
☐

b. List all property which has been in the hands of a custodian, receiver, or court-appointed official within **one year** immediately preceding the commencement of this case. (Married debtors filing under chapter 12 or chapter 13 must include information concerning property of either or both spouses whether or not a joint petition is filed, unless the spouses are separated and a joint petition is not filed.)

NAME AND ADDRESS OF CUSTODIAN	NAME AND LOCATION OF COURT CASE TITLE & NUMBER	DATE OF ORDER	DESCRIPTION AND VALUE Of PROPERTY

7.   Gifts

None
☐

List all gifts or charitable contributions made within **one year** immediately preceding the commencement of this case except ordinary and usual gifts to family members aggregating less than $200 in value per individual family member and charitable contributions aggregating less than $100 per recipient. (Married debtors filing under chapter 12 or chapter 13 must include gifts or contributions by either or both spouses whether or not a joint petition is filed, unless the spouses are separated and a joint petition is not filed.)

NAME AND ADDRESS OF PERSON OR ORGANIZATION	RELATIONSHIP TO DEBTOR, IF ANY	DATE OF GIFT	DESCRIPTION AND VALUE OF GIFT

8.   Losses

None
☐

List all losses from fire, theft, other casualty or gambling within **one year** immediately preceding the commencement of this case **or since the commencement of this case**. (Married debtors filing under chapter 12 or chapter 13 must include losses by either or both spouses whether or not a joint petition is filed, unless the spouses are separated and a joint petition is not filed.)

DESCRIPTION AND VALUE OF PROPERTY	DESCRIPTION OF CIRCUMSTANCES AND, IF LOSS WAS COVERED IN WHOLE OR IN PART BY INSURANCE, GIVE PARTICULARS	DATE OF LOSS

9. Payments related to debt counseling or bankruptcy

None   □

List all payments made or property transferred by or on behalf of the debtor to any persons, including attorneys, for consultation concerning debt consolidation, relief under the bankruptcy law or preparation of a petition in bankruptcy within **one year** immediately preceding the commencement of this case.

NAME AND ADDRESS OF PAYEE	DATE OF PAYMENT, NAME OF PAYER IF OTHER THAN DEBTOR	AMOUNT OF MONEY OR DESCRIPTION AND VALUE OF PROPERTY

10. Other transfers

None   □

a. List all other property, other than property transferred in the ordinary course of the business or financial affairs of the debtor, transferred either absolutely or as security within **two years** immediately preceding the commencement of this case. (Married debtors filing under chapter 12 or chapter 13 must include transfers by either or both spouses whether or not a joint petition is filed, unless the spouses are separated and a joint petition is not filed.)

NAME AND ADDRESS OF TRANSFEREE, RELATIONSHIP TO DEBTOR	DATE	DESCRIBE PROPERTY TRANSFERRED AND VALUE RECEIVED

None   □

b. List all property transferred by the debtor within **ten years** immediately preceding the commencement of this case to a self-settled trust or similar device of which the debtor is a beneficiary.

NAME OF TRUST OR OTHER DEVICE	DATE(S) OF TRANSFER(S)	AMOUNT OF MONEY OR DESCRIPTION AND VALUE OF PROPERTY OR DEBTOR'S INTEREST IN PROPERTY

11. Closed financial accounts

None   □

List all financial accounts and instruments held in the name of the debtor or for the benefit of the debtor which were closed, sold, or otherwise transferred within **one year** immediately preceding the commencement of this case. Include checking, savings, or other financial accounts, certificates of deposit, or other instruments; shares and share accounts held in banks, credit unions, pension funds, cooperatives, associations, brokerage houses and other financial institutions. (Married debtors filing under chapter 12 or chapter 13 must include information concerning accounts or instruments held by or for either or both spouses whether or not a joint petition is filed, unless the spouses are separated and a joint petition is not filed.)

NAME AND ADDRESS OF INSTITUTION	TYPE OF ACCOUNT, LAST FOUR DIGITS OF ACCOUNT NUMBER, AND AMOUNT OF FINAL BALANCE	AMOUNT AND DATE OF SALE OR CLOSING

12. Safe deposit boxes

None
☐

List each safe deposit or other box or depository in which the debtor has or had securities, cash, or other valuables within **one year** immediately preceding the commencement of this case. (Married debtors filing under chapter 12 or chapter 13 must include boxes or depositories of either or both spouses whether or not a joint petition is filed, unless the spouses are separated and a joint petition is not filed.)

NAME AND ADDRESS OF BANK OR OTHER DEPOSITORY	NAMES AND ADDRESSES OF THOSE WITH ACCESS TO BOX OR DEPOSITORY	DESCRIPTION OF CONTENTS	DATE OF TRANSFER OR SURRENDER, IF ANY

13. Setoffs

None
☐

List all setoffs made by any creditor, including a bank, against a debt or deposit of the debtor within **90 days** preceding the commencement of this case. (Married debtors filing under chapter 12 or chapter 13 must include information concerning either or both spouses whether or not a joint petition is filed, unless the spouses are separated and a joint petition is not filed.)

NAME AND ADDRESS OF CREDITOR	DATE OF SETOFF	AMOUNT OF SETOFF

14. Property held for another person

None
☐

List all property owned by another person that the debtor holds or controls.

NAME AND ADDRESS OF OWNER	DESCRIPTION AND VALUE OF PROPERTY	LOCATION OF PROPERTY

15. Prior address of debtor

None
☐

If debtor has moved within **three years** immediately preceding the commencement of this case, list all premises which the debtor occupied during that period and vacated prior to the commencement of this case. If a joint petition is filed, report also any separate address of either spouse.

ADDRESS	NAME USED	DATES OF OCCUPANCY

16. Spouses and Former Spouses

None

☐ If the debtor resides or resided in a community property state, commonwealth, or territory (including Alaska, Arizona, California, Idaho, Louisiana, Nevada, New Mexico, Puerto Rico, Texas, Washington, or Wisconsin) within **eight years** immediately preceding the commencement of the case, identify the name of the debtor's spouse and of any former spouse who resides or resided with the debtor in the community property state.

NAME

---

17. Environmental Information.

For the purpose of this question, the following definitions apply:

"Environmental Law" means any federal, state, or local statute or regulation regulating pollution, contamination, releases of hazardous or toxic substances, wastes or material into the air, land, soil, surface water, groundwater, or other medium, including, but not limited to, statutes or regulations regulating the cleanup of these substances, wastes, or material.

"Site" means any location, facility, or property as defined under any Environmental Law, whether or not presently or formerly owned or operated by the debtor, including, but not limited to, disposal sites.

"Hazardous Material" means anything defined as a hazardous waste, hazardous substance, toxic substance, hazardous material, pollutant, or contaminant or similar term under an Environmental Law.

None

☐ a. List the name and address of every site for which the debtor has received notice in writing by a governmental unit that it may be liable or potentially liable under or in violation of an Environmental Law. Indicate the governmental unit, the date of the notice, and, if known, the Environmental Law:

SITE NAME AND ADDRESS	NAME AND ADDRESS OF GOVERNMENTAL UNIT	DATE OF NOTICE	ENVIRONMENTAL LAW

None

☐ b. List the name and address of every site for which the debtor provided notice to a governmental unit of a release of Hazardous Material. Indicate the governmental unit to which the notice was sent and the date of the notice.

SITE NAME AND ADDRESS	NAME AND ADDRESS OF GOVERNMENTAL UNIT	DATE OF NOTICE	ENVIRONMENTAL LAW

None

☐ c. List all judicial or administrative proceedings, including settlements or orders, under any Environmental Law with respect to which the debtor is or was a party. Indicate the name and address of the governmental unit that is or was a party to the proceeding, and the docket number.

NAME AND ADDRESS OF GOVERNMENTAL UNIT	DOCKET NUMBER	STATUS OR DISPOSITION

---

18 . Nature, location and name of business

None

☐ a. *If the debtor is an individual*, list the names, addresses, taxpayer-identification numbers, nature of the businesses, and beginning and ending dates of all businesses in which the debtor was an officer, director, partner, or managing executive of a corporation, partner in a partnership, sole proprietor, or was self-employed in a trade, profession, or other activity either full- or part-time within **six years** immediately preceding the commencement of this case, or in which the debtor owned 5 percent or more of the voting or equity securities within **six years** immediately preceding the commencement of this case.

If the debtor is a partnership, list the names, addresses, taxpayer-identification numbers, nature of the businesses, and beginning and ending dates of all businesses in which the debtor was a partner or owned 5 percent or more of the voting or equity securities, within **six years** immediately preceding the commencement of this case.

If the debtor is a corporation, list the names, addresses, taxpayer-identification numbers, nature of the businesses, and beginning and ending dates of all businesses in which the debtor was a partner or owned 5 percent or more of the voting or equity securities within **six years** immediately preceding the commencement of this case.

NAME	LAST FOUR DIGITS OF SOCIAL-SECURITY OR OTHER INDIVIDUAL TAXPAYER-I.D. NO. (ITIN)/ COMPLETE EIN	ADDRESS	NATURE OF BUSINESS	BEGINNING AND ENDING DATES

None ☐

b. Identify any business listed in response to subdivision a., above, that is "single asset real estate" as defined in 11 U.S.C. § 101.

NAME	ADDRESS

The following questions are to be completed by every debtor that is a corporation or partnership and by any individual debtor who is or has been, within **six years** immediately preceding the commencement of this case, any of the following: an officer, director, managing executive, or owner of more than 5 percent of the voting or equity securities of a corporation; a partner, other than a limited partner, of a partnership, a sole proprietor, or self-employed in a trade, profession, or other activity, either full- or part-time.

*(An individual or joint debtor should complete this portion of the statement **only** if the debtor is or has been in business, as defined above, within six years immediately preceding the commencement of this case. A debtor who has not been in business within those six years should go directly to the signature page.)*

---

19. Books, records and financial statements

None ☐

a. List all bookkeepers and accountants who within **two years** immediately preceding the filing of this bankruptcy case kept or supervised the keeping of books of account and records of the debtor.

NAME AND ADDRESS	DATES SERVICES RENDERED

None ☐

b. List all firms or individuals who within **two years** immediately preceding the filing of this bankruptcy case have audited the books of account and records, or prepared a financial statement of the debtor.

NAME	ADDRESS	DATES SERVICES RENDERED

None ☐   c. List all firms or individuals who at the time of the commencement of this case were in possession of the books of account and records of the debtor. If any of the books of account and records are not available, explain.

NAME   ADDRESS

None ☐   d. List all financial institutions, creditors and other parties, including mercantile and trade agencies, to whom a financial statement was issued by the debtor within **two years** immediately preceding the commencement of this case.

NAME AND ADDRESS   DATE ISSUED

---

20. Inventories

None ☐   a. List the dates of the last two inventories taken of your property, the name of the person who supervised the taking of each inventory, and the dollar amount and basis of each inventory.

DATE OF INVENTORY   INVENTORY SUPERVISOR   DOLLAR AMOUNT
OF INVENTORY
(Specify cost, market or other basis)

None ☐   b. List the name and address of the person having possession of the records of each of the inventories reported in a., above.

DATE OF INVENTORY   NAME AND ADDRESSES
OF CUSTODIAN
OF INVENTORY RECORDS

---

21. Current Partners, Officers, Directors and Shareholders

None ☐   a. If the debtor is a partnership, list the nature and percentage of partnership interest of each member of the partnership.

NAME AND ADDRESS   NATURE OF INTEREST   PERCENTAGE OF INTEREST

None ☐   b. If the debtor is a corporation, list all officers and directors of the corporation, and each stockholder who directly or indirectly owns, controls, or holds 5 percent or more of the voting or equity securities of the corporation.

                                   NATURE AND PERCENTAGE
NAME AND ADDRESS   TITLE   OF STOCK OWNERSHIP

B7 (Official Form 7) (04/13)   10

22 . Former partners, officers, directors and shareholders

None   a.   If the debtor is a partnership, list each member who withdrew from the partnership within **one year** immediately
☐   preceding the commencement of this case.

NAME	ADDRESS	DATE OF WITHDRAWAL

None   b.   If the debtor is a corporation, list all officers or directors whose relationship with the corporation terminated
☐   within **one year** immediately preceding the commencement of this case.

NAME AND ADDRESS	TITLE	DATE OF TERMINATION

---

23 . Withdrawals from a partnership or distributions by a corporation

None   If the debtor is a partnership or corporation, list all withdrawals or distributions credited or given to an insider,
☐   including compensation in any form, bonuses, loans, stock redemptions, options exercised and any other perquisite
           during **one year** immediately preceding the commencement of this case.

NAME & ADDRESS OF RECIPIENT, RELATIONSHIP TO DEBTOR	DATE AND PURPOSE OF WITHDRAWAL	AMOUNT OF MONEY OR DESCRIPTION AND VALUE OF PROPERTY

---

24. Tax Consolidation Group.

None   If the debtor is a corporation, list the name and federal taxpayer-identification number of the parent corporation of any
☐   consolidated group for tax purposes of which the debtor has been a member at any time within **six years**
           immediately preceding the commencement of the case.

NAME OF PARENT CORPORATION	TAXPAYER-IDENTIFICATION NUMBER (EIN)

---

25. Pension Funds.

None   If the debtor is not an individual, list the name and federal taxpayer-identification number of any pension fund to
☐   which the debtor, as an employer, has been responsible for contributing at any time within **six years** immediately
           preceding the commencement of the case.

NAME OF PENSION FUND	TAXPAYER-IDENTIFICATION NUMBER (EIN)

* * * * * *

[If completed by an individual or individual and spouse]

I declare under penalty of perjury that I have read the answers contained in the foregoing statement of financial affairs and any attachments thereto and that they are true and correct.

Date _____   Signature of Debtor _____

Date _____   Signature of Joint Debtor (if any) _____

_____

[If completed on behalf of a partnership or corporation]

I declare under penalty of perjury that I have read the answers contained in the foregoing statement of financial affairs and any attachments thereto and that they are true and correct to the best of my knowledge, information and belief.

Date _____   Signature _____

Print Name and Title _____

[An individual signing on behalf of a partnership or corporation must indicate position or relationship to debtor.]

____continuation sheets attached

Penalty for making a false statement: Fine of up to $500,000 or imprisonment for up to 5 years, or both. 18 U.S.C. §§ 152 and 3571

DECLARATION AND SIGNATURE OF NON-ATTORNEY BANKRUPTCY PETITION PREPARER (See 11 U.S.C. § 110)

I declare under penalty of perjury that: (1) I am a bankruptcy petition preparer as defined in 11 U.S.C. § 110; (2) I prepared this document for compensation and have provided the debtor with a copy of this document and the notices and information required under 11 U.S.C. §§ 110(b), 110(h), and 342(b); and, (3) if rules or guidelines have been promulgated pursuant to 11 U.S.C. § 110(h) setting a maximum fee for services chargeable by bankruptcy petition preparers, I have given the debtor notice of the maximum amount before preparing any document for filing for a debtor or accepting any fee from the debtor, as required by that section.

_____   _____
Printed or Typed Name and Title, if any, of Bankruptcy Petition Preparer   Social-Security No. (Required by 11 U.S.C. § 110.)

If the bankruptcy petition preparer is not an individual, state the name, title (if any), address, and social-security number of the officer, principal, responsible person, or partner who signs this document.

_____
Address

_____   _____
Signature of Bankruptcy Petition Preparer   Date

Names and Social-Security numbers of all other individuals who prepared or assisted in preparing this document unless the bankruptcy petition preparer is not an individual:

If more than one person prepared this document, attach additional signed sheets conforming to the appropriate Official Form for each person

A bankruptcy petition preparer's failure to comply with the provisions of title 11 and the Federal Rules of Bankruptcy Procedure may result in fines or imprisonment or both. 18 U.S.C. § 156.

B 203
(12/94)

United States Bankruptcy Court

_____ District Of _____

In re

Case No. _____

Debtor

Chapter _____

DISCLOSURE OF COMPENSATION OF ATTORNEY FOR DEBTOR

1. Pursuant to 11 U.S.C. § 329(a) and Fed. Bankr. P. 2016(b), I certify that I am the attorney for the above-named debtor(s) and that compensation paid to me within one year before the filing of the petition in bankruptcy, or agreed to be paid to me, for services rendered or to be rendered on behalf of the debtor(s) in contemplation of or in connection with the bankruptcy case is as follows:

   For legal services, I have agreed to accept . . . . $_____

   Prior to the filing of this statement I have received   . . . . $_____

   Balance Due . . . . $_____

2. The source of the compensation paid to me was:

   ☐ Debtor   ☐ Other (specify)

3. The source of compensation to be paid to me is:

   ☐ Debtor   ☐ Other (specify)

4. ☐ I have not agreed to share the above-disclosed compensation with any other person unless they are members and associates of my law firm.

   ☐ I have agreed to share the above-disclosed compensation with a other person or persons who are not members or associates of my law firm. A copy of the agreement, together with a list of the names of the people sharing in the compensation, is attached.

5. In return for the above-disclosed fee, I have agreed to render legal service for all aspects of the bankruptcy case, including:

   a. Analysis of the debtor's financial situation, and rendering advice to the debtor in determining whether to file a petition in bankruptcy;

   b. Preparation and filing of any petition, schedules, statements of affairs and plan which may be required;

   c. Representation of the debtor at the meeting of creditors and confirmation hearing, and any adjourned hearings thereof;

DISCLOSURE OF COMPENSATION OF ATTORNEY FOR DEBTOR (Continued)

    d. Representation of the debtor in adversary proceedings and other contested bankruptcy matters;

    e. [Other provisions as needed]

6. By agreement with the debtor(s), the above-disclosed fee does not include the following services:

CERTIFICATION

    I certify that the foregoing is a complete statement of any agreement or arrangement for payment to me for representation of the debtor(s) in this bankruptcy proceedings.

_____   _____
        Date   *Signature of Attorney*

                               _____
                                    Name of law firm

B 8 (Official Form 8) (12/08)

UNITED STATES BANKRUPTCY COURT

In re _____,   Case No. _____
           Debtor   Chapter 7

CHAPTER 7 INDIVIDUAL DEBTOR'S STATEMENT OF INTENTION

PART A – Debts secured by property of the estate. *(Part A must be fully completed for **EACH** debt which is secured by property of the estate. Attach additional pages if necessary.)*

Property No. 1

Creditor's Name:	**Describe Property Securing Debt:**

Property will be *(check one)*:
   ❏ Surrendered   ❏ Retained

If retaining the property, I intend to *(check at least one)*:
   ❏ Redeem the property
   ❏ Reaffirm the debt
   ❏ Other. Explain _____ (for example, avoid lien using 11 U.S.C. § 522(f)).

Property is *(check one)*:
   ❏ Claimed as exempt   ❏ Not claimed as exempt

Property No. 2 *(if necessary)*

Creditor's Name:	**Describe Property Securing Debt:**

Property will be *(check one)*:
   ❏ Surrendered   ❏ Retained

If retaining the property, I intend to *(check at least one)*:
   ❏ Redeem the property
   ❏ Reaffirm the debt
   ❏ Other. Explain _____ (for example, avoid lien using 11 U.S.C. § 522(f)).

Property is *(check one)*:
   ❏ Claimed as exempt   ❏ Not claimed as exempt

PART B – Personal property subject to unexpired leases. *(All three columns of Part B must be completed for each unexpired lease. Attach additional pages if necessary.)*

Property No. 1		
Lessor's Name:	**Describe Leased Property:**	Lease will be Assumed pursuant to 11 U.S.C. § 365(p)(2): ❑ YES ❑ NO

Property No. 2 *(if necessary)*		
Lessor's Name:	**Describe Leased Property:**	Lease will be Assumed pursuant to 11 U.S.C. § 365(p)(2): ❑ YES ❑ NO

Property No. 3 *(if necessary)*		
Lessor's Name:	**Describe Leased Property:**	Lease will be Assumed pursuant to 11 U.S.C. § 365(p)(2): ❑ YES ❑ NO

_____ continuation sheets attached *(if any)*

I declare under penalty of perjury that the above indicates my intention as to any property of my estate securing a debt and/or personal property subject to an unexpired lease.

Date: _____

_____
Signature of Debtor

_____
Signature of Joint Debtor

CHAPTER 7 INDIVIDUAL DEBTOR'S STATEMENT OF INTENTION
(Continuation Sheet)

PART A - Continuation

Property No.	
Creditor's Name:	**Describe Property Securing Debt:**

Property will be *(check one)*:
❏ Surrendered   ❏ Retained

If retaining the property, I intend to *(check at least one)*:
❏ Redeem the property
❏ Reaffirm the debt
❏ Other. Explain _____ (for example, avoid lien
using 11 U.S.C. § 522(f)).

Property is *(check one)*:
❏ Claimed as exempt   ❏ Not claimed as exempt

PART B - Continuation

Property No.		
Lessor's Name:	**Describe Leased Property:**	Lease will be Assumed pursuant to 11 U.S.C. § 365(p)(2): ❏ YES ❏ NO

Property No.		
Lessor's Name:	**Describe Leased Property:**	Lease will be Assumed pursuant to 11 U.S.C. § 365(p)(2): ❏ YES ❏ NO

<table>
<tr><td>

Fill in this information to identify your case:

Debtor 1 _____
       First Name   Middle Name   Last Name

Debtor 2
(Spouse, if filing) _____
       First Name   Middle Name   Last Name

United States Bankruptcy Court for the: _____ District of _____

Case number _____
(If known)

</td><td>

Check one box only as directed in this form and in Form 22A-1Supp:

❑ 1. There is no presumption of abuse.

❑ 2. The calculation to determine if a presumption of abuse applies will be made under *Chapter 7 Means Test Calculation* (Official Form 22A–2).

❑ 3. The Means Test does not apply now because of qualified military service but it could apply later.

❑ Check if this is an amended filing

</td></tr>
</table>

OFFICIAL FORM B 22A1

Chapter 7 Statement of Your Current Monthly Income   12/14

Be as complete and accurate as possible. If two married people are filing together, both are equally responsible for being accurate. If more space is needed, attach a separate sheet to this form. Include the line number to which the additional information applies. On the top of any additional pages, write your name and case number (if known). If you believe that you are exempted from a presumption of abuse because you do not have primarily consumer debts or because of qualifying military service, complete and file *Statement of Exemption from Presumption of Abuse Under § 707(b)(2)* (Official Form 22A-1Supp) with this form.

Part 1:   Calculate Your Current Monthly Income

1. **What is your marital and filing status?** Check one only.

   ❑ **Not married.** Fill out Column A, lines 2-11.

   ❑ **Married and your spouse is filing with you.** Fill out both Columns A and B, lines 2-11.

   ❑ **Married and your spouse is NOT filing with you.** You and your spouse are:

      ❑ **Living in the same household and are not legally separated.** Fill out both Columns A and B, lines 2-11.

      ❑ **Living separately or are legally separated.** Fill out Column A, lines 2-11; do not fill out Column B. By checking this box, you declare under penalty of perjury that you and your spouse are legally separated under nonbankruptcy law that applies or that you and your spouse are living apart for reasons that do not include evading the Means Test requirements. 11 U.S.C. § 707(b)(7)(B).

   Fill in the average monthly income that you received from all sources, derived during the 6 full months before you file this bankruptcy case. 11 U.S.C. § 101(10A). For example, if you are filing on September 15, the 6-month period would be March 1 through August 31. If the amount of your monthly income varied during the 6 months, add the income for all 6 months and divide the total by 6. Fill in the result. Do not include any income amount more than once. For example, if both spouses own the same rental property, put the income from that property in one column only. If you have nothing to report for any line, write $0 in the space.

		Column A Debtor 1	Column B Debtor 2 or non-filing spouse
2.	**Your gross wages, salary, tips, bonuses, overtime, and commissions** (before all payroll deductions).	$_____	$_____
3.	**Alimony and maintenance payments.** Do not include payments from a spouse if Column B is filled in.	$_____	$_____
4.	**All amounts from any source which are regularly paid for household expenses of you or your dependents, including child support.** Include regular contributions from an unmarried partner, members of your household, your dependents, parents, and roommates. Include regular contributions from a spouse only if Column B is not filled in. Do not include payments you listed on line 3.	$_____	$_____

5. **Net income from operating a business, profession, or farm**

			Column A	Column B
	Gross receipts (before all deductions)	$_____		
	Ordinary and necessary operating expenses	– $_____		
	Net monthly income from a business, profession, or farm	$_____ **Copy here➔**	$_____	$_____

6. **Net income from rental and other real property**

			Column A	Column B
	Gross receipts (before all deductions)	$_____		
	Ordinary and necessary operating expenses	– $_____		
	Net monthly income from rental or other real property	$_____ **Copy here➔**	$_____	$_____

7.	**Interest, dividends, and royalties**	$_____	$_____

Debtor 1 _____   Case number *(if known)*_____
First Name   Middle Name   Last Name

	Column A Debtor 1	Column B Debtor 2 or non-filing spouse

8. **Unemployment compensation** $_____ $_____

Do not enter the amount if you contend that the amount received was a benefit
under the Social Security Act. Instead, list it here:.......................... ↓

For you .... $_____

For your spouse .... $_____

9. **Pension or retirement income.** Do not include any amount received that was a
benefit under the Social Security Act. $_____ $_____

10. **Income from all other sources not listed above.** Specify the source and amount.
Do not include any benefits received under the Social Security Act or payments received
as a victim of a war crime, a crime against humanity, or international or domestic
terrorism. If necessary, list other sources on a separate page and put the total on line 10c.

10a. _____ $_____ $_____

10b. _____ $_____ $_____

10c. Total amounts from separate pages, if any.   +$_____   +$_____

11. **Calculate your total current monthly income.** Add lines 2 through 10 for each
column. Then add the total for Column A to the total for Column B.

$_____ + $_____ = $_____

Total current monthly income

Part 2:	**Determine Whether the Means Test Applies to You**

12. **Calculate your current monthly income for the year.** Follow these steps:

12a.   Copy your total current monthly income from line 11..**Copy line 11 here** ➜ 12a. $_____

Multiply by 12 (the number of months in a year).   x 12

12b.   The result is your annual income for this part of the form.   12b. $_____

13. **Calculate the median family income that applies to you.** Follow these steps:

Fill in the state in which you live.   [_____]

Fill in the number of people in your household.   [_____]

Fill in the median family income for your state and size of household. ....   13. $_____

To find a list of applicable median income amounts, go online using the link specified in the separate
instructions for this form. This list may also be available at the bankruptcy clerk's office.

14. **How do the lines compare?**

14a. ☐ Line 12b is less than or equal to line 13. On the top of page 1, check box 1, *There is no presumption of abuse.*
Go to Part 3.

14b. ☐ Line 12b is more than line 13. On the top of page 1, check box 2, *The presumption of abuse is determined by Form 22A-2.*
Go to Part 3 and fill out Form 22A-2.

Part 3:	**Sign Below**

By signing here, I declare under penalty of perjury that the information on this statement and in any attachments is true and correct.

✗ _____   ✗ _____

Signature of Debtor 1   Signature of Debtor 2

Date _____   Date _____
MM / DD / YYYY   MM / DD / YYYY

If you checked line 14a, do NOT fill out or file Form 22A–2.

If you checked line 14b, fill out Form 22A–2 and file it with this form.

Official Form B 22A2 - Chapter 7 Means Test Calculation

Official Form B 22A2

Chapter 7 Means Test Calculation

12/14

To fill out this form, you will need your completed copy of *Chapter 7 Statement of Your Current Monthly Income* (Official Form 22A-1).

Be as complete and accurate as possible. If two married people are filing together, both are equally responsible for being accurate. If more space is needed, attach a separate sheet to this form. Include the line number to which the additional information applies. On the top of any additional pages, write your name and case number (if known).

Part 1:	Determine Your Adjusted Income

1. **Copy your total current monthly income.** .... Copy line 11 from Official Form 22A-1 here ➜ ....1. $_____

2. **Did you fill out Column B in Part 1 of Form 22A–1?**

    ☐ No. Fill in $0 on line 3d.

    ☐ Yes. Is your spouse filing with you?

        ☐ No. Go to line 3.

        ☐ Yes. Fill in $0 on line 3d.

3. **Adjust your current monthly income by subtracting any part of your spouse's income not used to pay for the household expenses of you or your dependents.** Follow these steps:

    On line 11, Column B of Form 22A–1, was any amount of the income you reported for your spouse NOT regularly used for the household expenses of you or your dependents?

    ☐ No. Fill in 0 on line 3d.

    ☐ Yes. Fill in the information below:

State each purpose for which the income was used For example, the income is used to pay your spouse's tax debt or to support people other than you or your dependents	**Fill in the amount you are subtracting from your spouse's income**
3a. _____	$_____
3b. _____	$_____
3c. _____	+ $_____
3d. **Total.** Add lines 3a, 3b, and 3c.	$_____ Copy total here ➜ ....3d. – $_____

4. **Adjust your current monthly income.** Subtract line 3d from line 1. $_____

Debtor 1 _____   Case number *(if known)*_____

First Name   Middle Name   Last Name

Part 2:   **Calculate Your Deductions from Your Income**

The Internal Revenue Service (IRS) issues National and Local Standards for certain expense amounts. Use these amounts to answer the questions in lines 6-15. To find the IRS standards, go online using the link specified in the separate instructions for this form. This information may also be available at the bankruptcy clerk's office.

Deduct the expense amounts set out in lines 6-15 regardless of your actual expense. In later parts of the form, you will use some of your actual expenses if they are higher than the standards. Do not deduct any amounts that you subtracted from your spouse's income in line 3 and do not deduct any operating expenses that you subtracted from income in lines 5 and 6 of Form 22A–1.

If your expenses differ from month to month, enter the average expense.

Whenever this part of the form refers to *you*, it means both you and your spouse if Column B of Form 22A–1 is filled in.

5. **The number of people used in determining your deductions from income**

   Fill in the number of people who could be claimed as exemptions on your federal income tax return, plus the number of any additional dependents whom you support. This number may be different from the number of people in your household.

   [ ]

National Standards   You must use the IRS National Standards to answer the questions in lines 6-7.

6. **Food, clothing, and other items:** Using the number of people you entered in line 5 and the IRS National Standards, fill in the dollar amount for food, clothing, and other items. $_____

7. **Out-of-pocket health care allowance:** Using the number of people you entered in line 5 and the IRS National Standards, fill in the dollar amount for out-of-pocket health care. The number of people is split into two categories—people who are under 65 and people who are 65 or older—because older people have a higher IRS allowance for health care costs. If your actual expenses are higher than this IRS amount, you may deduct the additional amount on line 22.

   People who are under 65 years of age

   7a. Out-of-pocket health care allowance per person $_____

   7b. Number of people who are under 65   X _____

   7c. **Subtotal.** Multiply line 7a by line 7b. $_____   Copy line 7c here ➔ .... $_____

   People who are 65 years of age or older

   7d. Out-of-pocket health care allowance per person $_____

   7e. Number of people who are 65 or older   X _____

   7f. **Subtotal.** Multiply line 7d by line 7e. $_____   Copy line 7f here ➔ ......   + $_____

   7g. **Total.** Add lines 7c and 7f... $_____   Copy total here ➔ .... 7g. $_____

Debtor 1 _____   Case number *(if known)*_____
First Name   Middle Name   Last Name

Local Standards	You must use the IRS Local Standards to answer the questions in lines 8-15.

Based on information from the IRS, the U.S. Trustee Program has divided the IRS Local Standard for housing for bankruptcy purposes into two parts:

- Housing and utilities – Insurance and operating expenses
- Housing and utilities – Mortgage or rent expenses

To answer the questions in lines 8-9, use the U.S. Trustee Program chart.

To find the chart, go online using the link specified in the separate instructions for this form. This chart may also be available at the bankruptcy clerk's office.

8. **Housing and utilities – Insurance and operating expenses:** Using the number of people you entered in line 5, fill in the dollar amount listed for your county for insurance and operating expenses. $_____

9. **Housing and utilities – Mortgage or rent expenses:**

   9a. Using the number of people you entered in line 5, fill in the dollar amount listed
   for your county for mortgage or rent expenses.   9a. $_____

   9b. Total average monthly payment for all mortgages and other debts secured by your home.

   To calculate the total average monthly payment, add all amounts that are contractually due to each secured creditor in the 60 months after you file for bankruptcy. Then divide by 60.

Name of the creditor	**Average monthly payment**
_____	$_____
_____	$_____
_____	+ $_____

   | 9b. Total average monthly payment | $_____ | **Copy line 9b here** ➔ | − $_____ | Repeat this amount on line 33a. |

   9c. Net mortgage or rent expense.
   Subtract line 9b (*total average monthly payment*) from line 9a (*mortgage or rent expense*). If this amount is less than $0, enter $0.   9c. $_____ **Copy line 9c here** ➔ $_____

10. **If you claim that the U.S. Trustee Program's division of the IRS Local Standard for housing is incorrect and affects the calculation of your monthly expenses, fill in any additional amount you claim.** $_____

    Explain
    why: _____
          _____

11. **Local transportation expenses:** Check the number of vehicles for which you claim an ownership or operating expense.

    ☐ 0. Go to line 14.
    ☐ 1. Go to line 12.
    ☐ 2 or more. Go to line 12.

12. **Vehicle operation expense:** Using the IRS Local Standards and the number of vehicles for which you claim the operating expenses, fill in the *Operating Costs* that apply for your Census region or metropolitan statistical area. $_____

Debtor 1 _____   Case number *(if known)*_____
           First Name   Middle Name   Last Name

13. **Vehicle ownership or lease expense:** Using the IRS Local Standards, calculate the net ownership or lease expense for each vehicle below. You may not claim the expense if you do not make any loan or lease payments on the vehicle. In addition, you may not claim the expense for more than two vehicles.

> **Vehicle 1**   **Describe Vehicle 1:**   _____
> _____

13a. Ownership or leasing costs using IRS Local Standard   13a. $_____

13b. Average monthly payment for all debts secured by Vehicle 1.
    Do not include costs for leased vehicles.

    To calculate the average monthly payment here and on line 13e, add all amounts that are contractually due to each secured creditor in the 60 months after you filed for bankruptcy. Then divide by 60.

Name of each creditor for Vehicle 1	Average monthly payment
_____	$_____

Copy 13b here ➔   — $_____   Repeat this amount on line 33b.

13c. Net Vehicle 1 ownership or lease expense
    Subtract line 13b from line 13a. If this amount is less than $0, enter $0.   13c. $_____   Copy net Vehicle 1 expense here..... ➔ $_____

> **Vehicle 2**   **Describe Vehicle 2:**   _____
> _____

13d. Ownership or leasing costs using IRS Local Standard   13d. $_____

13e. Average monthly payment for all debts secured by Vehicle 2. Do not include costs for leased vehicles.

Name of each creditor for Vehicle 2	Average monthly payment
_____	$_____

Copy 13e here ➔   — $_____   Repeat this amount on line 33c.

13f. Net Vehicle 2 ownership or lease expense
    Subtract line 13e from 13d. If this amount is less than $0, enter $0.   13f. $_____   Copy net Vehicle 2 expense here..... ➔ $_____

14. **Public transportation expense**: If you claimed 0 vehicles in line 11, using the IRS Local Standards, fill in the *Public Transportation* expense allowance regardless of whether you use public transportation. $_____

15. **Additional public transportation expense:** If you claimed 1 or more vehicles in line 11 and if you claim that you may also deduct a public transportation expense, you may fill in what you believe is the appropriate expense, but you may not claim more than the IRS Local Standard for *Public Transportation*. $_____

Debtor 1 _____   Case number (*if known*)_____
      First Name   Middle Name   Last Name

Other Necessary Expenses   In addition to the expense deductions listed above, you are allowed your monthly expenses for the following IRS categories.

16. **Taxes:** The total monthly amount that you will actually owe for federal, state and local taxes, such as income taxes, self-employment taxes, social security taxes, and Medicare taxes. You may include the monthly amount withheld from your pay for these taxes. However, if you expect to receive a tax refund, you must divide the expected refund by 12 and subtract that number from the total monthly amount that is withheld to pay for taxes.

    Do not include real estate, sales, or use taxes. $_____

17. **Involuntary deductions:** The total monthly payroll deductions that your job requires, such as retirement contributions, union dues, and uniform costs.

    Do not include amounts that are not required by your job, such as voluntary 401(k) contributions or payroll savings. $_____

18. **Life insurance:** The total monthly premiums that you pay for your own term life insurance. If two married people are filing together, include payments that you make for your spouse's term life insurance. Do not include premiums for life insurance on your dependents, for a non-filing spouse's life insurance, or for any form of life insurance other than term. $_____

19. **Court-ordered payments:** The total monthly amount that you pay as required by the order of a court or administrative agency, such as spousal or child support payments.

    Do not include payments on past due obligations for spousal or child support. You will list these obligations in line 35. $_____

20. **Education:** The total monthly amount that you pay for education that is either required:

    ■ as a condition for your job, or

    ■ for your physically or mentally challenged dependent child if no public education is available for similar services. $_____

21. **Childcare:** The total monthly amount that you pay for childcare, such as babysitting, daycare, nursery, and preschool.

    Do not include payments for any elementary or secondary school education. $_____

22. **Additional health care expenses, excluding insurance costs:** The monthly amount that you pay for health care that is required for the health and welfare of you or your dependents and that is not reimbursed by insurance or paid by a health savings account. Include only the amount that is more than the total entered in line 7.
Payments for health insurance or health savings accounts should be listed only in line 25. $_____

23. **Optional telephones and telephone services:** The total monthly amount that you pay for telecommunication services for you and your dependents, such as pagers, call waiting, caller identification, special long distance, or business cell phone service, to the extent necessary for your health and welfare or that of your dependents or for the production of income, if it is not reimbursed by your employer.   + $_____

    Do not include payments for basic home telephone, internet and cell phone service. Do not include self-employment expenses, such as those reported on line 5 of Official Form 22A-1, or any amount you previously deducted.

24. **Add all of the expenses allowed under the IRS expense allowances.**
Add lines 6 through 23. $_____

Debtor 1 _____   Case number (*if known*)_____
First Name   Middle Name   Last Name

Additional Expense Deductions	These are additional deductions allowed by the Means Test.
	Note: Do not include any expense allowances listed in lines 6-24.

25. **Health insurance, disability insurance, and health savings account expenses.** The monthly expenses for health
insurance, disability insurance, and health savings accounts that are reasonably necessary for yourself, your spouse, or your
dependents.

  Health insurance $_____

  Disability insurance $_____

  Health savings account   + $_____

  Total $_____   Copy total here ➔ .... $_____

  Do you actually spend this total amount?

  ☐ No. How much do you actually spend? $_____
  ☐ Yes

26. **Continued contributions to the care of household or family members.** The actual monthly expenses that you will
continue to pay for the reasonable and necessary care and support of an elderly, chronically ill, or disabled member of
your household or member of your immediate family who is unable to pay for such expenses. $_____

27. **Protection against family violence.** The reasonably necessary monthly expenses that you incur to maintain the safety
of you and your family under the Family Violence Prevention and Services Act or other federal laws that apply. $_____

  By law, the court must keep the nature of these expenses confidential.

28. **Additional home energy costs.** Your home energy costs are included in your non-mortgage housing and utilities
allowance on line 8.

  If you believe that you have home energy costs that are more than the home energy costs included in the non-mortgage
housing and utilities allowance, then fill in the excess amount of home energy costs. $_____

  You must give your case trustee documentation of your actual expenses, and you must show that the additional amount
claimed is reasonable and necessary.

29. **Education expenses for dependent children who are younger than 18.** The monthly expenses (not more than $156.25*
per child) that you pay for your dependent children who are younger than 18 years old to attend a private or public
elementary or secondary school. $_____

  You must give your case trustee documentation of your actual expenses, and you must explain why the amount claimed is
reasonable and necessary and not already accounted for in lines 6-23.

  * Subject to adjustment on 4/01/16, and every 3 years after that for cases begun on or after the date of adjustment.

30. **Additional food and clothing expense.** The monthly amount by which your actual food and clothing expenses are
higher than the combined food and clothing allowances in the IRS National Standards. That amount cannot be more than
5% of the food and clothing allowances in the IRS National Standards. $_____

  To find a chart showing the maximum additional allowance, go online using the link specified in the separate instructions for
this form. This chart may also be available at the bankruptcy clerk's office.

  You must show that the additional amount claimed is reasonable and necessary.

31. **Continuing charitable contributions.** The amount that you will continue to contribute in the form of cash or financial
instruments to a religious or charitable organization. 26 U.S.C. § 170(c)(1)-(2). $_____

32. **Add all of the additional expense deductions.**
Add lines 25 through 31. $_____

Debtor 1 _____   Case number (*if known*)_____
          First Name   Middle Name   Last Name

Deductions for Debt Payment

33. **For debts that are secured by an interest in property that you own, including home mortgages, vehicle loans, and other secured debt, fill in lines 33a through 33g.**

   To calculate the total average monthly payment, add all amounts that are contractually due to each secured creditor in the 60 months after you file for bankruptcy. Then divide by 60.

   Average monthly payment

   Mortgages on your home:

   33a. Copy line 9b here .... ➔ $_____

   Loans on your first two vehicles:

   33b. Copy line 13b here. .... ➔ $_____

   33c. Copy line 13e here. .... ➔ $_____

Name of each creditor for other secured debt	Identify property that secures the debt	Does payment include taxes or insurance?	
33d. _____	_____	☐ No ☐ Yes	$_____
33e. _____	_____	☐ No ☐ Yes	$_____
33f. _____	_____	☐ No ☐ Yes	+ $_____

   33g. Total average monthly payment. Add lines 33a through 33f. .... $_____   **Copy total here** ➔ $_____

34. **Are any debts that you listed in line 33 secured by your primary residence, a vehicle, or other property necessary for your support or the support of your dependents?**

   ☐ No. Go to line 35.

   ☐ Yes. State any amount that you must pay to a creditor, in addition to the payments listed in line 33, to keep possession of your property (called the *cure amount*). Next, divide by 60 and fill in the information below.

Name of the creditor	Identify property that secures the debt	Total cure amount		Monthly cure amount
_____	_____	$_____	÷ 60 =	$_____
_____	_____	$_____	÷ 60 =	$_____
_____	_____	$_____	÷ 60 =	+ $_____
		Total		$_____ **Copy total here** ➔ $_____

35. **Do you owe any priority claims such as a priority tax, child support, or alimony — that are past due as of the filing date of your bankruptcy case?** 11 U.S.C. § 507.

   ☐ No. Go to line 36.

   ☐ Yes. Fill in the total amount of all of these priority claims. Do not include current or ongoing priority claims, such as those you listed in line 19.

   Total amount of all past-due priority claims .... $_____   ÷ 60 = $_____

Debtor 1 _____   Case number *(if known)*_____

First Name   Middle Name   Last Name

36. **Are you eligible to file a case under Chapter 13?** 11 U.S.C. § 109(e).
   For more information, go online using the link for *Bankruptcy Basics* specified in the separate
   instructions for this form. *Bankruptcy Basics* may also be available at the bankruptcy clerk's office.

   ☐ No. Go to line 37.

   ☐ Yes. Fill in the following information.

   Projected monthly plan payment if you were filing under Chapter 13 $_____

   Current multiplier for your district as stated on the list issued by the
   Administrative Office of the United States Courts (for districts in Alabama and
   North Carolina) or by the Executive Office for United States Trustees (for all
   other districts).   x _____

   To find a list of district multipliers that includes your district, go online using the
   link specified in the separate instructions for this form. This list may also be
   available at the bankruptcy clerk's office.

   Average monthly administrative expense if you were filing under Chapter 13 $_____   Copy total here ➔ $_____

37. **Add all of the deductions for debt payment.**
   Add lines 33g through 36. $_____

Total Deductions from Income

38. **Add all of the allowed deductions.**

   Copy line 24, *All of the expenses allowed under IRS
   expense allowances* .... $_____

   Copy line 32, *All of the additional expense deductions* .... $_____

   Copy line 37, *All of the deductions for debt payment* .... **+** $_____

   Total deductions $_____   **Copy total here ➔** $_____

Part 3:   Determine Whether There Is a Presumption of Abuse

39. **Calculate monthly disposable income for 60 months**

   39a. Copy line 4, *adjusted current monthly income* ..... $_____

   39b. Copy line 38, *Total deductions*..........   **−** $_____

   39c. Monthly disposable income. 11 U.S.C. § 707(b)(2). $_____   Copy line $_____
   Subtract line 39b from line 39a.   39c here ➔

   For the next 60 months (5 years).......................................   **x 60**

   39d. **Total**. Multiply line 39c by 60. ....39d. $_____   Copy line 39d here ➔ $_____

40. **Find out whether there is a presumption of abuse.** Check the box that applies:

   ☐ **The line 39d is less than $7,475*.** On the top of page 1 of this form, check box 1, *There is no presumption of abuse.* Go
   to Part 5.

   ☐ **The line 39d is more than $12,475*.** On the top of page 1 of this form, check box 2, *There is a presumption of abuse.* You
   may fill out Part 4 if you claim special circumstances. Then go to Part 5.

   ☐ **The line 39d is at least $7,475*, but not more than $12,475*.** Go to line 41.

   *   Subject to adjustment on 4/01/16, and every 3 years after that for cases filed on or after the date of adjustment.

Debtor 1 _____   Case number (*if known*)_____

First Name   Middle Name   Last Name

---

41. 41a. **Fill in the amount of your total nonpriority unsecured debt.** If you filled out *A Summary of Your Assets and Liabilities and Certain Statistical Information Schedules* (Official Form 6), you may refer to line 5 on that form.

41a. $_____

x .25

41b. **25% of your total nonpriority unsecured debt.** 11 U.S.C. § 707(b)(2)(A)(i)(I)
Multiply line 41a by 0.25.

$_____   Copy here ➜ $_____

42. **Determine whether the income you have left over after subtracting all allowed deductions is enough to pay 25% of your unsecured, nonpriority debt.**
Check the box that applies:

☐ **Line 39d is less than line 41b.** On the top of page 1 of this form, check box 1, *There is no presumption of abuse.* Go to Part 5.

☐ **Line 39d is equal to or more than line 41b.** On the top of page 1 of this form, check box 2, *There is a presumption of abuse.* You may fill out Part 4 if you claim special circumstances. Then go to Part 5.

| Part 4: | **Give Details About Special Circumstances** |

43. **Do you have any special circumstances that justify additional expenses or adjustments of current monthly income for which there is no reasonable alternative?** 11 U.S.C. § 707(b)(2)(B).

☐ No. Go to Part 5.

☐ Yes. Fill in the following information. All figures should reflect your average monthly expense or income adjustment for each item. You may include expenses you listed in line 25.

You must give a detailed explanation of the special circumstances that make the expenses or income adjustments necessary and reasonable. You must also give your case trustee documentation of your actual expenses or income adjustments.

Give a detailed explanation of the special circumstances	Average monthly expense or income adjustment
_____	$_____
_____	$_____
_____	$_____
_____	$_____

| Part 5: | **Sign Below** |

By signing here, I declare under penalty of perjury that the information on this statement and in any attachments is true and correct.

✗ _____   ✗ _____
Signature of Debtor 1   Signature of Debtor 2

Date _____   Date _____
MM / DD / YYYY   MM / DD / YYYY

Chapter 13 - Statement of Currently Monthly Income and Calculation of Commitment Period and Disposable Income

Official Form 22C (Chapter 13) (12/08)

In re _____
                    Debtor(s)

Case Number: _____
                    (If known)

According to the calculations required by this statement:
☐ The applicable commitment period is 3 years.
☐ The applicable commitment period is 5 years.
☐ Disposable income is determined under § 1325(b)(3).
☐ Disposable income is not determined under § 1325(b)(3).
(Check the boxes as directed in Lines 17 and 23 of this statement.)

CHAPTER 13 STATEMENT OF CURRENT MONTHLY INCOME AND CALCULATION OF COMMITMENT PERIOD AND DISPOSABLE INCOME

In addition to Schedules I and J, this statement must be completed by every individual Chapter 13 debtor, whether or not filing jointly. Joint debtors may complete one statement only.

	Part I. REPORT OF INCOME		
1	**Marital/filing status.** Check the box that applies and complete the balance of this part of this statement as directed. a. ☐ **Unmarried.** Complete only Column A ("Debtor's Income") for Lines 2-10. b. ☐ **Married.** Complete both Column A ("Debtor's Income") and Column B ("Spouse's Income") for Lines 2-10.		
	All figures must reflect average monthly income received from all sources, derived during the six calendar months prior to filing the bankruptcy case, ending on the last day of the month before the filing. If the amount of monthly income varied during the six months, you must divide the six-month total by six, and enter the result on the appropriate line.	Column A Debtor's Income	Column B Spouse's Income
2	Gross wages, salary, tips, bonuses, overtime, commissions.	$	$
3	Income from the operation of a business, profession, or farm. Subtract Line b from Line a and enter the difference in the appropriate column(s) of Line 3. Do not enter a number less than zero. Do not include any part of the business expenses entered on Line b as a deduction in Part IV. <table><tr><td>a.</td><td>Gross receipts</td><td>$</td></tr><tr><td>b.</td><td>Ordinary and necessary business expenses</td><td>$</td></tr><tr><td>c.</td><td>Business income</td><td>Subtract Line b from Line a</td></tr></table>	$	$
4	Rent and other real property income. Subtract Line b from Line a and enter the difference in the appropriate column(s) of Line 4. Do not enter a number less than zero. Do not include any part of the operating expenses entered on Line b as a deduction in Part IV. <table><tr><td>a.</td><td>Gross receipts</td><td>$</td></tr><tr><td>b.</td><td>Ordinary and necessary operating expenses</td><td>$</td></tr><tr><td>c.</td><td>Rent and other real property income</td><td>Subtract Line b from Line a</td></tr></table>	$	$
5	Interest, dividends, and royalties.	$	$
6	Pension and retirement income.	$	$
7	Any amounts paid by another person or entity, on a regular basis, for the household expenses of the debtor or the debtor's dependents, including child or spousal support. Do not include amounts paid by the debtor's spouse.	$	$
8	Unemployment compensation. Enter the amount in the appropriate column(s) of Line 8. However, if you contend that unemployment compensation received by you or your spouse was a benefit under the Social Security Act, do not list the amount of such compensation in Column A or B, but instead state the amount in the space below: Unemployment compensation claimed to be a benefit under the Social Security Act Debtor $ _____ Spouse $ _____	$	$
9	Income from all other sources. Specify source and amount. If necessary, list additional sources on a separate page. Total and enter on Line 9. Do not include any benefits received under the Social Security Act or payments received as a victim of a war crime, crime against humanity, or as a victim of international or domestic terrorism. <table><tr><td>a.</td><td></td><td>$</td></tr><tr><td>b.</td><td></td><td>$</td></tr></table>	$	$
10	**Subtotal.** Add Lines 2 thru 9 in Column A, and, if Column B is completed, add Lines 2 through 9 in Column B. Enter the total(s).	$	$
11	**Total.** If Column B has been completed, add Line 10, Column A to Line 10, Column B, and enter the total. If Column B has not been completed, enter the amount from Line 10, Column A.	$	

	Part II. CALCULATION OF § 1325(b)(4) COMMITMENT PERIOD	
12	Enter the amount from Line 11.	
13	**Marital adjustment.** If you are married, but are not filing jointly with your spouse, AND if you contend that calculation of the commitment period under § 1325(b)(4) does not require inclusion of the income of your spouse, enter the amount of the income listed in Line 10, Column B that was NOT paid on a regular basis for the household expenses of you or your dependents. Otherwise, enter zero.	
14	Subtract Line 13 from Line 12 and enter the result.	
15	**Annualized current monthly income for § 1325(b)(4).** Multiply the amount from Line 14 by the number 12 and enter the result.	$
16	**Applicable median family income.** Enter the median family income for applicable state and household size. (This information is available by family size at www.usdoj.gov/ust/ or from the clerk of the bankruptcy court.) a. Enter debtor's state of residence: _____ b. Enter debtor's household size: _____	$
17	Application of § 1325(b)(4). Check the applicable box and proceed as directed. ☐ The amount on Line 15 is less than the amount on Line 16. Check the box for "The applicable commitment period is 3 years" at the top of page 1 of this statement and continue with this statement. ☐ The amount on Line 15 is not less than the amount on Line 16. Check the box for "The applicable commitment period is 5 years" at the top of page 1 of this statement and continue with this statement.	

	Part III. APPLICATION OF § 1325(b)(3) FOR DETERMINING DISPOSABLE INCOME	
18	Enter the amount from Line 11.	$
19	**Marital adjustment.** If you are married, but are not filing jointly with your spouse, enter the amount of the income listed in Line 10, Column B that was NOT paid on a regular basis for the household expenses of you or your dependents. If you are unmarried or married and filing jointly with your spouse, enter zero.	$
20	**Current monthly income for § 1325(b)(3).** Subtract Line 19 from Line 18 and enter the result.	
21	**Annualized current monthly income for § 1325(b)(3).** Multiply the amount from Line 20 by the number 12 and enter the result.	$
22	**Applicable median family income.** Enter the amount from Line 16.	$
23	Application of § 1325(b)(3). Check the applicable box and proceed as directed. ☐ The amount on Line 21 is more than the amount on Line 22. Check the box for "Disposable income is determined under § 1325(b)(3)" at the top of page 1 of this statement and complete the remaining parts of this statement. ☐ The amount on Line 21 is not more than the amount on Line 22. Check the box for "Disposable income is not determined under § 1325(b)(3)" at the top of page 1 of this statement and complete Part VII of this statement. Do not complete Parts IV, V, or VI.	

	Part IV. CALCULATION OF DEDUCTIONS ALLOWED UNDER § 707(b)(2)	
	Subpart A: Deductions under Standards of the Internal Revenue Service (IRS)	
24	**National Standards: food, clothing, household supplies, personal care, and miscellaneous.** Enter the "Total" amount from IRS National Standards for Allowable Living Expenses for the applicable family size and income level. (This information is available at www.usdoj.gov/ust/ or from the clerk of the bankruptcy court.)	$
25A	**Local Standards: housing and utilities; non-mortgage expenses.** Enter the amount of the IRS Housing and Utilities Standards; non-mortgage expenses for the applicable county and family size. (This information is available at www.usdoj.gov/ust/ or from the clerk of the bankruptcy court).	$

Official Form 22C (Chapter 13) (12/08)   3

25B	Local Standards: housing and utilities; mortgage/ rent expense. Enter, in Line a below, the amount of the IRS Housing and Utilities Standards; mortgage/rent expense for your county and family size (this information is available at www.usdoj.gov/ust/ or from the clerk of the bankruptcy court); enter on Line b the total of the Average Monthly Payments for any debts secured by your home, as stated in Line 47; subtract Line b from Line a and enter the result in Line 25B. Do not enter an amount less than zero.	

a.	IRS Housing and Utilities Standards; mortgage/rent expense	$	
b.	Average Monthly Payment for any debts secured by your home, if any, as stated in Line 47	$	
c.	Net mortgage/rental expense	Subtract Line b from Line a.	$

26	Local Standards: housing and utilities; adjustment. if you contend that the process set out in Lines 25A and 25B does not accurately compute the allowance to which you are entitled under the IRS Housing and Utilities Standards, enter any additional amount to which you contend you are entitled, and state the basis for your contention in the space below: _____ _____ _____ $

27	Local Standards: transportation; vehicle operation/ public transportation expense. You are entitled to an expense allowance in this category regardless of whether you pay the expenses of operating a vehicle and regardless of whether you use public transportation. Check the number of vehicles for which you pay the operating expenses or for which the operating expenses are included as a contribution to your household expenses in Line 7. ☐ 0 ☐ 1 ☐ 2 or more. Enter the amount from IRS Transportation Standards, Operating Costs & Public Transportation Costs for the applicable number of vehicles in the applicable Metropolitan Statistical Area or Census Region. (This information is available at www.usdoj.gov/ust/ or from the clerk of the bankruptcy court.) $

28	Local Standards: transportation ownership/ lease expense; Vehicle 1. Check the number of vehicles for which you claim an ownership/lease expense. (You may not claim an ownership/lease expense for more than two vehicles.) ☐ 1 ☐ 2 or more. Enter, in Line a below, the amount of the IRS Transportation Standards, Ownership Costs, First Car (available at www.usdoj.gov/ust/ or from the clerk of the bankruptcy court); enter in Line b the total of the Average Monthly Payments for any debts secured by Vehicle 1, as stated in Line 47; subtract Line b from Line a and enter the result in Line 28. Do not enter an amount less than zero.

a.	IRS Transportation Standards, Ownership Costs, First Car	$	
b.	Average Monthly Payment for any debts secured by Vehicle 1, as stated in Line 47	$	
c.	Net ownership/lease expense for Vehicle 1	Subtract Line b from Line a.	$

29	Local Standards: transportation ownership/ lease expense; Vehicle 2. Complete this Line only if you checked the "2 or more" Box in Line 28. Enter, in Line a below, the amount of the IRS Transportation Standards, Ownership Costs, Second Car (available at www.usdoj.gov/ust/ or from the clerk of the bankruptcy court); enter in Line b the total of the Average Monthly Payments for any debts secured by Vehicle 2, as stated in Line 47; subtract Line b from Line a and enter the result in Line 29. Do not enter an amount less than zero.

a.	IRS Transportation Standards, Ownership Costs, Second Car	$	
b.	Average Monthly Payment for any debts secured by Vehicle 2, as stated in Line 47	$	
c.	Net ownership/lease expense for Vehicle 2	Subtract Line b from Line a.	$

30	Other Necessary Expenses: taxes. Enter the total average monthly expense that you actually incur for all federal, state, and local taxes, other than real estate and sales taxes, such as income taxes, self employment taxes, social security taxes, and Medicare taxes. Do not include real estate or sales taxes.	$

31	Other Necessary Expenses: mandatory payroll deductions. Enter the total average monthly payroll deductions that are required for your employment, such as mandatory retirement contributions, union dues, and uniform costs. Do not include discretionary amounts, such as non-mandatory 401(k) contributions.	$

Official Form 22C (Chapter 13) (12/08)   4

32	**Other Necessary Expenses: life insurance.** Enter average monthly premiums that you actually pay for term life insurance for yourself. Do not include premiums for insurance on your dependents, for whole life or for any other form of insurance.	$
33	**Other Necessary Expenses: court-ordered payments.** Enter the total monthly amount that you are required to pay pursuant to court order, such as spousal or child support payments. Do not include payments on past due support obligations included in Line 49.	$
34	**Other Necessary Expenses: education for employment or for a physically or mentally challenged child.** Enter the total monthly amount that you actually expend for education that is a condition of employment and for education that is required for a physically or mentally challenged dependent child for whom no public education providing similar services is available.	
35	**Other Necessary Expenses: childcare.** Enter the average monthly amount that you actually expend on childcare—such as baby-sitting, day care, nursery and preschool. Do not include other educational payments.	$
36	**Other Necessary Expenses: health care.** Enter the average monthly amount that you actually expend on health care expenses that are not reimbursed by insurance or paid by a health savings account. Do not include payments for health insurance or health savings accounts listed in Line 39.	$
37	**Other Necessary Expenses: telecommunication services.** Enter the average monthly amount that you actually pay for telecommunication services other than your basic home telephone service—such as cell phones, pagers, call waiting, caller id, special long distance, or internet service—to the extent necessary for your health and welfare or that of your dependents. Do not include any amount previously deducted.	$
38	**Total Expenses Allowed under IRS Standards.** Enter the total of Lines 24 through 37.	$

Subpart B: Additional Expense Deductions under § 707(b)
Note: Do not include any expenses that you have listed in Lines 24-37

39	**Health Insurance, Disability Insurance, and Health Savings Account Expenses.** List and total the average monthly amounts that you actually pay for yourself, your spouse, or your dependents in the following categories.	
	a. Health Insurance — $ b. Disability Insurance — $ c. Health Savings Account — $ Total: Add Lines a, b, and c	$
40	**Continued contributions to the care of household or family members.** Enter the actual monthly expenses that you will continue to pay for the reasonable and necessary care and support of an elderly, chronically ill, or disabled member of your household or member of your immediate family who is unable to pay for such expenses. Do not include payments listed in Line 34.	$
41	**Protection against family violence.** Enter any average monthly expenses that you actually incurred to maintain the safety of your family under the Family Violence Prevention and Services Act or other applicable federal law. The nature of these expenses is required to be kept confidential by the court.	$
42	**Home energy costs.** Enter the average monthly amount, in excess of the allowance specified by IRS Local Standards for Housing and Utilities, that you actually expend for home energy costs. You must provide your case trustee with documentation demonstrating that the additional amount claimed is reasonable and necessary.	$
43	**Education expenses for dependent children under 18.** Enter the average monthly expenses that you actually incur, not to exceed $125 per child, in providing elementary and secondary education for your dependent children less than 18 years of age. You must provide your case trustee with documentation demonstrating that the amount claimed is reasonable and necessary and not already accounted for in the IRS Standards.	$
44	**Additional food and clothing expense.** Enter the average monthly amount by which your food and clothing expenses exceed the combined allowances for food and apparel in the IRS National Standards, not to exceed five percent of those combined allowances. (This information is available at www.usdoj.gov/ust/ or from the clerk of the bankruptcy court.) You must provide your case trustee with documentation demonstrating that the additional amount claimed is reasonable and necessary.	$
45	**Continued charitable contributions.** Enter the amount that you will continue to contribute in the form of cash or financial instruments to a charitable organization as defined in 26 U.S.C. § 170(c)(1)-(2).	$
46	**Total Additional Expense Deductions under § 707(b).** Enter the total of Lines 39 through 45.	$

Official Form 22C (Chapter 13) (12/08)   5

Subpart C: Deductions for Debt Payment			
47	**Future payments on secured claims.** For each of your debts that is secured by an interest in property that you own, list the name of the creditor, identify the property securing the debt, and state the Average Monthly Payment. The Average Monthly Payment is the total of all amounts contractually due to each Secured Creditor in the 60 months following the filing of the bankruptcy case, divided by 60. Mortgage debts should include payments of taxes and insurance required by the mortgage. If necessary, list additional entries on a separate page.		

	Name of Creditor	Property Securing the Debt	60-month Average Payment	
a.			$	
b.			$	
c.			$	
			Total: Add Lines a, b, and c	$

48	**Other payments on secured claims.** If any of debts listed in Line 47 are secured by your primary residence, a motor vehicle, or other property necessary for your support or the support of your dependents, you may include in your deduction 1/60th of any amount (the "cure amount") that you must pay the creditor in addition to the payments listed in Line 47, in order to maintain possession of the property. The cure amount would include any sums in default that must be paid in order to avoid repossession or foreclosure. List and total any such amounts in the following chart. If necessary, list additional entries on a separate page.

	Name of Creditor	Property Securing the Debt	1/60th of the Cure Amount	
a.			$	
b.			$	
c.			$	
			Total: Add Lines a, b, and c	$

49	**Payments on priority claims.** Enter the total amount of all priority claims (including priority child support and alimony claims), divided by 60.	$

50	**Chapter 13 administrative expenses.** Multiply the amount in Line a by the amount in Line b, and enter the resulting administrative expense.		
	a.	Projected average monthly Chapter 13 plan payment.	$
	b.	Current multiplier for your district as determined under schedules issued by the Executive Office for United States Trustees. (This information is available at www.usdoj.gov/ust/ or from the clerk of the bankruptcy court.)	x
	c.	Average monthly administrative expense of Chapter 13 case	Total: Multiply Lines a and b $

51	**Total Deductions for Debt Payment.** Enter the total of Lines 47 through 50.	$

Subpart D: Total Deductions Allowed under § 707(b)(2)	
52	**Total of all deductions allowed under § 707(b)(2).** Enter the total of Lines 38, 46, and 51.	$

Part V. DETERMINATION OF DISPOSABLE INCOME UNDER § 1325(b)(2)

53	**Total current monthly income.** Enter the amount from Line 20.	$
54	**Support income.** Enter the monthly average of any child support payments, foster care payments, or disability payments for a dependent child, included in Line 7, that you received in accordance with applicable nonbankruptcy law, to the extent reasonably necessary to be expended for such child.	$
55	**Qualified retirement deductions.** Enter the monthly average of (a) all contributions or wage deductions made to qualified retirement plans, as specified in § 541(b)(7) and (b) all repayments of loans from retirement plans, as specified in § 362(b)(19).	$
56	**Total of all deductions allowed under § 707(b)(2).** Enter the amount from Line 52.	$
57	**Total adjustments to determine disposable income.** Add the amounts on Lines 54, 55, and 56 and enter the result.	$

Official Form 22C (Chapter 13) (12/08) 6

| 58 | Monthly Disposable Income Under § 1325(b)(2). Subtract Line 57 from Line 53 and enter the result. | $ |

Part VI: ADDITIONAL EXPENSE CLAIMS

| 59 | Other Expenses. List and describe any monthly expenses, not otherwise stated in this form, that are required for the health and welfare of you and your family and that you contend should be an additional deduction from your current monthly income under § 707(b)(2)(A)(ii)(I). If necessary, list additional sources on a separate page. All figures should reflect your average monthly expense for each item. Total the expenses. |

	Expense Description	Monthly Amount
a.		$
b.		$
c.		$
	Total: Add Lines a, b, and c	$

Part VII: VERIFICATION

| 60 | I declare under penalty of perjury that the information provided in this statement is true and correct. *(If this is a joint case, both debtors must sign.)* |

Date: _____   Signature: _____
(Debtor)

Date: _____   Signature: _____
(Joint Debtor, if any)

UNITED STATES BANKRUPTCY COURT
DISTRICT OF MINNESOTA

In Re: Steven Allen Gewecke and Tamara Lynn Gewecke,

Debtors: Chapter 7 Case
Case No. BKY 09-41180-NCD.

NOTICE OF HEARING AND
MOTION FOR RELIEF FROM STAY

TO: The Debtors, Debtors' Attorney, Chapter 7 Trustee, United States Trustee, and the other parties in interest specified in Local Rule 1204(a).

1. **U.S. Bank National Association, as Trustee (Movant)**, a secured creditor of the Debtors herein, by its undersigned attorney, moves the Court for the relief requested below and gives notice of hearing herewith.

2. The Court will hold a hearing on this motion at 2:30 o'clock p.m., on April 23, 2009, before the Honorable Nancy C. Dreher, in Courtroom Number 7 West, United States Courthouse, 300 South Fourth Street, Minneapolis, Minnesota, 55415, or as soon thereafter as counsel can be heard.

3. Any response to this motion must be filed and delivered not later than April 20, 2009, which is three (3) days before the time set for the hearing (excluding Saturdays, Sundays, and holidays), or filed and served by mail not later than April 14, 2009, which is seven (7) days before the time set for the hearing (excluding Saturdays, Sundays, and holidays). UNLESS A RESPONSE OPPOSING THE MOTION IS TIMELY FILED, THE COURT MAY GRANT THE RELIEF REQUESTED IN THE MOTION WITHOUT A HEARING.

4. This motion is filed pursuant to Bankruptcy Rule 4001 and Local Rule 9013-2, and Movant seeks relief from the automatic stay of 11 U.S.C. §362 with respect to certain real property owned by the Debtors and subject to Movant's first mortgage lien.

5. The Petition commencing this Chapter 7 Case was filed on March 2, 2009, and the case is now pending in this Court. This Court has jurisdiction over this motion pursuant to 28 U.S.C. § 157(a), § 1334, 11 U.S.C. § 362(d), Bankruptcy Rule 5005, Local Rule 1070-1 and other applicable rules. This proceeding is a core proceeding.

6.   By certain mortgage dated September 5, 2006, in the original principal amount of $163,200.00 (**Mortgage**), Movant acquired a first mortgagee's interest in the following real property (**Property**):

Lot eight (8), Block one (1), in Northway Plat 5.

The Mortgage was filed for record in the office of the County Recorder, in and for Stearns County, Minnesota, on September 5, 2006, as document number 1206280.

8.   The subject property has a market value of $139,700.00. The total amount of debt secured by the subject property is $184,995.28 including Movant's mortgage. Hence, Debtors have little or no actual equity in the property.

9.   Debtors' fourteen (14) month delinquency under the terms of the Mortgage constitute cause, within the meaning of 11 U.S.C. § 362(d)(1), entitling Movant to relief from the automatic stay. Movant does not have, and has not been offered, adequate protection of its interest in the Property.

WHEREFORE, Movant, by its undersigned attorney, moves the Court for an order modifying the automatic stay of 11 U.S.C. § 362(a) so as to permit Movant to foreclose its Mortgage on the Property and for such other relief as the Court may deem to be just, fair and equitable.

Dated this 2nd day of April, 2009.

PETERSON, FRAM AND BERGMAN
A Professional Association

BY: /e/ Steven H. Bruns
Steven H. Bruns
Atty. Reg. #14888X
Attorneys for Movant
Suite 800, 55 East Fifth Street
St. Paul, Minnesota 55101
Telephone: (651) 291-8955

UNITED STATES BANKRUPTCY COURT
DISTRICT OF MINNESOTA

In Re: Steven Allen Gewecke and
     Tamara Lynn Gewecke,

Debtors: Chapter 7 Case
Case No. BKY 09-41180-NCD.

AFFIDAVIT IN SUPPORT OF
MOTION FOR RELIEF FROM STAY

STATE OF TEXAS   )
) ss.
COUNTY OF DALLAS   )

    I, Marsha Iokepa, your affiant, being first duly sworn on oath, state as follows:

    1.   I am an employee of Countrywide Home Loans Servicing, LP, servicer for

U.S. Bank National Association, as Trustee (Movant), and I have personal

knowledge of the facts stated herein.

    2.   I make this Affidavit in support of a motion to lift, modify or condition the

bankruptcy stay.

    3.   Debtors are the mortgagors on a mortgage dated September 5, 2006

which covers real property located in Stearns County and legally described as follows:

    Lot eight (8), Block one (1), in Northway Plat 5,

and which is commonly known as: 3013 15th Street North, St. Cloud, MN 56303. The mortgage was given to secure a promissory note. Copies of the note and the mortgage are attached hereto as Exhibit A and Exhibit B, respectively, and incorporated herein by this reference. The mortgage was assigned to Movant on September 10, 2008. A copy of the assignment is attached hereto as Exhibit C and incorporated herein by this reference.

4.   On or about March 2, 2009, Debtors filed a Petition under Chapter 7 of Title 11 U.S. Code in the United States Bankruptcy Court for the District of Minnesota.

5.   Debtors have failed to make fourteen (14) payments, resulting in an arrearage of $18,796.68, excluding late charges. The total mortgage debt is $184,995.28, which includes accrued interest through March 16, 2009. Thereafter, interest accrues on the unpaid principal balance at $41.02 per day.

6.   Based upon information and belief, the subject property has a market value of $139,700.00. The total amount of debt secured by the subject property is $184,995.28, including Movant's mortgage.

7.   I have read the Motion in this matter, and it is true to the best of my knowledge, information and belief.

Further, I saith not.

Marsha Iokepa

Subscribed and sworn to before me
this 25th day of March, 2009

Notary Public

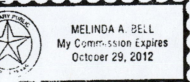

MELINDA A. BELL
My Commission Expires
October 29, 2012

UNITED STATES BANKRUPTCY COURT
DISTRICT OF MINNESOTA

In Re: Steven Allen Gewecke and
          Tamara Lynn Gewecke,

Debtors: Chapter 7 Case
Case No. BKY 09-41180-NCD.

MEMORANDUM OF LAW

U.S. Bank National Association, as Trustee (**Movant**) submits this memorandum of law in support of its motion for relief from the stay in the above-entitled matter.

FACTS

Movant holds a valid, duly perfected mortgage on certain real property owned by Debtors. The Debtors are delinquent with respect to payments due under the mortgage for the months of February 2008 through March 2009 in a total amount of $18,796.68, including late charges. The total mortgage debt is $184,995.28 which includes accrued interest through March 16, 2009. Thereafter, interest accrues on the unpaid principal balance at $41.02 per day.

The subject property has a market value of $139,700.00. The total amount of debt secured by the subject property is $184,995.28 including Movant's mortgage.

ARGUMENT

Under § 362(d)(1) of the Bankruptcy Code, relief from the automatic stay shall be granted upon request of a creditor "for cause, including the lack of adequate protection of an interest in property of such [creditor]." 11 U.S.C. § 362(d)(1). Debtors have failed to make payments due under the terms of the mortgage for a period of over fourteen (14) months. Debtors have little or no actual equity in the property; hence, Movant lacks adequate protection in the form of an equity cushion in the property. Furthermore, debtors have otherwise failed to provide Movant with adequate protection of its interest in the property.

Such circumstances constitute cause, within the meaning of § 362(d)(1), justifying relief from the stay. In Re Tainan, 48 B.R. 250 (Bkrtcy E.D. Pa. 1985); In Re Quinlan, 12 B.R. 516 (Bkrtcy. W.D. Wis. 1981).

Accordingly, Movant is entitled to an order terminating the stay of 11 U.S.C. § 362(a) and authorizing it to foreclose its mortgage on the property.

Dated this 2nd day April, of 2009.

PETERSON, FRAM AND BERGMAN
A Professional Association

BY: /e/ Steven H. Bruns
    Steven H. Bruns
    Atty. Reg. #14888X
Attorneys for Movant
Suite 800, 55 East Fifth Street
St. Paul, Minnesota 55101
Telephone: (651) 291-8955

UNITED STATES BANKRUPTCY COURT
DISTRICT OF MINNESOTA

In Re: Steven Allen Gewecke and
Tamara Lynn Gewecke,

Debtors: Chapter 7 Case
Case No. BKY 09-41180-NCD.

ORDER FOR RELIEF FROM AUTOMATIC STAY

The above-entitled matter came before the Court on the motion of U.S. Bank National Association, as Trustee (**Movant**) seeking relief from the automatic stay of 11 U.S.C. § 362(a). Based upon the files and records herein, the Court now finds that cause exists entitling Movant to the requested relief.

NOW, THEREFORE, IT IS HEREBY ORDERED that the automatic stay of 11 U.S.C. § 362(a) is immediately terminated as to Movant; and, Movant, its successors or assigns, are hereby authorized to foreclose <u>pursuant to Minnesota law</u> that certain Mortgage dated September 5, 2006, filed for record in the office of the County Recorder in and for Stearns County, Minnesota, on September 5, 2006, and recorded as Document No. 1206280 and covering real property located in Stearns County, Minnesota, which is legally described as follows:

Lot eight (8), Block one (1), in Northway Plat 5.

Notwithstanding Fed. R. Bankr. P. 4001(a)(3), this order is effective immediately.

Dated: _____

_____
Nancy C. Dreher
United States Bankruptcy Judge

AMRANE COHEN
CHAPTER 13 TRUSTEE
770 The City Drive South, Suite 8500
Orange CA, 92868
Tel: (714) 621-0200
Fax: (714) 621-0277

UNITED STATES BANKRUPTCY COURT CENTRAL
DISTRICT OF CALIFORNIA, SANTA ANA DIVISION

IN RE:
   ANTHONY RAMOS

	Chapter 13
	Case No.: 6:11-bk-25322-CB
	NOTICE OF MOTION AND VERIFIED
	MOTION FOR ORDER DISMISSING
	CHAPTER 13 PROCEEDING (11 U.S.C. -
Debtor(s).	**1307(c))**

PLEASE TAKE NOTICE THAT THE TRUSTEE HEREIN MOVES FOR AN ORDER DISMISSING THIS PROCEEDING ON OR AFTER 10/30/2011 UNLESS ARRANGEMENTS ARE MADE BY THE ABOVE-NAMED DEBTOR(S) TO CURE THE DELINQUENT PAYMENTS IN THE AMOUNT OF $6,375.00. IN ADDITION TO THE DELINQUENT AMOUNT LISTED, DEBTOR(S) MUST CURE ANY SUBSEQUENT TRUSTEE PAYMENT THAT MAY COME DUE AFTER THE DATE OF THIS NOTICE. THIS MOTION IS BASED ON THE FOLLOWING GROUNDS: MATERIAL DEFAULT BY THE DEBTOR(S) WITH RESPECT TO THE TERM OF THE CONFIRMED PLAN BY FAILING TO MAKE PAYMENTS ACCORDING TO THE PLAN (11 U.S.C. 1307(c)(6)).

THIS MOTION MAY BE GRANTED WITHOUT A HEARING, PURSUANT TO   LOCAL BANKRUPTCY RULE 9013-1(o). ANY PARTY IN INTEREST WHO WISHES TO OPPOSE THE MOTIONMUST OBTAINA HEARING DATE FROM   THE CLERK OF THE COURT FOR THE RIVERSIDE DIVISION AND MUST SERVE AND FILE HIS OPPOSITION PAPERS ON THE TRUSTEE WITHIN FOURTEEN(14) DAYS OF THE DATE OF SERVICE HEREOF.

                                     /S/AMRANE COHEN
                                     AMRANE COHEN

AMRANE COHEN DECLARES UNDER PENALTY OF PERJURY THAT HE IS THE DULY APPOINTED, QUALIFIED AND ACTING CHAPTER 13 TRUSTEE AND THE FOREGOING IS TRUE AND CORRECT. EXECUTED AT ORANGE, CALIFORNIA ON

DATED: 10/12/2011   **/S/AMRANE COHEN**
                                     AMRANE COHEN

Filer's Name, Address, Phone, Fax, Email:	UNITED STATES BANKRUPTCY COURT DISTRICT OF HAWAII 1132 Bishop Street, Suite 250 Honolulu, Hawaii 96813

hib_3015-1val (1/11)

Debtor Name: Address:	SSN (last 4 digits):	Case No.:
Jt Debtor Name: Address:	SSN (last 4 digits):	Chapter 13

CHAPTER 13 PLAN MOTION TO VALUE COLLATERAL; NOTICE OF DEADLINE TO OBJECT
[Do not include more than __one__ creditor or __one__ item of collateral per motion]

Name and address of creditor whose security interest is being modified ("stripped"):

Collateral (if real property, state address or tax map key; if vehicle, state Vehicle I.D. No., Year, Make, Model, Mileage):

Date debt incurred:	☐ If checked, subject property is debtor's principal residence.
Debtor's valuation: $	Value based on:

Chapter 13 Plan proposes treating this claim as secured to the extent of: (Balance of claim to be treated as general unsecured claim unless plan states otherwise.)	$

☐ **If checked, valuation may arguably be contrary to the Bankruptcy Code under 11 U.S.C. § 1325(a).**

Pursuant to 11 U.S.C. § 506(a) and Fed. R. Bankr. P. 3012, Debtor moves to value the above-described property and to modify the rights of the above-named creditor under 11 U.S.C. § 1322(b)(2). Based on the allegations stated below and in any supplemental documents, Debtor requests that the court make the valuation stated above. Debtor further requests that the valuation supersede any amount asserted as secured in the creditor's proof of claim. __ALL SECURITY INTERESTS IN THE SUBJECT PROPERTY ARE LISTED BELOW BY SENIORITY.__ __ANY INTEREST BEING MODIFIED IS CHECKED.__

Being Modified?	Creditor Name (List all, including interests not being modified)	Account No. (last 4 digits)	Balance due (good faith estimate)
☐			$
☐			$
☐			$
☐			$

NOTICE

NOTICE IS HEREBY GIVEN that this motion filed by the Debtor(s) concerns your interest in the above-described Property and is related to the Chapter 13 Plan being proposed by the Debtor(s), a copy of which should have been sent to you separately.

<u>**Your rights may be affected.**</u> **You should read the motion or application and the accompanying papers carefully and discuss them with your attorney if you have one in this bankruptcy case or proceeding. (If you do not have an attorney, you may wish to consult one.)**

If you do not want the court to approve the proposed treatment of your claim, or if you want the court to consider your views on the motion, then you or your attorney must file an Objection to Confirmation of Chapter 13 Plan <u>not later than 7 days before the confirmation hearing date, or 21 days after the filing of this motion, whichever is later.</u> Your objection will be considered at the confirmation hearing.

If you mail your response to the court for filing, you must mail it early enough so the court will **receive** it on or before the deadline stated above. Responses must be filed with the court at: **United States Bankruptcy Court, District of Hawaii, Suite 250, Honolulu, HI 96813**, and sent to the moving party at the address in the upper left corner of this document.

If you or your attorney do not file a timely objection, the court may decide that you do not oppose the relief sought in the motion and may enter an order granting the relief requested by the Debtor(s). The determination made in such an order will supersede any security interest stated in a proof of claim that you have filed or will file.

ADDITIONAL NOTICE OF PROVISION ARGUABLY CONTRARY TO BANKRUPTCY CODE

☐ IF CHECKED, FURTHER NOTICE IS GIVEN that one or more provisions in the proposed Chapter 13 Plan may arguably be contrary to the Bankruptcy Code. If so, the court may grant the motion to value collateral and confirm the plan **only** if you accept the treatment of your claim under the plan. **If you do not want to accept the plan, you must file a timely objection to this motion and the plan.** If you do not file a timely objection, you will have accepted the plan. If the court enters a confirmation order, the plan's provisions will be binding on you and the Debtor(s).

☐ The plan provides that you will NOT retain your lien in the subject property until paid in full under nonbankruptcy law or until a discharge is issued to the Debtor(s).

☐ The plan provides for less than full payment of a debt that (1) is secured by a purchase money security interest in the motor vehicle described above and (2) was incurred within 910 days preceding the date of the filing of the bankruptcy petition.

☐ The plan provides for less than full payment of a debt that (1) is secured by a purchase money security interest in the property described above and (2) was incurred within 1 year preceding the date of the filing of the bankruptcy petition.

Dated: _____   /s/ _____

Signature   (print name if original signature)

GLOSSARY

A

Actual fraud   A fraudulent transfer made within one year before the date of the filing of a bankruptcy petition and with the intent to hinder or defraud a creditor.

Adequate information   In a Chapter 11 bankruptcy, the debtor must supply creditors with enough data to evaluate the debtor's reorganization and make an informed decision in deciding whether to accept the debtor's proposed plan.

Adversary number   A separate docket number the bankruptcy court assigns to an adversary proceeding. This number is listed below the docket number for the main bankruptcy case.

Adversary proceeding   A separate lawsuit filed within a bankruptcy case, which must be resolved by the judge before the case may proceed to discharge. An adversary proceeding in a bankruptcy case is treated much like a civil lawsuit would be treated.

Adversary proceeding complaint   The initiating document in an **adversary proceeding**. The plaintiff files a formal complaint with the court and has that complaint served on the defendant.

Advisory Committee   A committee consisting of federal judges and bankruptcy attorneys that makes recommendations about bankruptcy rules, forms, and procedures.

Affidavit of Special Circumstances   A sworn document in which the debtor argues that such conditions exist, such as loss of employment, disability, injury, or unanticipated expenses, that the presumption of abuse should not be applied.

Alimony   Court-ordered financial support paid to an ex-spouse.

Allowed expenses   Expenses debtors may deduct from income for determining disposable income.

Attorney-client privilege   An ethical rule that prohibits an attorney from disclosing privileged information unless waived by the client, clearing the way for the attorney to discuss the contents of the communications with a third party.

Automatic Stay   An injunction against the debtor's creditors and claimants that stops all court lawsuits and collection efforts against the debtor until the stay is lifted, or removed, by the bankruptcy court or the case ends.

B

Bad faith   When a debtor conceals or misrepresents assets, income, or expenses; intends to avoid paying a large debt to a creditor; or spends lavishly without regard to where the money will come from to pay the bills.

Bankruptcy   A legal procedure established under federal law that allows a financially distressed individual, business, or municipality to obtain debt relief by either liquidating its assets or restructuring its debt so its creditors may be paid.

Bankruptcy Abuse Prevention and Consumer Protection Act of 2005 (BAPCPA)   Legislation that was enacted in April of 2005 that made several sweeping changes to the Bankruptcy Code.

Bankruptcy Appellate Panel (BAP)   The Bankruptcy Appellate Panel units of the federal courts of appeal; consist of a three-judge panel.

Bankruptcy attorney   An attorney that represents a debtor, creditor, or other interested party in a bankruptcy proceeding.

Bankruptcy Code   The bankruptcy laws, or statutes, created by Congress are found in Title 11 of the official United States Code or in the similarly titled unofficial U.S.C.A. published by Thomson-West or U.S.C.S. published by LexisNexis.

Bankruptcy court   A unit of the U.S. District Court; where the bankruptcy petition is filed and the system in which the bankruptcy case is processed.

Bankruptcy estate   All the legal and equitable interests that a debtor may own in property at the time of the filing of the Chapter 7 petition; also includes any property the debtor receives within 180 days of the filing date of the petition.

Bankruptcy examiner   An individual the court appoints in Chapter 11 cases to scrutinize the financial affairs of a debtor.

Bankruptcy judge   An individual who presides over the bankruptcy proceedings, serving for a 14-year term. The role of the bankruptcy judge is to hear arguments and resolve issues among the parties, rule on motions, conduct hearings, determine whether debtors qualify for relief under the Bankruptcy Code, administer rules under Bankruptcy Procedures and

Bankruptcy Code, and determine whether a debtor should receive a discharge.

Bankruptcy paralegal   A nonattorney who works under the supervision of a bankruptcy lawyer.

Bankruptcy petition   The initiating document that is filed along with a filing fee in the bankruptcy court of the federal district where the debtor is domiciled or resides with the intent to remain permanently. The petition includes Schedules, and the Statement of Financial Affairs, among other documents, which includes information regarding the debtor's assets, liabilities, expenses, and a list of creditors to whom debts are due.

Bankruptcy petition preparer   A person, other than an attorney for the debtor or an employee of such attorney under the direct supervision of such attorney, who prepares for compensation a document for filing.

Bankruptcy trustee   An individual the bankruptcy court appoints who is responsible for arranging the sale of the debtor's property and distributing the proceeds to the creditors.

Bankruptcy worksheet   A detailed questionnaire that guides the client in identifying the information necessary for the attorney to access the client's financial circumstances and determine the best course of action to take regarding the client's debt.

Blog   A webpage or website created by an individual or organizations who frequently express their views and opinions on various topics.

C

Cash collateral   Income the debtor generates during the course of a Chapter 11 bankruptcy case.

Chapter 11   A bankruptcy chapter available for business debtors who want to remain in business and are allowed to maintain control over their assets under the supervision of the bankruptcy court.

Chapter 12   A bankruptcy chapter specifically created for family farmers and family fishers with regular income; similar to a reorganization under Chapter 11.

Chapter 13   A bankruptcy chapter filed by an individual who has a regular source of income and can propose a plan of repayment rather than liquidation.

Chapter 7   The most common type of bankruptcy chapter filed to liquidate the debtor's obligations. Also known as **straight bankruptcy**, **total bankruptcy**, or **complete bankruptcy**.

Chapter 9   A bankruptcy chapter municipalities file seeking to restructure their debt and propose a repayment plan.

Claims   A creditor's right to receive payment for debts owed them.

Closed bankruptcy   A status indicating that there is no longer any activity in the debtor's bankruptcy case.

CM/ECF (Case Management/Electronic Case Files)   Acronym for **Case Management/ Electronic Case Files**, a system that enables attorneys and paralegals to file and download documents related to bankruptcy cases when the firm represents the debtor, creditor, or other interested party.

Co-debtor stay   Legal protection under the Automatic Stay that is also extended to co-debtors in Chapter 13 cases and remains in effect until the debtor's case is closed.

Co-debtors   People, in addition to the debtor, who are potentially liable for one or more of the debts listed in the bankruptcy schedules.

Collateral   An asset or specific of property pledged in exchange for a secured loan.

Committee Notes   Notes the Judicial Conference Advisory Committee on Rules of Bankruptcy Procedure creates that provide details of the changes in bankruptcy forms and the reasons for the revisions.

Compensation   Payment for legal services. The rules of ethics require attorney compensation or fees to be reasonable; the attorney must provide an explanation to the client regarding the scope of representation and the basis of the fee.

Competency   An ethical rule that requires attorneys and paralegals to possess the knowledge, skill, preparation, and thoroughness to represent bankruptcy clients adequately.

Complete bankruptcy   Another term that describes a Chapter 7 bankruptcy.

Confidentiality   An ethical rule that prohibits attorneys from disclosing information regarding the client's case to a third party unless the client consents or the attorney is required to do so under the law.

Confirmation   The bankruptcy court's process of approving the debtor's reorganization plan.

Confirmation hearing   A hearing in which the bankruptcy court judge determines whether to accept the debtor's repayment plan.

Conflict of interest   Relationships or circumstances that compromise the duty of loyalty attorneys and paralegals owe to their clients.

Conflicts check   A formal review of the law firm's client database to determine whether the firm has formerly or is currently representing a client whose interest might conflict with a potential new client.

Constructive fraud   A fraudulent transfer by which the debtor transfers assets for grossly inadequate consideration.

Consumer bankruptcy   Another term to define a Chapter 7 bankruptcy.

Consumer debt   Nonbusiness-related debt.

Contemporaneous exchange   A transfer by which the debtor received sufficient new value from the creditor in return for the exchange.

Contingent debt   A debt that depends on an event happening such as a loan that the debtor co-signed that has not defaulted.

Conversion   A legal process by which the debtor's original bankruptcy filing status is changed, either voluntarily or involuntarily, from one chapter to another.

Cosigner   Person or persons who cosign on a loan with the debtor prior to the debtor's bankruptcy case.

Cramdown   Court-ordered modifications made to loans that are basically crammed down the creditors' throats, which they are forced to accept.

Credit counseling course   A mandatory course that provides debtors with alternatives to bankruptcy and explores the possibility of working out a payment plan with creditors instead.

Credit repair organization (CRO)   Businesses that promise to repair a client's credit report for a fee.

Credit Repair Organizations Act (CROA)   A federal law passed in 1996 designed to protect the public from unfair or deceptive advertising and business practices by credit repair organizations.

Credit report   A detailed snapshot of an individual's financial history.

Credit score   A number that summarizes the information in an individual's credit report. Credit scores range from 300 to 850. The rule is that the higher the credit score, the more creditworthy the debtor.

Creditors' committee   A group appointed by the United States trustee who represents creditors that have claims against a business in a bankruptcy proceeding.

The creditors' committee is divided between secured and unsecured creditors.

Criminal law exception   An exception to the Automatic Stay. The commencement or continuation of any criminal action or proceeding against an individual who has committed a crime under the laws of the federal or state government is not stayed under the Bankruptcy Code.

Cross-border insolvency case   A term that refers to cases filed under Chapter 15 of the Bankruptcy Code. Chapter 15 applies to debtors and creditors and other parties in interest when more than one country is involved.

Custodial parent   The parent with residential custody of the minor children.

D

Debt consolidation   A bankruptcy alternative that requires the debtor to obtain a large loan to pay off existing debts.

Debt management agencies   Nonprofit entities that promise to negotiate a payment plan with creditors.

Debt relief agency   Any person who provides any bankruptcy assistance to an assisted person in return for the payment of money or other valuable consideration or who is a bankruptcy petition preparer.

Debt settlement   A lump sum payment to the creditor, from 30% to 50% of the total debt, in satisfaction of the entire obligation.

Debtor   An individual, corporation, partnership, or municipality seeking relief in the bankruptcy court from debts owed to creditors.

Debtor education course (financial management course)   A mandatory course for debtors filing for Chapter 7 relief that must be completed within 60 days of the initial date set for the meeting of creditors.

Debtor in possession (DIP)   An individual or business that files for Chapter 11 relief while retaining control over their assets and continues operating the business without having to seek court approval.

Debtors' prison   A special facility where individuals who were in debt were incarcerated.

Deed of trust   A legal arrangement by which a lender, such as a bank, loans a borrower the money to purchase real estate.

Defalcation   A culpable state-of-mind requirement involving knowledge of, or gross recklessness in respect to, the improper nature of the fiduciary behavior.

Denial of discharge Declaring a debt nondischargeable that normally would have been discharged,

DIP financing New debt that a business obtains in the process of a reorganization under Chapter 11 that has priority over existing debt, equity, and security claims. DIP financing allows businesses filing for Chapter 11 to obtain loans to continue their day-to-day operations during the reorganization process.

Discharge A document issued by a bankruptcy judge that releases the debtor from liability and prohibits the creditor from pursuing any legal action to collect those debts.

Discharge of debt A ruling issued by a bankruptcy judge that releases the debtor from liability and prohibits the creditor from pursuing any legal action to collect those debts.

Dischargeability Determining whether a debt may be eliminated in bankruptcy.

Disclosure agreement or disclosure statement A document that lists all the mandatory disclosures required in 11 U.S.C. § 527, Section 527. It includes information such as the financial details of the debtor's business, enough to allow the creditors to determine how their interests will be affected.

Discretionary income Income remaining after taxes are paid and used to pay for food, shelter, utility bills, and other necessary items such as clothing and toiletries.

Disgorge The bankruptcy court's authority to order professional persons to disgorge or give up excessive fees.

Disinterested party Someone who does not have any interest materially adverse to a creditor because of his or her association with the debtor.

Dismissal When the bankruptcy court closes the case without granting the debtor the benefit of a fresh start. The debtor's obligations are still due, and the court will take no further action on the case. The point at which the bankruptcy court ceases administration of the case and no longer has jurisdiction over the matter, including any adversary proceedings that have been filed.

Dismissed with prejudice The bankruptcy court dismisses a debtor's case and limits or prohibits the debtor from filing for bankruptcy at a later time due to the debtor's bad faith or abuse of the bankruptcy process.

Dismissed without prejudice The bankruptcy court dismisses the debtor's case, allowing the debtor to file for bankruptcy again immediately and discharge the same debts included in the first petition.

Disposable income Income remaining after the debtor pays for certain expenses the Bankruptcy Code allows such as mortgage payments, health insurance payments, medical bills, and food bills.

Disputed debt Debt where the debtor and creditor disagree regarding the amount.

Due diligence The process of verifying the client's financial information.

E

Economic unit approach A method adopted by a majority of the circuit courts and used to calculate the size of the debtor's household. This method looks at the household as a single economic unit and takes into account who is making financial contributions and who depends on the debtor for support.

E-filing Electronic filing of legal pleadings an documents; implemented in many courts across the country.

Embezzlement Misappropriating the funds of another person

Emergency filing A situation where the debtor needs the protection of the Automatic Stay but cannot wait longer than a day or two for all the forms and schedules to be filed.

Enabling loan A security instrument a creditor records for property it provided to the debtor.

Equitable rights Individual rights concerned with enforcing rules or statutes and often involving a court ordering someone to do or refrain from doing something.

Equity security holder One who holds an ownership interest in a business.

Eviction exception An exception to the Automatic Stay, allowing the property owner to proceed with an eviction.

Examiner The individual the court appoints to investigate cases of alleged fraud, dishonesty, misconduct, or irregularity in the current or former management of the debtor's affairs.

Exclusivity period The debtor's exclusive right to propose a plan of reorganization during the first 120 days after Chapter 11 has been filed.

Executory contract A contract executed when insufficient or incomplete performance on either side of the contract has occurred.

Exempt property The term referring to property that is exempt from seizure by creditors.

F

Fair Credit Reporting Act   A federal law that prohibits reporting inaccurate or incomplete information on the client's credit report.

Family law exception   One of the most common exceptions to the Automatic Stay concerning family law matters.

Federal Rules of Bankruptcy Procedure or Fed. R. Bankr. P. (FRBP)   A supplement to the Bankruptcy Code that includes the mechanics of processing a bankruptcy case. It is abbreviated in the formal *Bluebook* citation form as **Fed. R. Bankr. P.** or the more informal **FRBP**; often referred to by legal practitioners as the Bankruptcy Rules.

Fiduciary   One who holds a position of trust and generally manages the money of another person or persons and has similar powers to that of a Chapter 11 trustee.

Fillable   Electronic forms that may be completed online and saved for later use or to work on later.

Final order   A court order that resolves the dispute between the parties.

Financial therapy industry   Professional mental health counselors specializing in assisting debtors dealing with the emotionality of being in financial distress and the accompanying problems they face.

First day motions   A series of pleadings the debtor files on the first day the Chapter 11 petition is filed to obtain court approval to engage in activities that are not allowed under the Bankruptcy Code.

First meeting of the creditors (341 hearing)   A hearing held within 40 days after the bankruptcy petition is filed; the trustee reviews the debtor's petitions, schedules, and statements and provides the invited creditors to do the same.

Fixed or flat fee   A one-time fee an attorney charges for filing the bankruptcy case and assisting the client through the bankruptcy administration process.

Forced conversion   A bankruptcy court-ordered liquidation triggered when the debtor fails to create a Chapter 13 plan or successfully make payments under the Chapter 13 plan or engages in some unreasonable delay that will cause harm to the creditors.

Foreclosure   A legal proceeding a lender, usually a bank or mortgage trust company, files against a debtor who fails to make payments on a mortgage loan on a parcel of real property. The lender seeks to force the sale of the property to recover the money and interest plus legal costs of foreclosure.

Fraudulent conveyance   A transfer of assets to a third party for the purpose of preventing creditors from satisfying their claims.

Fresh start   The ultimate goal in bankruptcy; either the debtor's obligations are wiped away or he or she is given the opportunity to reorganize the debt in a manner that is more manageable and realistic.

G

Gramm-Leach-Bliley Act of 1999 (Financial Services Modernization Act of 1999)   Also known as the **Financial Services Modernization Act of 1999**. A federal law that requires financial institutions to limit disclosure of consumers' personal financial state, advise consumers of the institution's privacy policies, and allow consumers to opt out of sharing their personal financial information.

H

Heads-on-beds approach   A method used to calculate the size of the debtor's household adopted by a minority of the circuit courts. This method uses the U.S. Bureau of the Census's definition, which is a head count of everyone who resides in the home.

Hourly fee   An arrangement for the payment of legal fees by which a client is billed for every hour the attorney or paralegal spends working on the case.

I

Impaired class   A class of creditors who will not receive the full value of their claims.

Income tax–dependent approach   A method to calculate the size of the debtor's household based on the number of dependents claimed on the debtor's tax return; adopted by a minority of circuit courts,.

Indentured servants   An individual who paid for his or her passage, including expenses and maintenance, by contracting to work for a period of years for his or her sponsors.

Initial client interview   The bankruptcy client's first meeting with the attorney and his or her paralegal. It is when the attorney provides the client with legal advice; takes the initial steps to determine which bankruptcy chapter is appropriate, considering the client's circumstances; and establishes the attorney–client relationship.

Insider   A person or entity that has a close relationship to the debtor.

Institutional creditors   Creditors such as banks or other lending institutions who want their loans paid back and may wish to liquidate the debtor's business to satisfy their claims.

Intangible property   Items that have value but cannot be felt or touched, such as stock in a company.

Interlocutory order   An interim or temporary court order on issues that arise during the case.

Intersection   Area of legal practice that is influenced by another area of the law.

Involuntary conversion   A bankruptcy conversion that is not initiated by the debtor but, rather, by the trustee, creditor, other party in interest, or the bankruptcy court.

Involuntary dismissal   A dismissal initiated by the bankruptcy court judge acting on his or her own or by motion of the U.S. trustee.

Involuntary petition   A petition that is brought against the debtor by several creditors.

Involuntary transfer   A transfer that is not within the debtor's control, such as a repossession, a lien, or garnishment against the debtor, which the trustee may reverse if it occurred within 90 days of the debtor's bankruptcy filing.

J

Judgment proof   The inability of a creditor to collect on a debt, even though he or she has obtained a judgment, because the debtor has no property to attach or wages to garnish.

Jurisdiction   The power or authority of a court to hear and resolve a case.

L

Legal rights   Individual rights concerned with the recovery of property or money in a lawsuit because of something the plaintiff is owed or has lost.

License   The right to use another's creative work under certain terms and conditions.

Lien stripping   If the debtor has a second, or even a third mortgage or a home equity line of credit on his or her property, that secondary loan can be literally stripped away from the primary loan on the property;

a benefit usually available only to Chapter 13 debtors with regard to the primary residence.

Liquidated   The legal process by which the trustee sells nonexempt property and in turn pays the administration expenses associated with the bankruptcy case.

Liquidation   A bankruptcy filing by a debtor who has very little or no ability to pay back his or her debts and whose income level qualifies under the Bankruptcy Abuse Prevention and Consumer Protection Act of 2005. The goal of the liquidation bankruptcy is to discharge the debtor's debt, resulting in a fresh start.

Liquidation bankruptcy   Another term for a Chapter 7 bankruptcy.

Local bankruptcy forms   Bankruptcy forms created by the individual district courts that may vary from one federal district to another.

Local bankruptcy rules   Bankruptcy rules drafted by individual district courts specifically for the administration and case management of bankruptcy matters in that particular court system.

Local Standards   Expense costs used in calculating the Means Test that are based on the average housing, utilities, and transportation expenses in the state and county where the debtor lives.

M

Malicious injury   A wrongful, intentional act that causes injury to another or his or her property.

Mandatory credit counseling   Required counseling that focuses on training the debtor how to handle his or her own finances.

Material fact   Facts on which one or both parties rely when deciding to enter into a contract with the other.

Means Test   A formula designed to determine whether debtors have income and the ability to restructure their debt and pay off their creditors.

Median household income   The income level that falls exactly in the middle of the range of incomes for a particular family size in the debtor's state.

Mediation   A form of alternate dispute resolution by which the parties seek to resolve their legal dispute through means other than expensive and time-consuming litigation.

Mediator   A neutral party who facilitates a discussion between the parties in mediation and proposes possible solutions.

Meeting of the creditors (341 hearing) The first court appearance the debtor makes in a bankruptcy case. This meeting may also be referred to as the **341 meeting**, named after the Bankruptcy Code section where it is found. The debtor must attend this meeting or risk dismissal of his or her case by the court.

Mortgage A loan to finance the purchase of real estate payable over a period of years and at a rate of interest.

Motion A request filed by a party in a legal case when a court ruling is required on important issues or in contested matters requiring a resolution by the judge.

Motion for relief from Automatic Stay A motion a creditor files in a bankruptcy case, asking the Automatic Stay to be lifted so the creditor may proceed with legal proceedings or collection against the debtor.

Motion to use cash collateral or obtain DIP financing Motion a debtor files along with a Chapter 11 petition, asking the court to allow the debtor to obtain loans or use income he or she generates to pay certain expenses so the business may continue.

Motion to value the collateral A motion a debtor must file to invoke either the cramdown or lien stripping benefits of a Chapter 13 filing. Here, the bankruptcy court determines the value of the collateral, compares it with the amount of the secured creditor's claim, and makes the determination regarding the unsecured portion of the creditor's claim.

Multi-user license A license that allows more than one person to use software.

N

National Standards Monthly expense amounts based on nationwide figures and considered allowable living expenses, depending on the size of the family.

Necessary expense test An inquiry into the expenses needed to provide for the health, welfare, and/or the production of income for the debtor and the debtor's family.

No-asset case A bankruptcy case in which most of the debtor's assets are exempt from the proceedings, leaving no nonexempt property for the trustee to sell.

Nondischargeable Certain debts that cannot be eliminated in bankruptcy due to public policy concerns.

Nonexempt property Property that becomes part of the bankruptcy estate and may be sold by the bankruptcy trustee to raise funds to pay back creditors.

Nonpriority unsecured claims Creditor claims that are not entitled to priority, and no collateral secures their interest.

Notice of conversion A court notice sent to creditors and other parties in interest, informing them of a case's potential change of status, allowing them to raise objections.

Notice of non-representation A disclosure statement informing the client that the attorney–client relationship is not established until the client signs a retainer agreement and pays the attorney's fee.

O

Objection to discharge A creditor's or the trustee's formal opposition to the bankruptcy court's decision to grant a discharge to the debtor.

Official Bankruptcy Forms The forms that are approved by the Judicial Conference of the United States that include the Petition, Schedules of the debtors assets and debts, and Statement of Financial Affairs.

Operative chapters Sections of the Bankruptcy Code that define the specific types of bankruptcy filings a debtor may file, depending on his or her eligibility and income level.

P

PACER (Public Access to Court Electronic Records) An acronym for **Public Access to Court Electronic Records**, an Internet-based public access system that allows registered users to obtain basic case information, docket information, opinions, and documents filed in federal appellate, district, and bankruptcy courts.

Panel trustee An individual who serves on a panel in a particular judicial district and is assigned Chapter 7 bankruptcies and functions similar to an executor in a probate estate.

Parties in interest Any party who has an interest in the amount of money a creditor is claiming; may file an objection the creditor's proof of claim.

Payday loans Short-term, high-interest loans made usually to financially strapped individuals who need an infusion of cash for one reason or another between paychecks.

Payment plan   A fee arrangement that allows the client to pay the attorney in installments.

Perfecting the security interest in the property   The process by which the creditor records a secured financing agreement with the office of the secretary of state in the jurisdiction where the business is located.

Personal guarantee   An agreement, a business owner signs that allows the creditor to pursue the personal assets of the owner for the debts the business entity owes. If the business cannot pay its debts, the business owner is sued in his or her personal capacity.

Personal guarantee insurance   Insurance coverage purchased to minimize the risk of loss to a business owner's personal assets if the liquidated business assets cannot satisfy its debts. The insurance may cover a percentage of the business debts so that the personal consequences to the owner are not so severe that they require a personal bankruptcy filing.

Personally identifiable information   Any information that can be used to identify a specific individual; must be protected from public view whether the information is filed electronically or in paper form.

Petition for writ of certiorari   A document the petitioner files with the U.S. Supreme Court, asking the Court to review the lower court's decision.

Plan of reorganization or Chapter 11 plan   A process by which the business debtor creates a plan designed to restructure the creditor's financial claims so that the debtor's business may remain viable and stand on its own without the legal protections of Chapter 11.

Prepackaged bankruptcy or prepack   A Chapter 11 reorganization that has been prenegotiated between the debtor and its creditors.

Pre-petition certificate   Documentary proof of debtor's completion of credit counseling requirement.

Pre-petition credit counseling   The legal requirement that forces debtors to participate in consumer credit counseling prior to filing the bankruptcy petition.

Presumption of abuse   A presumption that arises when a calculation of the Means Test reveals that the debtor has enough disposable income to arrange a payment plan with creditors under Chapter 13.

Priority creditor   A creditor to whom the debtor has not pledged any type of collateral to satisfy the loan if the debtor defaults on payment; unsecured creditors whose claims take precedence over the claims of other creditors.

Priority unsecured claims   Claims that take precedence over the claims of other creditors.

Private Trustees   Individuals the U.S. trustee appoints to administer bankruptcy estates filed under Chapters 7, 12, and 13. Private trustees are not considered government employees but are private attorneys supervised by and who work in conjunction with the U.S. trustee.

Proof of Claim   A court form a creditor files that contains the amount of debt owed and the reason for the debt. The creditor must include evidence proving the debt, such as an invoice, statement, or receipts.

Property of the estate   Encompasses all the debtor's legal and equitable interests in property anywhere or in anyone's possession.

Purchase money security interest (PMSI)   A clause in a credit card agreement that gives the creditor the right to repossess the goods if the debtor does not make payments in a timely fashion.

R

Reaffirmation   The debtor agrees to reassume the responsibility of paying off the loan. The creditor agrees not to seize the property as long as the debtor continues to make payments.

Reaffirmation agreement   A contract between the debtor and creditor by which the debtor reassumes the responsibility of paying off the loan.

Reaffirmation of debt   A situation where the debtor reinstates the debt on a secured loan.

Real property   Land owned by the debtor or any property that has a direct relationship to the land such as a house or other type of permanent structure.

Redacting   Striking out the confidential words, phrases, or numbers by blacking out the information with a marker or using computer software that performs the process through electronic means.

Redemption   A situation where the debtor pays either the value or the loan balance on a piece of exempt property, whichever figure is less.

Regular income   Debtor's income from traditional employment, pension payments, public benefits, domestic support (child support and alimony), unemployment benefits, social security, and payments received from royalties and rents.

Relief from the Automatic Stay   Creditor's request for the court to lift or remove the Automatic Stay.

REO (real estate owned) properties   Bank-owned properties.

Reopened bankruptcy   A bankruptcy case that is reactivated for further proceedings.

Reorganization   A bankruptcy filed by a business or individual who works closely with the bankruptcy court, directly or with the assistance of a bankruptcy attorney, to restructure or reorganize his or her debt.

Repayment plan   The debtor's proposal for how the money he or she owes to the creditors will be paid back and the monthly amount of such payments.

Retainer agreement   An agreement entered into between an attorney or law firm and a client to provide the client with legal services.

Revocation of discharge   The bankruptcy court's removal of a debtor's discharge.

S

Section 363 sale   A procedure that allows a bankruptcy trustee or debtor in possession to sell the bankruptcy estate's assets free and clear of any interest in such property Chapter 11.

Secured claim   A loan granted to the debtor in exchange for a lien on the property. Secured claims receive top priority in repayment of debts in a bankruptcy proceeding.

Secured credit card   A credit card issued to an individual with poor credit; the cardholder provides the credit card company with a monetary deposit, which serves as a security similar to how a property owner collects a security deposit prior to leasing property to the lessee.

Secured creditors   Creditors that have a claim against the debtor; the property is secured as collateral in exchange for extension of credit.

Secured financing agreement   A contract between the creditor and the debtor whereby the debtor agrees to give the creditor an interest in specific assets pledged as collateral.

Single-user license   A license that allows one person to use the software.

Standing trustees   An individual responsible for administering Chapter 12 and Chapter 13 bankruptcies in designated geographic areas within the judicial district.

Statement of Intentions   A form filed in a Chapter 7 case that informs the creditors, trustee, and bankruptcy court of how the debtor intends to deal with secured debts within the context of the bankruptcy.

Statutory lien   A mechanic's lien or a tax lien.

Straight bankruptcy   Another term for a Chapter 7 bankruptcy.

Sua sponte   An action a court takes on its own motion.

T

Tangible property   Personal property that can be seen or felt, such as cars or furniture.

Taxing authority exception   Exception to Automatic Stay regarding owed taxes.

Total bankruptcy   A term used to define a Chapter 7 bankruptcy.

Trade creditors   Creditors who supply goods or services to the debtor's business; the business is given a grace period to pay its debt.

Trustee   An individual typically appointed in a Chapter 11 case when the bankruptcy court finds that the current management has engaged in some type of fraud, dishonesty, incompetence, or gross mismanagement.

Tutorial   An online resource that provides the user with step-by-step instruction in how to use the bankruptcy software; an invaluable resource when learning new software.

U

Unexpired lease   A lease that is still in effect.

Uniform Commercial Code (UCC) filing   Often used by creditors to secure rights to collateral specified in secured financing agreements. The creditor files the agreement with the secretary of state's office lender, which puts the public on notice that the creditor is a legally recognized interest in the collateral until it is fully paid for; also establishes the creditor's legal title in the assets if the debtor defaults.

United States trustee (U.S. trustee)   A federal official the government employs, appointed by the U.S. Attorney General; responsible for enforcing the civil provisions of the bankruptcy laws of the United States by supervising the administration of bankruptcy cases and the functions of private trustees.

Universal chapters Chapters 1, 3, and 5 of the Bankruptcy Code that operate as an instruction manual or rule book of sorts for the remaining chapters of the code known as the operative chapters.

Unliquidated debt A debt of which the amount has yet to be determined.

Unsecured claim A debt that is not secured by collateral. Unsecured creditors have less protection because there is no collateral behind the debt, and the creditor will receive only a pro rata share if anything is remaining to divide among the creditors.

Unsecured creditor A creditor whose debt is not securedby collateral.

Unsecured nonpriority creditor A creditor that does not receive any priority treatment in bankruptcy liquidation or reorganization.

Unsecured priority creditor (often simply referred to as a priority creditor) A creditor given priority over non-priority secured debtors in a bankruptcy liquidation or reorganization. Examples include custodial parents owed child support payments and employees owed back wages.

V

Valuation Motion (Motion to Value Collateral) A motion filed to ask the court to determine the value of the collateral securing a particular loan or loans.

Voidable preference or voidable transfer A transfer the debtor makes to a creditor prior to filing for bankruptcy. Here the debtor pays a preferred or favored creditor in full while the rest are left to divide a pro rata share after a bankruptcy case is filed.

Voluntary conversion When the debtor seeks to change his or her bankruptcy filing status from one chapter to another.

Voluntary dismissal Voluntary dismissal When the debtor decides not to pursue the bankruptcy case and consents to its dismissal.

Voluntary petition A court form, similar to an application, that the debtor must complete in order to be eligible for bankruptcy relief.

W

Wage garnishment A wage deduction of a certain amount of money that the debtor owes usually pursuant to a court order.

INDEX

CREDITS